The Mystery of Appearance

Conversations Between
Ten British Post-War Painters

Catherine Lampert
Tom Hunt

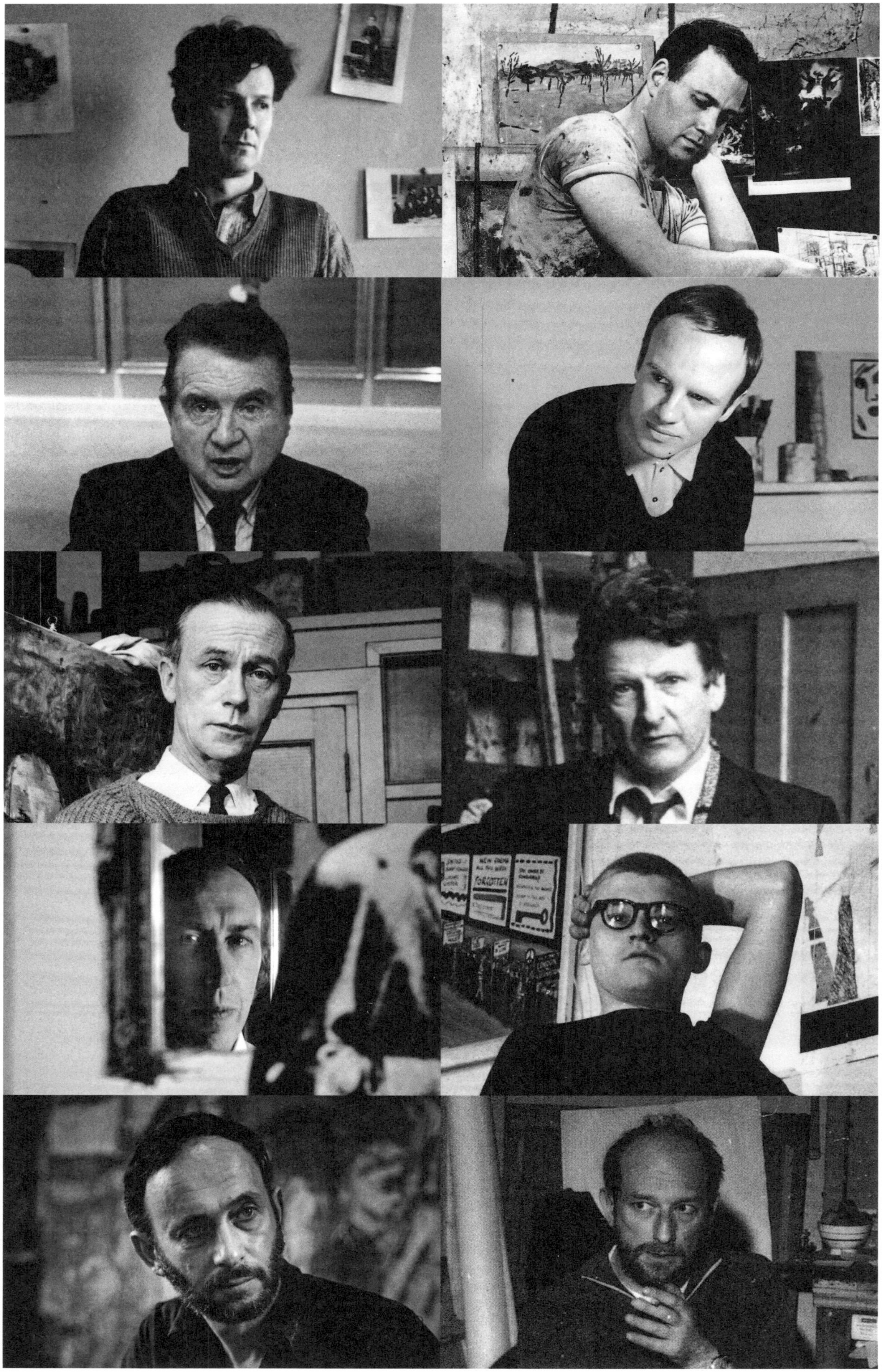
NEW CINEMA
ALL THIS WEEK
FORGOTTEN

The Mystery of Appearance

Conversations Between
Ten British Post-War Painters

Michael Andrews
Frank Auerbach
Francis Bacon
Patrick Caulfield
William Coldstream
Lucian Freud
Richard Hamilton
David Hockney
Leon Kossoff
Euan Uglow

Haunch of Venison

To me, the mystery of
painting today is how
can appearance be made.
I know it can be illustrated,
I know it can be photographed.
But how can this thing
be made so that you catch
the mystery of appearance
within the mystery of
the making? . . . one knows
that by some accidental brush-
marks suddenly appearance
comes in with a vividness
that no accepted way of doing
it would have brought about.

— Francis Bacon

Contents

Introduction

Amongst the most celebrated artists working in Britain since the end of the Second World War are a group of figurative painters, distinguished by a profound commitment to the medium, a powerful sense of the need to make grand and articulate yet mysterious images that speak of the human condition, a dedication to the highest traditions of historic painting, and a disregard for the vagaries of fashion.

It is many years now since R.B. Kitaj's speculative proposal for a "School of London" hardened into art historical cliché around five key figures: Francis Bacon, Lucian Freud, Frank Auerbach, Leon Kossoff, and Michael Andrews. However, while there are many reasons to justify viewing these artists together, they are each very individual and to position them thus is to remove them from a context that is vital for an understanding of their work. It also gives a skewed sense of the artistic milieu in which they worked. Art history likes to place artists within distinct categories; so it is that in usual readings of the pluralistic art scene of post-war Britain distinctions are drawn between different groups and movements; between St Ives Abstraction and Constructionism, Pop Art and "Kitchen Sink" realism and so on. Yet this reductive view doesn't take account of the crossovers, the "conversations," that took place, and which profoundly enriched the work of artists working in very different modes. Within the orbits of the core artists of the so-called "School of London" we find at different times Pop artists including Richard Hamilton, David Hockney, Patrick Caulfield, R.B. Kitaj, Eduardo Paolozzi, and Peter Blake, as well as painters as varied as John Craxton, Howard Hodgkin, Patrick George, Karl Weschke, Paula Rego, and Victor Willing. In every instance the "conversation" was a dialogue, an exchange.

This exhibition revives a sense of these overlapping spheres of influence and engagement within a dynamic and varied artistic community. It testifies to the extraordinary and ongoing vitality of figurative painting in London in the decades after the war.

The exhibition is timely. These artists, and the relationships between them, warrant re-examination now, not only because of the enduring achievements of the individual artists across uncommonly long careers, but because their work continues to exert an extraordinary influence upon the contemporary art landscape, informing and affecting the work of major figures as varied as Damien Hirst, Peter Doig, Michael Landy, Keith Coventry, Glenn Brown, Wilhelm Sasnal, Elizabeth Peyton, and Adrian Ghenie. Here influence is often not just formal, but a question of attitude, of commitment. At the same time, the idea of a "School of London" has become so pervasive that it is important to question it, to open it up to debate. That there have been no institutional surveys of this phenomenon in more than a decade makes the need for such an investigation more current.

This exhibition does not attempt a definitive overview of the subject. It is very much a personal selection made by the exhibition's curator, Catherine Lampert. Her extended essay for this publication brilliantly articulates the interconnections between very different artists and draws out points of connection and difference. Tom Hunt's essay explores their ongoing influence.

This project has been long in its development and realisation and many people need to be thanked for their commitment, patience and generosity. We are especially grateful to the lenders to the show, both museums and private individuals. Their support makes such a project possible. Above all, we are indebted to the artists. It was very gratifying that Frank Auerbach, Leon Kossoff, and David Hockney supported and contributed to the project from the beginning. In addition, Lucian Freud and Richard Hamilton endorsed the project and were involved before their recent deaths.

Finally, our thanks are due to Catherine Lampert. Catherine responded to our initial invitation to make an exhibition exploring this subject with great enthusiasm. Drawing on her long personal associations with the artists she has brought together a group of works that suggests revealing new perspectives. Her enduring long-term commitment to this group of artists since the 1970s—as curator, writer, sitter, and friend—is inspiring.

Ben Tufnell
Director of Exhibitions, Haunch of Venison

The Mystery of Appearance

Catherine Lampert

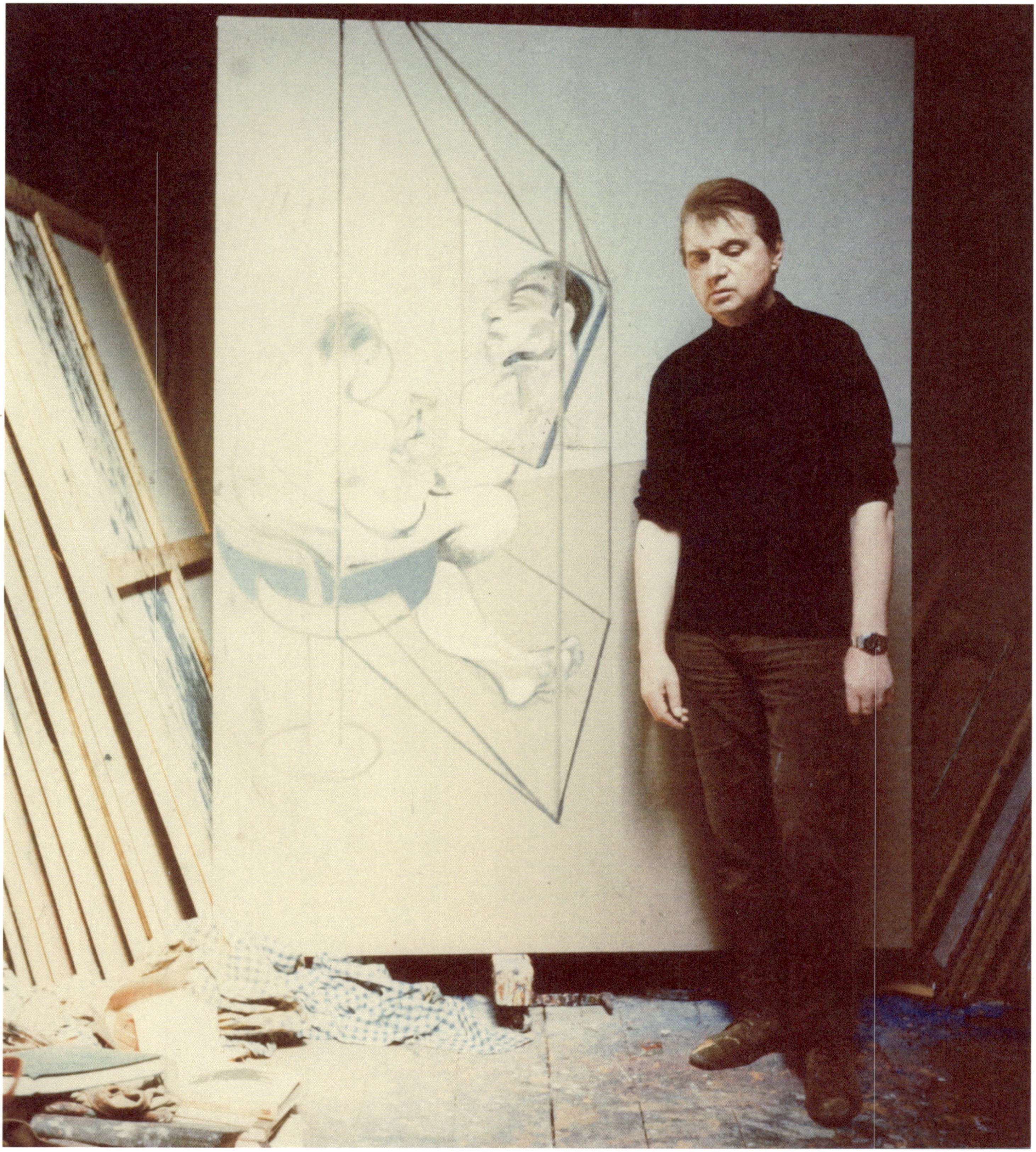

[1] Francis Bacon, in *David Sylvester, Interviews with Francis Bacon* (London, 1980), p. 105.

[2] R.B. Kitaj, *Art Works: British and Contemporary Art 1960–2000*, Deutsche Bank (London, 2000).

[3] Richard Hamilton, *The Artist's Eye*, exh. cat., National Gallery (London,1978), reprinted in *Richard Hamilton, Collected Words. 1953–1982* (London, 1982), pp. 264–65.

Left: Francis Bacon in 1978, in front of the left panel of *Three Studies of the Male Back*, 1970. Photo: Michael Pergolani

> To me, the mystery of painting today is how can appearance be made. I know it can be illustrated, I know it can be photographed. But how can this thing be made so that you catch the mystery of appearance within the mystery of the making? . . . one knows that by some accidental brushmarks suddenly appearance comes in with a vividness that no accepted way of doing it would have brought about.[1]
>
> — *Francis Bacon*

Introduction

The Mystery of Appearance is intended to remind visitors of the extraordinary quality and liveliness of the work of ten artists and with its catalogue to suggest fresh, tangential connections. Their achievements are still persistently under-rated in non-British accounts so another reason for the juxtapositions (albeit with a limited number) is to challenge the orthodox story of post-war art. Too often British painting in the 1950s is cast as art made in the shadow of the terrible trauma of the Second World War, with abstract art tagged as a progressive escape route and the new confidence and subject matter emerging in the 1960s, lit up by the buzz of Pop art and swinging London, defined as a golden moment. But this account falters not just by trying to simplify the artists into distinct movements and generations—it underestimates the self-aware way each insisted upon pinning down raw observations and breathing a fresh existence into found imagery. Their paintings often aim for grand effect but also for clarity and an authentic, stirring equivalent of space, their idioms unprecedented and always changing. As the quotation from Bacon suggests, it is difficult to put these things—their feats—into words.

Within a relatively small post-war British art world the most ambitious artists tended to be aware of each other and to engage in "conversations." Unfortunately the various attempts to draw a line around a "School of London," which began in the late 1940s and gathered speed in the late 1970s, created a false history associated with "representational" art (as if a moral virtue) and the suggestion of a "club" (tagged to a photograph taken at Wheeler's restaurant in 1962). R.B. Kitaj regretted the attention the phrase received; in the catalogue for *The Human Clay,* an Arts Council purchase exhibition staged in 1976, he chose a generous group of "fifty artists, both known and unknown" working in his "then adopted city."[2] The question of whether painting had contemporary relevance was raised in *A New Spirit of Painting* at the Royal Academy of Arts in 1981, however, with a few exceptions British artists remained on the periphery of international art discourse, only Bacon and Freud rivalling Warhol and Richter in name recognition.

The least one could say is that these artists feel a kindred relationship to the great art displayed in museums, and their persistence and focus over a lifetime of unrelenting self-discipline has led to work of extraordinary invention right up to the end. Richard Hamilton, writing with respect to his selection for the National Gallery's second *Artist's Eye* exhibition in 1978 said something rather prophetic when he commended the kind of expression where "there is no rhetoric, only a calm resolution in the undertaking of a remarkably daring endeavour."[3]

Into the display of paintings from the collection by Mantegna, Goya, Poussin, Saenredam, Turner and others—he inserted a television and a reproduction of Van Gogh's sunflowers, an indication of being attuned to the ever-growing public fascination with iconic images and an emphasis on the life stories of artists.

We begin with a selection of paintings of single people, not classic portraits or nudes but a product of "the sitter and the artist." The next section includes pictures with direct reference to the art in museum collections and to neglected genres like still-life. This is followed by a group of paintings realised by way of very rich, organic forms derived from people and nature, the forms nurtured in a subtly tactile way whereas in the final space the art registers the outside world, sometimes using the filter of photographs, and preparatory studies or set-ups, the colour fresh and at times hyper-real.

The gallery's initial idea was to stage an exhibition of British figurative painting that would be in a sense a successor to David Anfam's reading of Abstract Expressionism (Haunch of Venison New York, *Abstract Expressionism— A World Elsewhere,* 2008). In the back of the curators' minds was why the best British art of the mid-1950s to late 1970s was always about "something" whereas American painters of the same time looked for a more all-over wholeness, insisting on a strange equation of gestural, or formal, handling of paint with conceptual universality. A famous statement by Barnett Newman asserts that advanced art shares the goal of "freeing ourselves of the impediments of memory, association, nostalgia, legend, myth, or what have you that have been the devices of Western European painting."[4]

As a way of indicating the British preference for facts and experience, as well as understatement, rather than such Gnostic pronouncements, one is reminded of David Hockney's anecdote. Comparing Newman and Degas he accepted that any good artist is engaged with theory, "But it's Degas's eye and attitudes that matter, the responses he got, the responses he in part felt. In Barnett Newman's work it isn't like that at all. I'm not praising one over another, we all know who is the better artist, I'm sure Barnett Newman wouldn't say he was as good as Degas. He loved Degas, actually, as I do. Once Newman came to one of the first shows I had in New York, and he said to me, 'You know, I used to paint like this myself.' And I said to him, 'Do you mean I'm going to finish up painting blue stripes?' And he laughed. He was a sweet man."[5]

The confidence, or perversity, to nurture a prosaic subject in a traditional medium went against a prevailing ethos in the 1950s. Francis Bacon's subject is a man eating a leg of chicken. William Coldstream takes on a commission to paint the Provost of University College London as an experiment in the impartial registration of personality. Leon Kossoff draws *Old People's Party at Bethnal Green,* 1958–59. Richard Hamilton is fascinated by the ideas around depicting movement on a picture plane and begins with diagrammatic studies of a model in the life room. There is a sense that to admit interest in authentic records of human behaviour and to respect an empirical method was intentionally in opposition to attitudes and opinions coming from prominent critics. Herbert Read, once linked to Surrealism, when championing the work of artists like Henry Moore, Reg Butler and Graham Sutherland, praised their attenuated forms as progressive, as echoing the grim fear of nuclear devastation, while claiming that a purging, cryptic reductiveness could be socially redemptive. On the other hand Read condemned the New York School as lost in "a vacuous nihilism that renounces the visible world and even the inner world of the imagination, and scribbles a graph of its uncertainty on the surface of a blank consciousness."[6]

This essay begins with the dilemma and voice of William Coldstream (1908–87), partly as a way of bridging the pre- and post-war periods, partly to avoid an account mainly mediated by the voice of critics and most of all because he was an exceptionally intelligent and perceptive artist whose radical work is presently almost invisible. John Russell, in 1981, looking back on the period of this exhibition, called him "a buoy by which to steer."[7] Later, one-to-one contacts and conversations between the individual artists are privileged (though not as exhaustively as one would like). A digression to introduce the Arts Council-organised exhibitions in 1965 and 1966 of Giacometti and Duchamp at the Tate is justified because of the involvement of eight of these artists in their realisation and because the documentary material flushes out subtle differences in their way of relating to contingent issues of representation and iconoclasm. There are obviously other outstanding paint-

[4] David Anfam, *Abstract Expressionism—A World Elsewhere,* exh. cat., Haunch of Venison (New York, 2008), p. 15, quoting Newman, "The Sublime is Now." (1948)

[5] *David Hockney by David Hockney. My Early Years,* ed. Nikos Stangos (London, 1976), p. 62.

[6] Herbert Read, "A Blot on the Scutcheon," *Encounter,* July 1955, pp. 54–57, and *Contemporary British Art,* 1951, revised 1954. When the ICA opened in 1948 (and moved to Dover Street in 1950) Read was President, and Penrose, Chairman of the Board.

[7] John Russell, "The Pervasive Presence of William Coldstream," *New York Times,* 8 November, 1981, p. 27.

Right: Visitors and work in *The Artist's Eye* exhibition by Richard Hamilton, The National Gallery, 1978.

Below left: Francis Bacon, *Study of a Portrait of Lucian Freud (Sideways)*, 1971.

Below right: Francis Bacon, *Man Eating a Leg of Chicken*, 1952. Collezione Maramotti.

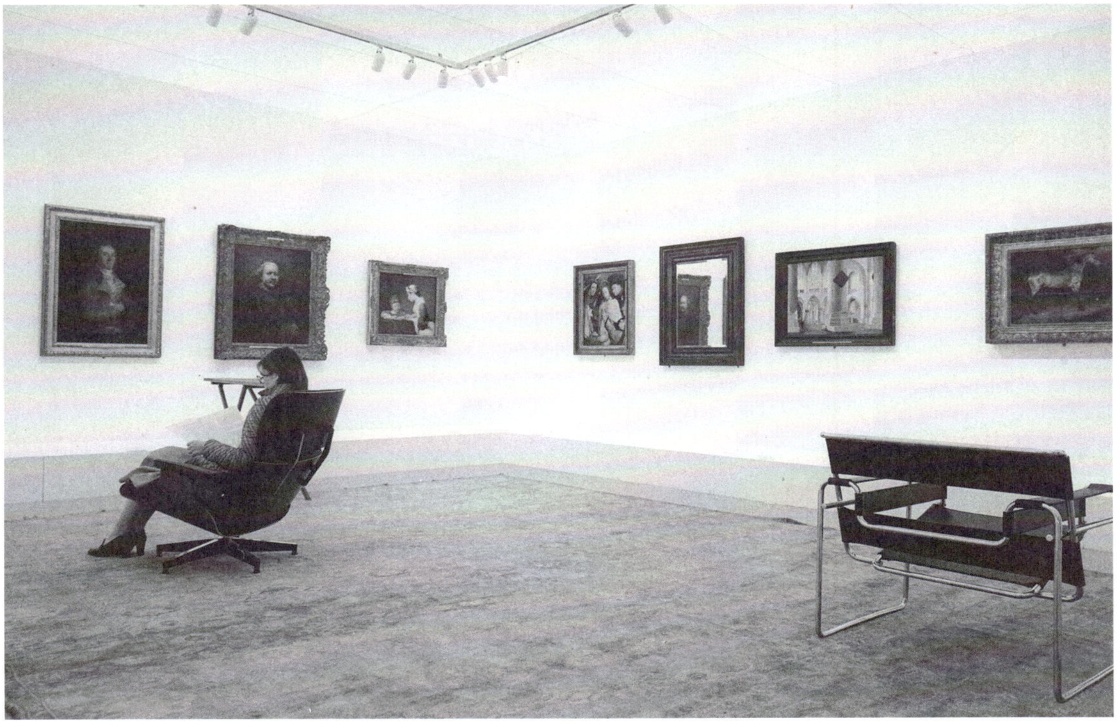

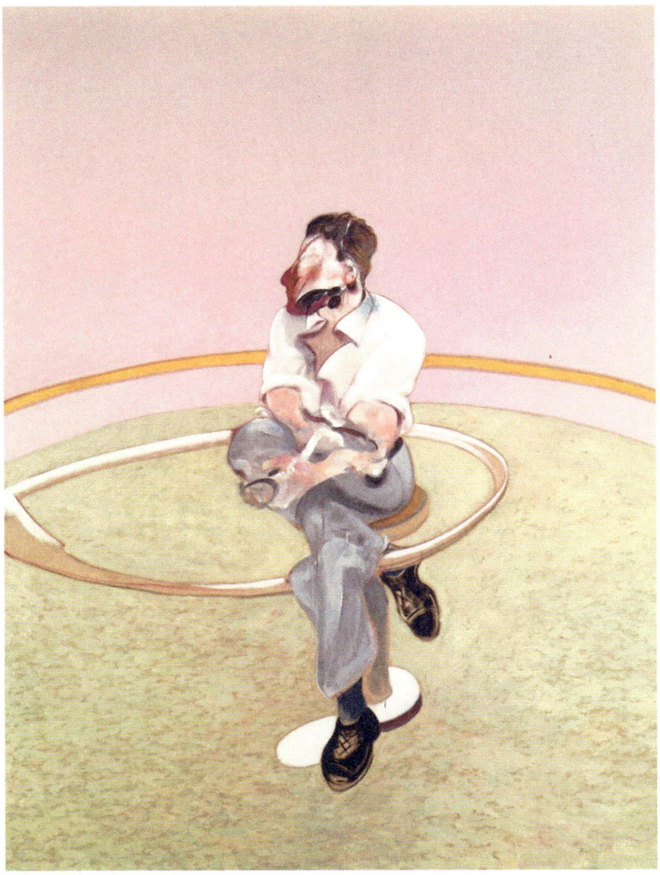

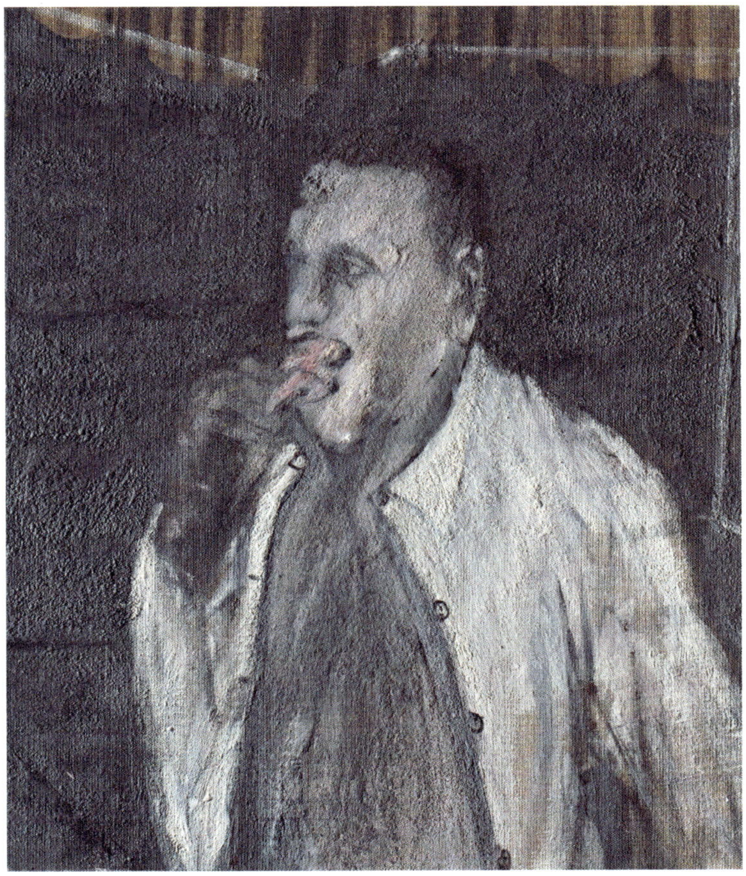

William Coldstream

Born 1908 in Bedford, Northumberland

After originally intending to study medicine, Coldstream decided to study art at the Slade School of Fine Art, entering in 1926, and leaving in 1929 without a diploma. He travelled to France, Greece, and Italy, and became friends with W.H. Auden, Victor Pasmore, and Graham Bell. Continually uncertain which direction to take and how to support himself, he worked with the G.P.O. Film Unit from1934–37, which was led by Geoffrey Grigson, but he also made a painting in Bolton under the Mass Observation project, which helped confirm the direction he would take. In 1937 he was one of the founders of the School of Drawing and Painting in the Euston Road, which survived until the war began. After teaching at Camberwell School of Arts and Crafts, he was appointed Slade Professor of Fine Art, University College, in 1949, introducing a wide range of tutors, including, as well as artists, several art historians (Rudolph Wittkower and Ernst Gombrich), and opening a film department run by Thorold Dickinson. Knighted in 1956, Coldstream was Chairman of the National Advisory Council on Art Education (1958–71), a role that lead to the reshaping of art education in Britain—the Second Coldstream Report was published in 1970. An Arts Council solo exhibition opened at the South London Art Gallery in 1962 and toured for six months. Coldstream died in 1987. His posthumous Tate retrospective in 1990 was selected by Lawrence Gowing and David Sylvester.

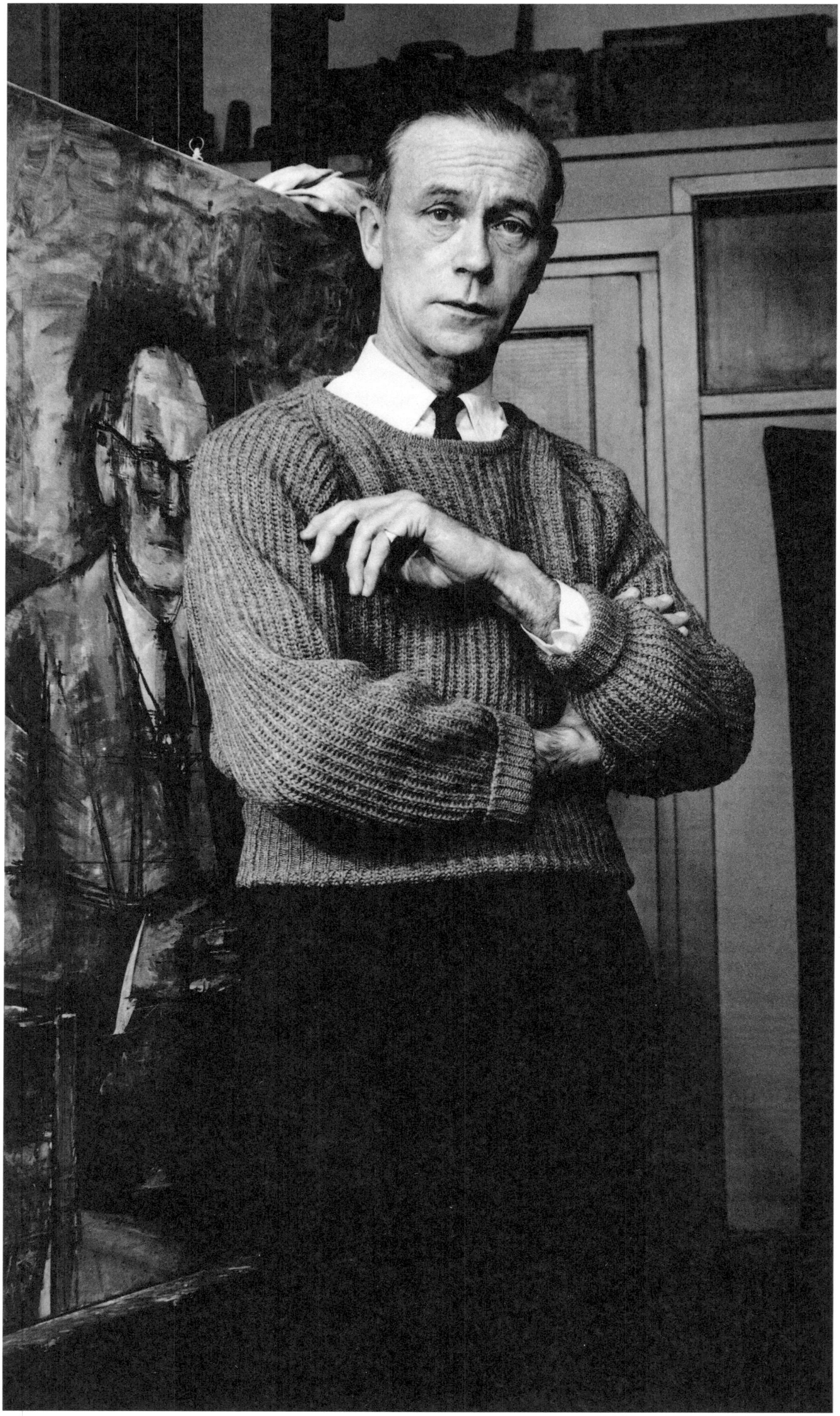

Right: Jorge Lewinski, *William Coldstream*, 1963.

I William Coldstream, letter to John Rake, 7 August, 1947, Tate archive.

II William Coldstream, interview with David Sylvester, *Burlington Magazine*, 1962.

Van Gogh could paint pictures with an idea from nature because he painted them off bang in one go and left them. But the reason that the long protracted Cézannes are true and successful is that Cézanne had no preconceived idea—he let the picture unfold; and accepted fully the changes in the aspect of his most stable subject matter he could find . . . [I]

Oh, there's no going over. I mean I never rub out. I just gradually build up. I like to feel that the whole surface in a way is sort of coming along together up to a point. It isn't that I don't work sometimes a very long time in one corner, but I like to feel that the whole surface is remaining somehow in balance at any moment. That's to say, I don't like to feel there's a hole in the canvas, so I like it to be even and to grow evenly . . . One doesn't read the figure in the way that one reads the expression in the face and therefore this tremendously concentrated and expressive focal point, yet indissolubly attached to the figure—somehow it's a piquant contrast which I think is moving and interesting. [II]

[8] Lampert organised/curated exhibitions at the Hayward Gallery (Auerbach, 1978; Andrews, 1980; Freud, 1988), Serpentine Gallery (Caro, 1984; Gowing, 1983); Whitechapel Gallery (Uglow, 1974, 1989; Andrews, 1991; Freud, 1993); Royal Academy of Arts (Auerbach, 2001); Irish Museum of Modern Art, Dublin (Freud, 2007) and has written on most of the artists in this exhibition. She has sat for Auerbach since 1978.

[9] William Coldstream to Dr John S. Rake, 17 January, 1932, Tate archive.

[10] Ibid., 15 July, 1932.

[11] Lawrence Gowing, referring to the *Objective Abstraction* exhibition, Zwemmer's Gallery, London, 1934, in *Rodrigo Moynihan*, exh. cat., Royal Academy of Arts (London, 1998), p. 8.

ers and sculptors of similar age who are very relevant to the "British" story, yet to keep the concentration appropriate to the scale of the space and occasion, the focus is limited to ten, evidencing their "mature" style in the 1950s and 1960s, extending to the 1970s and early 1980s when I began to know them, sit for Auerbach, and organise exhibitions for the Hayward, Serpentine, and Whitechapel galleries.[8] Happily, three are alive and working at the very highest level.

What you can believe in: William Coldstream

While studying at the Slade (1926–29) Coldstream received a "traditional" grounding in drawing but remembered being more stimulated by the wayward opinions and work of Walter Richard Sickert (1860–1942), and by French painting, some of it hung in the newly established Modern Foreign Gallery at the Tate, paintings by Matisse hung in the Gargoyle Club, and more art experienced on visits to the continent. Reading his long-term correspondence with a friend who became a doctor, John Rake, we learn he was experimenting with abstraction in the manner of Braque in 1932. "All the time I have in the back of my mind the feeling that painting must rise above purism and take back humanity if it is to be really vital again."[9] "However much we may admire the art of primitive peoples which is always imaginative and not connected with objective vision it must be impossible for us to profit from it in any practical way. The surrealism and other non-visual (or imaginative painters) one imagines have been influenced by primitive and oriental work. But just as the attempt of the pre-Raphaelites was wrong because it was a mimicry of old painting and not a parallel so it seems to me that the attempt of such people as Klee is wrong."[10]

Two of Coldstream's friends, Rodrigo Moynihan and Geoffrey Tibble, were among those who gathered briefly in 1934 under the label Objective Abstraction. Adopting a loose "stream of consciousness" application of paint, their experiments focused on the material aspect of art, as the artist Lawrence Gowing described it: "The contention was that objectively painting consisted simply of paint, the brush marks themselves, and the painter's commitment to them. Objectively a Monet was the crust of pigment."[11] Coldstream, after making an unsuccessful attempt, was unconvinced. "Someone I know said that the logical development of objectivism in painting must eventually lead to regarding the canvas itself as the object—something to be worked on

[12] Coldstream-Rake, 8 March, 1933, Tate archive.

[13] Ibid., September 1936. Coldstream's article "How I Paint," *Listener*, 15 September, 1937, pp. 570–72, describes how "the 1930 slump" affected his generation.

[14] Coldstream-Rake, first quarter, 1936. Auden went off to Spain in January 1939, volunteering to drive an ambulance (Coldstream's portrait was made soon after his return in March and before he left for the United States).

[15] Foreword by Benedict Nicolson to an interview with David Sylvester, 13 April, 1962, published in the *Burlington Magazine*, p. 263. Various artists, notably the photographer Humphrey Jennings, participated in the Mass Observation movement. Coldstream and Graham Bell were sent to Bolton in the north to paint the industrial landscape.

[16] Catherine Lampert and Richard Kendall, *Euan Uglow. The Complete Paintings* (London and New Haven, 2007), p.lv citing a radio interview with Blunt, 25 July, 1938.

[17] William Townsend, *The Townsend Journals. An Artist's Record of his Times 1928–51* (London, 1976), 24 June, 1937, pp. 40–41. Spender recalled "It was a very miserable picture, a sheet of paper with about two lines on it. I thought he might have done a bit better." See also Jake Auerbach interviewing Spender, "Brushes with genius, Picasso's sculpture," *The Independent*, 6 February, 1984.

[18] Ibid., 16 March, 1938, p. 43.

[19] *The Whitechapel Art Gallery Centenary Review*, ed. Catherine Lampert and Andrea Tarsia (London, 2001), contains articles on historic Whitechapel exhibitions. Hamilton and Uglow spoke to the author about the peripheral pleasures of the American-sponsored events.

as a carpenter works on a chair. The illusion is expelled. But this is really absurd because painting is the exploitation of vision not of material."[12] In 1935, uncertain of his own direction and frustrated in his attempt to support a family as an artist, at the suggestion of W.H. Auden, he approached John Grierson, a documentary film maker and head of public relations at the Post Office and was asked to join the G.P.O. Film Unit. One can spot Coldstream's hallmark wit and clarity in several very lively instructive films like *The King's Stamp, Night Mail* (with words by Auden), and the amusing *The Fairy of the Phone,* which he directed (the chorus line was made up of the girl telephone operators).

Slowly regaining his determination to paint, Coldstream began teaching in the Mary Ward settlement in the East End in September 1936. "I find that I can only paint in front of the thing now and I really am not much interested in doing anything but faces."[13] He reports that Auden laments "that the most interesting thing in the world at the moment was a civil war," an opinion shared by their friend the poet Stephen Spender and others. "I had social realist ideas in the sense that I would like to paint in a kind of way which people who might not know an enormous amount about painting would find interesting."[14] Ultimately, as the art historian Benedict Nicolson observed, Coldstream was ill-equipped "to appeal to a wider public because he lacked the 'illustrative capacity' . . . his honesty forbade him from going beyond what his imagination dictated."[15]

Anthony Blunt, head of the Courtauld Institute, praised Coldstream as sharing with the Mexican muralists Diego Rivera and José Clemente Orozco the desire to establish a figurative movement that was capable of "helping the proletariat," whereas in the same recorded conversation Coldstream demurred, "It's no good painting a certain way merely because you think you 'ought' to, unless such a subject or such a treatment comes naturally to you . . . "[16] A number of artists participated in the Peace rally in the Albert Hall in June 1937 in support of the Spanish Republican cause. Picasso sent regrets (he was finishing *Guernica*) but donated a drawing for auction; Paul Robeson "bestrode this meeting so that the negroes and the Spaniards seemed the same thing . . . the oppressed everywhere and all the generous aspirations of the unoppressed as well."[17] Roland Penrose, artist and future founder of the ICA, and Stephen Spender were central players in the fight against fascism. They were also protagonists in the debates between artists where there was a level of tolerance and good humour. The left-leaning group, the A.I.A., pitted the Surrealists against the Realists in March 1938. The Surrealists (represented by Penrose, Julian Trevelyan, and Humphrey Jennings) were, according to William Townsend, the more brilliant debaters (works by Picasso and Miró hung behind them) while the other side (Graham Bell, Coldstream, and the Social Realist sculptor of Hungarian origin, Peter Peri) protested that Surrealism was too restricted in its pictorial aims.[18]

In January 1939, with Penrose's encouragement, it was arranged for Picasso's *Guernica* to be displayed for two weeks in the West End (where Hamilton remembered seeing the accompanying drawings as well as the enormous canvas) and another two at the Whitechapel Gallery under the auspices of the East London Aid Spain committee of the Stepney Trades Council (a local organisation with Communist Party members). In a photograph the Labour Party leader Clement Attlee addresses the group, Roland Penrose, seated on the right. Gowing, Pasmore, Moynihan, and their friends produced large banners with motifs from Goya's Disasters of War series to use for the Trafalgar Square demonstration in February 1939, *Arms for Spain* and the Whitechapel's *Art for the People* was arranged in distinct sections (surrealism, abstraction and realism) in order that modern art might be understood by a broad audience.[19]

A few painters, initially Claude Rogers, joined by Graham Bell, Victor Pasmore and Coldstream, rented studios in autumn 1937 on Fitzroy Street, and then in a larger space

[20] Lawrence Gowing, "Remembering Coldstream," *William Coldstream*, exh. cat., Tate (London, 1990), p. 12 and p. 15. See also Bruce Laughton, *William Coldstream* (London and New Haven, 2004), Chapter 5.

on the Euston Road. During the two years this rather "atelier" model of artists working alongside students survived, Rogers was the main instructor. Coldstream never taught there regularly, yet his intellectual rigour was valued and his method of overcoming the difficulty of rendering a curved visual field on a flat surface emulated. Holding a brush at a right angle to the artist's extended arm, the head steady but the open eye moving, the marks on the canvas were part of a "struggle for verifiable definition," at least to determine positions and proportional relationships. The difficulty of representation, the phenomena of seeing, was embraced; if his system of measurements became more laborious than nearly any other painter would tolerate, as Gowing reckoned, it "opened to Coldstream a degree of objective certainty that none of his contemporaries had any idea of."[20] It also steadied the nerves of an artist almost ashamed of his acutely heightened perceptions; inspecting masterpieces like *Winifred Burger,* 1936–37, with its airy, parallel strokes, or the light-filled *St Pancras Station L.M.S.,* 1938 (which began with photographs taken on site), we can appreciate how much he departed from a literal description. According to the painter, Patrick George, Coldstream's fascination with measurement was deep-rooted. On a daily basis he would guess ages and heights on the underground, the distance between lampposts

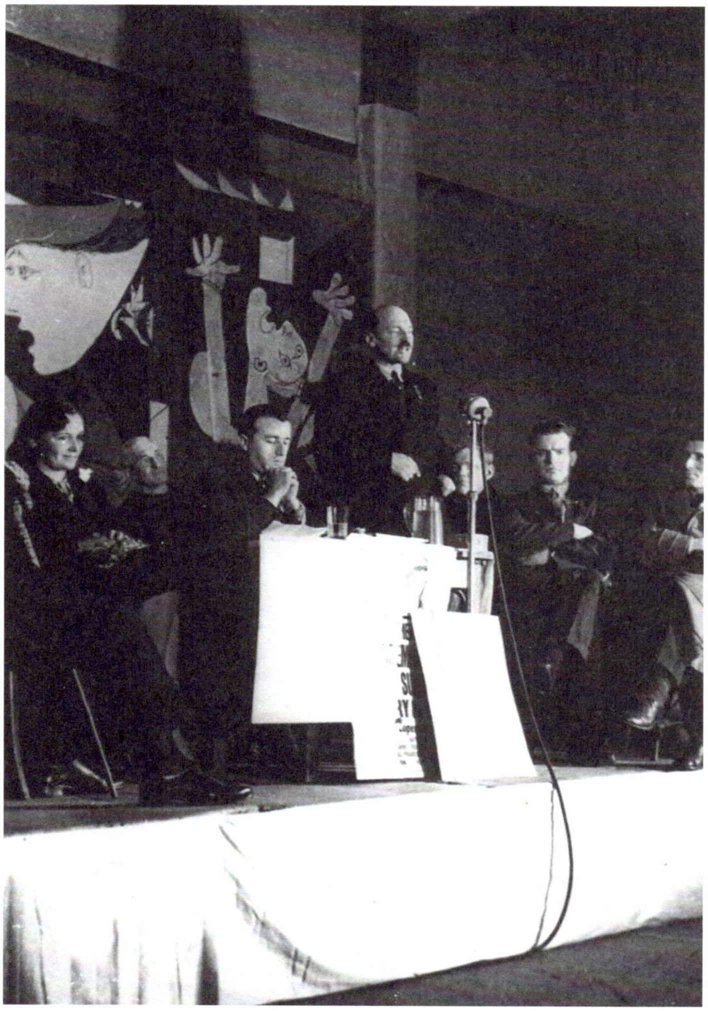

Below: Clement Atlee at Whitechapel Gallery (Roland Penrose far right), London, England, 1939.

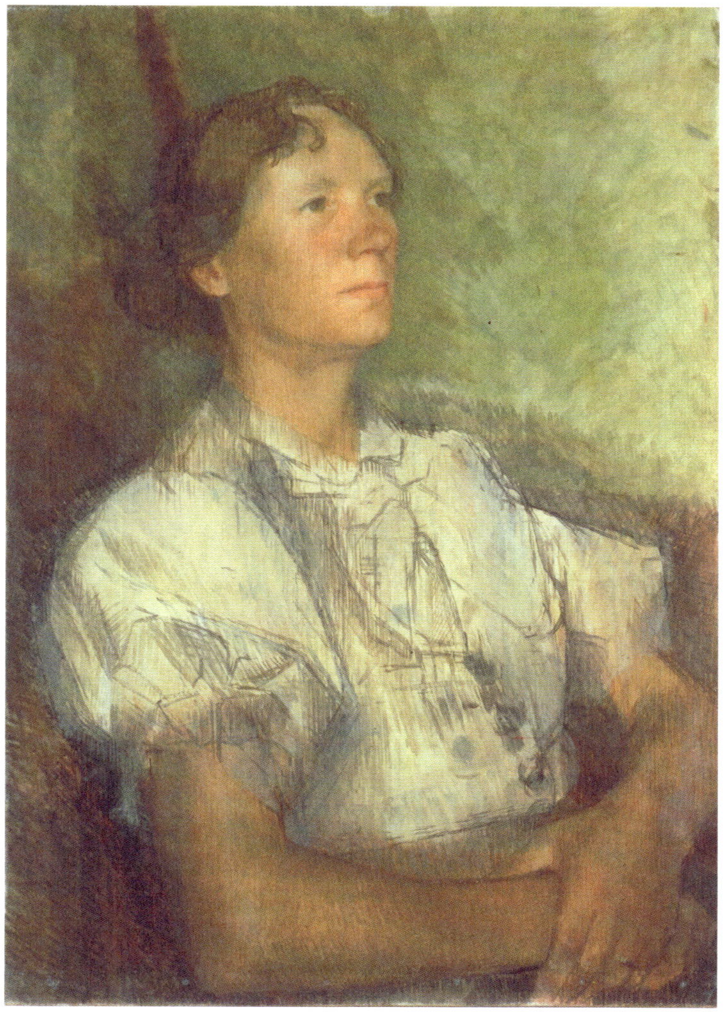

Below right: William Coldstream, *Winifred Burger,* 1937. Tate, London.

[21] Patrick George, speaking at Tate Britain, 2008. Adrian Stokes on Coldstream "a great modern master, as 'extreme' and isolated as Rothko" quoted in Uglow, 2007, p. xix.

[22] Al Alvarez, *Leon Kossoff. From the Early Years 1957–67,* exh. cat., Mitchell-Innes Nash (New York, 2009), p. 13.

[23] The direct involvement in military service differed, not least due to age (National Service, the compulsory call-up, ended in 1960). Coldstream enlisted in the Royal Artillery, moving via camouflage officer to Official War Artist. Legend (well-informed) has it that the night before his medical examination Francis Bacon slept next to a dog so that his asthma would seem alarmingly evident but he was engaged in home service. Freud and his family arrived from Berlin in 1933. Three weeks before the rules of the internment of foreigners took effect, they were naturalised, an exception facilitated by Sigmund Freud's disciple, Princess Marie Bonaparte, and her Greek husband's connections to the Royal family. Freud signed on as a merchant seaman on a ship leaving Liverpool for Nova Scotia (he survived a near miss when German aircraft attacked the convoy) and on his return he was invalided out with tonsillitis. Having worked as a jig and tool draughtsman after the outbreak of war, 1940–45, Hamilton resumed study at the RA Schools, was expelled, and continued studying at the Slade. Kossoff had been evacuated from the East End to Suffolk where his temporary family encouraged him to paint. After serving three years in Europe with the Royal Fusiliers, attached to 2nd Battalion Jewish Brigade, 1945–48, in 1949 he enrolled at St Martins. Auerbach failed his army medical; Hockney and Uglow (evacuated as a child to Cornwall) became conscientious objectors (doing hospital and building duties); Caulfield signed up for three years with the Royal Air Force.

and the weight of babies.[21] A much later work, the *Seated Nude (Catherine Kessler),* 1972–73, indicates how such direct looking and measuring helped to overcome the artificiality of painting a young woman nude, seated in the same armchair used for the portrait commissions, invariably mature men. Serene, she makes eye contact with the artist. His brush touches the planes that depict the corner of the room in a way that seems recklessly beautiful and complementary to her compact form held together by the blood-flushed hands lying in her lap.

But a practice that allows for a heightened emotional state and accurate drawing is not only achieved by a gradual application of marks. The writer Al Alvarez describes the Kossoff painting *Seated Woman No.2,* 1959, which he has owned for decades: "a perfect example of Coleridge's 'aloofness.' The impulse behind it may be expressionist—grieving and wild—but the execution is restrained and the final effect is almost classical. The finished picture seems to have emerged from the dense mass of pigment terribly slowly and only as a result of great labour and concentration."[22]

Around the art schools and the galleries after the war

After leaving the army in 1945, where he had served as a camouflage officer and then Official War Artist, Coldstream headed the painting department at Camberwell School of Art and began to have a public voice and various responsibilities, for example, he recorded his thoughts on Courbet's *Burial at Ornans* for a BBC television programme in 1947, and later became a trustee of the National Gallery, the Tate, and head of the British Film Institute.[23] Soon after being appointed Professor at the Slade School of Art in 1949, he brought in younger artists as tutors—Patrick George, Lucian Freud, and Andrew Forge—and visitors from a spectrum as broad as Fernand Léger, Robert Medley, and Keith Vaughan. Rudolph Wittkower and Ernst Gombrich were invited to teach art history and the first Film Unit in an art college, run by the director Thorold Dickinson, opened in 1960. A number of "mature," ex-service, ex-industry students were already enrolled, amongst them Hamilton, Eduardo Paolozzi, Nigel Henderson, and William Turnbull. Hamilton, who got on well with Coldstream, said simply "the atmosphere was marvelous at that time."[24]

A key source and area of research that attracted young artists during the 1950s was the book *On Growth and Form* by the Scottish morphologist, D'Arcy Wentworth Thompson (1917, re-issued in 1944), the text accompanied by intriguing illustrations and cross-sections of organisms. Hamilton and Turnbull began "spending hours in the Natural History Museum examining fantastic biological forms from the fossil collection."[25] This extended to investigating various systems of representation, like James J. Gibson's writing on the question of vision in motion, and Hamilton devised an exhibition around *Growth and Form* as the ICA's contribution to the Festival of Britain in 1951. Such pursuits sometimes crossed with erudite analysis of the mathematics and perspective used in early Renaissance art (especially in the work of Piero Della Francesca) led by Wittkower and another tutor, Sam Carter. Euan Uglow, in his last year at the Slade, 1954, set out to make a painting using all the "old" methods of perspective, his *Musicians.*[26] As well as Eadweard Muybridge's photographic studies, a book often cited in connection with Francis Bacon, K.C. Clark's *Positioning in Radiography* (1939) was in the libraries of several artists. For Uglow it suggested unconventional ways to pose models; one sees this later in the 1960s when the angle of vision is very arbitrary and the recess in which the model sits or lies is contrived as with diorama or laboratory-like precision.

To realise the paintings *Respective,* 1951, and *Trainsition III,* 1954, Hamilton interpreted delicate three-dimensional readings of objects in space, the tone and shading controlled with finesse, as he recalled: "These paintings took a major characteristic of Cézanne's method, that of structuring the surface through straight

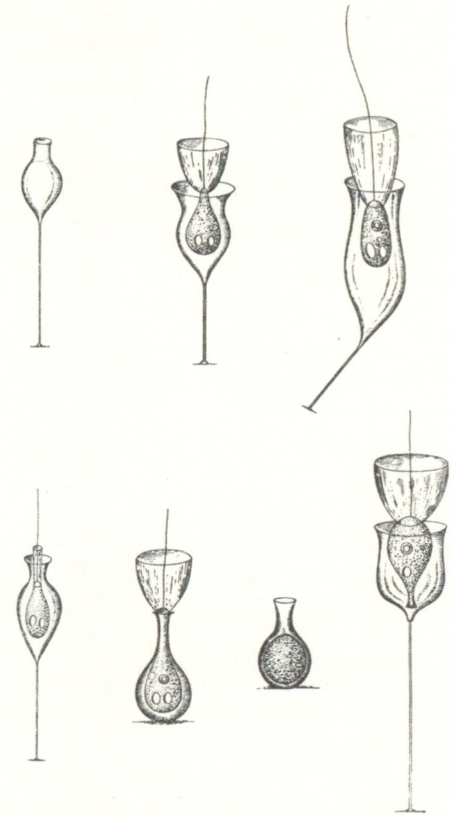

Fig. 20. Various species of *Salpingoeca.* After Saville Kent.

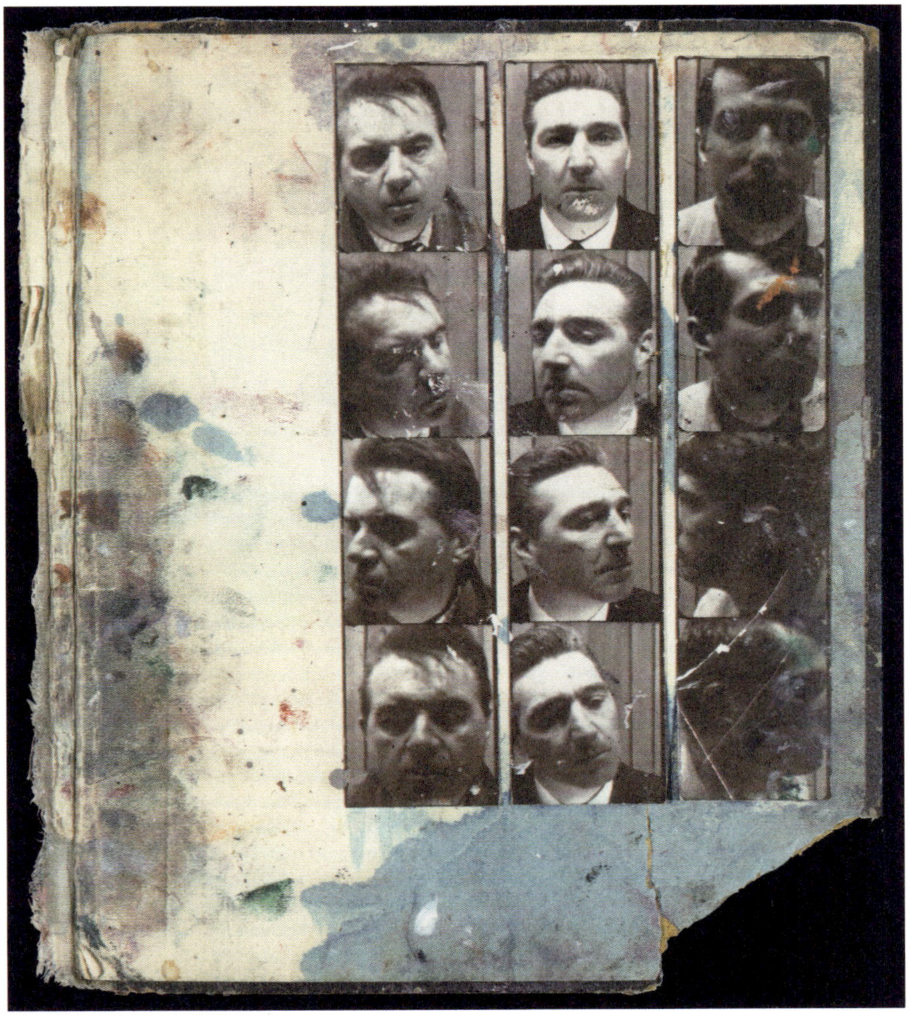

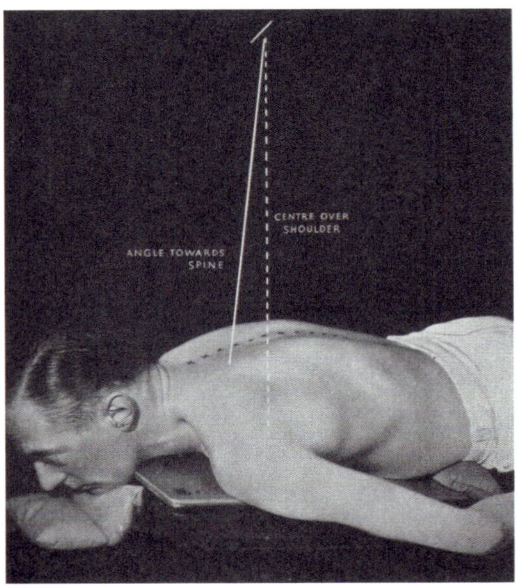

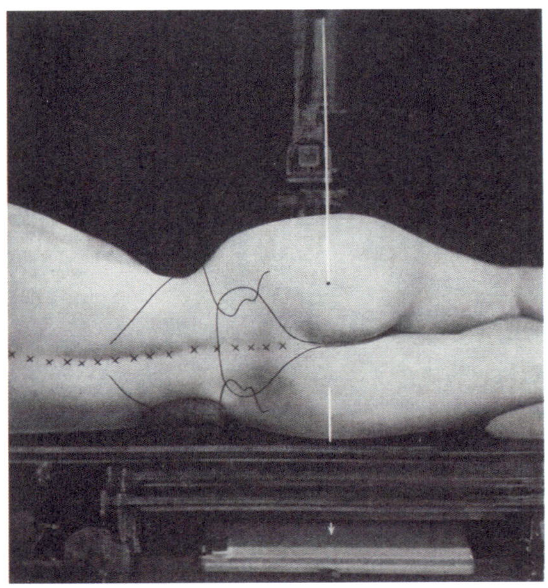

Above left: Illustrations from *On Growth and Form,* 1917, by D'Arcy Wentworth Thompson, p. 83.

Above right: Working document: three photomat strips, of Bacon, George Dyer, and David Plante, taken in Aix-en-Provence, 1966, pasted onto the inside rear cover of an unidentified book, c. 1966–67.

Right: Illustrations from K.C. Clark's *Positioning in Radiography,* 1939.

Francis Bacon

Born 1909 in Dublin

Bacon spent his youth in Ireland and England, before going to Paris in 1927 and to Germany in 1929. In the 1930s he began to work as an interior designer of furniture and rugs, while also painting and exhibiting. In the 1940s he became friends with Graham Sutherland, who introduced him to Erica Brausen, who opened the Hanover Gallery, exhibiting Bacon in 1949. His work became known to an American audience, partly through Sam Hunter's article "Francis Bacon: The Anatomy of Horror," in *Magazine of Art,* 1952. Paintings after Velázquez's *Innocent X* appear from 1951. During the 1950s and 1960s Bacon travelled constantly, spending time in Monaco, Italy, Paris, and Tangiers. From 1960 to his death he was represented by Marlborough Fine Art. Photographs were one source for his images, although Bacon protested that he didn't "use them at all as a model," regarding them as fundamentally mere illustrations. His retrospective at the Grand Palais in Paris in 1971 was marked by the death of his lover George Dyer on the eve of the opening, an event later visualised by several memorial triptychs. David Sylvester published *Interviews with Francis Bacon,* first in 1975 (the texts subsequently extended and revised.) Bacon's cluttered studio in Reece Mews, South Kensington, London, where he moved in 1961, was relocated to the Dublin City Gallery The Hugh Lane, and the contents digitally archived. Bacon died in Madrid in 1992.

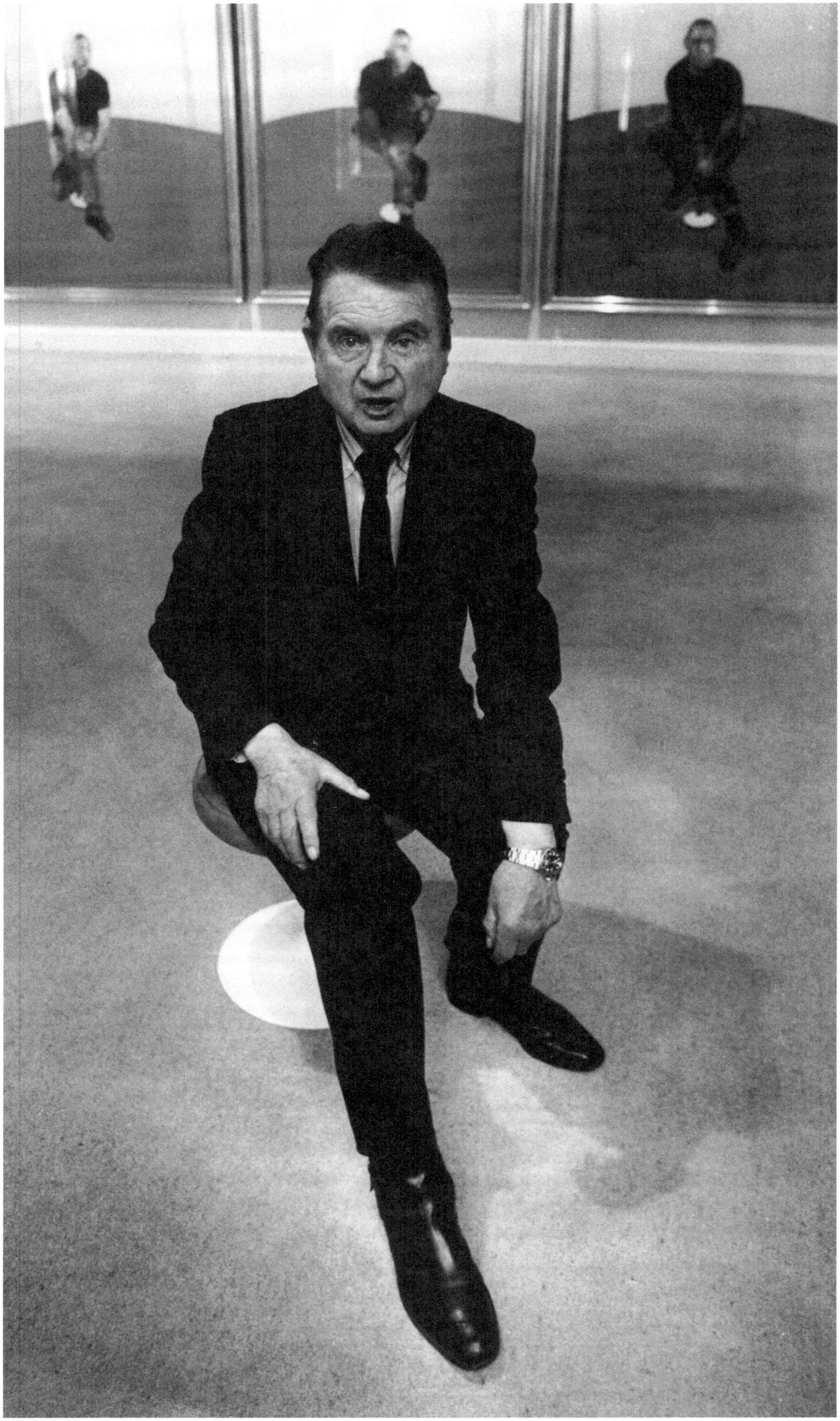

Right: Mark Ellidge, *Francis Bacon,* 1987.

I Francis Bacon, quoted in Rothenstein, *Francis Bacon*, exh. cat., Tate (London, 1962), introduction.

II Ibid.

III Francis Bacon, speaking of the early painting *Figure in a Landscape*, 1945, Sylvester interviews (1980 edition).

IV Ibid.

What one requires is intelligence and awareness just to the edge, and beyond that to trust to instinct. [I]

'How can I take an interest in my work,' he asked me, 'when I don't like it?' [II]

The Junta [by Goya, in Castres] is a very special painting because the figures seem to have been woven out of the air in such a mysterious way, as though the air actually entered into the being of each image of each person. [III]

Actually there is no paint at all on the suit apart from a very thin grey wash on which I put dust from the floor . . . I don't know about the lastingness of things. But that is how it was because I thought: well, how I can make that slightly furry quality of a flannel suit? And then I suddenly thought: well, I'll get some dust.

I am working for myself; what else have I got to work for? How can you work for an audience . . . I have got nobody to excite except myself, so I am always surprised if anybody else likes my work sometimes . . . I want my life to be as free as possible, I just want the best kind of atmosphere to work in. And so in politics I have tended to vote for the Right because they are less idealistic than the Left, and therefore one is left freer than one would be if encumbered by the idealism of the Left. [IV]

[24] Hamilton interview with Michael Craig-Martin, Richard Hamilton, *October files 10*, (Cambridge, MA, 2010), p. 3 and p. 43. Hamilton acknowledges his debt to Nigel Henderson, who had run the Peggy Guggenheim Gallery in London and owned an example of Duchamp's *Green Box*. He introduced him to Roland Penrose and Bacon. See Victoria Walsh, *Nigel Henderson. Parallel of Life and Art* (London, 2001), footnote 41.

[25] Ibid., p. 43. *On Growth and Form* was also a favourite book of Uglow and figures like the diagram of hexagonal-cells inspired the patterns he inscribed as background.

[26] Catherine Lampert and Richard Kendall, *Euan Uglow: The Complete Paintings* (London, 2007), and the account in Martin Golding, "Euan Uglow's Nudes," *Euan Uglow*, exh. cat., Whitechapel Gallery (London, 1989), p. 59, "He deliberately set out to use 'all the old methods,' trying to give an imagined subject a greater reality through measuring. This was an isolated experiment and in later years he deliberately ignored perspective and preferred to construct an ordered rectangle."

linear relationships, and investigated it in a very narrow sense. The theoretical arguments justifying the primacy of the painted surface had been much discussed in the early part of this century; considerations which had led to an assumption that the logical consequence of Cézanne's example must be a commitment to the perfect integrity of the painted surface: so "abstract" painting was granted its motivation."[27] In a curious way works by Hamilton and Coldstream share qualities, for example, slight changes in position and their way of registering their regard for the surface and the edges of the rectangle. Although Coldstream thought it a mistake for artists to make a virtue of leaving traces of their method, he confessed, "I do, I must say, I get great pleasure in actually touching the canvas and in the sort of configurations I'm making under the cloak of representing what I see . . . And if there seems to be a certain necessity about them it's very satisfying. Of course, very often there isn't, and with a great many paintings one paints they simply don't 'take.' Painting is rather like an inoculation, you know. I mean, you scratch the surface and you hope it will take and swell up."[28]

While the post-war mood in Europe is generally described as being overshadowed by the Cold War and the nuclear threat, and thus pessimistic, amongst these artists, it would better be described as rather perilous and unpredictable. As Bacon insisted, each individual must fabricate meaning out of daily existence which is always a transitory phenomenon without purpose or afterlife; to attempt to portray the horror of the world, would be to reduce art to a language that was merely illustrational. Auerbach, who was orphaned during the holocaust, left boarding school in 1947 and moved to the city. He recalls the atmosphere as invigorating. "There was a curious feeling of liberty about because everybody who was living there had escaped death in some way. It was sexy in a way, this semi-destroyed London."[29] He and Kossoff began haunting various building sites, dodging the workers as they drew. Although they only worked together at one site, Smithfields, both developed a lifelong attraction to gritty urban panoramas. Auerbach explained, "A city fully functional is to me a somewhat formally boring collection of cubic rectilinear shapes, but London after the war was a marvellous landscape with precipice and mountain and crags, full of drama."[30]

The *Picasso/Matisse* exhibition at the Victoria & Albert Museum in December 1945 represented the re-opening of cultural contact between England and the Continent. Picasso's spokesman, Christian Zervos, claimed the subjects of the twenty-four paintings from 1942–43 were "inspired by the extermination camps." In the parallel catalogue introduction Jean Cassou described Matisse's work as linked to "an exquisite, dazzling and irresistibly seductive grace manifest in the invention of these creatures."[31] In the wake of these opposite characterizations of the two prime inventors of modernist figuration, there was a reaction somehow linked to existentialism and another kind of unpredictability. It was natural that Bacon's howling figures crouching behind a grisaille screen were compared initially to Picasso's brutal rendering of form. From the beginning his admirers made connections to the films of Sergei Eisenstein, and Luis Buñuel.[32]

At the time many artists and critics expressed ambivalent reactions to Bacon's improvised, nearly amateur facture, and his increasing claim to forefront "accident." Gowing recalled the first Bacon exhibition at the Hanover Gallery, opening at Christmas 1949: "It was an outrage, a disloyalty to the existential principle, a mimic capitulation to tradition, a profane pietism like inverted intellectual snobbery, a surrender also to tonal painting, which earnestly progressive painters have never forgiven. It was everything unpardonable. The paradoxical appearance at once of pastiche and of iconoclasm was indeed one of Bacon's most original strokes. The picture [*Head VI,* 1949, purchased by the Arts Council] remains one of his masterpieces, and one of the least conventional, least foreseeable pictures of the twentieth century. Like really important pictures, it inaugurated a dimension that we could not have imagined and still cannot wholly describe. Such pictures are never without their detractors, and there is a body of opinion that cannot tolerate either the traditionalism in Bacon's painterly style or the invariable element of the irrational in his standpoint."[33]

Pope I, 1951, was one of three completed paintings of this subject (those begun early in 1951 were destroyed) and apart from referencing a reproduction of Velázquez's *Pope Innocent X,* 1650, it is said to have been inspired by a photograph of Pope Pius XII borne on a *sedia gestatoria,* carried high through the vaulted rooms of the Vatican.[34] When Bruce Bernard, the writer and picture editor, close friend of many of these artists, was preparing a monograph on Bacon in the 1980s (never published), Michael Andrews drafted a testament setting down still vivid memories: "The supremely significant thing as far as I was concerned about Francis's pictures, when I first became familiar with them as a Slade student in 1949–53, was that they were of mature adults, responsible, culpable, corruptible, vulnerable men, and occasionally women—not boys and girls. And that together with the fact that if they had no clothes on, what was remarkable was nakedness rather than nudity—contemporary adults undressed. That's what struck me first and foremost, immediately, and still does."[35]

Lucian Freud's situation at this time was, as ever, singular. Freud began renting rooms in Paddington in 1943, engaging friends within its working-class Irish population, some adolescents, as models. Meanwhile his West End social life was also fairly fantastic, revolving sometimes around the *Horizon* magazine set (Spender, Cyril Connolly, and Peter Watson) and sometimes the upper classes. He attended the masked balls, for example, at Warwick House, the home of Ann Fleming while still Lady Rothemere. Crossing the channel at the first opportunity after the war, the summer of 1946, he stopped in Paris, en route to stay with John Craxton in Greece, and the city became a second home for the next ten years. Freud had introductions to Picasso via his nephew Javier Vilató, to Christian Bérard, and to Giacometti from Watson. These ambitious artists, along

[27] Richard Hamilton, *Collected Words* (London, 1982), p. 12.

[28] Interview with Sylvester recorded in 1962, reprinted in *The Paintings of William Coldstream 1908–1987,* exh. cat., Tate (London, 1990), p. 27.

[29] Auerbach to Martin Gayford, *Apollo,* 2009, p. 59. For a wider discussion of this period see *Let us Face the Future,* curated by Andrew Dempsey and Richard Riley, Miró Foundation, Barcelona, November 2010; Margaret Garlake, *New Art New World, British Art in Postwar Society* (New Haven and London, 1998).

[30] Auerbach to Barnaby Wright, *Frank Auerbach. Building Sites 1952–62,* exh. cat., Courtauld Institute (London, 2009), pp. 14–15.

[31] *Picasso/Matisse,* exh. cat., Victoria & Albert Museum (London, 1945). Spender, having lunch with Picasso and Paul Eluard in 1950, recalled a great feeling of camaraderie that was really the basis of the artist's Communism; almost like Joseph Beuys twenty years later, Picasso claimed art as a cure for conflict: "He did seem to think of the world as a place where everyone could be creating the whole time, and that if they were doing that they wouldn't be aggressive, they wouldn't be fighting wars. Indeed at lunch he never stopped making things. Almost unconsciously while he was talking he would take the bread and model it into different shapes, a napkin, almost anything became raw material for him."

[32] For example, Robert Melville, "Francis Bacon," *Horizon,* vol. xx, no.12021, December 1949–January 1950, pp. 419–20. Picasso's, Matta's, Duchamp's, and several other artists' relationship to Bacon is also examined.

[33] Lawrence Gowing, *Francis Bacon. The Human Presence,* exh. cat., Hirshhorn Museum and Sculpture Garden (Washington,1990), p. 15.

Opposite: Francis Bacon, *Portrait of Isabel Rawsthorne Standing in a Street in Soho,* 1967. Staatliche Museen zu Berlin, Nationalgalerie.

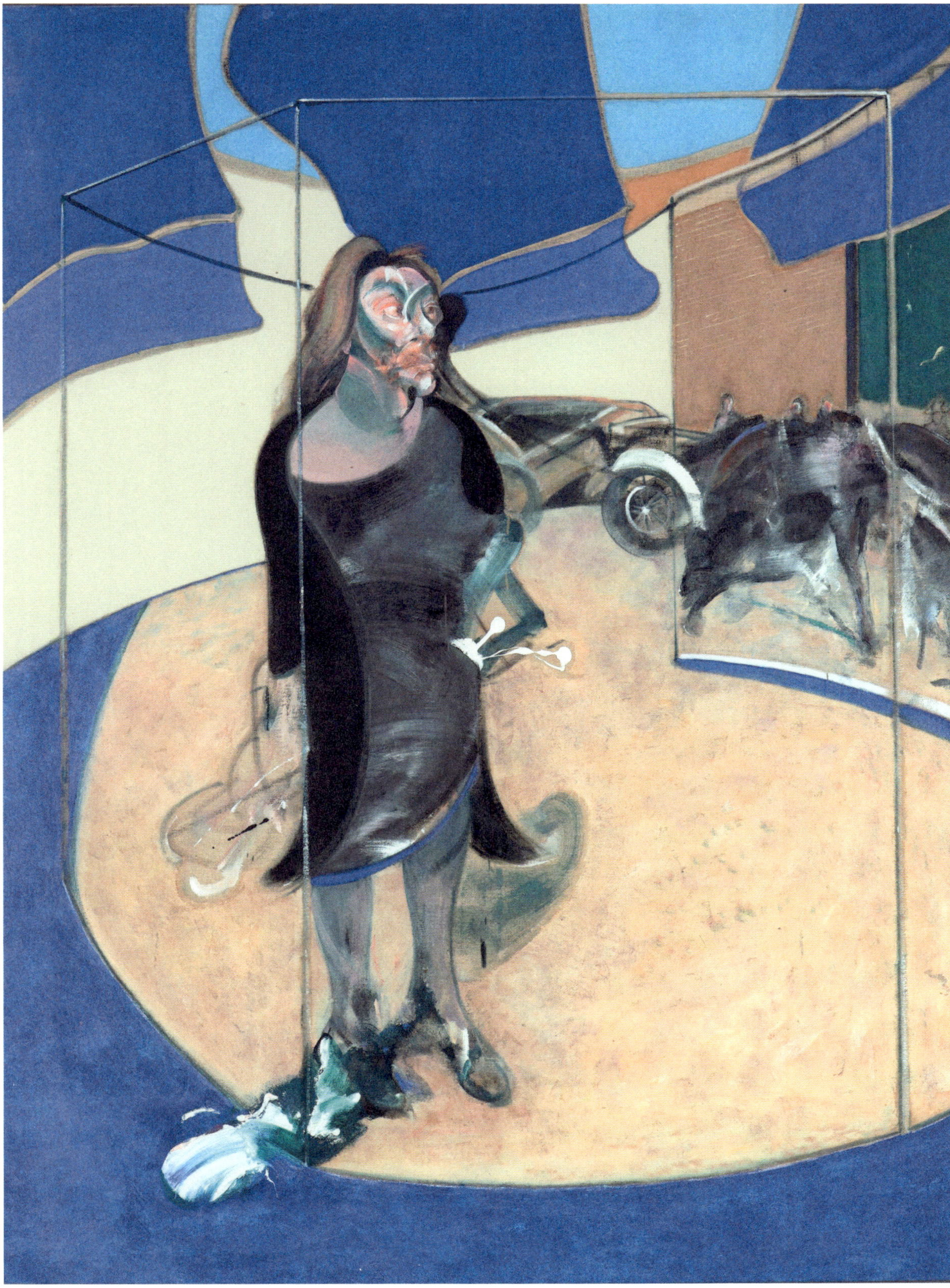

Lucian Freud
Born in 1922 in Berlin

The son of Sigmund Freud's youngest child. The family left Germany in 1933 and Freud spent a term at the Central School of Arts and Crafts, London, and, sporadically, the East Anglian School of Painting and Drawing. Freud's first solo exhibition was at Alex Reid and Lefevre Gallery, London, in 1944, and his widely admired drawings were published in *Horizon* magazine and as illustrations for books. After the war Freud spent long periods in Paris and Ireland. A large painting, *Interior in Paddington*, won a purchase prize at the Festival of Britain in 1951, and Freud represented Britain at the Venice Biennale in 1954 (with Ben Nicolson and Francis Bacon). In the mid-1950s his handling of paint became looser, the artist standing to paint, the subjects often scrutinised from above. His first retrospective was at the Hayward Gallery in 1974, and from 1987 onwards his international reputation grew, culminating in exhibitions at the Museum of Modern Art, New York, in 2007 (*The Painter's Etchings*) and at the Centre Pompidou, Paris, in 2010. Freud was awarded Britain's highest honours, CH and OM, and died in July 2011.

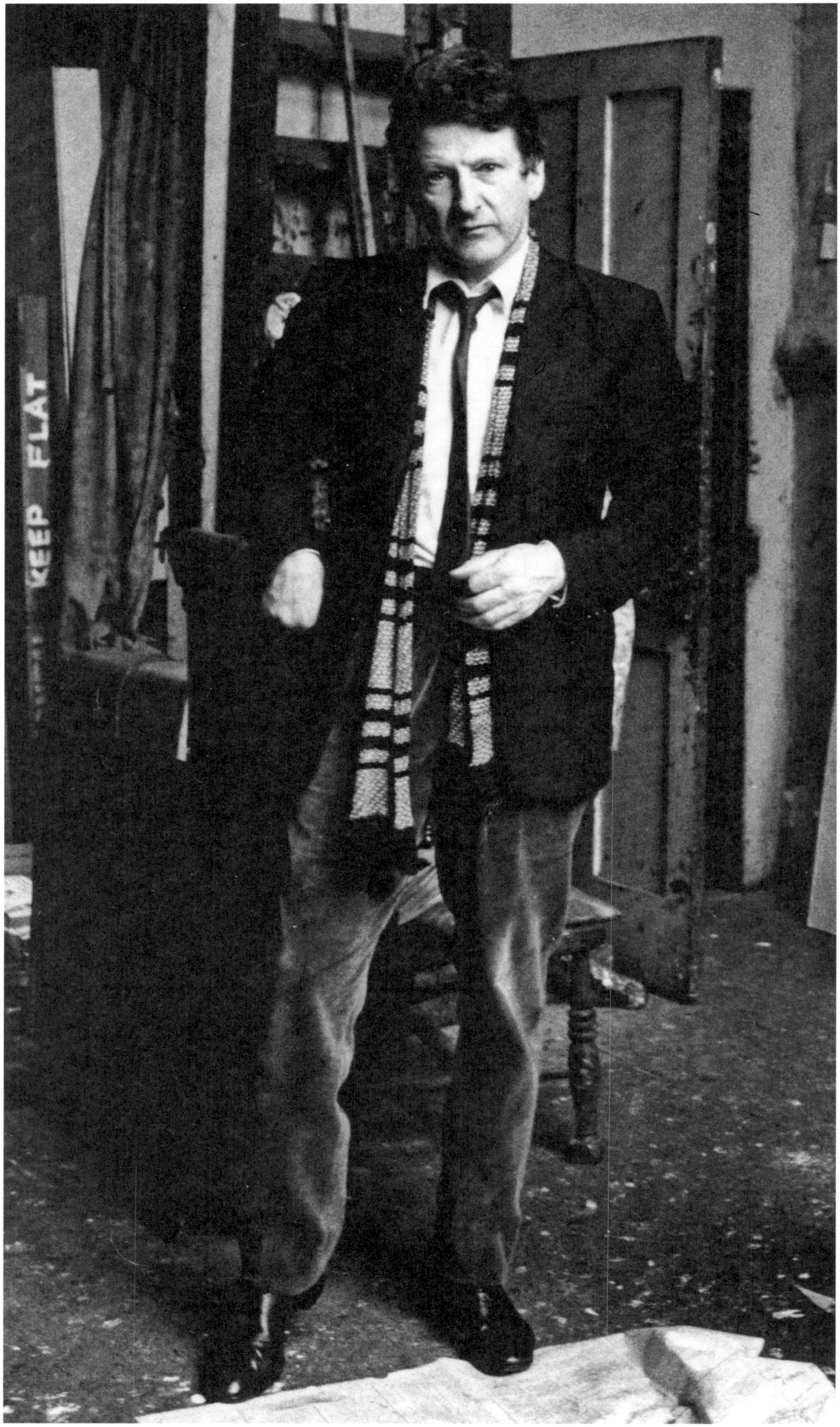

Right: Harry Diamond, *Lucian Freud*, 1975.

[I] Lucian Freud, quoted in *Cambridge Opinion* 37, 1963, p. 47. The quote appeared above *Sleeping Head*, 1962, at Marlborough Fine Art, London, 1963.

[II] Lucian Freud, "Artscene, Private View," *Tatler*, March 2004.

When man finally sealed his destiny by inventing his own inevitable destruction he also gave art absolute gravity by adding a new dimension: this new dimension, having the end in sight can give the artist supreme control, daring and such awareness of his bearings in existence that he will (in Nietzsche's words) create conditions under which 'a thousand secrets of the past crawl out of their hideout into his sun.[I]

A painter's relationship with the paint is the most important artistic relationship there is —on a par with behaviour in life. If you cover yourself with paint from head to foot, you may well learn more about painting than by going to an art school.[II]

[34] This image was reproduced in *Magazine of Art*, XLV, January 1952, p. 12, with other images from Bacon's studio. The painting was in the Hanover Gallery exhibition opening in December 1951.

[35] Andrews, unpublished text, courtesy Virginia Verran.

[36] *British Masters*, BBC, July 2011.

[37] David Sylvester, "Two Painters," *Britain Today*, June 1950.

[38] Catherine Lampert, "Notes on the pictures and the times, 1940–58," *Lucian Freud. Early Works 1940–58*, exh. cat., Hazlitt Holland-Hibbert (London, 2008), p. 67, quoting Freud to Méraud Guinness, Tate archive.

[39] Freud, "Some thoughts on painting," *Encounter*, London, July 1954 (reprinted *Lucian Freud Naked Portraits*, exh. cat., MMK Museum für Moderne Kunst (Frankfurt, 2001), pp. 282–83.

with Balthus, one can surmise, became role models. Letters and diaries from the period rather diminish a reading of Freud's work as being largely responsive to external events or parochial arguments about the direction of art, for example, those views voiced by James Fox in his 2011 BBC programme about British masters. Fox describes the painting *Girl with a Kitten*, 1947, now at the Tate, as belonging to the responses of artists to "evil on such a vast scale" and in Freud's case sees within it "the horrors he escaped haunted his painting, a little Virgin Mary of the twentieth century . . . a theatre of agitated energy."[36] As Sylvester wrote in 1950, Freud's "pictures suggest that he has hypnotized the subject, rendering it intensely strange and perverse," but possessed with an inevitability.[37] The limpid cool grey of Kitty Garman's eyes and silk shirt harmonize as does the tawny ground and skin, the solemnity punctuated by the amusing stare of the kitten, the painting transmitting through their eyes the aura the artist engendered, intimidating, and sometimes very pleasurable. For example, in the summer of 1947, after holidaying on the Riviera with Kitty, Freud thanks his host for a week spent enjoying "the most delicious, luxurious and tranquil sequence of days [that] pass in dreamy winy harmony" and makes plans to return to Provence that autumn in the company of Graham and Kathleen Sutherland.[38]

Much of the extraordinary depiction of the inner life of Freud's sitters depends on exceptional trust and complicity of outlook. The subject of *Portrait of a Woman*, c. 1950, is Anne Tree, sister of the Duke of Devonshire. It feels like each curl, each vein beneath her translucent skin, every variance in tone across the face and neck, paint applied in an increasingly looser manner, is true. At this time Freud expressed the conviction that close observation of the subject "will eventually reveal the all without which selection itself is not possible," while above all "the model should only serve the very private function for the painter of providing the starting point for his excitement. The picture is all he feels about it, all he thinks worth preserving of it, all he invests it with."[39]

Exhibition reviews from this period suggest the writer's familiarity with the subject, indeed the article "Portraits by Lucian Freud" in *Vogue*, 1954, names the women (including Mrs. Beryl Chance, Mrs. Michael Wishart, formerly Miss Anne Dunn). Many writers were themselves artists; one especially admires the reviews by Andrew Forge, John Berger, Patrick Heron, and Lawrence Gowing as well as critics like Sylvester, Robert Melville, and John Russell. Their judgments, changing year by year, seem very different from the more distant assessments and ratings applied today to high profile retrospectives or high profile group exhibitions, with theoretical perspectives selected by curators. In addition we can sense from anecdote and later memories how familiar artists were with each other, especially with the link between art colleges (it is said Robin Darwin, head of the RCA, and Coldstream were on the phone daily).

Hamilton was a neighbour of Freud and

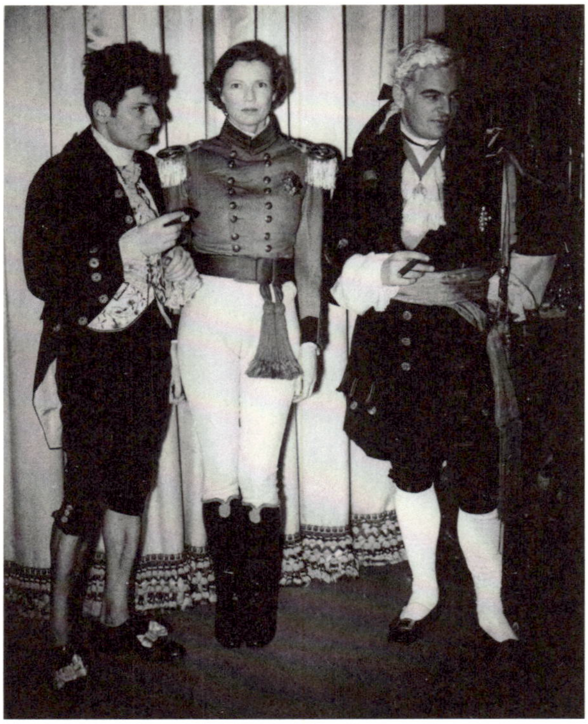

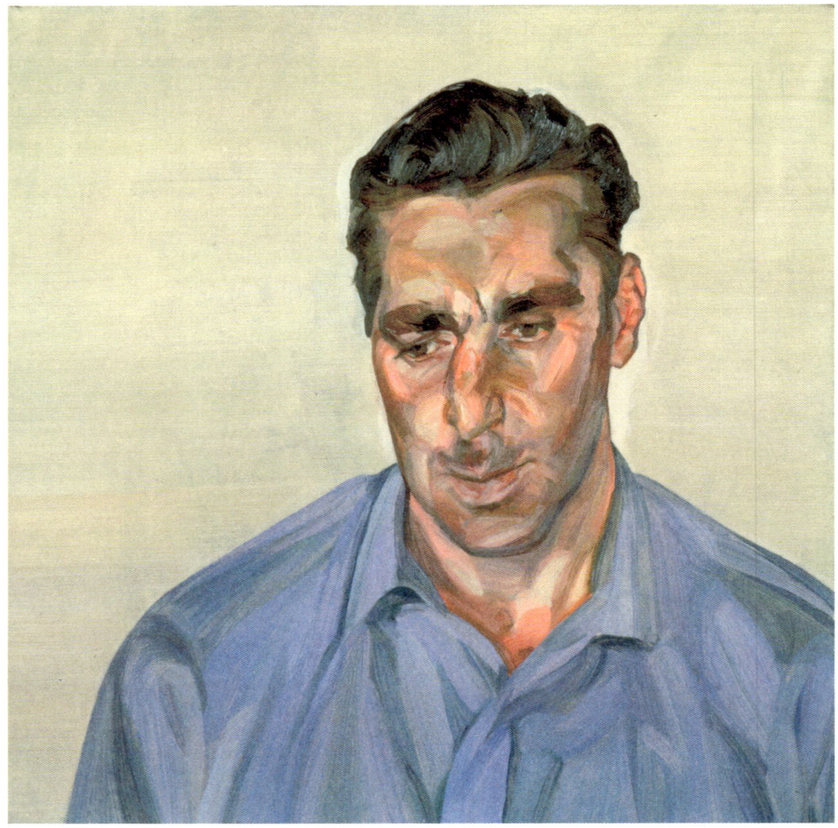

Kitty in St John's Wood in 1950, engaged himself in very finely executed scenes from episodes in Joyce's *Ulysses,* like the watercolour of Molly and Bloom under the covers, *Going to dark bed,* 1949. Both born in 1922 (and dying the same year) they had friends in common like Peter Watson, Penrose, the poet, artist and critic Toni del Renzio, and Sonia Brownell Orwell (briefly a companion of Coldstream before he went into the army and she married George at the end of his life). Coming into the Slade at the beginning of an autumn term in the early 1950s, asking Freud about his summer, Hamilton was told it was one of three nervous breakdowns. "Yours?," "No, ones I've caused." Their intermittent conversations brought out their differences: one assessing the overall direction appropriate to contemporary art and society while devising an experimental process for his own work, and the other relying on nerve and concentration to render virtually kinetic as well as instinctive responses to the subject, intimately connected to a secretive and sometimes perilous life.[40]

William Townsend described accompanying Coldstream to Freud's house to celebrate the opening of his exhibition at the Hanover Gallery in April 1950. "All the furniture was cleared except one large red-lush-carved settee, two screens, one of them covered in tiger skin, and a table from which were served champagne and whisky. This was a company in which Bill and I were like strangers, matter of fact and banal. [Apart from a bearded man] . . . the rest of the men were beautifully hairless . . . Had a long talk with Francis Bacon who is fantastic enough, but charming and immensely intelligent."[41]

Graham Sutherland brought Freud together with Bacon when he invited them both to Wales in 1944. Freud began going around to Bacon's studio in Cromwell Place in the afternoons. Bacon "would have ideas which he put down and then destroyed and then quickly put

[40] Hamilton to Lampert, July 2010. Hamilton remembers rescuing Freud's wife Kitty when she ran out of money at Christmas time, c. 1950, and Freud was absent. See Freud quoted by Martin Gayford, *Lucian Freud,* exh. cat., Irish Museum of Moden Art (Dublin, 2007), p. 13, and *Man with a Blue Scarf* (London, 2010), pp. 177–78, on his recollection of a conversation with Hamilton who asks "'I can't see the point in it, why do you do it?' I told him not to worry about it."

[41] Townsend 1976, 19 April, 1950, p. 88.

Opposite left: Lucian Freud with Joan and Patrick Leigh Fermour in fancy dress.

Opposite right
Lucian Freud, *Man in a Blue Shirt,* 1965, (portrait of George Dyer).

Right:
Bruce Bernard, *Lucian Freud, posing as a Henry Moore,* 1983.

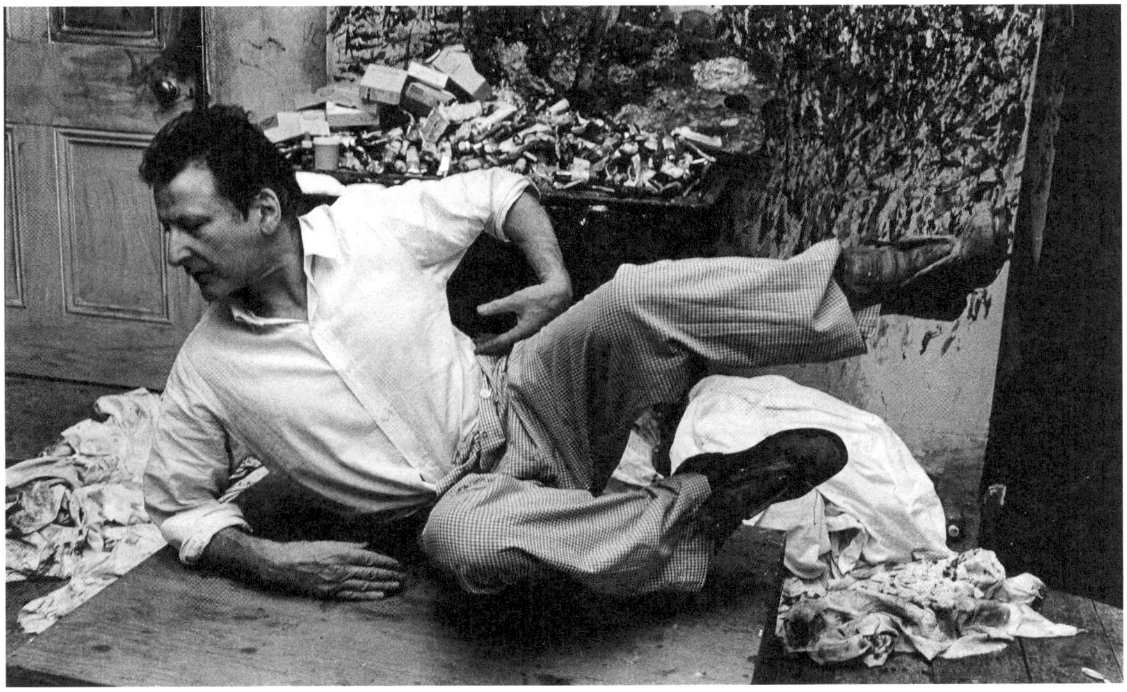

[42] Sebastian Smee, "A Late-Night Conversation with Lucian Freud," *Freud at Work* (London, 2006), p. 16.

[43] William Feaver, "Freud at the Correr: Fifty Years," *Lucian Freud*, exh. cat., Museo Correr (Venice 2005), p. 33.

[44] James Kirkman letter to Ronald Alley, 12 September, 1963, Tate archive.

down again. It was his attitude that I admired. The way he was completely ruthless about his own work."[42] "He talked about packing a lot of things into one single brushstroke which amused and excited me, and I realised that it was a million miles from anything I could ever do."[43]

The first of more than a dozen portraits by Bacon of Freud, a standing figure rather like a stiff walk-on actor, from 1951, is now in the Whitworth Art Gallery. Supplying information to his dealer James Kirkman, Freud explained that when he arrived to pose "he found the portrait almost completely finished and he says it was an extremely good likeness: Francis merely said that he wanted to work on the feet, but then he changed it altogether a great deal. Apparently it was inspired by a picture of Kafka leaning against a wall."[44] The result is not much like the often-cited source photo or its subject although in other paintings Bacon conjures up Freud's physical magnetism and his oblique way of facing another person. Elements of John Deakin's familiar photographs (taken on behalf of Bacon) transfer between paintings, often the protagonists seem composite, talismanic. In *Study for Self-Portrait,* 1964, Bacon introduces his own facial features with the torso of George Dyer in his underwear, right leg folded over left, and something of Freud's strong physique, his white shirt with rolled-up sleeves. Bacon sat for Freud in 1952, and again in 1964, as well as for three amazing drawings where the pose has a preening aspect, the trouser fly partially unbuttoned to display his slender hips. Dyer appears in a triptych by Bacon in 1964, and posed for Freud twice in 1965–66. Increasingly the two artists drew apart. Years before, Freud had deplored Francis's addiction to his lover, Peter Lacy, while sensing that when he, in turn, became successful and his work fetched good prices, Bacon became "bitter and bitchy." On the other hand, Bacon's memorable image of men making love, *Two Figures,* 1953, hung in his bedroom in Kensington.

Bacon was occupying Rodrigo Moynihan's studio at the Royal College when Auerbach arrived there to study in 1950 and they became aware of each other. Six years later, after viewing Auerbach's first one-person exhibition, Bacon boasted to Freud about this young artist

Frank Auerbach

Born in 1931 in Berlin

Shortly before his eighth birthday, with war approaching, Auerbach was sent to England by his parents, never seeing them again. The boarding school Bunce Court was a sympathetic environment with an emphasis on self-sufficiency, staffed mainly by refugees and conscientious objectors, and when Auerbach left in 1947 he moved to London, where he has remained. As well as acting in small parts, he enrolled at the Borough Polytechnic Institute in 1948, continuing to attend David Bomberg's classes until 1954, as well as studying at St Martin's School of Art and then the Royal College of Art. He moved to his studio in Camden in 1954, close to the landscapes he has painted, the area around Mornington Crescent and Primrose Hill. Auerbach began showing at the Beaux Arts Gallery in 1956, and since 1965 at Marlborough Fine Art. The catalogue for his Arts Council retrospective in 1978, opening at the Hayward Gallery, included a text by Leon Kossoff, and a conversation with Catherine Lampert. He represented Britain at the Venice Biennale in 1986 and shared the Golden Lion with Sigmar Polke (the works toured to Hamburg, Essen, and Madrid) and in 1989 the Rijksmusueum, Amsterdam, staged an exhibition; in 2001 there was a solo exhibition in the main galleries at the Royal Academy of Arts. Robert Hughes wrote a monograph in 1990, and in 2009, at the time of the exhibition of *Building Sites, 1952–62*, at the Courtauld Institute, a book authored by William Feaver reproduced Auerbach's paintings from 1953–2009. Auerbach is known for painting and drawing the same people for decades, most famously E.O.W. and J.Y.M., but also his wife, son, and a few friends.

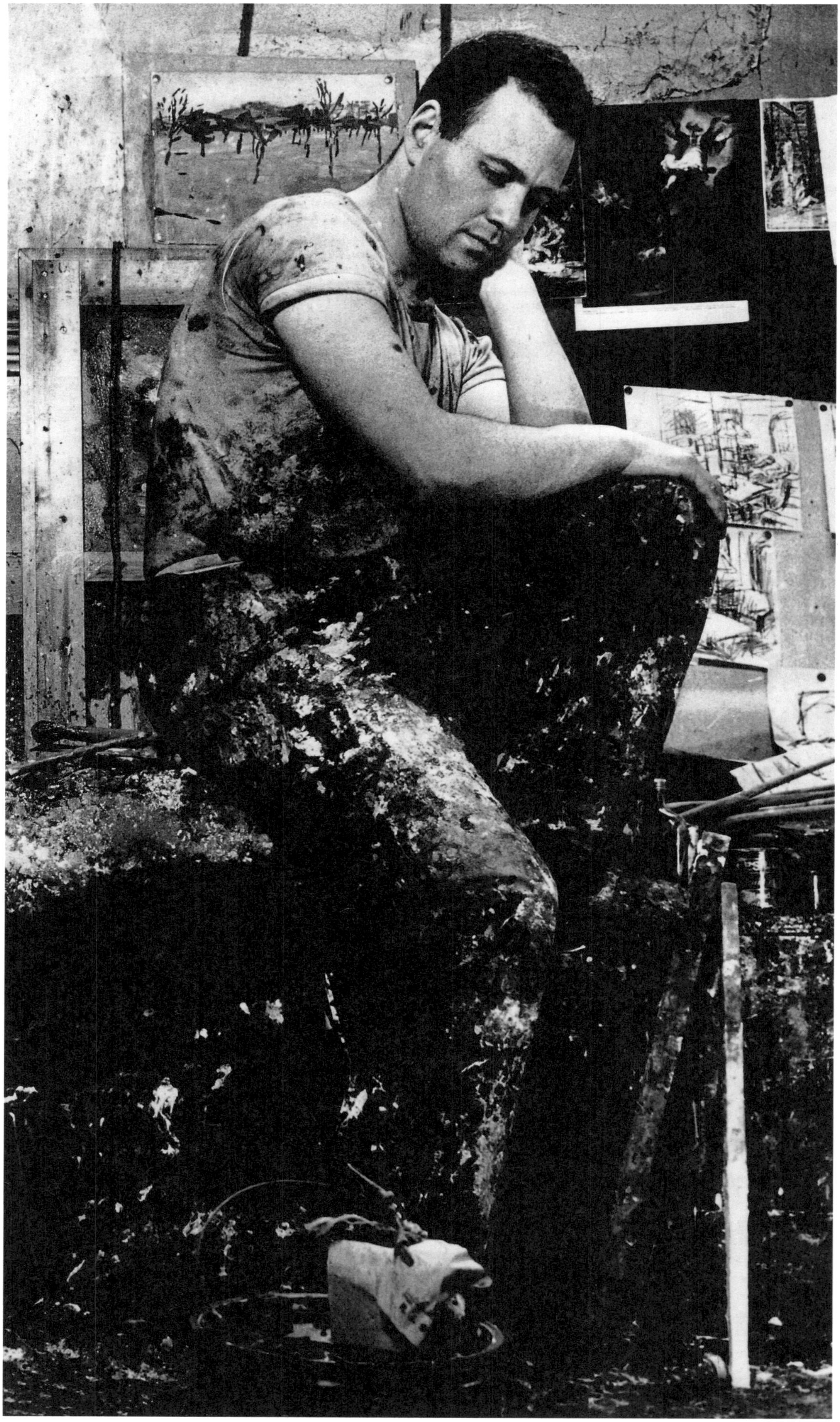

Right: Jorge Lewinski, *Frank Auerbach*, 1963.

I Frank Auerbach, talking to John Cristopher Battye, *Art and Artists*, January 1971.

II Frank Auerbach, speaking to Andrew Lambirth, *The Spectator*, 13 October, 2009.

I'm not especially moved by a photograph—nor by the look of something by itself. I don't keep souvenirs. But, the touch and the curious way in which an object experienced by touch is entirely different to one's visual experience of it, seems to go right to the core of my nervous system. You have the greatest painting in the world in a room and look around you . . . look at the chairs, the tables, and the people moving about… in some way they always seem more alive, more exciting, more extraordinary and more odd than the picture—than the greatest painting in the world—*Las Meninas*, or a great Rembrandt or a great Matisse, or anything. There would be no motive or painting if the painting seemed to somehow conquer the existing world. So one tries to catch hold of the world of fact and experience at some point at which it hasn't been caught hold of before, so that one remakes it in a sense which speaks to oneself directly—so that every mark, proportion and weight in some way conforms to one's deepest desires without betraying its essence or identity—so that the stress of the real world and the stress on the newness of the painting are really a stress on the same thing. [I]

I never visualise a picture before I start . . . I have an impulse and I try to find a form for that impulse. The great benefit of manuring the thing with reality is that reality continually belies one's expectations: where one expects the grand sweep it suddenly starts becoming petty, where one expects it to be hard it becomes soft, the proportions—almost every day one goes out there, one has different sensations about them. [II]

[45] David Sylvester interviewed by Andrew Brighton, Tate Modern, June, 2000.

[46] Smee (London, 2006), p. 17 and p. 26.

[47] John Berger, "A stick in the dark," *New Statesman*, 28 November, 1959.

[48] Andrew Forge, "Auerbach and Paolozzi," *New Statesman*, 12 September, 1963.

[49] Martin Gayford, "Auerbach's London," *Apollo*, October 2009, p. 61 (mentioning Kossoff, Freud, Andrews, and Uglow). Many of the artists in this exhibition sat for each other (Freud for Coldstream in 1976 and for a charcoal drawing and an etching by Auerbach in 1981; Bacon made a diptych with Auerbach and Freud in 1964, Hockney and Freud worked from each other in 2002, Hamilton produced a collotype and screenprint from a Polaroid photograph by Bacon and was portrayed in *A portrait of the artist by Francis Bacon*, 1970–71; Kossoff and Auerbach sat for each other 1951–57.)

of great promise, "I go and talk to this very good-looking painter in the French pub." Sylvester, speaking to Andrew Brighton in 2000[45] made the unexpected comment that Bacon learned to speak about art things from Lucian, "his language is all there in that first interview," and added that in the 1950s Hamilton and Auerbach were the artists that most influenced his way of painting.[46]

John Berger had viewed Auerbach's work in 1959, praised its extraordinary physical presence and recognised an impetus to create from discontent, "always aware of the richness of life."[47] In 1963 Andrew Forge spoke of Auerbach's portraits in a way that might have goaded Bacon to depart from the flatness of the photographic source: "The familiarity of the subject binds him and frees him at the same time. It is as though he is deliberately screwing down on any arbitrary variation, cutting out any opportunity for freshness and difference that comes from outside himself . . . He uses it [the material presence] to gamble with the image, coaxing or bullying features out of the vagaries of its surface, so that you are all the time stumbling on a chin or a brow defined abruptly in a cliff-edge of paint."[48]

Shared galleries included the Beaux Arts, Hanover, Marlborough, Robert Fraser, Kasmin, Waddington, and several abroad. Auerbach speaks for most of these artists: "I had that curious sense which one has if one's lucky of having quick-witted, intelligent companions with whom I could talk excited drivel for hours and occasionally stumble on a nugget of sense. I suppose I actually spoke about painting more with Francis Bacon than to anyone else, partly because he liked making statements, formulating dogma, laying down the rules. Of course they changed all the time."[49] Continuing in this vain as he looked back from the perspective of 2009, "There's always something in the air; good painting always captures in a way what is around, and these Americans had gripped large and made splendid an impulse that, partly as a reaction against what had been going on—the mannered formalised painting that had preceded them—made these particular images. They did it large and they did it with conviction and they did it so that any-

Leon Kossoff

Born in 1926 in East London

Kossoff spent his childhood in Shoreditch, Bethnal Green, and Hackney, where he drew the city and his family. In 1939 he was evacuated to King's Lynn, Norfolk, where he was encouraged to become an artist. He began a commercial art course at St Martin's School of Art which was interrupted by military service. He retuned to the fine art course at St Martin's and then at the Royal College of Art, attending evening classes with David Bomberg at the Borough Polytechnic. In 1966 he moved to his present studio in Willesden Green. His urban landscapes began with the Building Site paintings and drawings of the 1950s, and have treated underground stations, schools, railroad junctions, and his back garden, as well as a local swimming pool, and Hawksmoor's Christchurch in Spitalfields. He began showing with the Beaux Arts Gallery in 1956 and after its closure with various galleries, including Fischer Fine Art, London, and in recent years L.A. Louver, Venice, California, Mitchell-Innes & Nash, New York, and Annely Juda Fine Art, London. Kossoff is particularly known for drawings and prints after old masters. A group after Poussin were shown at the Los Angeles County Museum in 2000, and at the Metropolitan Museum in New York, and the National Gallery of Australia, Canberra, as well as in a memorable exhibition of drawing from painting at the National Gallery, London, in 2007. Kossoff represented Britain in the Venice Biennale in 1995.

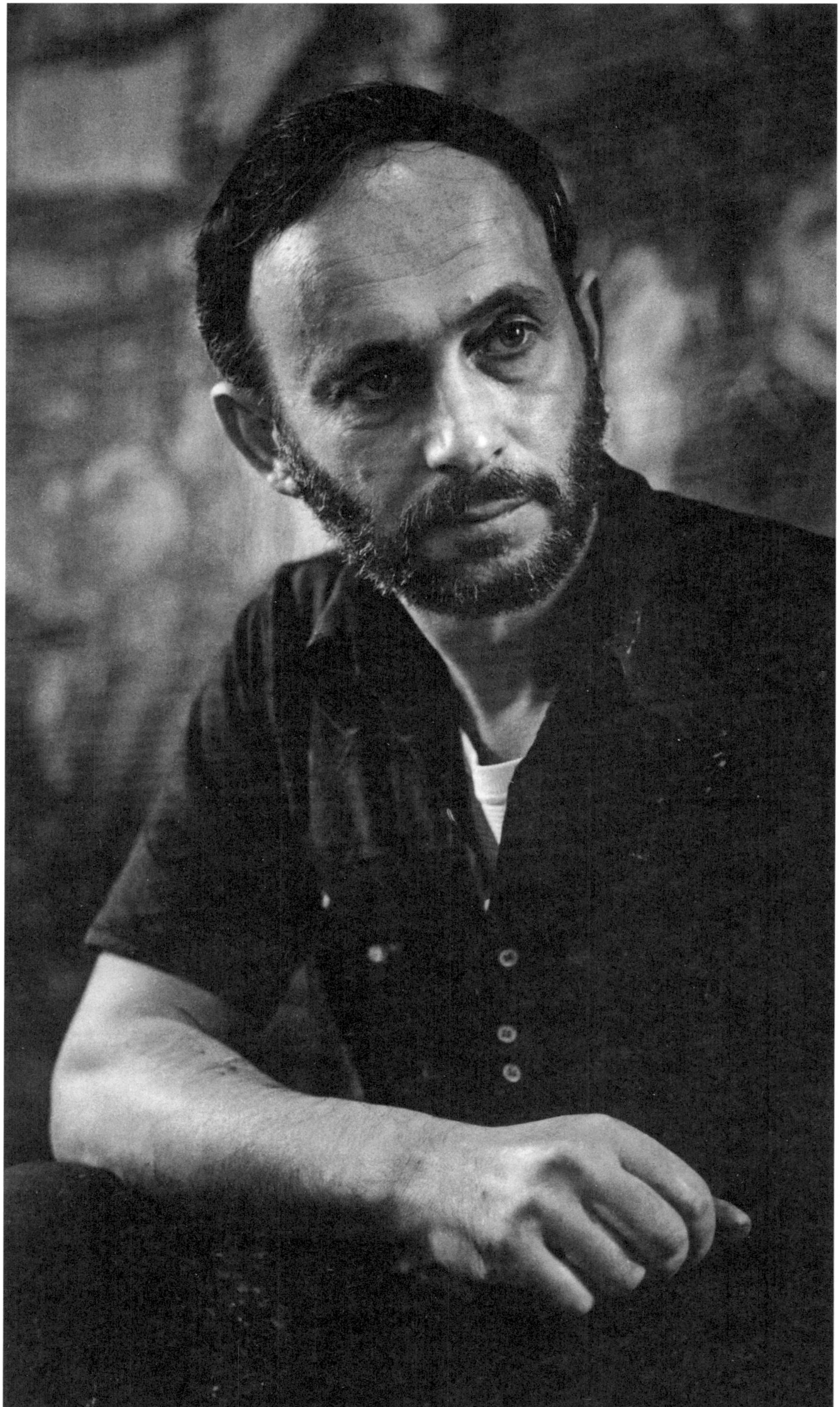

Right: S.S. Walia, *Leon Kossoff.*

I *Leon Kossoff, Recent Drawings and Paintings*, Fischer Fine Art Limited, January–February.

II Kossoff's reply to a letter from John Berger, *The Shape of a Pocket* (London, 2003).

The strange ever changing light, the endless streets and the shuddering feel of the sprawling city lingers in my mind like a faintly glimmering memory of a long forgotten, perhaps never experienced childhood, which, if rediscovered and illuminated, would ameliorate the pain of the present.

I have also, ever since I can remember, drawn and painted my father and I have worked from others close to me who were able to persevere with the sittings.

Although I have drawn and painted from landscapes and people constantly I have never finished a picture without first experiencing a huge emptying of all factual and topographical knowledge. And always, the moment before finishing, the painting disappears, sometimes into greyness for ever, or sometimes into a huge heap on the floor to be reclaimed, redrawn and committed to an image which makes itself. [I]

'Thereness' follows nothingness. It is impossible to premeditate. It is to do with the collaboration of the sitter, as you say, but also to do with the disappearance of the sitter the moment the image emerges. Is this what you mean by 'the self-effacement of the good host'? The Fayum portraits of course emerge out of an attitude to life and death quite different from our own. In the pyramids there was life after death and the life was in the 'thereness' of the portraits. If there is something of this quality in the painting of Pilar it has more to do with the processes I am involved with than trying to paint a certain picture. [II]

[50] Frank Auerbach in conversation with William Feaver, *Frank Auerbach* (New York, 2009), p. 233.

[51] Auerbach to Penny Marcus, 16 March, 1972, Tate archive.

[52] David Mercer, "To Leon Kossoff," *Leon Kossoff*, exh. cat., Whitechapel Gallery (London, 1972). See also Paul Moorhouse, "The eye sees more than the heart knows. The Work of Leon Kossoff," *Leon Kossoff*, exh. cat., Tate (London, 1996), p. 18.

[53] Coldstream to Sylvester in 1962, (London, 1990), p. 26.

body could see. But, having worked in Bomberg's class, having an emphasis on being, as it were, inside the painting and that what one did was one's gesture that arose out of one's sensations, then a Kline or a Pollock, although admirable, was in no sense news."[50]

Starting the day with quick drawings, referring to the Primrose Hill paintings, Auerbach explained he did this "so as to have an impulse, an idea, a new fact, a newly discovered structure, to work from—and then to paint with older and newer drawings pinned up"; the painting, "the end result of hundreds of transmutations."[51] The hope was for a unity arising out of plotting such ever-changing factors, those in the head as well as in nature. The bold linear drawing, loopy and angular shapes representing clouds and moving, oblique tree branches suggest exhilarating speed and discontent.

In 1961 Leon Kossoff rented a studio in a former garage close to Willesden Junction. Nearby a bridge stretched over the railway lines and a vast panorama of sky was visible. This man-made landscape and similar railway vistas at King's Cross, as well as the huge edifice of the Shell building rising up on the South Bank, are represented by almost throbbing rhythms of voids and hard material—railway arches, windows, platforms, electric lines. David Mercer, the playwright, entered the mind of Kossoff and through him the motifs, seeing a connection between the landscapes and the paintings of people. In the catalogue for Kossoff's exhibition at the Whitechapel in 1972 he wrote: "But everything is restless. And constantly that word 'redemptive' comes to mind. Love is restored, mourning is restored, the transience of life and the somber fact of death are redeemed. A painted nude sprawls just above one's eye-line. Her flesh seems to hover uncertainly between putrescence and vigorous sensuality."[52]

A similar ruthless revision of one's work was advocated by Bomberg, but is curiously just as present in the outlook of Coldstream: "And I think that while one's painting on a picture it always seems to me that every time you start you've got to be willing to risk everything, and if there's a passage you happen to like you always feel, you know, you've got to be prepared to put your brush right through it."[53] In a rare statement printed in the catalogue

[54] Kossoff in Venice Biennale catalogue, 1995, and speaking to Jon Snow, 2007, at the National Gallery.

[55] Martin Golding (London, 1989), p. 17. 'DS taught at both schools, and compared Royal College students at this time ("rocks") with those at the Slade ("mods"), Martin Harrison, *Transition. The London Art Scene in the 50s*, exh. cat., Barbican Art Gallery (London, 2002), footnote 31/32. See also quote from 1966, re-printed in David Sylvester, *Looking Back at Francis Bacon* (London, 2000), p. 246.

when Kossoff showed at the 1995 Venice Biennale, he explained, "Every time the model sits everything has changed. You have changed, she has changed . . . the directions you try to remember are no longer there and, whether working from the model or landscape drawings, everything has to be reconstructed daily, many many times," or as he repeated in 2007, he has to "learn to draw" anew every time he picks up a pencil and confronts a motif.[54]

Mercer's description could be adapted to the paintings of a lifelong artist friend of Kossoff, Euan Uglow. His large nude, *Lady C* (the subject Coldstream's future wife, Monica Hoyer), was painted in 1960 when she was modelling at the Slade. It begins with the integration of the proportions of the rectangle (3:4) and the daylight striking the rear wall, the human form built up with close attention to each shift in tone. During a Slade seminar on Realism in 1953, David Sylvester argued that Courbet was indebted to the past, even to Italian art, but modern art should not represent objects and individuals but a "series of perceptions." The young Uglow protested that the issue was never verisimilitude, a picture could be "right" without being "like."[55] Sometimes Uglow's convictions and empirical methods compare more readily to artists that might be thought to be at the opposite end of a spectrum from painting from life, closer to his tutors at Camberwell like Kenneth Martin (who also ran an adult class at St Martin's in the late 1940s) and Victor Pasmore. They endorsed rigorous mathematical and conceptual starting points, aiming for a purer abstraction than that of the St Ives group. In the small publication *Broadsheet No. 1*, 1951, Martin wrote, "What is generally termed abstract is not to be confused with the abstraction from nature which is concerned with the visual aspect of nature and its reduction and distortion to a pictorial form . . . abstract art . . . has become a construction or concretion coming from within. The abstract painting is the result of a creative process absolutely the opposite to abstraction."[56]

Below left: Leon Kossoff, *Head of Frank Auerbach*, 1953.

Below right: Frank Auerbach, *Head of Catherine Lampert II*, 1985.

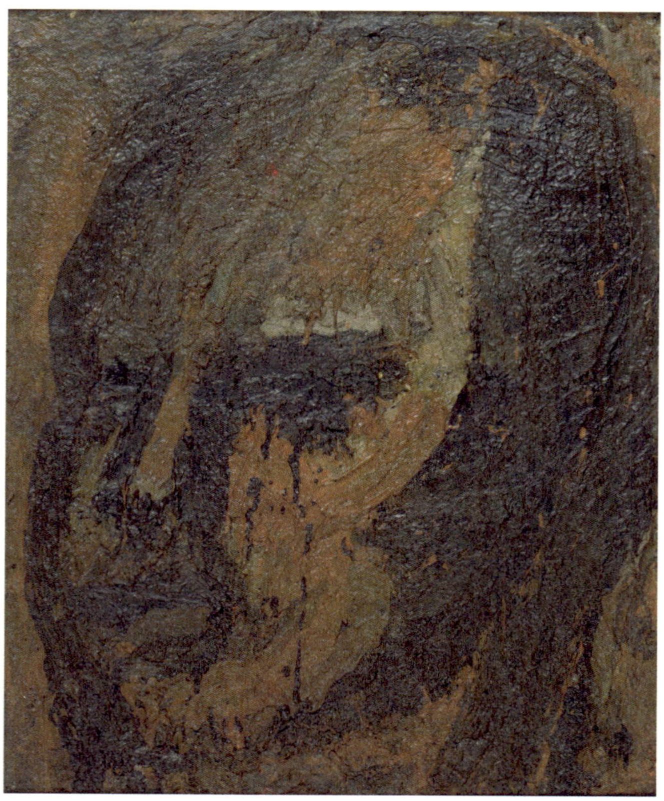

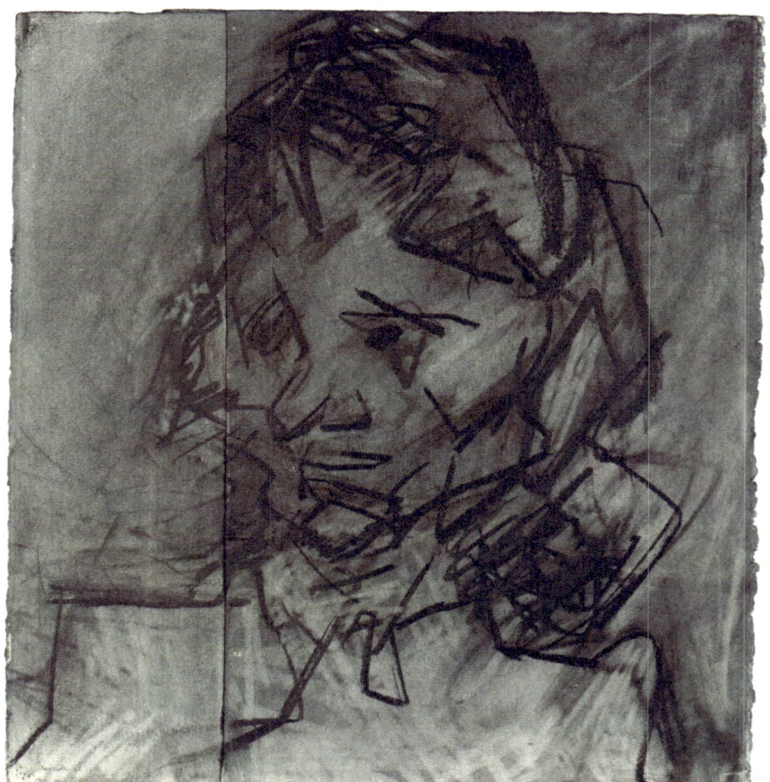

[56] Kenneth Martin, "Abstract Art," *Broadsheet No. 1* (London, 1951). Martin made his first mobile sculpture at the home of Nigel Henderson, with Paolozzi advising on the materials, and stated a case for such radical abstraction in the discussion, "The Strange Case of Abstract Art," chaired by Herbert Read at the ICA in 1950. See catalogues for his exhibitions at the Serpentine (1985), Annely Juda Fine Art (1987), and Camden Arts Centre (2007).

[57] These events are analysed in James Hyman, *The Battle for Realism* (London and New Haven, 2001) and explored in articles like Jonathan Jones, "John Berger and Looking Forward," *The Whitechapel Art Gallery Centenary Review*, ed. Catherine Lampert and Andrea Tarsia (London, 2001). Various specialists of the period have also made comparisons to the ideas of figures like the philosopher A.J. Ayer, Frederick Antal, and Bishop Berkeley.

[58] David Sylvester, *About Modern Art. Critical Essays 1948–97* (London, 1997), p. 19.

[59] Harrison 2002, p. 54. See also Victoria Walsh, *Nigel Henderson. Parallel of Life and Art* (London, 2001).

[60] Martin Harrison, *In Camera: Francis Bacon* (London, 2005), p. 86.

[61] *Nine Young Painters* exh. cat., ICA (London, 1952).

Modernism and popular culture debated

By the mid 1950s many artists whose work was "referential" could be seen to be following one of two paths—a modernist realism with emphasis on spatial structure, the kind praised by David Sylvester, or a social realism, advocated by John Berger, who maintained that "every artist has the duty to communicate with the minimum of ambiguity."[57] In the exhibition *Looking Forward* (Whitechapel, 1952) Berger included painters who placed their subjects in a domestic context like Jack Smith and John Bratby (and were described as "kitchen sink" painters, a phrase that first appeared in a 1954 review by Sylvester). He also selected other artists working in a "humanist" tradition —Rodrigo Moynihan, Carel Weight, and Claude Rogers—but explicitly excluded Freud and Coldstream. James Hyman's excellent account of the period, *The Battle for Realism,* follows the critics year by year, naturally revising their opinions and allegiances. David Sylvester, for example, in 1950 advocated a future "School of London" that would embrace the ideas and forms associated with the art of André Masson, Paul Klee, and Henry Moore. Writing an article in the American magazine *The Nation,* he criticised Gorky and de Kooning, although in reality his remarks were directed more against the formalist position of Clement Greenberg. Sylvester underwent, in his words, a "Damascene conversion" one evening in 1956 visiting the Tate exhibition, *Modern Art in the United States*.[57] Thereafter, American art by this generation of Abstract Expressionists, and later the work of Jasper Johns and Richard Serra, earned his highest esteem while Berger remains especially alive to new art aligned to a critical moral and interior vision, a champion of Juan Muñoz and Miquel Barceló, among others.

The more one scrutinizes the records of exhibitions and debates, the more one sees how interlinked some of the artists and critics were, and sometimes how personalised the arguments became. For example, during an ICA debate on 15 January, 1952, Sylvester criticises the work of Renato Guttuso, an attack on Berger, and champions Bacon. At *Points of View* (ICA, March 1952), one of the participants, Peter Rose Pulham, affirmed the importance of found photographs, especially those taken by journalists working for the press and "reproduced through a course screen on bad paper," his argument referencing both Bacon's work and the possibilities of collage sourced from mass media.[59] One of the many fascinating observations in Martin Harrison's book *In Camera: Francis Bacon,* based on Bacon's virtual and studio archive, is that one of Nigel Henderson's experiments in "post-visualisation" (*a lantern slide of bathers,* c.1953) revels in a screen-like "pleating of the image, which Henderson had subsequently re-photographed and re-printed"—an experiment that may have inspired Bacon to try something similar.[60]

The selection committees for group exhibitions embraced opposing views, for example Berger, Penrose, Del Renzio, Sylvester, and Watson chose Michael Andrews and Richard Hamilton, as well as Edward Middleditch, Harold Cohen, and Victor Willing for the exhibition *Nine Young Painters* (ICA, 1952). The catalogue admitted their deliberations were undertaken "laboriously and polemically, almost pugilistic ally and perhaps unexpectedly, considering the differences of opinion expressed" and went on to describe the artists' commonality as the way they "treat subjects and build up formal structures of a fairly complex kind and although they owe nothing to the English romantic tradition of Blake and Palmer, they are 'romantic painters.'"[61]

Bryan Robertson, newly appointed director at the Whitechapel in 1952, suffered the Berger exhibition *Looking Forward* and subsequently, at least in the 1950s, avoided almost all artists that drew or painted from life. One rationale Robertson gave to his bias was that he wished to overcome the association of the Jewish East End, where the gallery was located, with depressing representational art that pandered to the man in the street, and in contrast to offer visitors the work of painters and sculptors

[62] Jonathan Jones, *Whitechapel Art Gallery Centenary Review*, 2001, p. 66, and references in other articles including an account of *This is Tomorrow* by the participants still living, and Bryan Robertson's lively account of the Nicholas de Staël controversies, where Douglas Cooper and Graham Sutherland figure, "Supping with the Devil."

[63] "Richard Hamilton in Conversation with Michael Craig-Martin," Richard Hamilton, *October files 10* (Cambridge, MA and London, 2010), p. 8, and authors conversations with other artists. "Alloway took his colleagues to task for their lack of enthusiasm in an article in which he analysed the gestural painting of Pollock, de Kooning, and Franz Kline in such as way as to incorporate it into the nexus of European humanism. He pointed out that within Abstract Expressionism 'a picture is not painting according to pre-existing ideas but . . . it is a structure that results from the activity of its making. The tracks of these actions are not primarily decorative but charged with the humanity of the man who makes them.'" "US Modern: painting," *Art News & Review*, 21 January, 1956.

whose preference for fresh colour and formal invention might have a cheering effect.[62] He was responsive to Patrick Heron, who referenced the formal lessons of Brancusi, Bonnard, Moore, and Nicholson; he exhibited the work of Michael Ayrton, Robert Colquhoun, Alan Davie, and Sidney Nolan. The historic exhibitions, including Mondrian and Malevich, were, of course, thrilling for a wide span of artists, as were Robertson's timely appropriations of the exciting travelling exhibitions initiated by the International Council of the Museum of Modern Art, New York, the first one Jackson Pollock in 1958, followed by Mark Rothko, and Philip Guston.

Despite later denunciations condemning these U.S.I.S-funded tours as a Cold War strategy to promote Abstract Expressionism as an alternative to Soviet realism, the American influence on the cultural life in London was generally welcomed and the Embassy in Regent's Park a destination, particularly as their library stocked desirable illustrated magazines, and they hosted glamorous cocktail parties. First visits to America were memorable events. Hamilton, over forty when he went in 1963 to attend the opening of the Duchamp exhibition in Pasadena, recalled meeting his contemporaries, Oldenburg and Warhol. His badge *Epiphany,* 1964, refers to his ongoing investigation into the codes of modernism and satirizes his own timidity ("I couldn't refrain from making a lyrical little passage somewhere. I thought: these guys don't care!")[63]

During the next decade younger artists continued to be described, at least by the previous generation, as working in relation to existentialism. In 1963, for example, Roland Penrose assembled an exhibition, *Fear,* the title allowing him to gather reproductions of 237 works by artists as various as George Bellows, Henri Michaux, and Max Beckmann, a small section of original works by Paul Nash, Chaim Soutine, Edward Burra, Henry Moore and others, and a few paintings by the younger "international" generation, including David Hockney's *Teeth Cleaning,* 1962, and Mel Ramos's *Tiger Girl,* 1963.

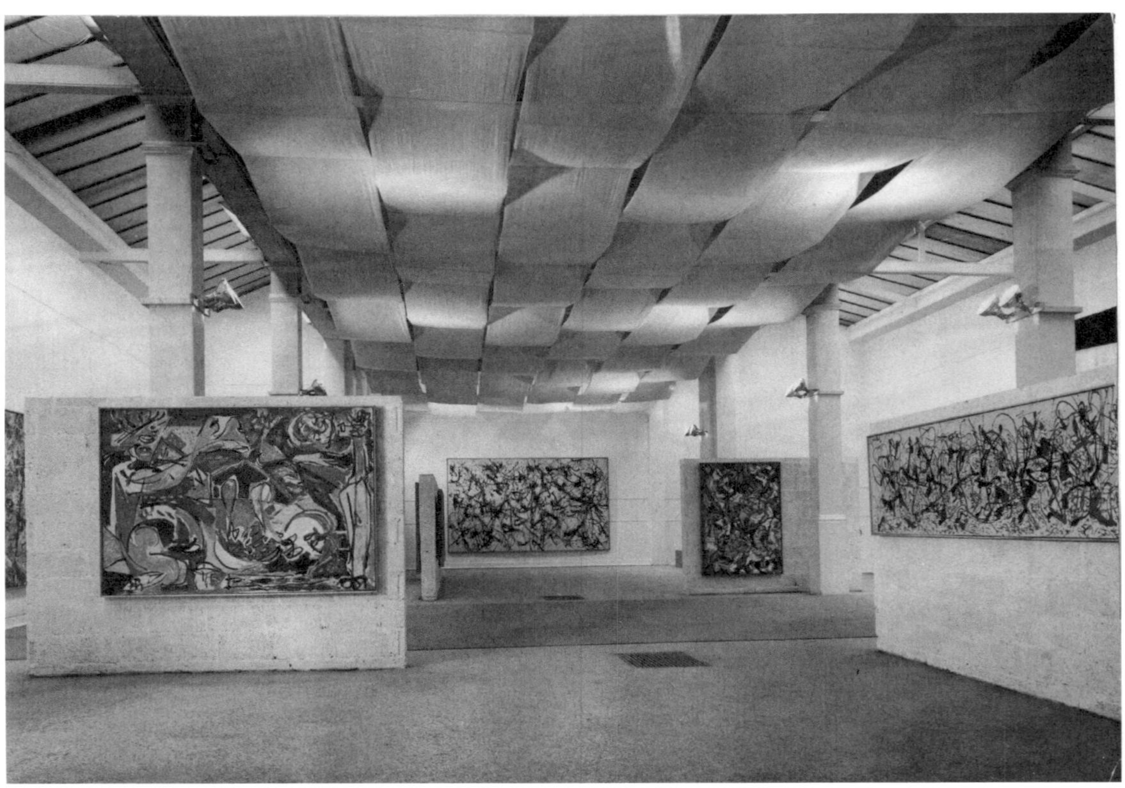

Right: Jackson Pollock exhibition, designed by Trevor Dannett, Whitechapel Gallery, 1958.

Right: Richard Hamilton, *Man, Machine and Motion,* Hatton Gallery, Newcastle upon Tyne, 1955.

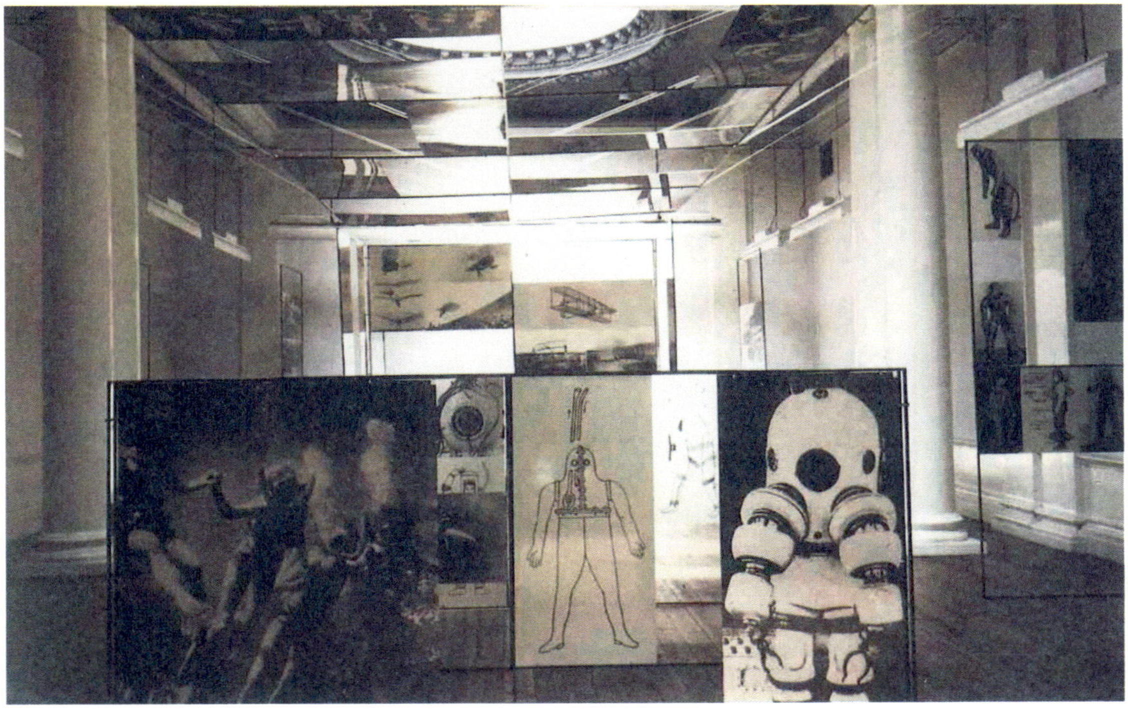

He argued that artists could express violence in a distinctly personal way; "If he burns, slashes, crushes, treads into the earth or blows up his own creation, the artist does so in order to convey to us not only his inner turmoil but also his delight in a wilful and sometimes exuberant violation of inertia"; thus "We participate in the act of violence without suffering its evil consequences . . . Its non-violent power has a therapeutic and catalytic influence."[64]

The first phase of English Pop art (1953–58) was strongly linked with technology and consumerism, the "pin-board" aesthetic practiced by those who amassed found material from popular culture and advertising. Nigel Henderson, Eduardo Paolozzi, William Turnbull, and Hamilton were pioneers and in an ongoing way there was a link with Surrealism, reinforced by the contributions of Toni del Renzio, by now a graphic designer and art editor, and Robert Melville, as well as with contact with foreign groups like the French *Nouveau Réalists,* and the Situationists. Hamilton reminds us that the Independent Group, which met at the ICA, was a forum for debating subjects of common interest, "it wasn't like the Cedar Bar in New York, where painters got drunk and argued out the ideas that led to Abstract Expressionism. The Independent Group consisted of people with many different backgrounds and professional aspirations [architects, writers] . . . We could discuss Elvis Presley; we could discuss what went on in the cinema; we presented papers to each other."[65] According to Lawrence Alloway, "One result of our discussions was to take Pop culture out of the realm of 'escapism,' 'sheer entertainment,' 'relaxation,' and to treat it with the seriousness of art. These interests put us in opposition both to the supporters of indigenous folk art and to anti-American opinion in Britain."[66] Sometimes their enthusiasms were taken beyond these intellectual forums, for example, Hamilton addressed teachers in his lecture "Popular Culture and Personal Responsibility" (NUT, Westminster, 1960). Nigel Henderson observed: "If there was one binding spirit amongst the people at the Independent Group, it was a distaste for Herbert Read's attitudes."[67]

Lawrence Gowing, always receptive to the convictions of very singular, inspired artists and a colleague of Hamilton at Newcastle Uni-

[64] Roland Penrose, *Fear,* exh. cat., ICA (London, 1962), introduction.

[65] Hamilton, Richard Hamilton, *October files 10* (Cambridge, MA and London, 2010), pp. 4–5.

[66] Lawrence Alloway, "The Development of Pop Art," Lucy R. Lippard, *Pop Art* (London, 1966), arguing against Greenberg's 1961 article "Avant Garde and Kitsch," p. 36. Alloway became a curator at the Guggenheim Museum in 1961.

[67] Victoria Walsh, *Nigel Henderson. Parallel of Life and Art* (London, 2001), quoting Charlie Jackson, "Nigel Henderson," dissertation, Hornsey College of Art, 1973. Hamilton coined the phrase "Pop art" in 1957 in a note to Alison and Peter Smithson: "Pop art is Popular (designed for a mass audience), Transient (short-term solution), Expendable (easily forgotten), Low Cost, Mass Produced, Young (aimed at youth), Wicked, Sexy, Gimmicky, Glamorous, Big Business" (Interview with Rachel Cooke, *The Observer,* 14 February 2010).

Richard Hamilton

Born in 1922 in London

Hamilton grew up in London and left school with no formal qualifications. He attended various evening classes, including courses at the Royal Academy and the Slade, as well as working during the war years as a technical draughtsman. He made drawings and prints, illustrating *Ulysses* in 1948–49 (and returned to the project in 1981). He devised exhibitions at the ICA in London, and collaborated on *Man, Machine & Motion*, 1955, at the Hatton Gallery, Newcastle upon Tyne, and *This is Tomorrow*, 1956, at the Whitechapel. In addition, he organised events associated with the Independent Group to do with popular culture and American products, or "the continuum with at one end Piccasso and the other Elvis Presley." Hamilton taught at King's College, University of Durham, 1953–1966. He became immersed in Duchamp's *Large Glass*, transcribing the text. Hamilton is known for his paintings and sophisticated, multi-state prints, especially those subjects derived from photographs and film stills like Bing Crosby in *I'm Dreaming of a White Christmas*, and *Swingeing London*, an image that captures Robert Fraser and Mick Jagger as they were arrested and handcuffed on drugs charges. Hamilton has exhibited internationally, and in 2009–10 his political and protest works were seen in Edinburgh and London, the best known of which, *The Citizen*, honours the Republican political prisoners in the H blocks at the Maze prison in Ireland—the 'dirty' protest. He died in September 2011.

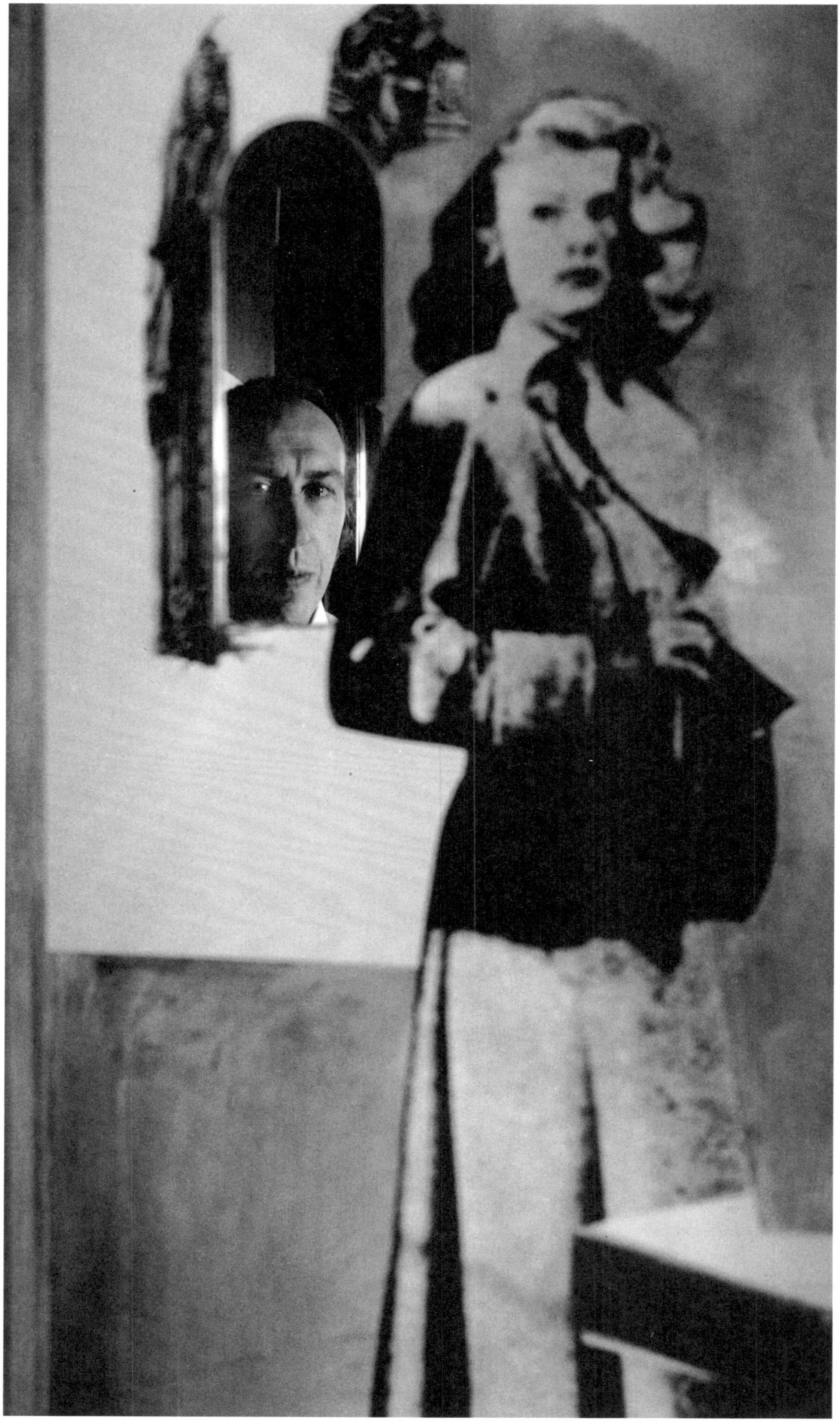

Right: Jorge Lewinski, *Richard Hamilton*, 1966.

I Richard Hamilton, *Collected Words 1953–1982* (London, 1982), pp. 66–68.

II Hamilton, speaking (in the 3rd person), in the context of *Shit and Flowers 1970–80*, Alan Cristea Gallery, London, 2010, on a series which preceeded *Mother and Child*.

One postcard, of the beach at Whitley Bay, has produced several variations: a medium-sized painting, a print on a photographic base, a postcard, a one-off 'multiple' and the cover for the March 1969 issue of *Studio International*. This particular postcard is itself a true photographic print without an intruding reproduction screen . . . I find it astonishing that a flick of a shutter over a coating of silver emulsion can snatch so much information about that millisecond of activity over half a mile of beach at Whitley Bay one summer's day. As this texture of anonymous humanity is penetrated, it yields more fragments of knowledge about individuals isolated within it as well as endless patterns of group relationships. Ultimately, enlargement takes us into unreadable, abstract clumps of silver halides. The attempts of some non-figurative artists to create paintings or objects without external reference (however admirable the results) seem to me to be not only futile but retrograde. I marvel that marks and shapes, simple or complex, have the capacity to enlarge consciousness, can allude back to an ever-widening history of mankind, can force emotional responses as well as aesthetic ones and permit both internal and external associations to germinate the imagination of the spectator. [I]

"I've always been an old style artist, a fine artist in the commonly accepted sense: that was my student training and that's what I've remained." *Soft blue landscape* demonstrates a talent that could be turned on and off at will and one which he enjoyed. Photographic grain and the reprographic dots of halftone could be converted into brushstrokes or used as part of the surface texture, differences of scale and configuration in the marks added up to an abstraction. Whether broadly gestural or small and painstakingly contrived, each mark competed in a struggle for recognition. [II]

[68] *Richard Hamilton. Collected Words* (London, 1982), pp. 19–20.

[69] Ibid.

[70] Richard Hamilton, quoted in "Works of Political and Moral Motivation," by Michael Bracewell, *Richard Hamilton. Modern Moral Matters*, exh. cat., Serpentine Gallery (London, 2010), p. 22.

versity, collaborated on the text to accompany one of Hamilton's most experimental exhibitions, *Man, Machine and Motion,* staged at the University's Hatton Gallery in 1955. The authors point out that the photograph of an early aviator "in his spider web," a plane hardly fit to fly, embodies man in a new, complex relationship, more moving that that of horse and rider; man and machine "liberates a deeper, more fearsome human impulse," best expressed in poetry and art, "man has no other means of assimilating disruptive experience to the balanced fabric of thought and feeling."[68]

Hamilton showed paintings at the Hanover Gallery in 1955 (without commercial success) and professed to mixing idioms, comparing himself with R.B. Kitaj, who even as a student at the Royal College of Art in 1960, mixed styles, the avoidance of an organic wholeness intended "to preserve the identity of different sources; though a diversifying of language is, I like to think, a mutual objective."[69] Acknowledging that the disadvantage (as well as the great virtue) of the *This is Tomorrow* exhibition at the Whitechapel was its incoherence and obscurity of language (it was presented in twelve separate sections, each a different team's effort), Hamilton found, nevertheless, "There was a turning point in my life, in 1956, where I thought that art doesn't need to come out of looking at reality . . . all I needed for stimulation was second-hand pictures in film and TV magazines, newspapers . . . things that had been pre-digested and 'two-dimensionalised' . . . however irrational these visual relationships were, that very fact created an excitement in the image that wouldn't be there if it was too coherent. Everything comes out of that understanding—even the recognition later, that this was the characteristic of Pop art. It wasn't the subject matter, it was the fact that it was second-hand imagery, not directly derived from nature."[70] As his art developed from the famous collage *Just what is it that makes today's homes so different, so appealing?,* 1956, with the muscle man holding the American chewy confection, the Tootsie Pop, Hamilton continued to respond to disparate

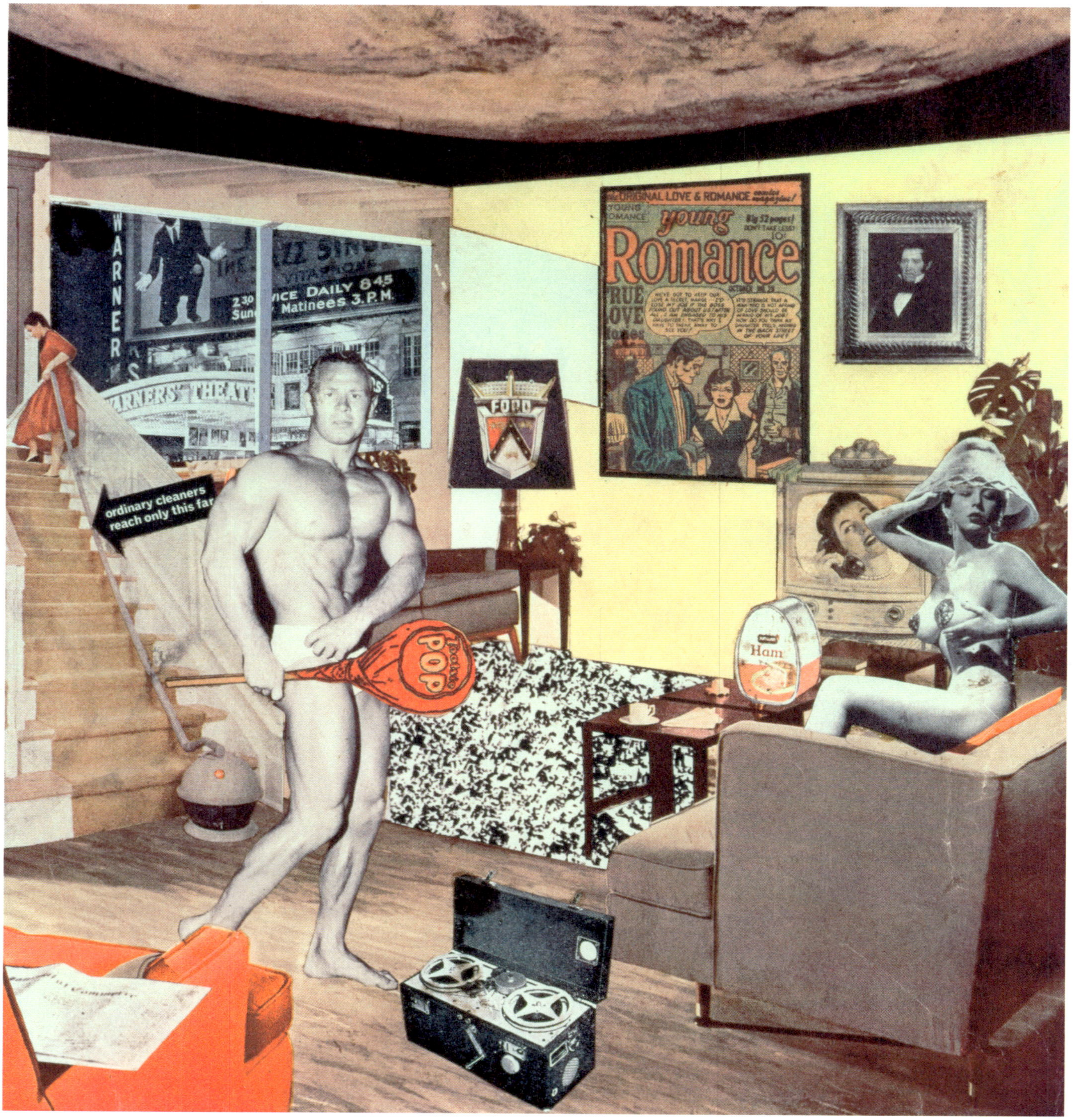

Above: Richard Hamilton,
What is it that makes today's homes so different, so appealing?, 1956.
Kunsthalle Tübingen, Tübingen.

[71] *Richard Hamilton. Collected Words* (London, 1982), p. 38.

[72] Rawsthorne letters, Tate archive, and *Isabel and Other Intimate Strangers: Portraits by Alberto Giacometti and Francis Bacon* (New York, 2008).

[73] Celia Paul to Lampert, 2009.

[74] Sylvester, *About Modern Art* (London, 1997), p. 16.

[75] Bruce Laughton, "Coldstream and Giacometti in London," *The British Art Journal*, Vol. IX, no.2, Autumn 2008.

[76] Andrew Forge, *Observation: Notation*, exh. cat., New York Studio School (New York, 2000), np. Quoted in Laughton, London, 2008.

[77] Arts Council archive at the V&A, Blyth Road; "A personal reminiscence by Robin Campbell," *Studio International*, Feb 1966, vol. 171, no.874, p. 47 and Auerbach to author, also in variations in Daniel Farson's biography of Bacon, *The Gilded Gutter Life of Francis Bacon* (London, 1994), p. 167. Campbell, then Deputy Director of Art at the Arts Council, was a friend of many of the artists in this exhibition. See too *Francis Bacon and the Tradition of Art* (Vienna, 2004), the essays by Barbara Steffen, Michael Peppiatt, and the interview with Sylvester and Michel Archimbaud reprinted there, as well as text in *Crossing the Channel*, by Pilar Ordovas, Gagosian Gallery, London 2010. The contrary details arise partly because Giacometti came to London in September 1964, and in July and August 1965.

idioms and sources while insisting that ideas "be explicit and separable, so the plastic entities must retain their identity as tokens. The elements hold their integrity because they are voiced in different plastic dialects within the unified whole."[71]

Giacometti

For eight of the artists in this exhibition contact with Alberto Giacometti and Marcel Duchamp was face to face, and intense at the time of the 1965 and 1966 Tate exhibitions, selected by Sylvester and Hamilton respectively. An important English conduit to Giacometti was the artist Isabel (Lambert) Rawsthorne. Early in her life Rawsthorne, formerly the mistress of Jacob Epstein (Freud's first father-in-law), became Giacometti's muse and early companion, and met Sartre, Simone de Beauvoir, Michel Leiris, and Georges Bataille. Picasso claimed that she made love with Annette [Giacometti's new wife, who also favoured Freud] and that she had a splendid muscular body, and was a keen skier. After the war she married the composer Alan Rawsthorne, continued to go to Paris, exhibited at E.L.T. Mesens's London Gallery, then at Marlborough, and was the subject of unforgettable works by Bacon, most famously the portrait of her on Dean Street in Soho, which began with a John Deakin photograph.[72]

Freud frequented Giacometti's studio on the rue Hippolyte-Maindron where he posed for drawings and the two men saw each other alone in Paris and London. Freud claimed to feel and think the opposite of what Giacometti believed and told a friend of his, the artist Celia Paul, that the divergence fostered their friendship rather than the opposite.[73] To him, Giacometti's sculpture seemed very tentative, especially the touch, perhaps because Freud's own work was more finished and precise, and he liked more the paintings.

David Sylvester was in regular contact with Giacometti after they met in autumn 1948, reporting back to London friends on each development, for example, in 1950, how Giacometti had resumed making sculpture from nature as well as memory. In his judgment Giacometti was the one artist taking figurative art into a domain, "more complex, more specific, richer in human content" and beyond the range of abstract art.[74] At the time of the 1955 Arts Council exhibition in their space in St James's Square, which Sylvester arranged, he brought Giacometti, visiting London for the first time, to the Slade to meet Coldstream and tour the school, no doubt viewing one of the portraits in progress in the studio, perhaps that of a bishop. They went for a long dinner at L'Escargot that ended in a drinking session at the Regent's Palace bar, and in the following years exchanged messages and gifts (the last a drawing made in his hotel room in 1965). Bruce Laughton has studied their relationship and notes that Coldstream "allowed his gaze to roam evenly over the field of vision, and tended to play down depth in favour of the picture plane" whereas Giacometti returned the model's gaze.[75] Uglow, who met Giacometti first in 1957, explained that he could never look the models in the eye, much less see them nude, except when he was painting. Coldstream's heavily scored portrait of *Lord Ifor Evans,* 1958–60, places emphasis on the man's body encased in a suit; this only increases the oddities of visual experience, as Andrew Forge wrote, the "endless half-threatening mysteries."[76]

While Giacometti's 1965 exhibition was being installed at the Tate, space in the warehouse was cleared so he could work, surrounded by empty packing cases, on several unfinished plasters and, if he liked, begin painting on two large canvases procured by Andrew Forge. He had met Bacon only the previous summer of 1964 when he came to London with Michel Leiris and his wife. A day was spent at the British Museum and Sir John Soane's Museum (and admiring the Hogarths). This time he went to L'Escargot with Bacon, George Dyer, and Auerbach, the conversation conducted in English, French, and German. Annette made jokes about the skinny figures Alberto made and Bacon, fairly drunk, tried to argue with Giacometti.[77] Bacon's comments about Gia-

Below left: Alberto Giacometti, *Seated Man,* 1949. Tate, London.

Below right: Marcel Duchamp, *Nude Descending a Staircase (No.2),* 1912. Philadelphia Museum of Art.

cometti's work, typically half-complimentary, half-dismissive, are often quoted, and their mutual use of a frame/cage/line around the figure frequently compared, with their conflicted sexual lives proposed as a clue to the interpretation of the portraits of Caroline and Dyer. Yet this seems tenuous, at least in comparison to a deeper engagement with similar problems in the work of those painters who worked from life, and placed emphasis on drawing.

Sylvester's point of reference often returned to Giacometti, for example, writing on Kossoff in 1995, he begins with the challenge of Cézanne, the further pursuit of the problems of appearance in two dimensions by Giacometti, before describing Kossoff's use of paint almost as if clay, "its density, its pliability," the long trails of pigment asserting the existence of the object as a living thing, referential and gestural, as well as endowed with a luminosity that contradicts the materiality. Thus, "the result is a dialectic between rapid realisation of the image and sustained involvement with a subject."[78]

Before his death in February 1966 Giacometti expressed his ambition to work in parallel on the same head both from life and when alone from memory, "Because in working from life, you always see much more than you can cope with, so you get lost in too many complications. In working from memory you try to retain what

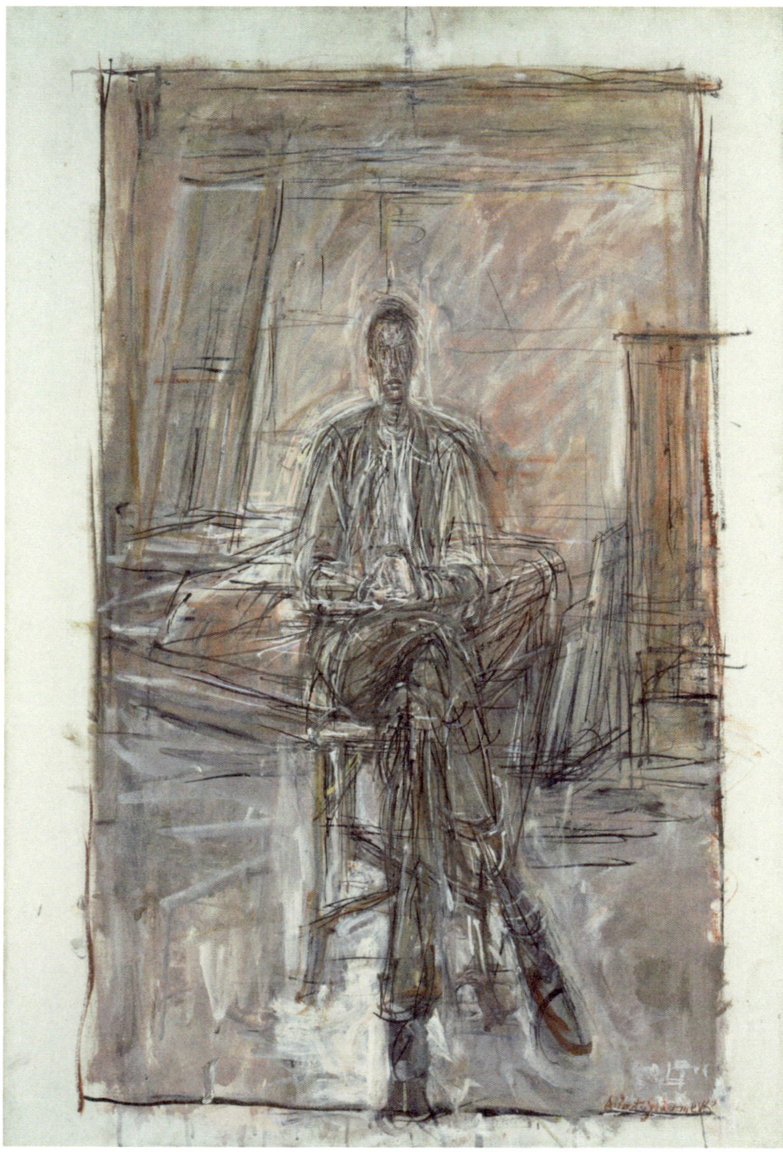

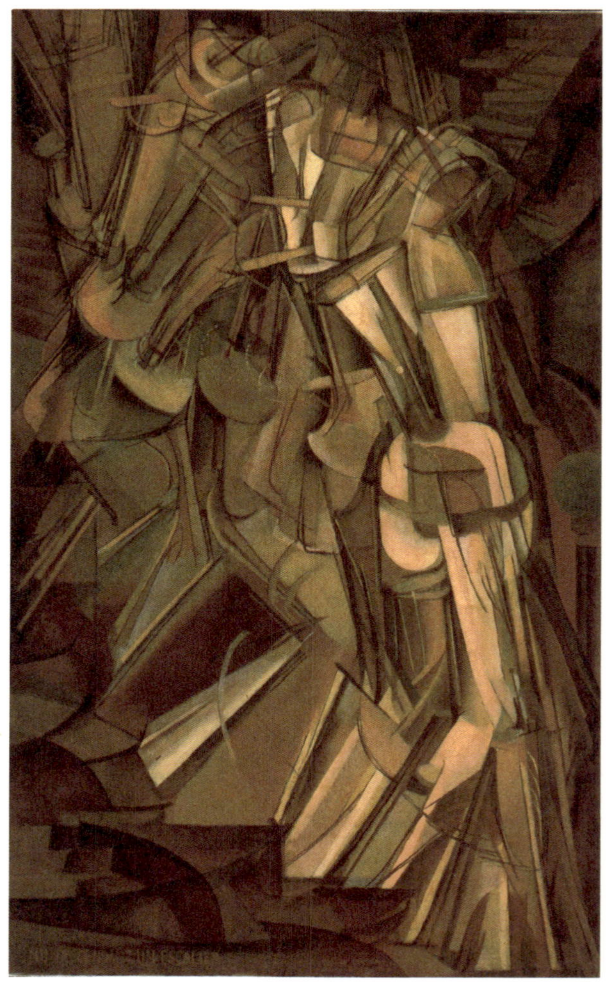

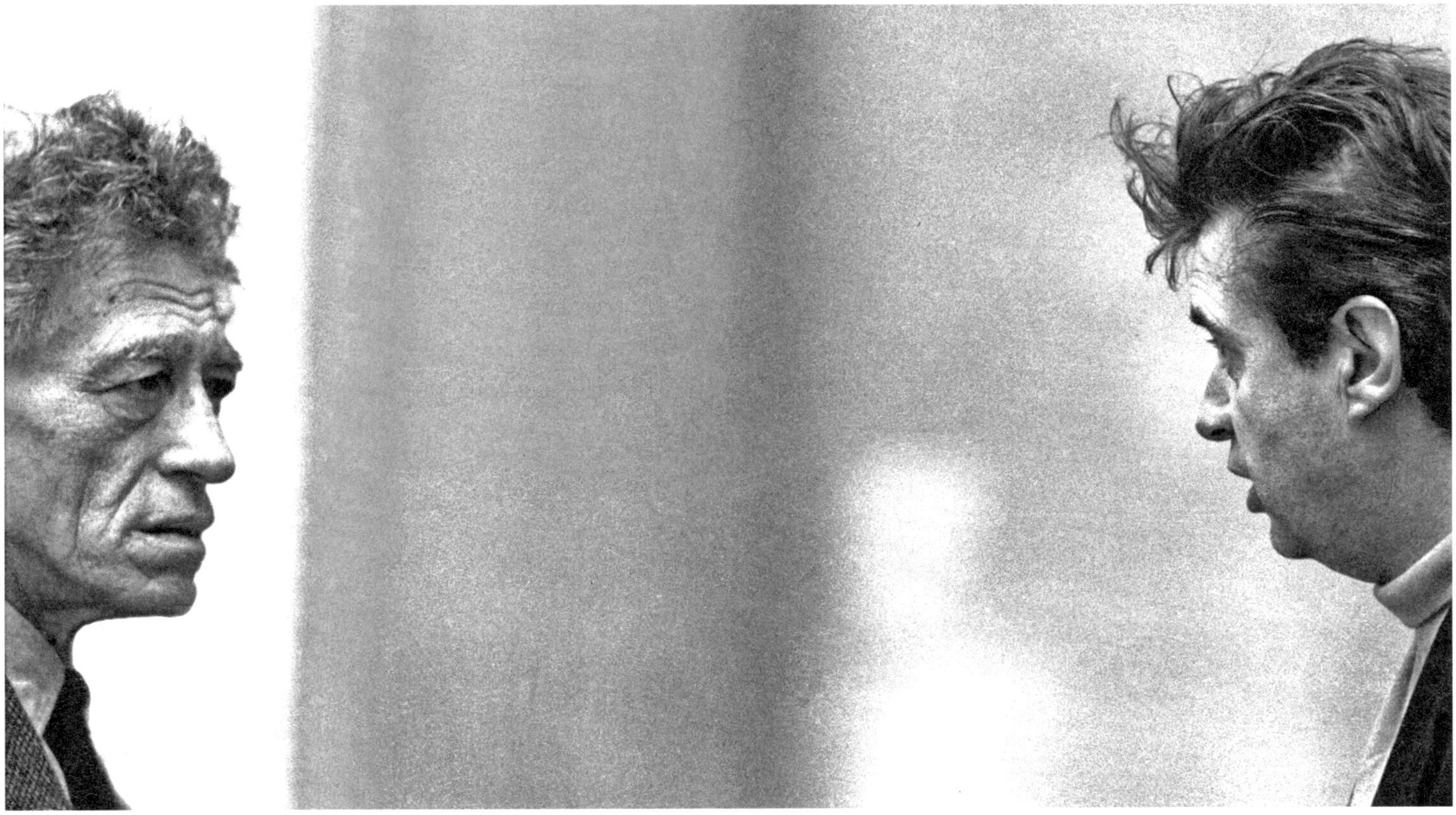

[78] David Sylvester, "Nothing is ever the same," *Leon Kossoff*, exh. cat., XLVI, Venice Biennale (London, 1995), p. 25.

[79] David Sylvester interviewing Giacometti in 1964, *Looking at Giacometti* (London, 1994), pp. 227, 239.

[80] Freud to Méraud Guinness, summer 1947, Tate archive.

[81] Richard Hamilton in *The almost complete works of Marcel Duchamp*, exh. cat., Tate (London, 1966), introduction.

Above: Alberto Giacometti and Francis Bacon at Tate, 1965. Photo: Graham Keen.

has struck you most forcibly. At the same time it helps you to go on working from life. Ultimately, my idea would be to work in exactly the same way whether from memory or from life—that the two should overlap completely."[79]

Duchamp

The last great Surrealist exhibition devised by André Breton opened at Galerie Maeght in July 1947, the outlandish installation designed by Frederick Kiesler in collaboration with Duchamp. Maria Martins's sculpture *L'impossible*—its theme attraction and repulsion—was displayed on a billiard table in the "Rain Room." The twenty-four year old Freud attended the preview and sent a postcard to a friend: "The Surrealist exhibition is very dark and rainy and beautifully built and arranged like the ideal home exhibition."[80] Richard Hamilton encountered Duchamp's *Green Box* at this time through Nigel Henderson (whose father ran Peggy Guggenheim's London gallery before the war). In 1957 he was entrusted with a typographic translation of its written contents which led to collaboration between the two men in the making of a replica of the *Large Glass,* virtually destroyed in 1926. It was a main feature of *The almost complete works of Marcel Duchamp* at the Tate. In the catalogue introduction Hamilton tried to define the Duchamp "enigma," his dedicated rejection of commitment and principled "indifference," telling the readers that Duchamp's "search for an object without aesthetic merit, one 'with the least virtue' that he could find to allege his conviction that 'taste is the enemy of art,' has proved futile. His essentially artistic genius won out. It was with just a tinge of sadness that Duchamp admitted in 1961, 'I'm nothing else but an artist . . . I couldn't be very much more iconoclastic any more.'"[81]

The day after the exhibition opened,

[82] A two-hour interview with Duchamp for the Arts Council of Great Britain, 19 June, 1966, *Alexina and Marcel Duchamp Papers, 3:2*, Philadelphia Museum of Art, unpaginated, quoted by kind permission of the Arts Council England and the PMA.

19 June, 1966, Hamilton invited four friends—William Coldstream, R.B. Kitaj, Robert Melville, and David Sylvester—to his Highgate home with the intention of recording a conversation with Duchamp. Kitaj begins by trying to entice Duchamp to articulate what he thinks about "art for art's sake," autonomous art in "radical abstract modes," by which Kitaj means art which he deplores and believes widens the gap between contemporary art and a general audience.[82] Duchamp explains that public receptivity to Abstract Expressionism, indeed their love of it, is only a post-war phenomenon ("the less the public is invited to judge, the better I have felt all my life.") Kitaj argues that since Manet, "paintings have begun to concern themselves more with themselves; and it's reached an apex in our own time." Duchamp reminds the others that the patron had already lost ground with the arrival of Courbet, artists became self-directed, revered like saints. Hamilton shifts the focus, surely Duchamp must have conceived the *Large Glass* "in a very emotional way, because in the note that describes it you infer sexuality, 'Blossoming being the sum total of her splendid vibrations.'" Duchamp doesn't deny this reading even when "the deity in this case could be eroticism," however, he brings up the case of Fra Angelico, not principally an artist, a young man "who had to paint and serve his God" and hopes he too can make something not judged by the retina (especially despising colour combinations) but rather art that re-introduces something beyond the anecdotal, where "the grey matter would come in as an instrument of measure."

The conversation was dominated by Sylvester and Melville until Coldstream finally interjects and asks whether Duchamp agrees that it is a feature of the twentieth century that artists "have felt compulsion to take up a stand which is other"; wasn't it true that with the ready-mades "you wanted to take up a stand that was new," analogous to the ambition of contemporary artists? Duchamp agrees and furthermore suggests making art is not a question of emulating scientific progress, the aim of most artists is to make something that has "no trace of traditional learning or something that he has known before." Duchamp concedes that it is hard to make something truly "indifferent," taste comes into it.

Coldstream continues. That morning he met a young artist who was very interested that he was going to have a chance of seeing Duchamp, "what I would like to ask Mr. Duchamp is why he has made such few works for such a long time?—because what I like about Mr. Duchamp is all the work he hasn't made." He wasn't being ironical, Coldstream adds, he wanted to know "if it required a great effort of will not to do any work." Duchamp prevaricates: "those things I haven't done were still below indifference in a certain [way]"; he is no longer tempted to do ready-mades, but has not made a vow. Nowadays oil painting doesn't tempt him because it would use the "self-same process." The painters he most enjoys are Seurat and Mondrian, as neither, contrary to received opinion, he would call "retinal," and he could still find the motivation to work "as long as you let me work very slowly."

Coldstream persists. Could Duchamp use someone else to make those things that depend on grey matter, "Or do you find when you are making them that you get involved in something other than the idea?" Duchamp could use someone else, "But I am interested enough to do it myself. You see, I am manual at the same time. I am not completely spatial. I like manual execution," for example, although his "windows" were made by a carpenter, "I did the black glass which is leather and should be shined every morning like shoes." Coldstream's favourite object in the newly opened exhibition is an ordinary waistcoat on a hangar (*no. 179*, made for Benjamin Peret in November 1958). Duchamp concedes that he likes it best of his "ready-mades" as no one would be able to say whether it was good or bad.

Chance in Duchamp's terms paralleled the "notion of removing his hand from the operation so that he gained the advantage of precision," a notion that also fascinated Bacon. Most obviously one thinks of his paint so liberally and instinctively applied that the

Right: Andrew Forge, "In Duchamp's Footsteps." Richard Hamilton's reconstrucion of Marcel Duchamp's *The bride stripped bare by her bachelors, even* (the *Large Glass*) of 1915–23. Photographs by Richard Hamilton and Mark Lancaster, *Studio International,* vol. 171, no. 878, 1966.

Below: Installation shot of *The Almost Complete Works of Marcel Duchamp,* Tate, 1966.

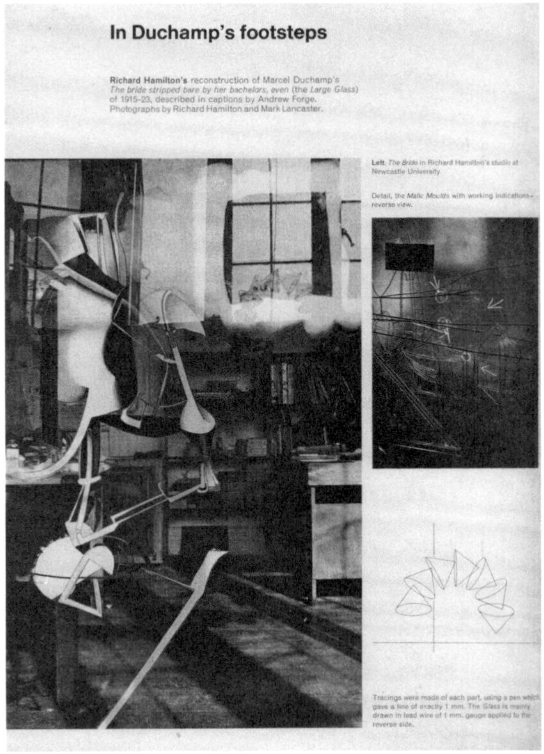

In Duchamp's footsteps

Richard Hamilton's reconstruction of Marcel Duchamp's *The bride stripped bare by her bachelors, even* (the *Large Glass*) of 1915-23, described in captions by Andrew Forge. Photographs by Richard Hamilton and Mark Lancaster.

Left. *The Bride* in Richard Hamilton's studio at Newcastle University.

Detail, the *Malic Moulds* with working indications–reverse view.

Tracings were made of each part, using a pen which gave a line of exactly 1 mm. The *Glass* is mainly drawn in lead wire of 1 mm. gauge applied to the reverse side.

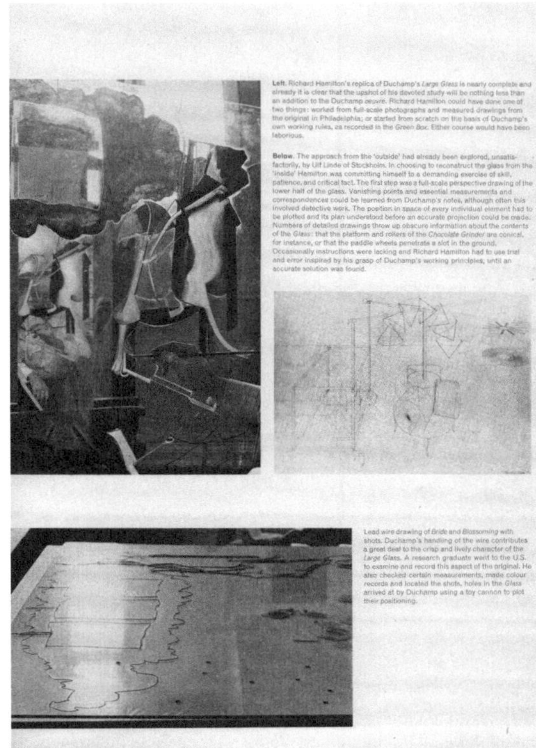

Left. Richard Hamilton's replica of Duchamp's *Large Glass* is nearly complete and already it is clear that the upshot of his devoted study will be nothing less than an addition to the Duchamp *oeuvre*. Richard Hamilton could have done one of two things: worked from full-scale photographs and measured drawings from the original in Philadelphia; or started from scratch on the basis of Duchamp's own working rules, as recorded in the *Green Box*. Either course would have been laborious.

Below. The approach from the 'outside' had already been explored, unsatisfactorily, by Ulf Linde of Stockholm. In choosing to reconstruct the glass from the 'inside' Hamilton was committing himself to a demanding exercise of skill, patience, and critical tact. The first step was a full-scale perspective drawing of the lower half of the glass. Vanishing points and essential measurements and correspondences could be learned from Duchamp's notes, although often this involved detective work. The position in space of every individual element had to be plotted and its plan understood before an accurate projection could be made. Numbers of detailed drawings throw up obscure information about the contents of the *Glass*: that the platform and rollers of the *Chocolate Grinder* are conical, for instance, or that the paddle wheels penetrate a slot in the ground. Occasionally instructions were lacking and Richard Hamilton had to use trial and error inspired by his grasp of Duchamp's working principles, until an accurate solution was found.

Lead wire drawing of *Bride* and *Blossoming* with shots. Duchamp's handling of the wire contributes a great deal to the crisp and lively character of the *Large Glass*. A research graduate went to the U.S. to examine and record this aspect of the original. He also checked certain measurements, made colour records and located the shots, holes in the *Glass* arrived at by Duchamp using a toy cannon to plot their positioning.

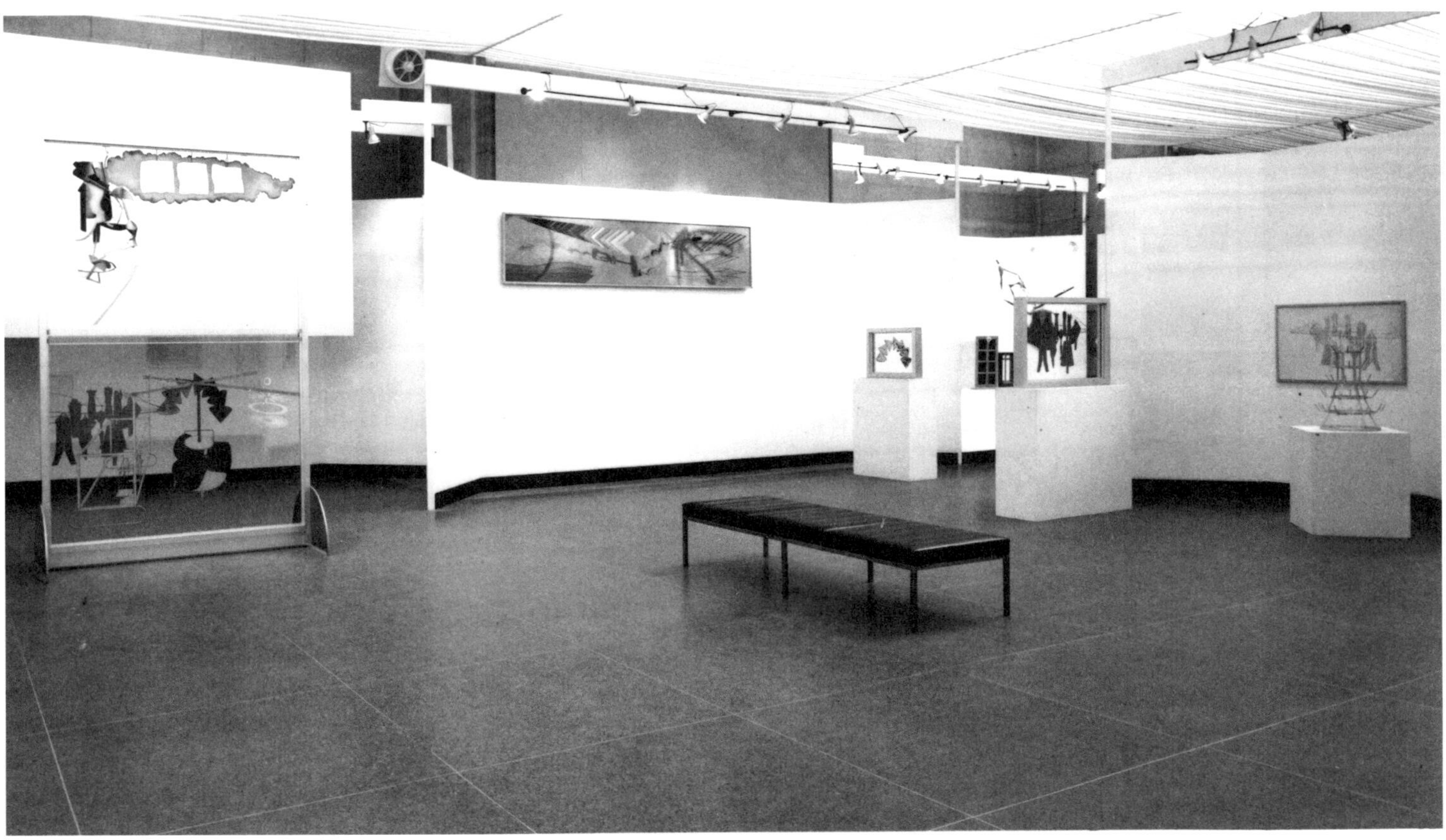

David Hockney
Born 1937 in Bradford

Hockney studied at the Royal College of Art from 1959–62, his student works demonstrating a candid attitude to homosexual love and alternative art styles, for example, *We Two Boys Together Clinging*, 1961, and *The First Marriage (Marriage of Styles)*, 1962. On his second visit to New York, in 1963, Hockney met Andy Warhol, Dennis Hopper, and Henry Geldzahler, followed by an initial exposure to California which inspired landscapes of downtown Los Angeles, as well as figures in swimming pools. Hockney travelled continually, usually with direct results for his art: for example, making drawings for the etchings related to the poems of C.P. Cavafy in Beirut. His retrospective at the Whitechapel opened in 1970 and travelled to Germany. After a concentration on portrait drawings and paintings, as well as lithographs, Hockney began to work extensively in photography in 1976, using a photocopier, fax machine, and lately advanced digital technology. His theatre sets and costume designs in Covent Garden, Glyndebourne, and the Metropolitan Opera, were widely praised. In the late 1990s an investigation into the historic use by artists of the *camera lucida* occupied his attention, resulting in the book *Secret Knowledge: Rediscovering the lost techniques of the Old Masters*, 2001. Although retaining studios in Los Angeles and Pembroke Studios, London, in recent years Hockney has painted the East Yorkshire landscape, sometimes using a multi-canvas format. In 2012 the Royal Academy of Arts will stage a major retrospective.

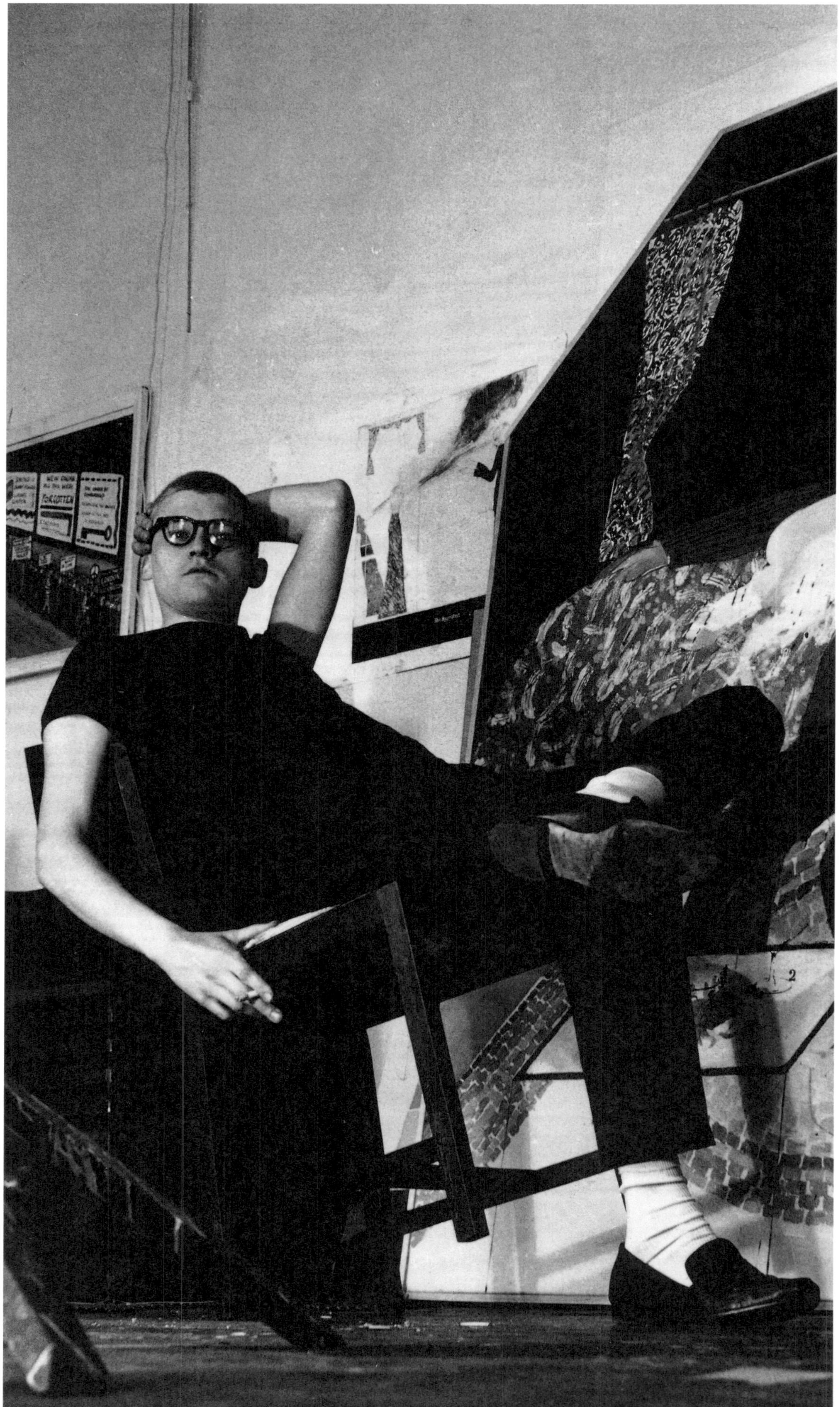

Right: Jorge Lewinski, *David Hockney*, 1963.

[I] *Hockney on Hockney* (London, 1976), p. 41.

[II] David Hockney, on the paintings of late 1961, painted on Hessian in imitation of Bacon, *Hockney on Hockney*, p. 67.

In 1956 there'd been a big exhibition at the Tate of American Abstract Expressionist painting, and then Bryan Robertson had done shows at the Whitechapel of Pollock and in 1961 Rothko. And this was the latest thing. This was painting that had been done just two or three years before in America. Young students had realized that American painting was more interesting than French painting. The idea of French painting disappeared really, and American Abstract Expressionism was the great influence. So I tried my hand at it, I did a few pictures, about twenty on three feet by four feet pieces of hardboard that were based on a kind of mixture of Alan Davie cum Jackson Pollock cum Roger Hilton. And I did them for a while, and then I couldn't. It was too barren for me. [I]

It was his style [Dubuffet's] of doing images, the kind of childish drawing he used, that attracted me. You see, I was in a dilemma which was probably similar to Francis Bacon's; he always said he did want to draw—he never draws now—because it would make his pictures very different if he could draw well. You can see the point. His images have a crudity and vigour which help the impact of the pictures . . . At the time I could draw figures quite well in an academic way. But that's not what I wanted in the paintings . . . I also liked his [Dubuffet] work's similarity to children's art, which is like Egyptian art in that it's all the same. So I felt that using that kind of thing was using an anonymous style; and it occurred all the time in those pictures. [II]

[83] Transcript of a conversation between Richard Hamilton, David Alan Mellor, and Nicola Roberts, *Francis Bacon. The Barry Joule Archive*, exh. cat., Irish Museum of Modern Art (Dublin, 2000), p. 32.

[84] Auerbach to Lampert.

[85] Bacon, 1966, in David Sylvester, *Looking Back at Francis Bacon* (London, 2000), p. 246.

[86] Hamilton, *The Barry Joule Archive* (Dublin, 2000), p. 32.

[87] Richard Kendall quoting from interviews with Uglow, *Uglow: The Complete Paintings* (London and New Haven, 2007), p. liii.

[88] Smee (London, 2006), pp. 26–27.

marks left on the canvas could be described as "accidental." This claim is increasingly seen as an attempt to conceal Bacon's fascination with manipulated images. Hamilton viewed the diagram Bacon had drawn on a newspaper photograph of a group of rugby players, he described it connecting their pricks, eyes, and backsides with lines, associating the result with Duchamp's *Nine Malic Moulds,* 1914–15 the focus of both works the "horizontal plane of sex," tops and bottoms unaligned ("I am quite sure that Francis was aware of his source.")[83] On the other hand when Bacon went around the 1966 Duchamp show with his friend Denis Wirth-Miller, glancing at *Tu'm,* 1918, he shrewdly remarked, "I don't think that one works" (ironically it was Sylvester's favorite painting but according to Duchamp, more a commission to go above a patron's bookshelf and "a recapitulation of previous ideas.")[84]

Bacon invariably described the work of his contemporaries as disappointing. For example, "I saw the Rothkos at the Whitechapel Gallery (1961) and I hoped to see marvellous abstract Turners, and what I saw were rather dismal variations on colour, which at any rate, from my point of view, gave me no excitement and no possibility of entering or communicating whatsoever."[85] On the other hand Hamilton and Rita Donagh recalled long conversations with Bacon, Bacon praising Manet for his sheer painterly skill, he [Bacon] "would talk at great length about a rose on a Manet painting: the fact that the brush marks didn't describe the structure of a rose—they created a rose."[86]

Early in the careers of both Hamilton and Uglow they painted their own variations of Duchamp's *Nude Descending a Staircase, No.2,* 1912. For Uglow was it about "trapping movement," a girl and a winding staircase, a challenge that he addressed in numerous works of his own, some that required set-ups as elaborate as the construction of *Étant Donnés,* 1946–66 only revealed after Duchamp's death. Uglow explained, "Basically I am trying to paint a structured painting full of controlled, and therefore potent, emotion." "I don't do wristy paintings because I want the brain to intervene between the observation and the mark."[87] Freud spoke of the moments in Duchamp when "the quality is so extraordinary and lively—and secretive! His general idea was to get rid of everything except pure intelligence. He wanted to be the last artist . . . in a way you could say he was saying, 'I dare you to do something actually good that lasts.'"[88]

[89] Auerbach to Lampert, Lawrence Alloway, *Young Contemporaries 1961*, RBA Galleries, London, 1961.

An abundance of styles and directions

When Kitaj and David Hockney met at the Royal College the more worldly American, Kitaj, encouraged the young man from Bradford to forget about emulating the current enthusiasm for semi-abstraction, and instead to foreground his personal interests (which at the time were vegetarianism, politics, and a few heroes). Hockney listened, changed course and began scrawling words on his images, like "Gandhi" and "to Queens" and applying titles as evocative as *I'm in the Mood for Love,* 1961. Auerbach remembers when the early graffiti-ish works by Hockney came before the jury of the *Young Contemporaries* in January 1961. He put up his hand, and challenged by the chair, Lawrence Alloway, defended these paintings as urgent and memorable, like the drawing on lavatory walls. The others assented and writing in the catalogue Alloway analysed the common threads in this remarkable generation of RCA students that included Allen Jones, Peter Phillips, Derek Boshier, and Patrick Caulfield: "The impact of popular art is present, but checked by puzzles and paradoxes about the play of signs at different levels of signification in their work, which combines real objects, same-size representation, sketchy notation, and writing."[89]

Hockney describes meeting Hamilton when he came to critique the student sketch club. "Nobody knew much about him, although he

Below: David Hockney, *Christopher Isherwood and Don Bachardy,* 1968.

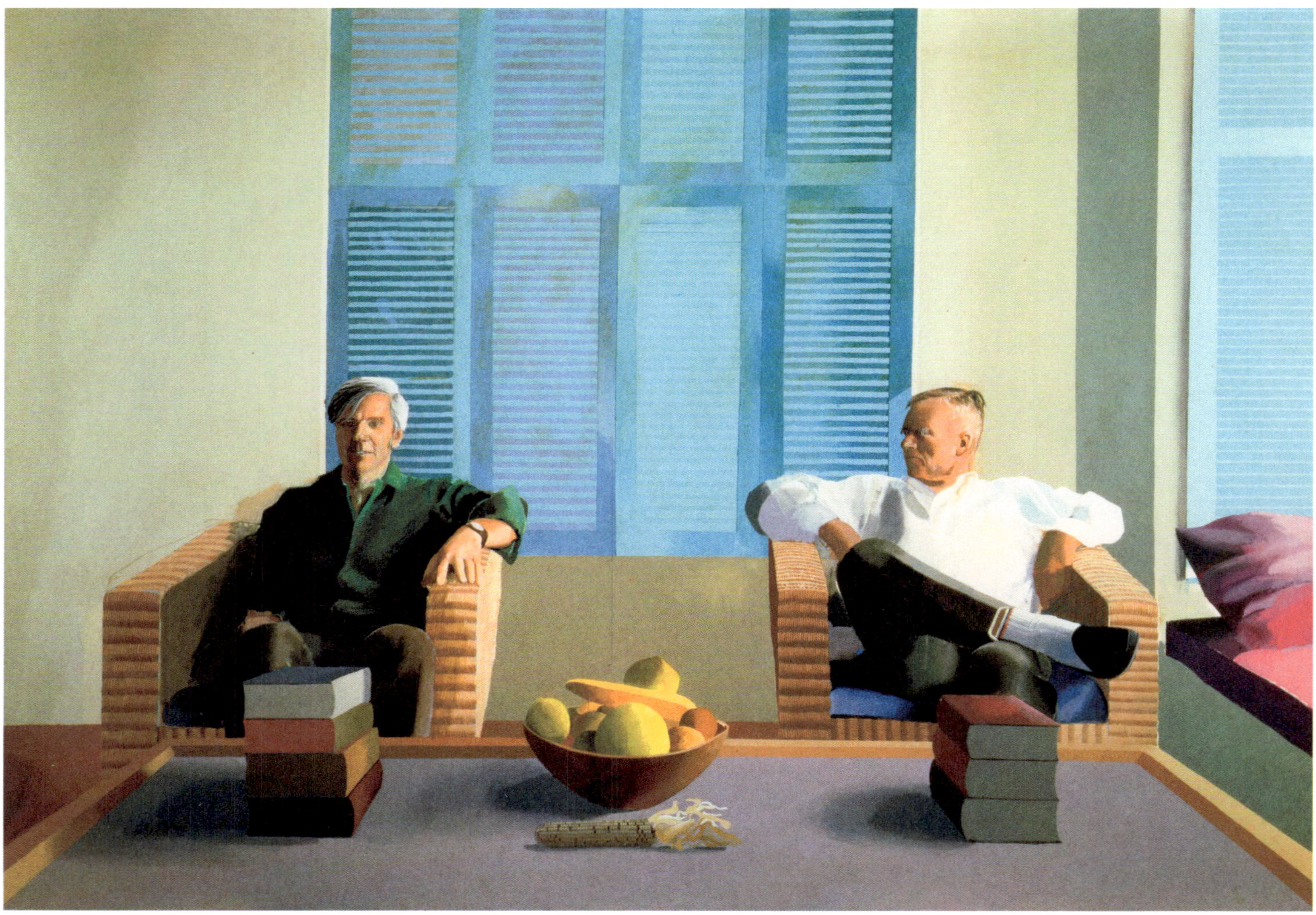

Right: David Hockney, *A Bigger Splash*, 1967. Tate, London.

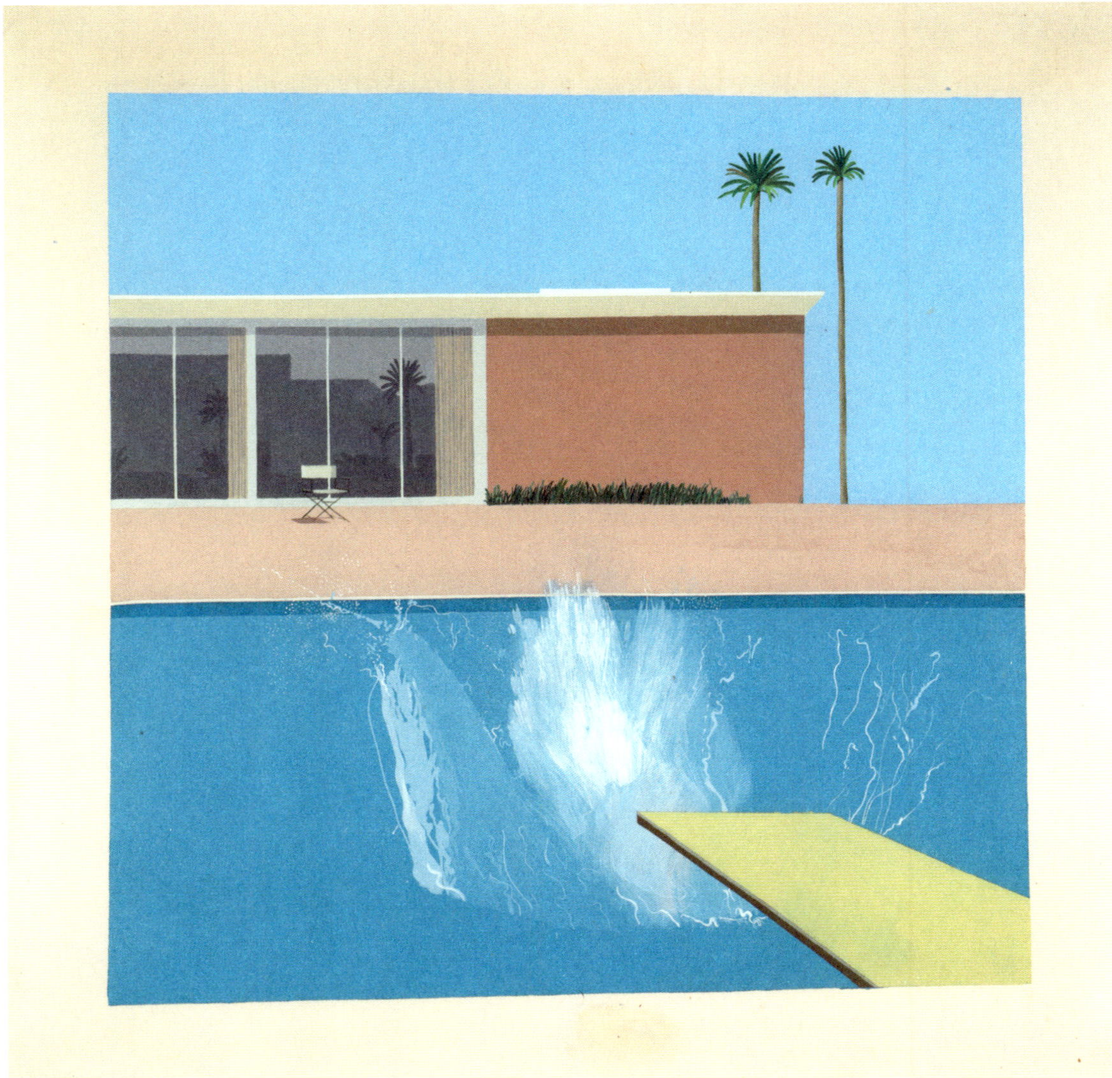

[90] *Hockney on Hockney*, 1976, p. 41.

[91] Ibid., p. 42.

[92] Andrew Brighton, "Hockney's Courage," *David Hockney 1960–1968: A Marriage of Styles*, exh. cat., Nottingham Contemporary (Nottingham, 2009), discusses this subject.

was teaching in the school of interior design . . . He gave a prize to Ron [Kitaj] and a prize to me, and from that moment on the staff of the College never said a word to me about my work being awful."[90] Hockney remembered being influenced by Bacon (the blocks of colour, the choice of Hessian similar to Bacon's use of the back side of the canvas). He also appreciated the work of the American painter Larry Rivers, another visitor to the college, and in a letter to him explained his paintings of 1962 in terms of a fascination with style: "I deliberately set out to prove I could do four entirely different sorts of picture like Picasso. They all had a subtitle and each was in a different style, Egyptian, illusionistic, flat—but looking at them later I realised the attitude is basically the same and you come to see yourself there a bit."[91] *Man in a Museum (Or You're in the Wrong Movie)*, 1962, was chosen for the next *Young Contemporaries*. John Berger singled Hockney out in his *Observer* review, commending him for the emphasis on subject, relieved that at last there were paintings you could talk about again, instead of just abstract pictures, while allegedly William Scott denigrated Hockney as merely "a colour supplement artist."[92]

Michael Andrews

Born in 1928 in Norwich

Andrews studied at the Slade, 1949–53, where he painted *A Man Who Suddenly Fell Over*, 1952, the first of many paintings that responded to the behaviour of people in public. He first exhibited at the Beaux Arts Gallery in 1958, and lived for periods in Norwich, Hertfordshire, and London, until 1961, when he settled in London, taking a studio in Pembroke Gardens in 1968. During the 1960s Andrews made a number of works about parties, including *The Deer Park*, 1962, and complex works such as *The Lord Mayor's Reception...*, which combined images of rock stars as well as local people and his relatives. The Lights series derives its name from Rimbaud's *Illuminations*; a hot-air balloon carries a metaphor for the theme of "sudden enlightenment," the balloon looking for an ideal place to land. *Melanie and Me Swimming*, 1978–9 (owned by the Tate), began with a holiday photograph of his daughter swimming in Scotland, whereas the next group of paintings extended the idea of a pilgrimage to the sacred mountain of the Aborigines, Ayers Rock, and idea of spiritual solace from the hymn "Let me hide myself in Thee." This series was shown in its entirety in 1991 in an exhibition of recent work including portraits at the Whitechapel (which toured to Paris and New York). After returning to London in 1992, Andrews began working on the theme of the Thames near Albert Bridge at low tide and the river estuary, adapting his use of paint to convey the undertow and muddy banks. He had a first retrospective at the Hayward in 1980, and a posthumous retrospective at the Tate in 2001. Andrews died in 1995.

Right: John Deakin, *Michael Andrews*, c. 1961.

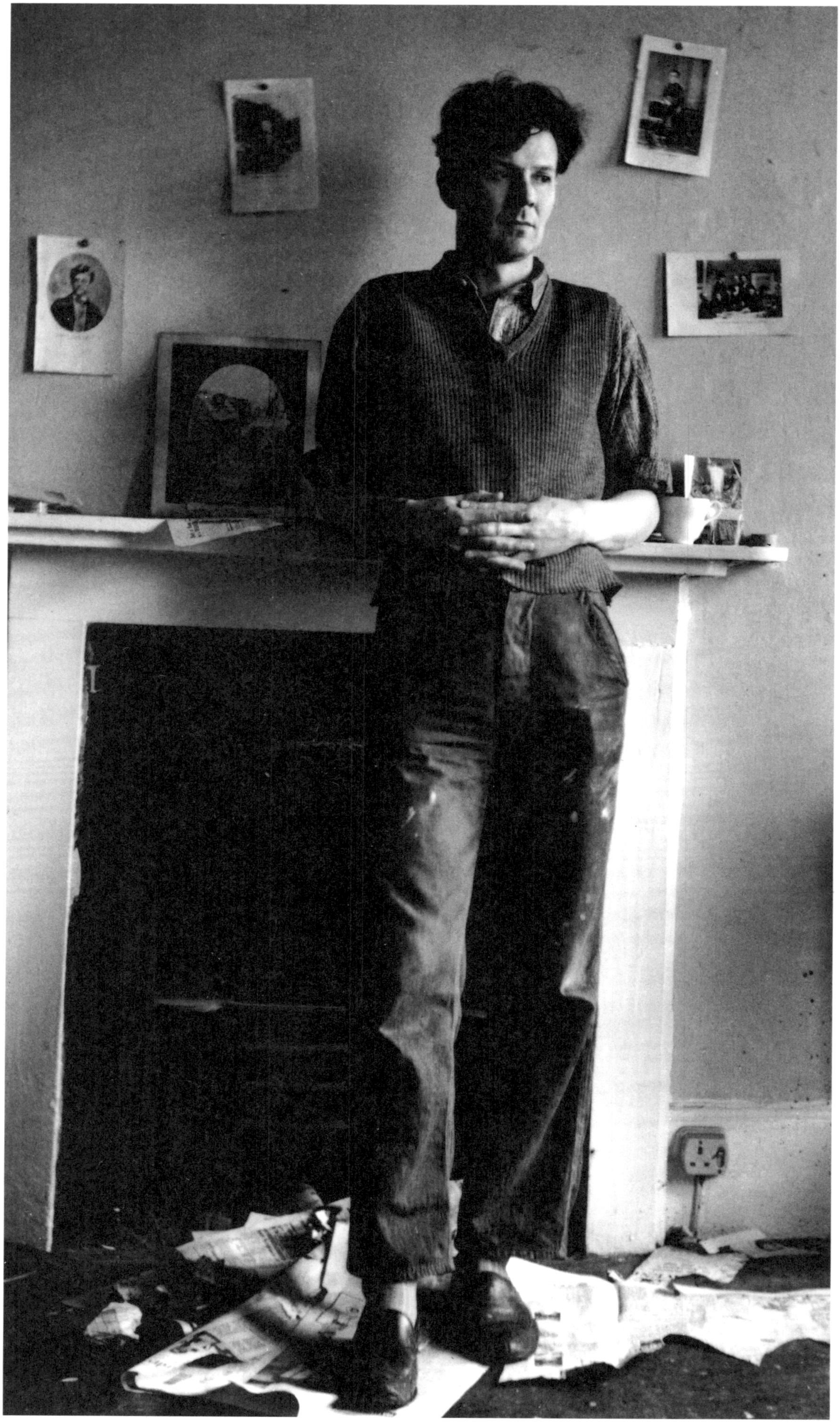

I Michael Andrews, looking at the link between Kierkegaard and Zen Buddhism, unpublished conversation with Catherine Lampert, 1980.

II Michael Andrews, speaking of the heads with the party scenes, unpublished conversation with Catherine Lampert, 1980.

The interesting thing about Kierkegaard was that he didn't believe that a systematic philosophy was possible, he didn't believe that everything could be put within a hard and fast framework, and either Kierkegaard coined the phrase, or Sartre later, which I think is still the definition of existentialism if ever one wanted a pat one, which is that existence precedes essence, which I take to mean living comes before ideas, living takes precedence over ideas. I think the original phrase is better—existence precedes essence. And that happens all the time—it's inevitable, whatever system of ideas you set up, fresh circumstances arise in life to disqualify them in some respect, so living always take precedence over ideas [I]

In a sort of way it's pointless and it reduces the universality by naming because you start to consider in what way it is like the person, the anonymity is more valuable . . . In 1965 the Museums Committee asked me if I would do a picture for them . . . they told me that the Chancellor for the new University was to be installed and there would be a huge party at the Castle Museum in Norwich and I thought "marvellous," I would be able to crystallise all my views of Norwich people . . . all human life would be there so to speak. Every kind of person from Lord Lieutenant of the County to rude mechanics . . . I took a local photographer who was used to taking wedding groups so that when I said take this or that he would immediately attempt to pose people in groups! So I had hundreds of photographs of groups grinning. I'd been reading a lot of R.D. Laing and I'd become intrigued with certain metaphors, like "someone dissolving into tears" and "someone feeling deflated," "somebody feeling buoyant," "light-headed" . . . I'd also become very interested in the notion that the ego was not a thing but a concept and Laing, I think it was, went further and used the expression "skin-encapsulated ego." [II]

[93] Ibid., pp. 76–77.

[94] *Hockney on Hockney*, 1976, p. 42.

Such widespread enthusiasm contrasted with Herbert Read's accusation that the audience for Hockney and his type was content with stimulus as "brief and banal as any side show in an amusement park"; or as Andrew Brighton suggests, Read's denigration of Pop art came from his accusation that it merely appealed to those "incapable of the concentration and effort required by genuine art."[93]

With money from early sales, Hockney flew to Los Angeles in 1963, purchased a bicycle, and when that proved impractical in a sprawling city, obtained a car and a driver's license. He rented a studio in Venice, all within a week. "And I thought, it's just how I imagined it would be."[94] Hockney's first Californian series, paintings of several local boulevards, matched the terrific clear light of the Pacific coast with a sense of emptiness, not much more than the heads of rare pedestrians and the street sign. His sun-flushed blue came to be associated with what the English imagined was a hedonistic life, the colour of swimming pools and cloudless skies. Curiously the Reckett's blue that Uglow applied to the wall of his studio served as background to masterpieces like his *Summer Picture,* 1971–72, and in its association with his longing to be next to the Mediterranean Sea, as he had been painting the *Mosque at Çiftlik Koyou,* 1966. Hockney's *The Room, Tarzana,* 1967, carries something of the observational strictures applied to painting a studio nude, however, the clean lines of the décor in this bedroom in an L.A. neighbourhood contrast so perfectly with the affectionate intimacy attached to the male subject that we feel he's inventing a new genre.

Marco Livingstone accepts the picture-postcard prettiness in Patrick Caulfield's works like

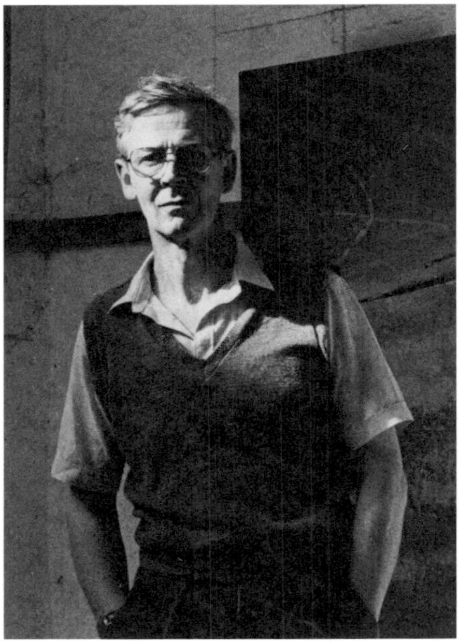

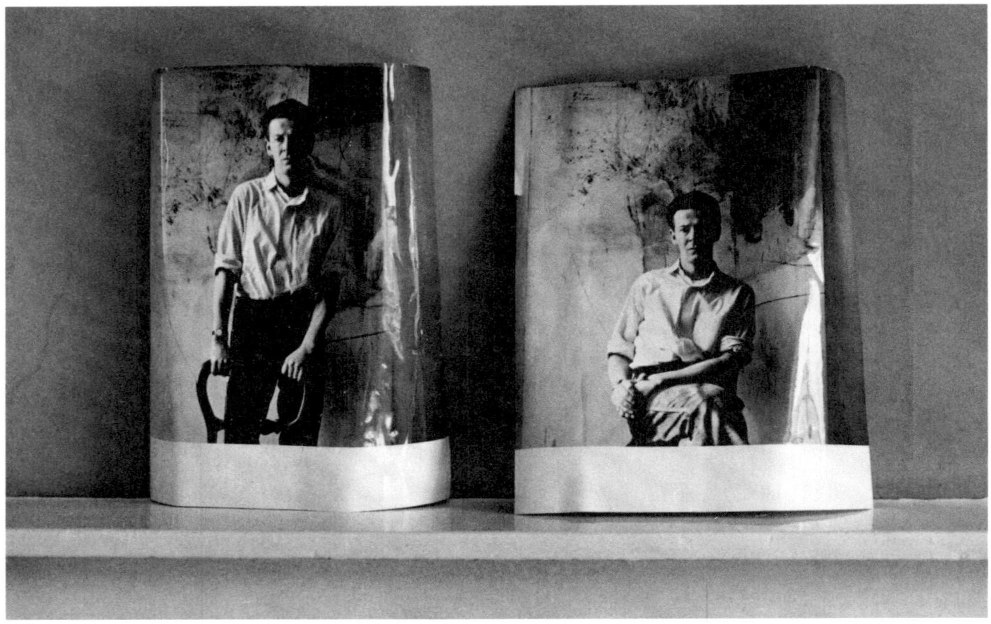

Above left: Robert Mason, *Michael Andrews in his Tasburgh studio, Norfolk,* 1984.

Above right: Bruce Bernard, *Two prints of Michael Andrews by John Deakin, 1955,* c. 1988.

View of the Bay, 1964, its mood taken from an escapist travel brochure-like image mixed with post-Fauve summary notations, but comments that the end mood, even in this early period, is invariably one of despair and ennui. Caulfield was a frequent visitor to the Victoria and Albert Museum, down the road from the Royal College, and the central motif of *Still life with necklace,* 1964, comes from Islamic vases on display, "Because they're pots, they don't envelop one like wallpaper. And they have beautiful calligraphy."[95]

In the same period he made an "after Delacroix" as well as pictures exploring the style and motifs of neglected painters like Juan Gris and Raoul Dufy. His general suspicion of high culture was expressed by references to a vernacular language with different roots: "I was reading a lot of American literature. Hemingway, Faulkner, Dos Passos, Caldwell, Lewis, Steinbeck, Thomas Wolfe. I didn't read much contemporary English literature because I felt divorced from it, quite remote. It seemed to deal with a middle-to-upper-class society that I didn't know anything about and it meant nothing to me."[96] Another instinct was to "make life difficult for himself as an artist, to flirt with the most discredited conventions of his chosen medium in order to breath new life into them," something his Pop artist contemporaries were doing but also motivation for artists turning to painting in the late 1980s, dissidents like Glenn Brown and Peter Doig.

From the beginning Caulfield preferred to lay down a flat ground, and for the rest of his working life this hardly changed. Sometimes the depiction was primarily linear, without shadow, later he combined light and shade. Although he planned the large interiors of the 1970s by making pencil and pen drawings with well-resolved angles to organize the architecture in recessional perspective and proportion, he was reluctant to exhibit these, despite their marvelous detail, like ingenious thrillers that convey an air of expectation and sometimes menace.

Around 1963 Michael Andrews became preoccupied with the theme of how metropolitan people behaved at parties, borrowing elements from advertisements in the Sunday supplements and adding specific references to British scandals, as William Feaver put it, "where jet set meets demi-monde, scandal brews."[97] *All Night Long* (which referenced a

[95] Marco Livingstone quoting Caulfield, *Patrick Caulfield Paintings* (London, 2005) p. 33.

[96] Ibid., p. 33.

[97] William Feaver, "An Actual Present Atmosphere," *Michael Andrews,* exh. cat., Tate (London, 2001), p. 52, and Catherine Lampert, notes on the works, *Michael Andrews,* exh. cat., Hayward Gallery (London, 1980).

[98] Information kindly supplied by Lynda Morris; Andrews quoted by Lampert from interview (and unpublished full manuscript), Hayward Gallery, London 1980; and Tate retrospective 2001.

Below: Michael Andrews, *The Deer Park*, 1962. Tate, London.

British Airways advertisement and a newspaper clipping captioned "All Steamed up to Romp in the Snow") was followed by an ambitious triptych *Good and Bad at Games*, 1964–68, a line-up of small heads attached to spectral bodies (devised from torn strips of paper used as templates, their elongated forms inspired by the photograph used for the private view card of the 1965 Giacometti exhibition). The same year Andrews bravely accepted a commission from the Norwich Museums Committee, the subject the official reception the night before the installation of the first Chancellor of the new University of East Anglia. He had resisted earning money from official portraits, like those his tutor Coldstream executed, but "I had long wanted to paint a picture about Norwich people."[98] A large number of photographs were assembled, some taken from photographs of

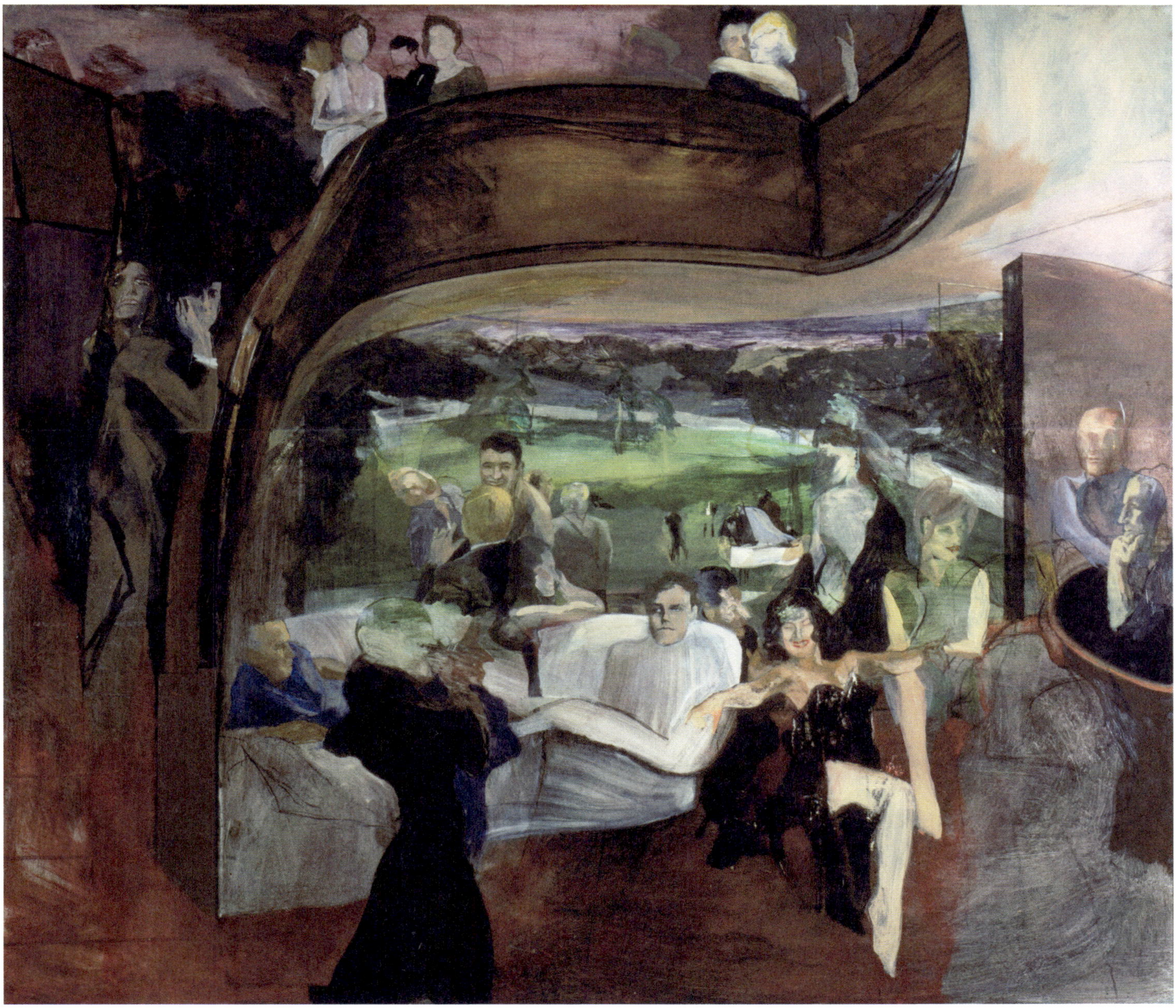

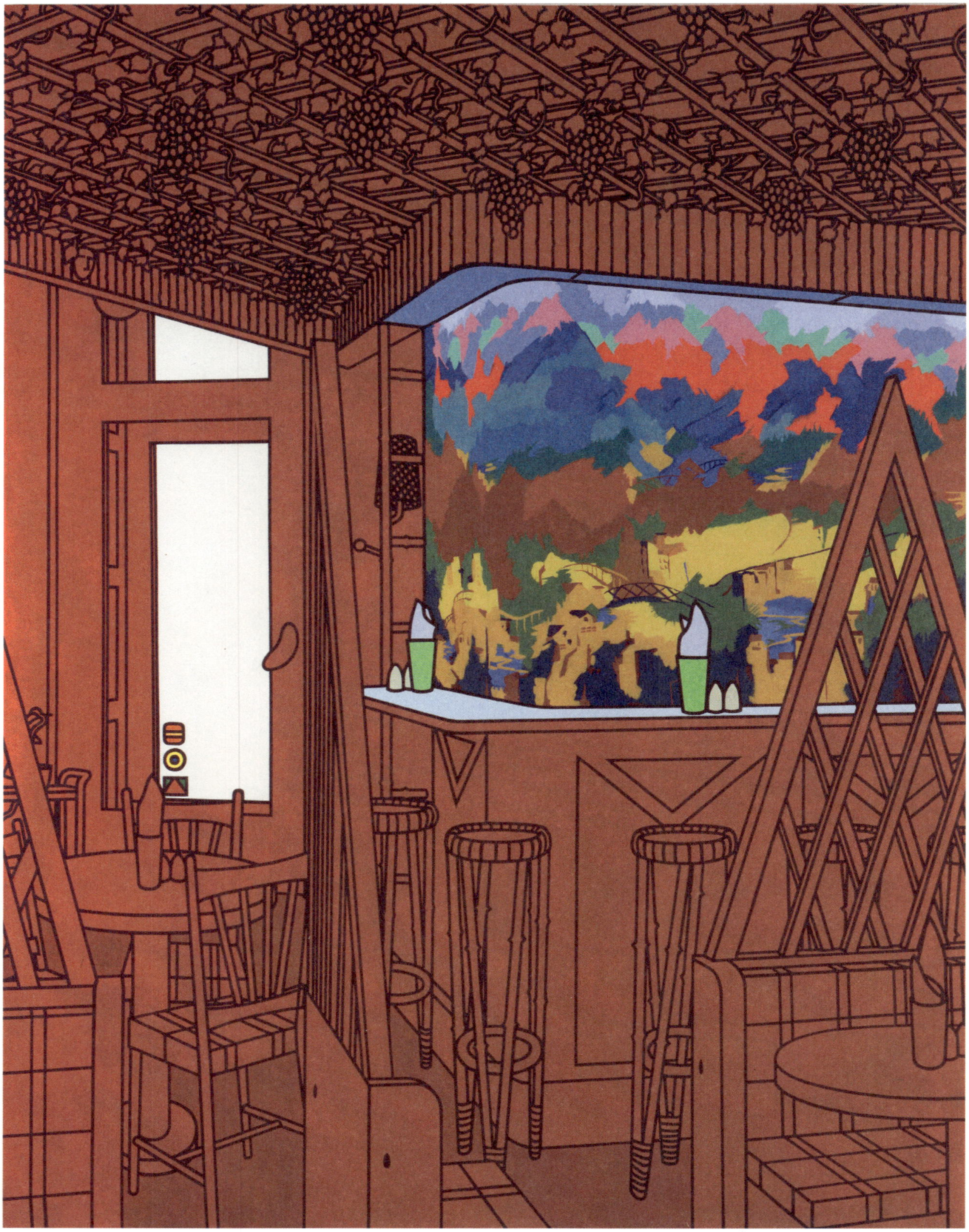

[99] Stephen Bann, "Exteriors/Interiors 1990," in *October*, 2010, p. 79.

the guests and others from a variety of media sources, "contemporary luminaries" like Mick Jagger and Dave Brubeck, plus an anonymous war criminal, his Aunts Ivy and Florrie and ex-Slade friends such as Victor Willing, Myles Murphy, and Craigie Aitchison. Nigel Henderson helped on the technical side (the transfer of photographs by the "turaphot" technique, the collage). The studies went on for a year, the large picture completed after moving to Pembroke Gardens in 1968 where Hockney occupied another studio. The artist's preoccupation with ideas about the "ego" and self-consciousness, his fascination with Zen Buddhism and Kierkegaard, informed the Lights series at the beginning of the 1970s. The protagonist was a hot air balloon that floated high over cities and coastlines, the bathers on the beach and the headlamps of cars on the highway registering as tiny spots in comparison to the panoramic scale.

There are parallels to Hamilton's imagery and approach. In *Bathers II,* 1965, and *Whitley Bay,* 1965, "Hamilton has utilised our perceptual capacities (developed and fostered by the experimental work of artists like Monet) to demonstrate a kind of threshold between chaos and legibility reducing the visual clues in *People* [a collaboration of 1968 with Dieter Roth] to the point where only our recognition of the photographic schemata will persuade us of the image's residual verisimilitude and building them up again, in *Bathers II,* to incite a virtuoso reinterpretation of the whole scene."[99] Apart from the inventive distillation of the image by various techniques (hand-colouring,

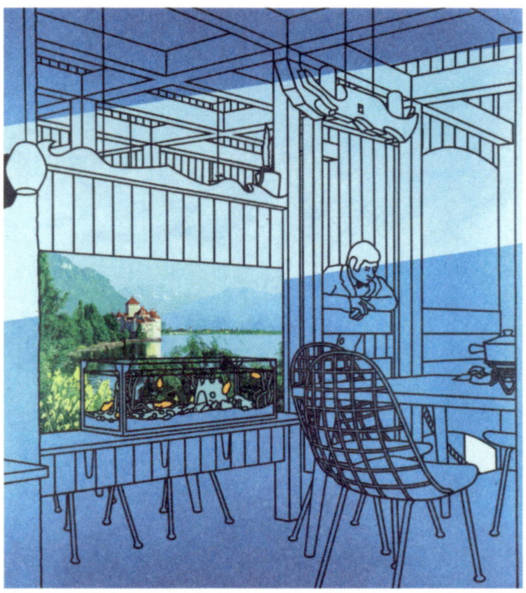

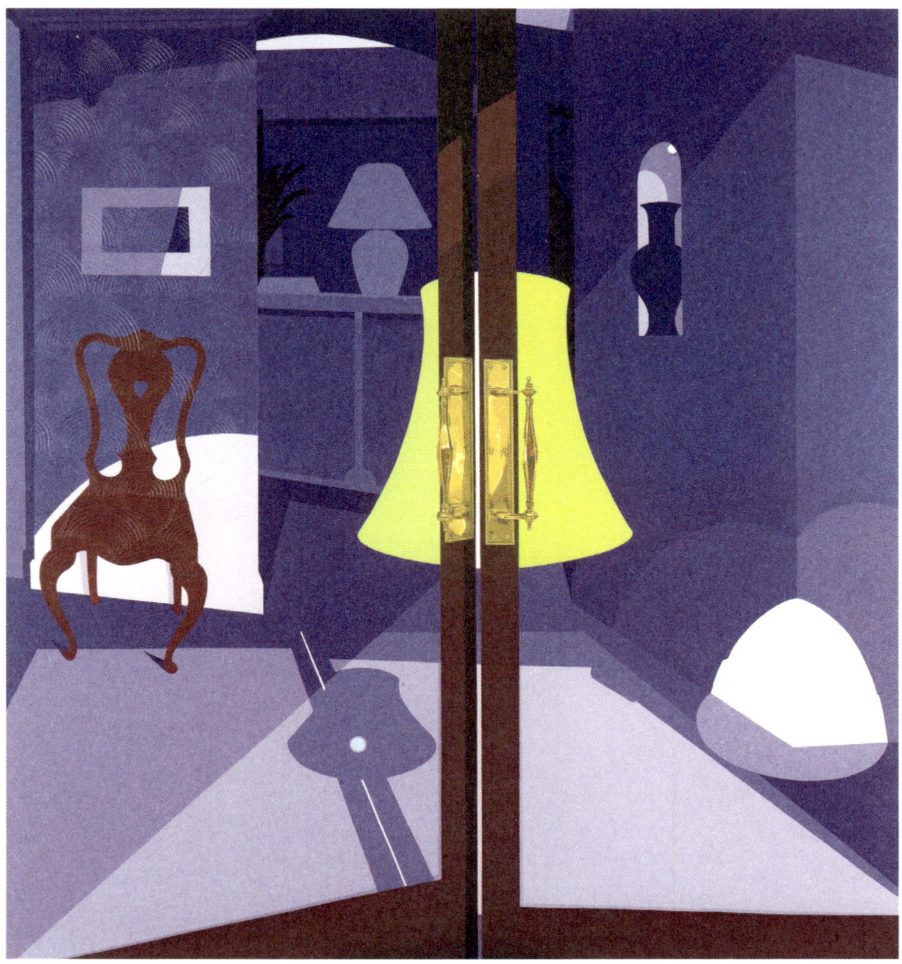

Left: Patrick Caulfield, *Paradise Bar,* 1974. Virginia MFA, Richmond, The Sydney and Frances Lewis Contemporary Art Fund.

Above: Patrick Caulfield, *After Lunch,* 1975. Tate, London.

Right: Patrick Caulfield, *Bishop's,* 2004.

Patrick Caulfield

Born 1936 in South Acton, London

After spending the war years in Bolton, with his family, he began working at fifteen, followed by evening classes in commercial art at Harrow School of Art while he was in military service. At Chelsea School of Art the new principal Lawrence Gowing encouraged him to continue studying at the Royal College of Art, entering in 1960, one year after the class that included David Hockney, Allen Jones, and Derek Boshier. His work was selected for the *Young Contemporaries* in 1960–63, and in the 1964 *New Generation* exhibition at the Whitechapel he showed works in a landscape format, depicting objects like Turkish pots, and Mughal daggers. Caulfield spoke of his admiration for Juan Gris and Edward Hopper, as well as shop signs, objects of industrial design, and images from films. His first exhibition in the US was at the Robert Elkon Gallery, New York, and when the Robert Fraser Gallery closed in 1968 he joined Waddington Galleries. Gradually the work increased in scale, the materials changed from decorator's paint on hardboard to acrylic on canvas, and several large interiors were realised in monochrome. The seated figure in *Bistro*, 1970, was the painter John Hoyland, who also worked at Primrose Hill Studios at the time. Caulfield became known for his highly regarded screenprints and in 1973 Petersburg Press produced a limited-edition book with twenty-two illustrations for *Some Poems of Jules Laforgue*. Caulfield was commissioned to make mosaics, cathedral doors, and carpets, as well as costume and set designs. In 1985–87 he had a solo exhibition touring Latin America, and a retrospective at the Hayward Gallery in 1999, touring to Luxembourg, Lisbon, and New Haven. Caulfield died in 2005..

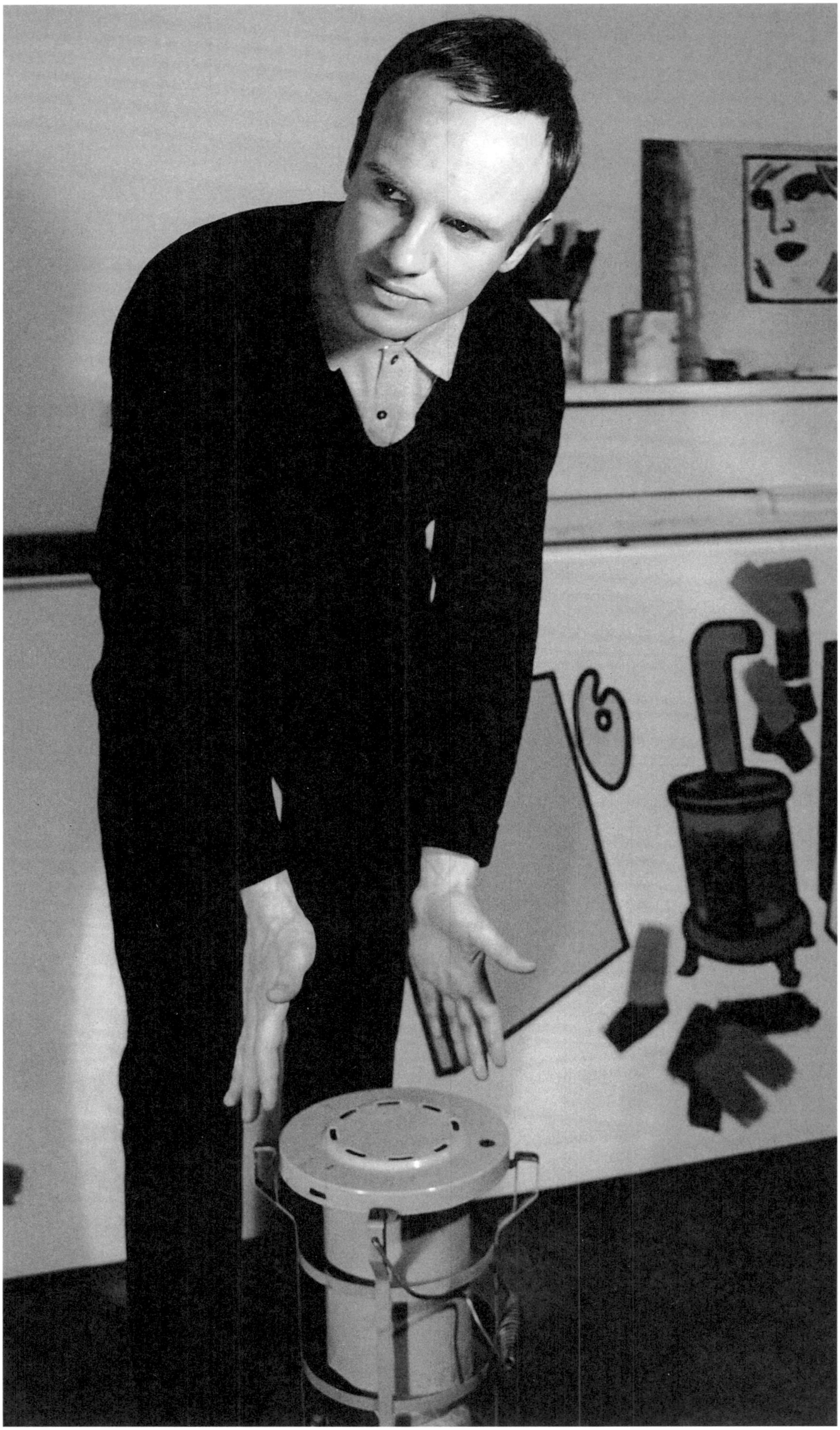

Right: Jorge Lewinski, *Patrick Caulfield*, 1965.

I Patrick Caulfield, quoted in Livingstone (London, 2005).

II Patrick Caulfield, speaking of Dieric Bouts, *Portrait of a Man, 1462*, selected for his *Artist's Eye* exhibition at the National Gallery, London, 1986.

I'm not actually painting from observation of light, I'm making up an idea of how light could appear to be. The angles of light in naturalistic terms could be totally wrong, but they either help the composition of the picture or they help the feeling of light more strongly. [I]

I also like the shift from shallow to deep space, which occurs in several of my choices, I notice—here through the device of the window with its landscape view. I don't quite know why I like it, but I think it's something to do with getting more for your money . . . there are more levels of information when space is played about with like this—the hands resting on the ledge is another device, bringing the space one step forward—than if the subject was enclosed . I incorporate the same sort of shifts in my own painting. It's playing games, to some extent! [II]

[100] Corrine Diserens, *Le Grand Dechiffreur: Richard Hamilton on Marcel Duchamp* (Paris and Zürich, 2009), p. 173.

[101] Richard Hamilton in conversation with Michael Craig-Martin, 1990, in Richard Hamilton, *October files* (Cambridge, MA 2010), pp. 10–12.

[102] Lynda Morris, *Pictures of Pictures* (Arnolfini, Bristol, and Norwich Gallery, 1999), p. 20, and speaking to the author.

enlargement, printing lab techniques) one feels these paintings are also about envy of those whose pleasures are the visits to seaside in the company of their families. Hamilton went himself to Cadaques on the Costa Brava where the Duchamps spent summers and where Hockney visited one year. Yet the artist is hardly relaxing; he writes to Marcel in November 1965 that his "head is buried pretty deep in the immediate tasks. I am doing a full size perspective drawing of the bachelor machine," and continues with thoughts surprisingly like those of Coldstream and Uglow, "should I make my perspective wrong to make it resemble your proportions?"[100]

In 1969, while working in Milan, Hamilton had admired a snapshot the printer had taken of his wife and child, took it home as a gift, and in 1984 came across the document, its genuine feeling and enduring subject seeming an appropriate starting point for a print he was committed to make for a series to benefit women demonstrating for nuclear disarmament at Greenham Common. The *contre-jour* lighting and cropping puts the focus on the adored child, the translation to pale greens and yellow referencing the values of Post-Impressionist painting as well as female-oriented advertising. The liberties Hamilton allowed himself when making a painted version are testament to his self-confidence and experimental attitude. Speaking of his decision in the mid-1960s to reverse the Duchampian idea that painting should be anti-retinal, Richard Hamilton recalled that he "began to paint romantic subjects in an overly sentimental manner, and of course they were seen as absurd in the context of conceptualism. It was taken to be a retreat into fuddy-duddyism, senility, especially when it got to painting flowers and turds, girls in the woods, romantic landscapes, and sunlight coming through the trees. They were certainly not perceived as iconoclastic by their audience, but they were against the prevailing mood and nonetheless conceptual for me. What I was really concerned with was the crisis of modern art which occurred at the middle of this century. The first half of the century showed a move towards abstraction. You end up in a Malevich black square. So everybody in the 1950s, I think, was looking to where you go beyond this. A lot of the most interesting people found the Pop solution. You go towards figuration again, but you do it in a different way."[101]

Lynda Morris has pointed out Gerhard Richter's feeling that he and Hamilton were working in parallel even before they met in New York in 1973 (at Richter's insistence). She cites the link between Hamilton's *Kent State,* 1970, taken from TV news footage of the American student slain by the National Guard and Richter's *18 October,* 1977, made in part from Stammheim Prison video footage: "They both used the objective eye of the camera to let them get away with political painting."[102]

Euan Uglow

Born in 1932 in London

Uglow began studying art at the Junior Art School at Camberwell School of Arts and Crafts in 1947, where he was exposed to the ideas of a wide variety of tutors, including Victor Pasmore, Claude Rogers, Kenneth Martin, and William Coldstream, before moving to the Slade in 1950 and continuing as a tutor for the rest of his life. Nearly all Uglow's works were made in his studio in Turnchapel Mews, Battersea, which he occupied from 1959. However, on a number of occasions he painted landscapes in Mediterranean countries, like the mosque overlooking the sea at Çiftlik Koyou, on the west coast of Turkey. Although he exhibited regularly in private galleries (at the Beaux Arts Gallery in 1961, and with Browse & Darby from 1977) the two retrospective exhibitions in his lifetime both opened at the Whitechapel, in 1974 and 1989, before touring. Uglow won first prize in the John Moores Exhibition in 1972. He insisted his paintings began with an idea, one that often required a particular studio set-up that controlled the light and the relation of painter to subject, these factors incorporated into the notes written by Catherine Lampert for the catalogue raisonné published by Yale University Press in 2007. Uglow died in 2000.

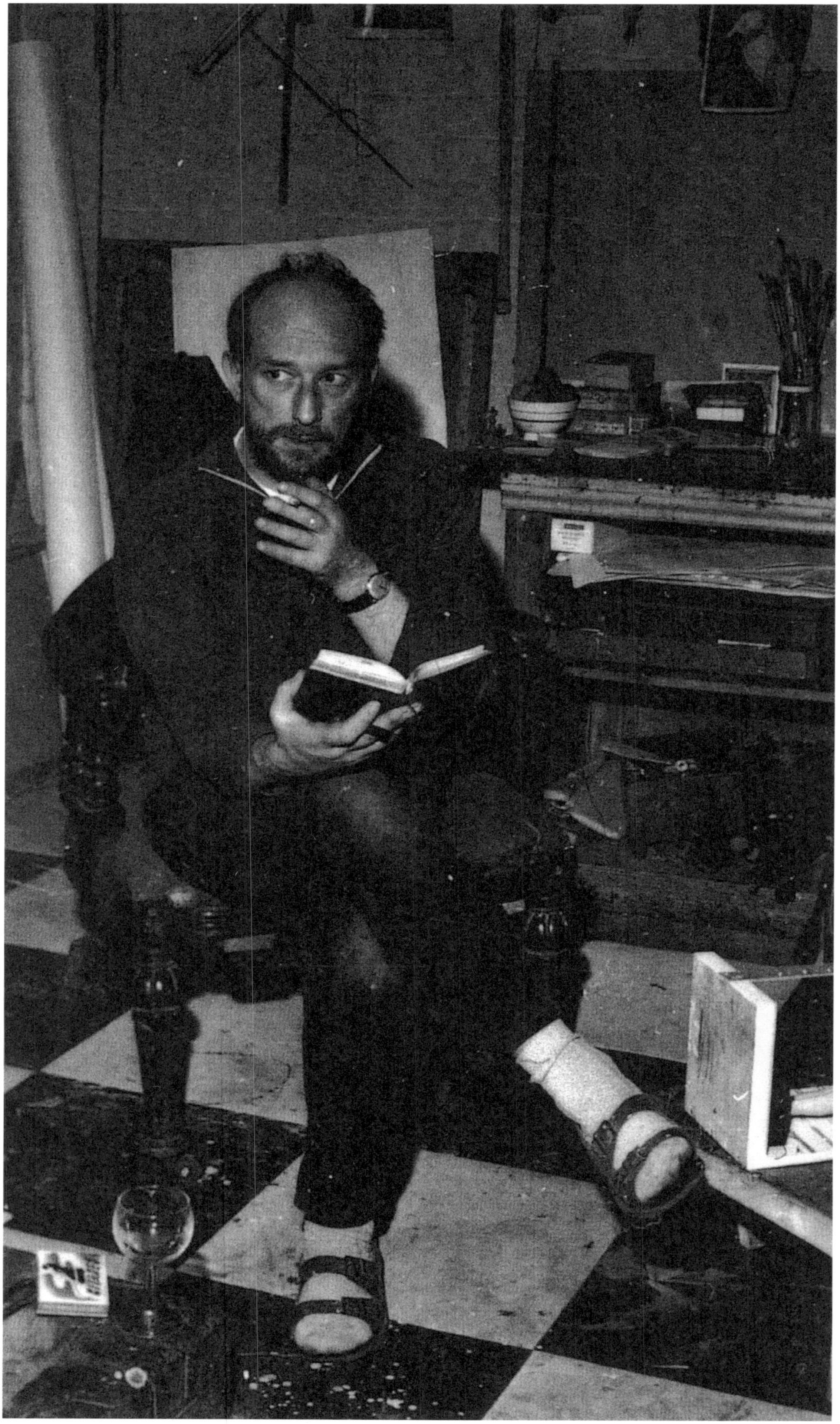

Right: Euan Uglow, photographed during the course of being filmed by *Aquarius* television, 1986.

I Euan Uglow, conversation with Martin Gayford, *Modern Painters*, reprinted in Richard Kendall and Martin Gayford, *Euan Uglow. Controlled Passion*, exh. cat., Abbot Hall Art Gallery (Kendal, 2003).

II Euan Uglow, to Martin Golding on the subject of painting a nude, *Euan Uglow*, exh. cat., Whitechapel Gallery (London, 1989), p. 23.

I don't know what true to life is. Painting's artifice, isn't it. It's nothing to do with being true to life. You're trying to construct a new world so that it can stand. Nothing to do with illusionism, I can't bear the idea. You get a marvelous smile from a girl: what does that mean? . . . I may want to be able to say something about that visual idea, but it wouldn't be 'true to life'. It has to be transferred into another world. Well, I think so.

I'm not interested in that [painting from photographs] because I like the poignancy of the right light at the right time hitting a bit of colour. Everybody's trying to make an image, but we have different ways of getting at it. [I]

It's like trying to paint a moving snake all the time: one's got to try to look at its tail at the same time as its tongue—that is the important about painting anything which is alive. [II]

[103] Livingstone (London, 2005), p. 22.

[104] Richard Kendall, *Drawn to Painting: Leon Kossoff's Drawings and Paintings After Nicholas Poussin*, exh. cat., Los Angeles County Museum of Art (Los Angeles, 2000), pp. 10–11.

[105] Philip Conisbee, "From Poussin," *Leon Kossoff. Drawing From Painting*, exh. cat., National Gallery (London, 2007), p. 93.

Art about something

The young Caulfield had begun studying graphic design at Chelsea in 1956, and with the support of Gowing, who was confident of his ability, gained a place at the Royal College. Like Hockney he found himself out of step with an avant-garde orthodoxy not so dissimilar from that which prevailed in the 1930s and failed to convince Coldstream and Hamilton: "It was a sort of popularistic idea that the development of an artist in the twentieth century was that you started by doing very good tight drawings, and eventually some good figurative work, and then gradually becoming more abstract, until your work became more or less totally abstract, rather like Mondrian."[103] *Red, White and Black Still Life,* 1966/1984, has an interesting story. Caulfield initially painted it as two bottles and a glass but returned to it fifteen or so years later, made the black bottle appear to be a shadow of the red bottle and added more of the diagrammatic grid lines on the left and right sides of the picture. The mark at the bottom right, which is like an enlarged version of the red and black ellipses scattered over the surface, suggests a thumb-print and denotes his signature.

The National Gallery is London's Louvre, as Cézanne put it, "*le livre où nous apprenons à lire.*" As a boy of ten, Kossoff remembers being struck by a work of Rembrandt, *A Woman Bathing in a Stream,* 1654. It gave him the feeling "that I could learn to draw from this painting."[104] Scanning the tablet-shaped copy he made in 1982, her body so near and natural, the sensuality in the folds of her white shift echoed in the murky undergrowth and the flash of crimson on the bank. The painting is one of many examples of Kossoff's great ability to enter the same space, to identify with the Old Masters and in consequence to lose inhibitions about conjuring up subjects that require clusters of naked, agitated people. In May 1979, Kossoff's exhibition at Fischer Fine Art included three oil paintings based on Poussin's *Cephalus and Aurora,* 1629–30. He re-encountered this modest-sized work, in his own words, as "a painting about love" and began to make drawings and etchings. As Philip Conisbee put it, "These figures from classical mythology act out an all-too-human moral dilemma, a story of love and of love denied . . . [Kossoff's] subtle additions of colour to the most resolved of these drawings brings an undeniable aura of sensuality."[105]

Poussin appealed to Uglow from student days, when he copied *Cephalus and Aurora* in 1953, and when around 1982 he engaged with *Rinaldo and Armida,* c.1630, hanging in the Dulwich Picture Gallery. Uglow explained his

[106] Lampert and Kendall, (London, 2007), p. 141.

compulsion from time to time to make copies as a case of locating a bond with those artists he could get near to—like Courbet and Poussin—while respecting the fact that he would never approach others whose work he also responded to, like Masaccio and Bellini. "I'm not trying to make a better picture or a worse picture (silly trying to make a worse picture) but just to say, here's a marvellous picture."[106] His version of *The Massacre of the Innocents,* 1628–29, in the Musée Conde, Chantilly, began with inspecting the canvas unframed to ascertain the geometry of the rectangle (whether the column on the left was a third of the whole). In the end the sweep of arms, the wonderful hands, and sole of the baby's foot in the Poussin, and the luminous colour characterise his translation. This same painting was the first work to affect Bacon; in 1927 he was struck by the crying mouth of the kneeling woman which made a "terrible" impression.

Comparison of the choices for the *Artist's Eye* series and the whole of these artists' paintings, drawings, and etchings "after" the Old Masters might offer a sort of morphological map of affinities and catalysts; it would extend to other contemporaries like Anthony Caro and Howard Hodgkin. Paula Rego, the National Gallery's first associate artist, while working there in 1990–91, made a touching, superb interpretation of Phillipe de Champaigne's *The Dream of Saint Joseph,* 1642–43, for which her friend Rudi Nassauer, the writer and wine merchant, a collector and friend of Uglow, Kossoff and Caulfield, posed as Joseph.

Late in his life Freud, when pressed to come to the National Gallery and encouraged to make telling observations about Titian's *Diana and Actaeon,* 1556-9, (as part of the national campaign to prevent a private sale and export), demurred from analysis, something really "convincing" had a more visceral effect,

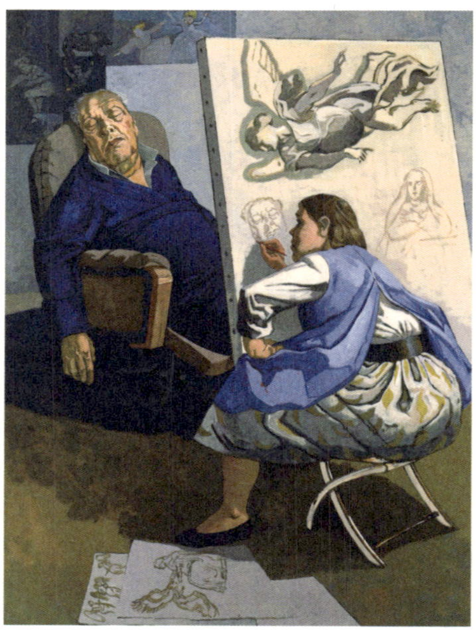

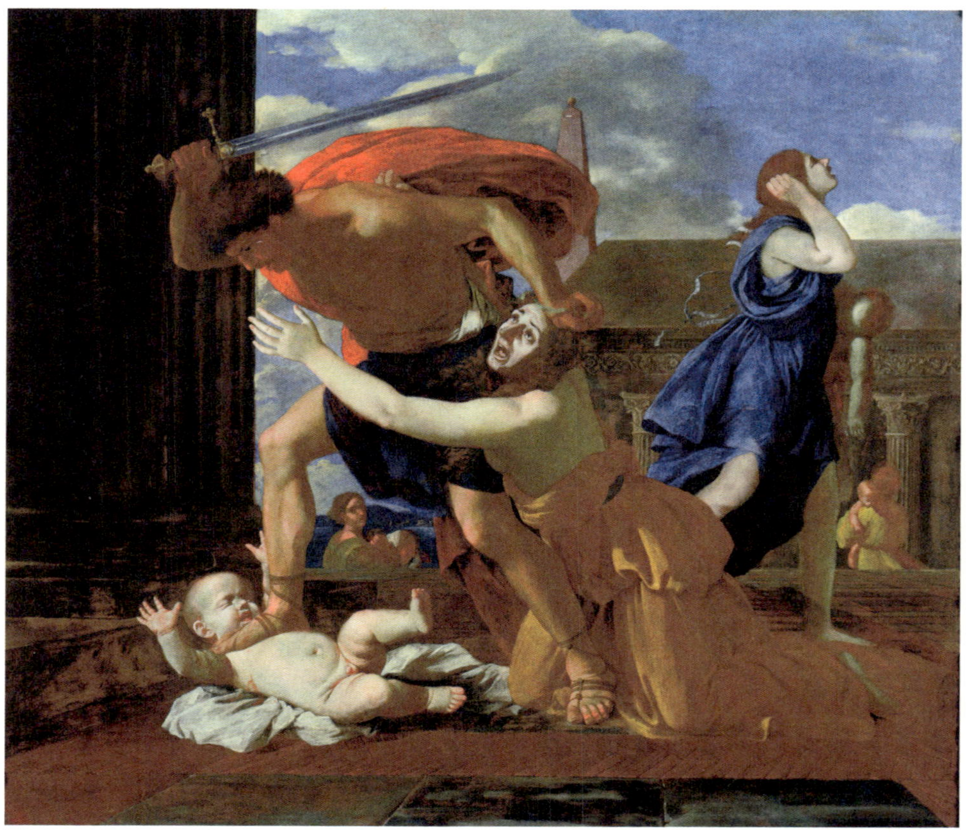

Above: Paula Rego, *Joseph's Dream,* 1990.

Right: Nicolas Poussin (1594–1665), *The Massacre of the Innocents,* c.1628–29. Musée Condé, Chantilly, France.

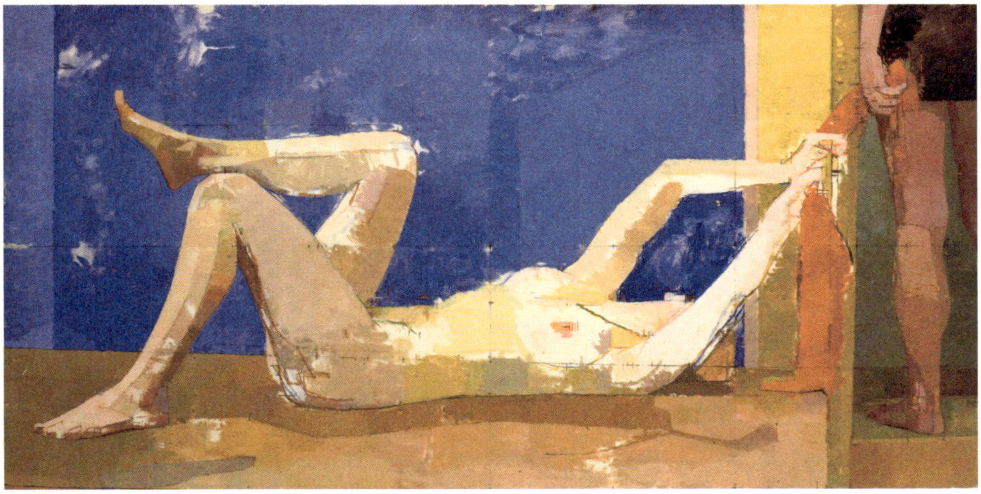

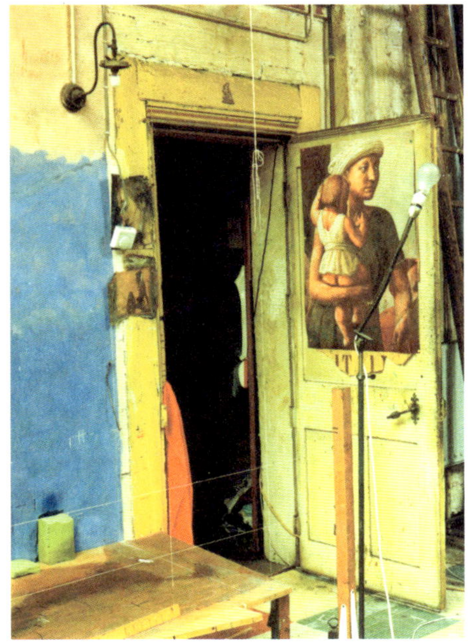

[107] Freud with Nicholas Penny on *Diana and Actaeon,* in a conversation recorded by Nicholas Glass, 28 October, 2008.

[108] Michael Craig-Martin, quoted by Ben Miller, *Between the Lines,* reviewing the exhibition and panel discussion at Pallant House Gallery, Chichester, for *culture 24,* 17 April, 2009.

[109] Caulfield quoted by Livingstone (London, 2005), p. 101.

Above left: Euan Uglow, *Potiphar's Wife,* 2000.

Above right: Set-up for a picture, Uglow's studio, Turnchapel Mews, London, 2000. Photo: Steve Pocklington.

acting as a stimulant. Asked about the colour, "I'm not scholarly in that way, because on the whole I go to see pictures like going to the doctor, to get help in fact." Asked about the question of influence, "I would have thought not. I've always had a natural, or perhaps an unnatural resistance against being influenced by things. And I like looking and looking and taking them in but if I thought they had emerged in some way that related to what I was looking at [in the studio], I wouldn't feel free about working like that."[107]

The relationship of artists to the past and to admired artists living in their own lifetime remains complicated. When the exhibition *Metamorphosis* opens at the National Gallery in summer 2012, we will see Mark Wallinger, Chris Ofili, and Conrad Shawcross responding to Titian's *Diana and Actaeon,* a London Olympic commission that relates to stage and costume designs for new productions at the Royal Opera House. The National Gallery will present a Hamilton exhibition in 2012 planned by the artist, in detail, up until his death in September 2011. Kossoff's extraordinary paintings of the cherry tree in his back garden, completed in 2010, were read partly as a comment on the life span of organic matter and an elegy to lost friends, but like Hockney's landscapes of Bridlington, they are also about experimental methods, formal departures, and joy.

Michael Craig-Martin voiced his admiration for Caulfield's fully-realised, multi-part scenes, "Patrick made grand works but disguised them in modesty."[108] One thinks of his late interiors like *Bishops,* 2004, or *Paradise Bar,* 1975, and his words, "The spaces and interiors we see in real life are always more surprising than those we could invent. Since one can't actually compete with the unexpectedness of reality, I feel free to invent any contortions of space as long as they work for me. At the same time I don't want to do something which is so artificial that it becomes Surrealism. I want it to have some link with reality."[109] Uglow, a friend of Caulfield (they shared an enthusiasm for playing cricket and for good wine) also began with similarly distinctive and economic drawings, some as aids to determine the precise position of the model (or object) in relationship to the two-dimensional area. The motif might be an ordinary subject like iced buns or a pear observed as it shrivels and sinks. Uglow's *Potiphar's Wife* was on the easel when he died in 2000; like so many of his highly original works it depends upon a colour and an almost heavenly light, here an orange cloth held by the reclining figure in

[110] Colin St John Wilson, *The Artist at Work. On the Working Methods of William Coldstream and Michael Andrews* (London, 1999), pp. 55–57.

[111] Smee 2006, p. 33.

daylight and the standing one leaving the studio. Private intuitions of mortality permeate Andrews' last series of paintings about the Thames, which he began by writing "BE BOLD" on the studio wall. From the high vantage point of the Albert Bridge he drew and then interpreted in grainy-silty paint the grab-chains and ladder, two barges, and the lines of the land-drains and culverts on the beach, making the marvelous landscape *The Thames at Low Tide,* 1994–95.[110]

When these pictures and those by the other artists are studied in fifty years' time, something about British understatement and this wide-generation's feeling that existence is brief may be evident; their way of arriving at unprecedented creations requiring both synthesis and fearless simplicity. "Late" subjects draw from a lifetime of pictorial and moral research, guided by a desire to add to the grand tradition of painting, inhibitions subtly loosened. Freud's brush invents a new language to describe the material warmth and smell surrounding the Skewbald mare standing in the straw-filled stable in 2004. The work fulfills his ambition, to convey "the feeling of individuality and the intensity of the regard and the focus on the specific . . . I think the most boring thing you can say about a work of art is that it's 'timeless.'"[111]

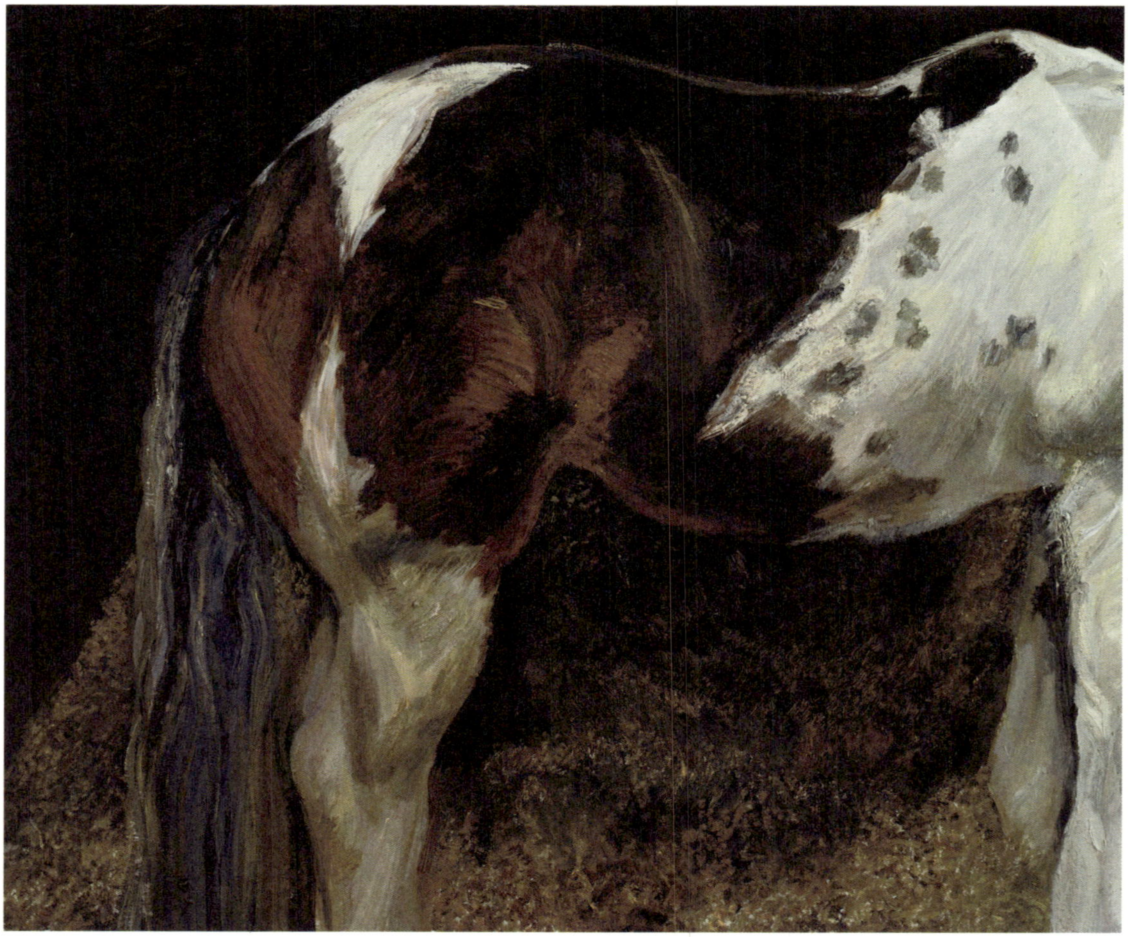

Right: Lucian Freud, *Skewbald Mare,* 2004.

Conversations Between
Ten British Post-War Painters

Michael Andrews
Frank Auerbach
Francis Bacon
Patrick Caulfield
William Coldstream
Lucian Freud
Richard Hamilton
David Hockney
Leon Kossoff
Euan Uglow

Lucian Freud

Francis Bacon (Study), 1951
Pencil and charcoal on paper
54.7 × 42 cm

Private collection

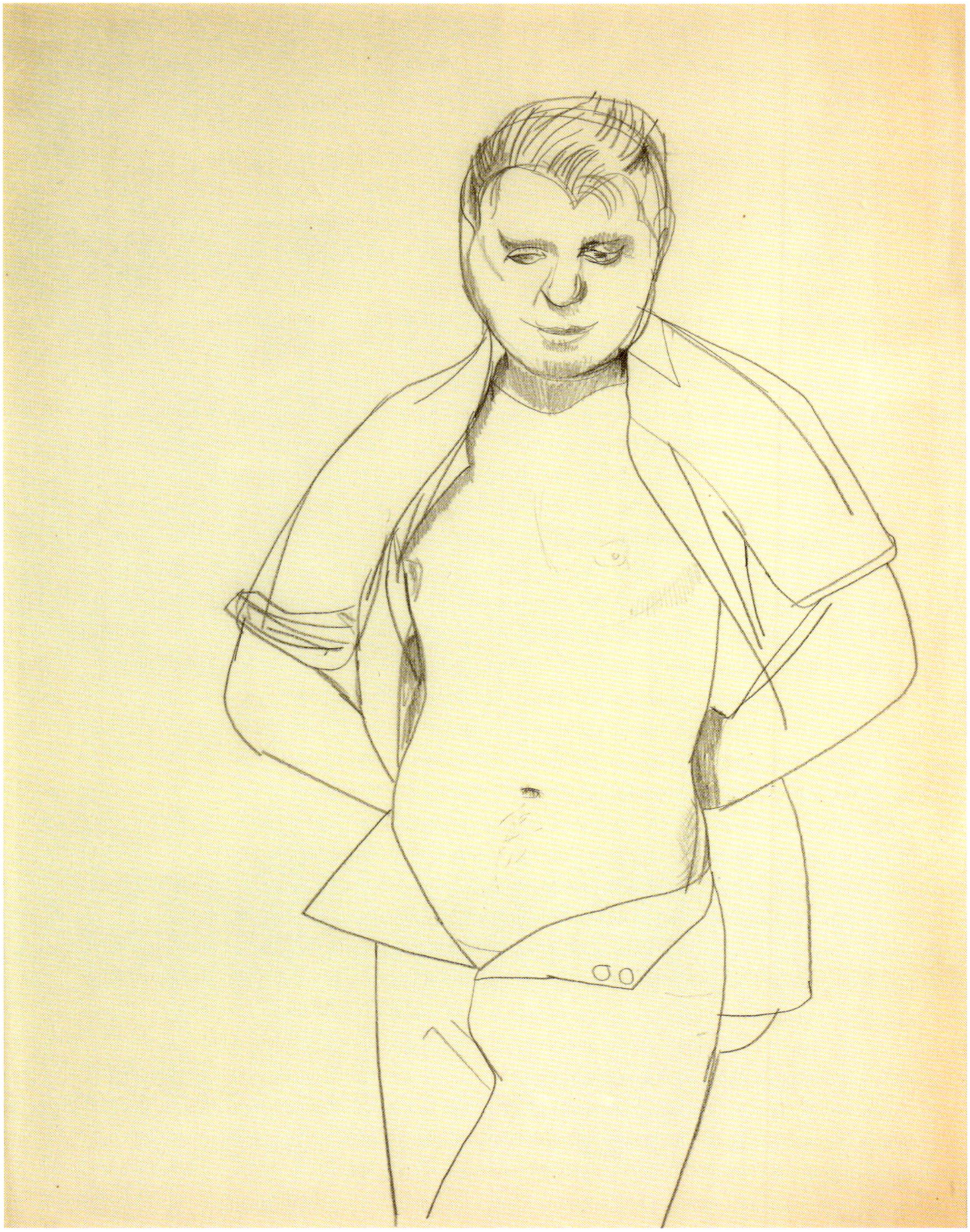

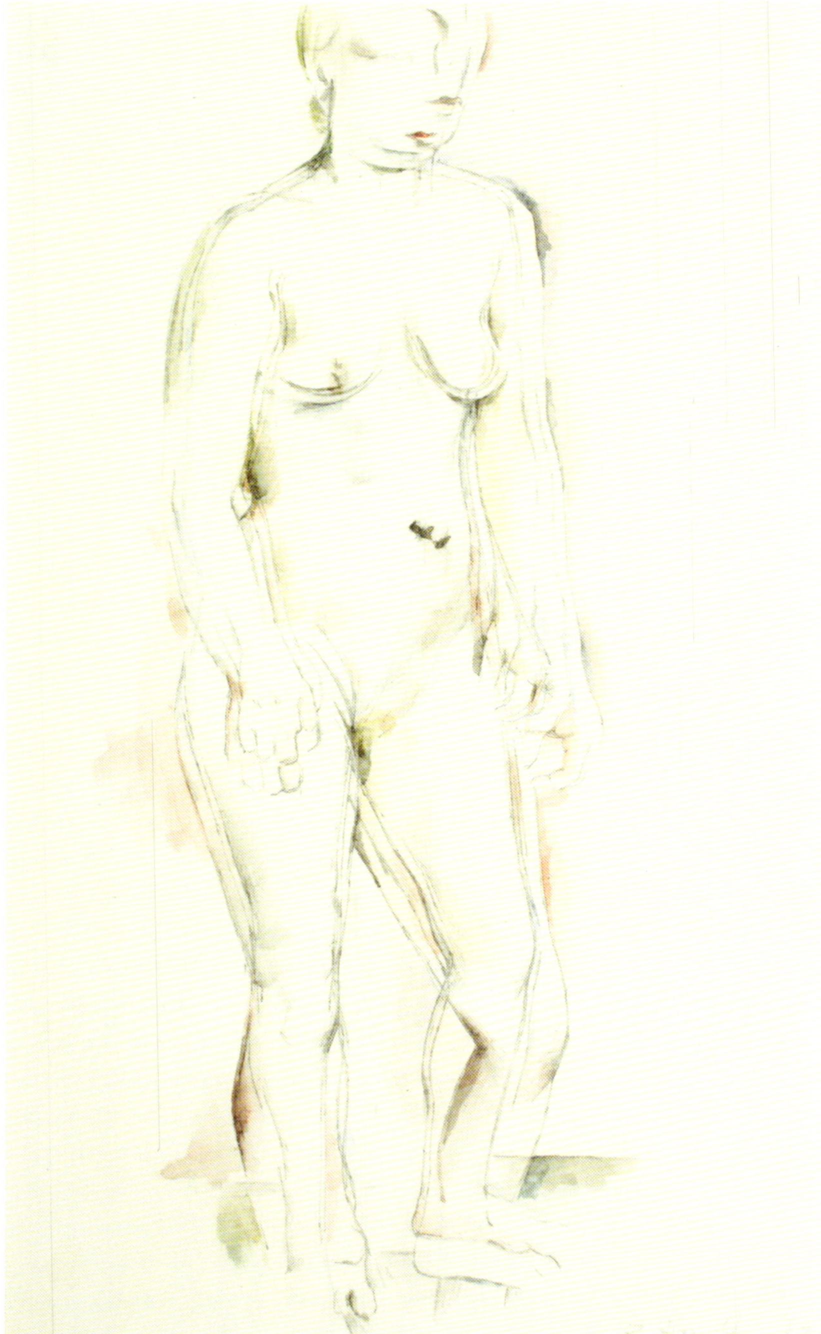

Richard Hamilton

reNude Study, 1954
Pencil and watercolour on paper
37 × 22.7 cm

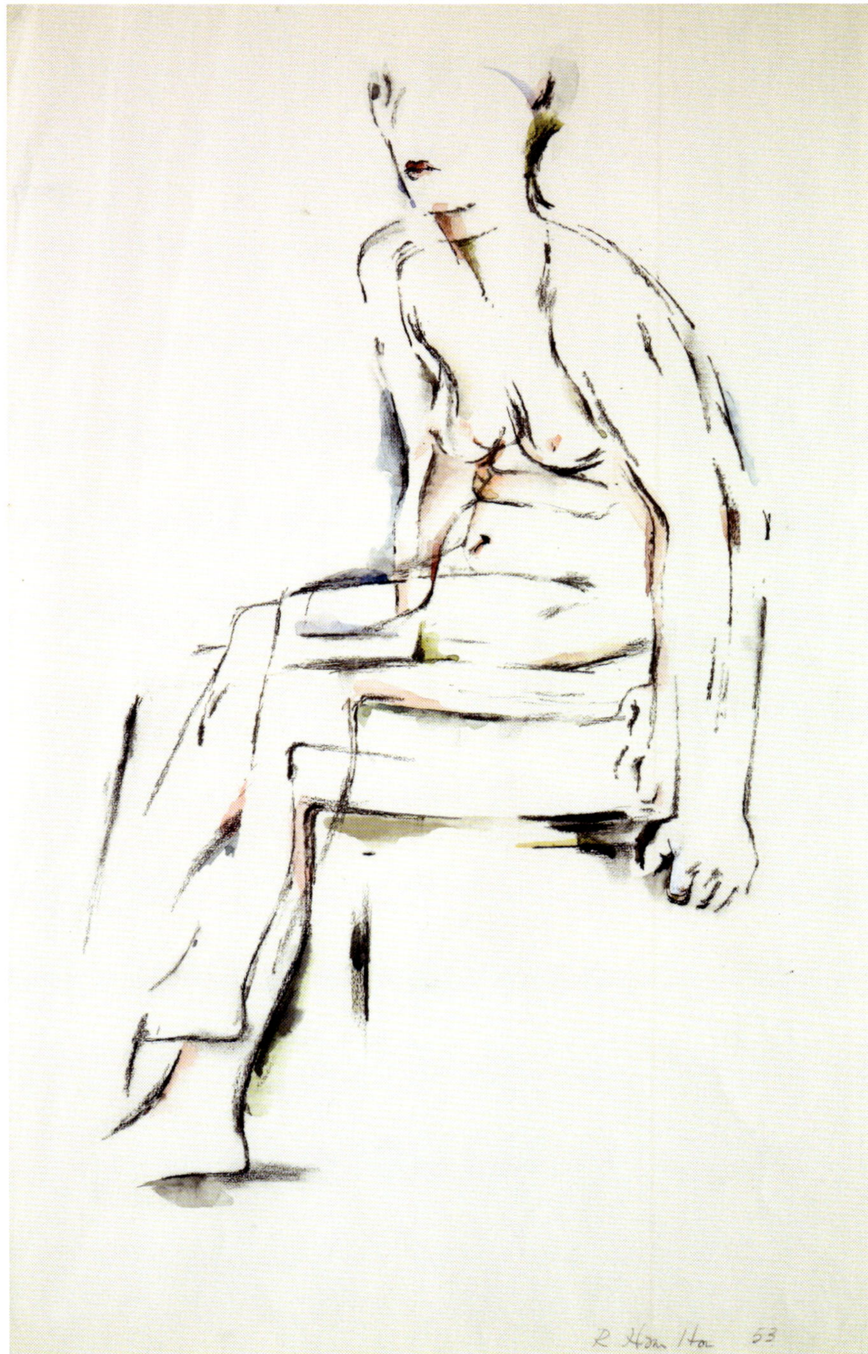

Richard Hamilton

Study for reNude, 1953
Pencil and watercolour on paper
53 × 33.6 cm

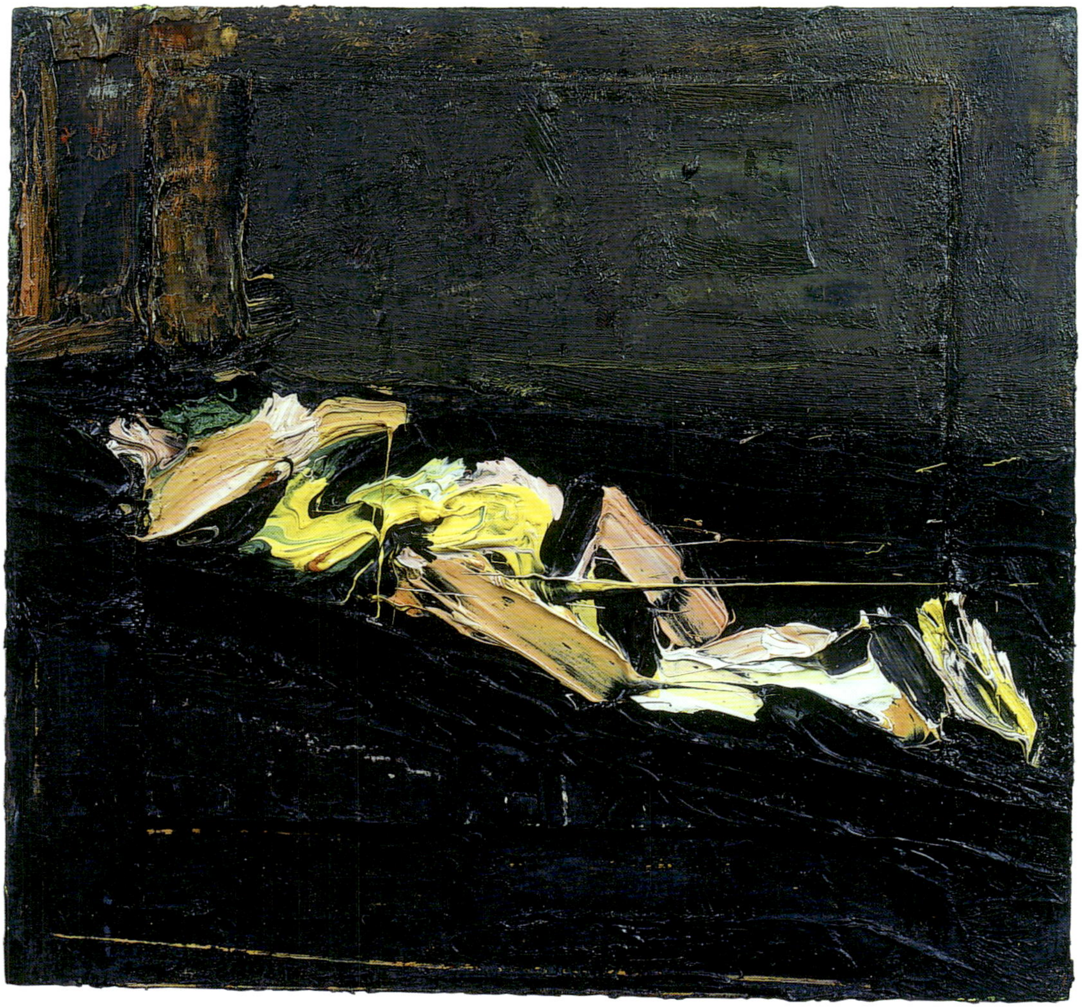

Frank Auerbach

Reclining Figure, 1972
Oil on board
38.1 × 40.6 cm

Private Collection, NY

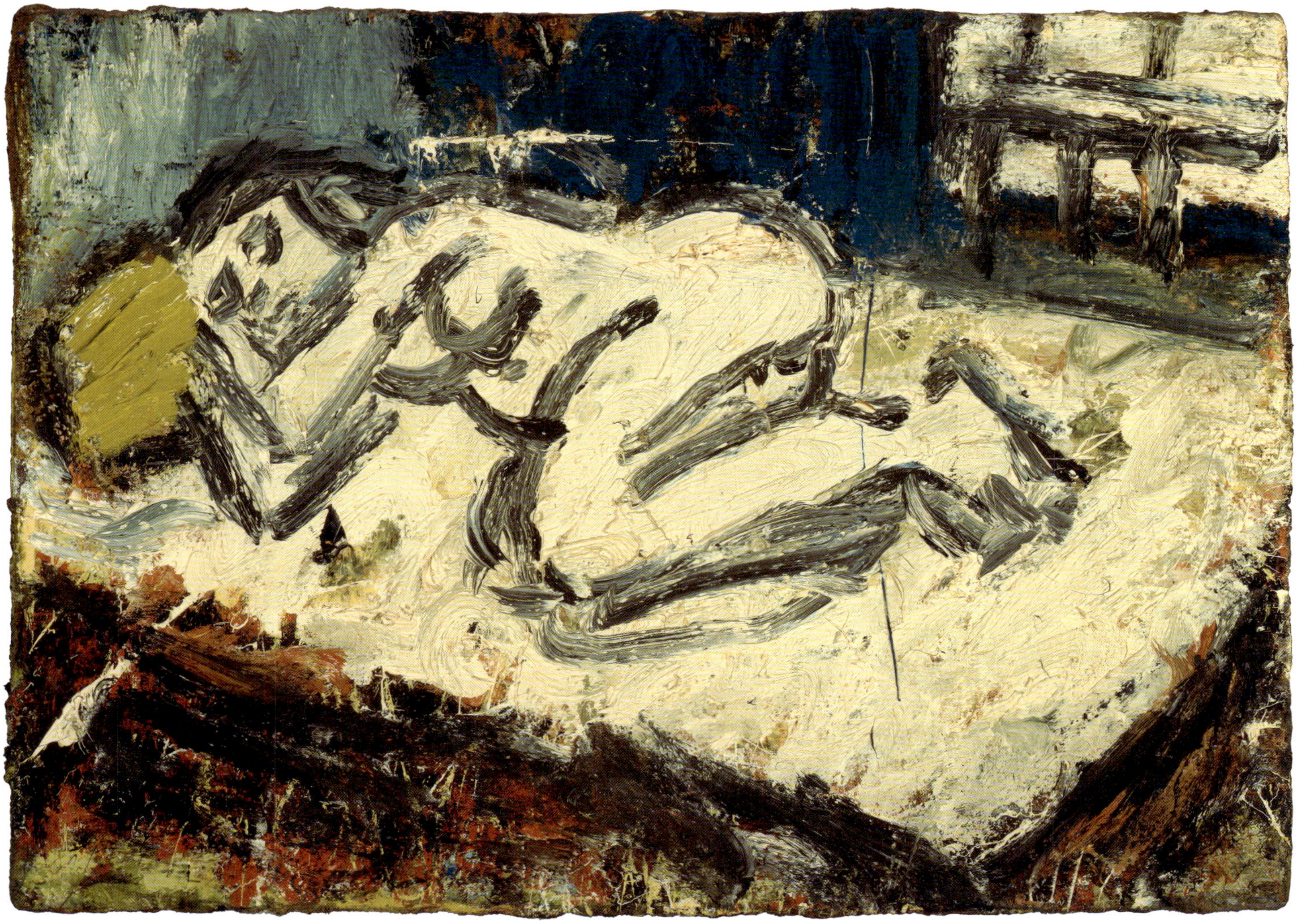

Leon Kossoff

Nude (Autumn Morning), 1971
Oil on board
81 × 111 cm

Private collection

William Coldstream

Seated Nude, 1972–73
Oil on canvas
110.6 × 61.4 cm

Private collection

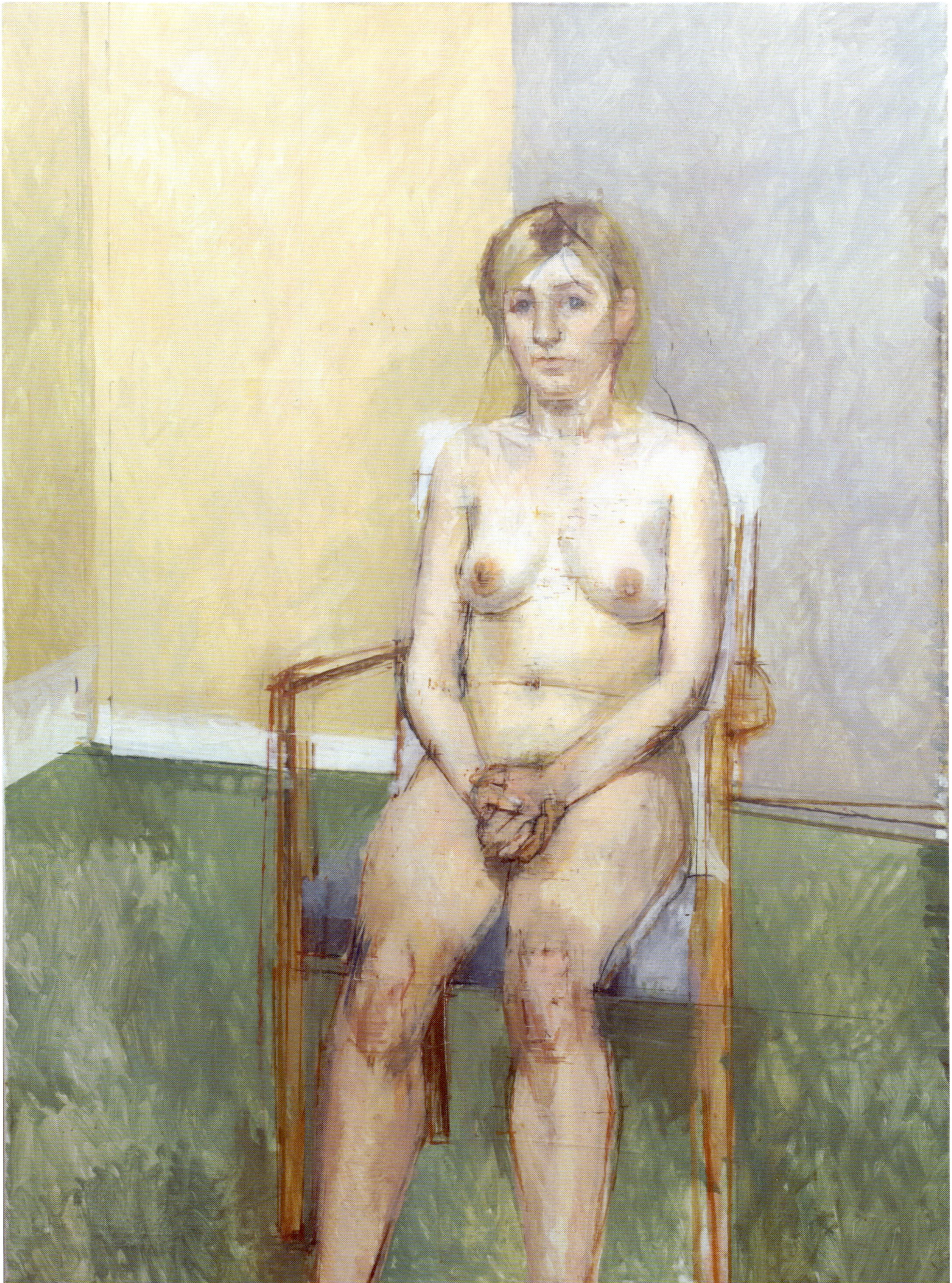

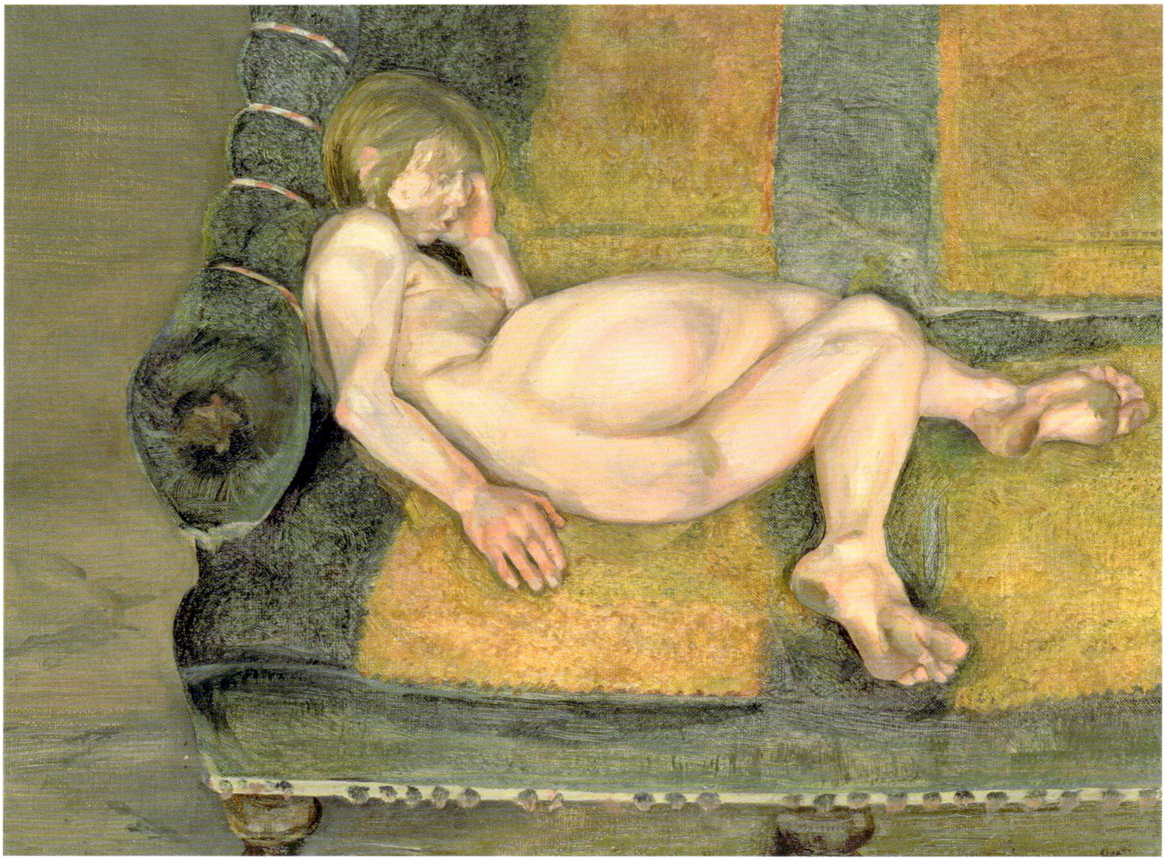

Lucian Freud

Girl on a Turkish Sofa, 1966
Oil on canvas
26.7 × 34.9 cm

Private collection

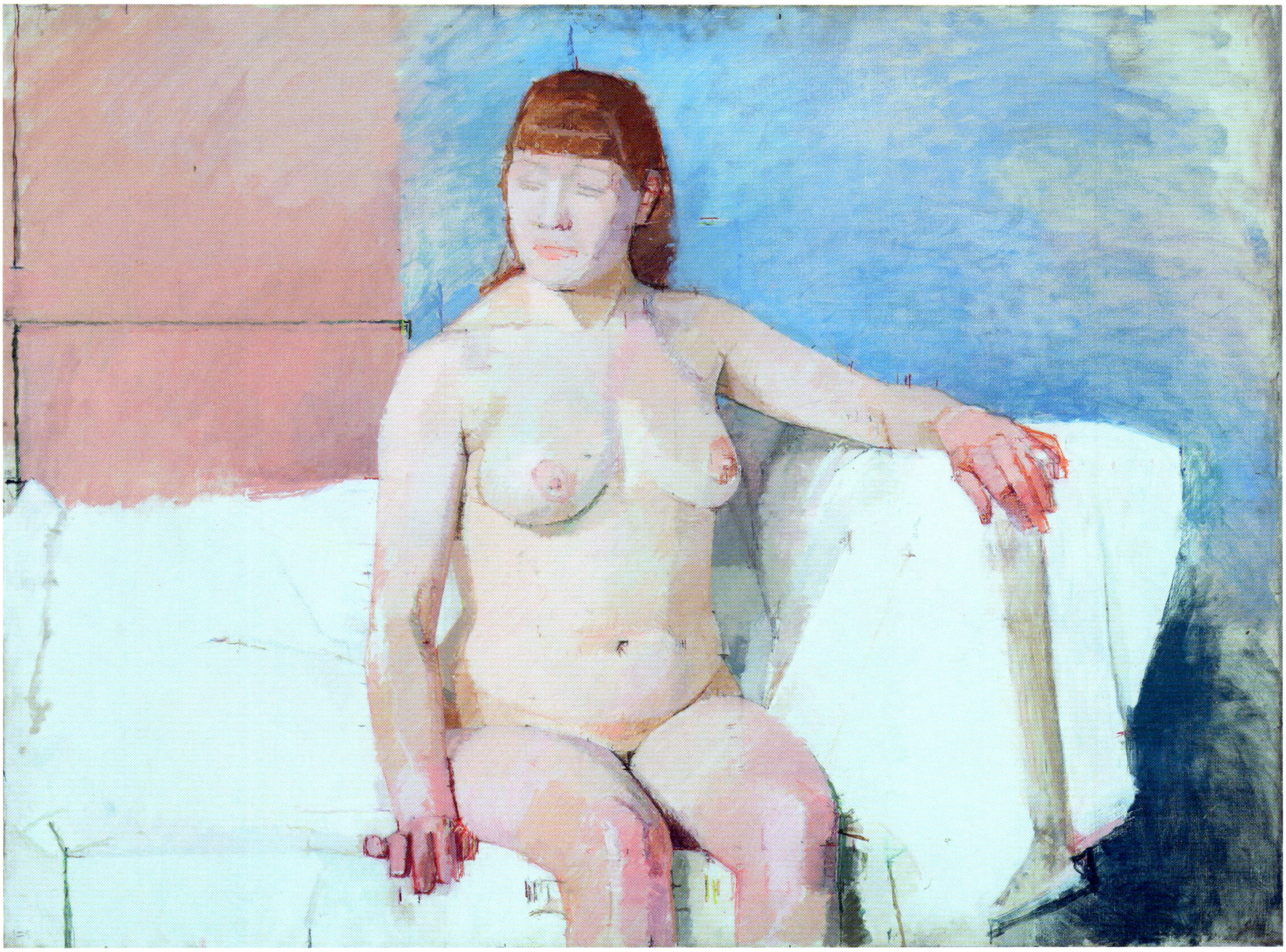

Euan Uglow

Nude, Lady C, 1959–60
Oil on canvas
75 × 101.5 cm

John and Julia Scott

Francis Bacon

Pope I—Study after Pope Innocent X by Velázquez, 1951
Oil on canvas
197.8 × 137.4 cm

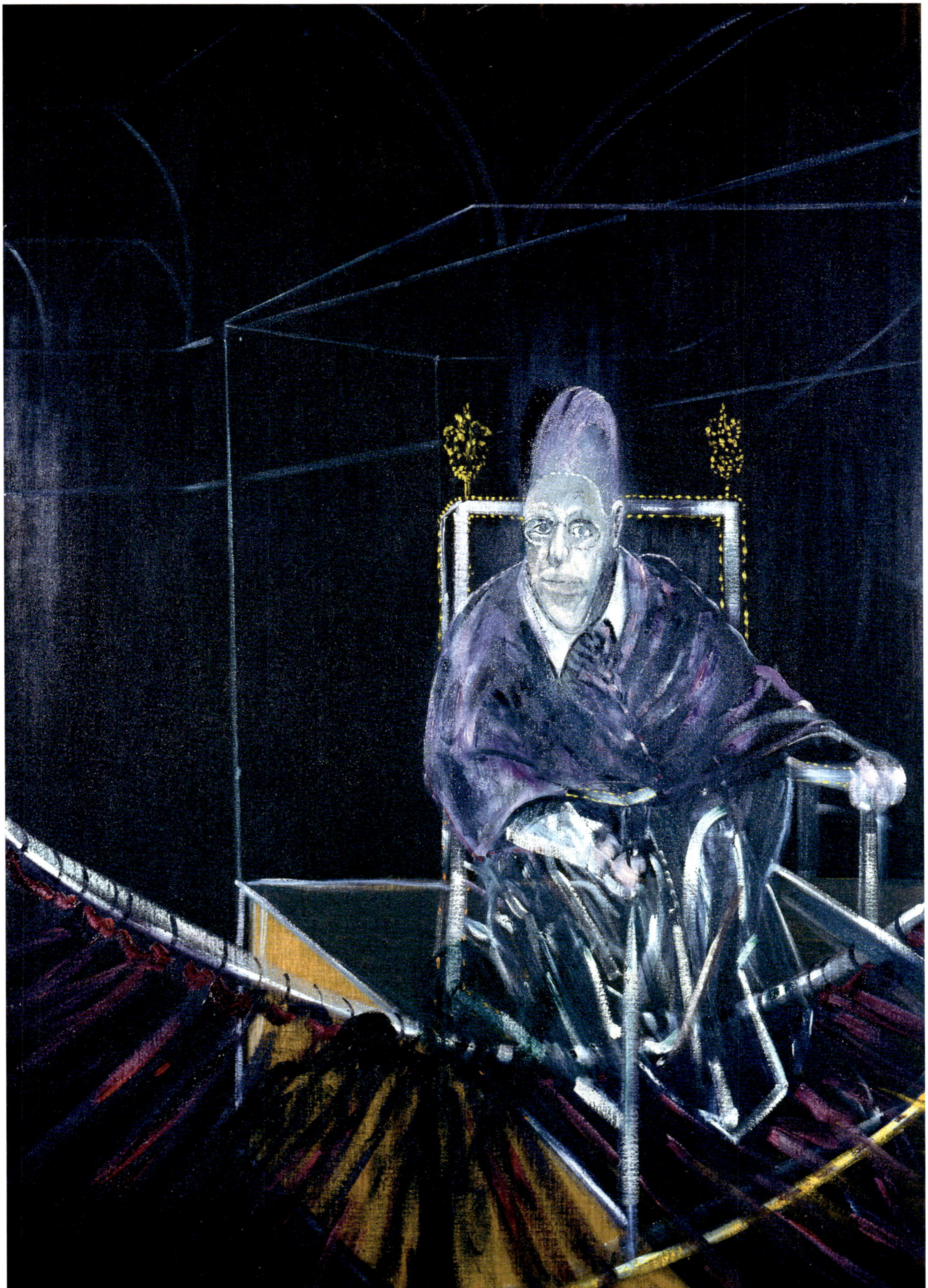

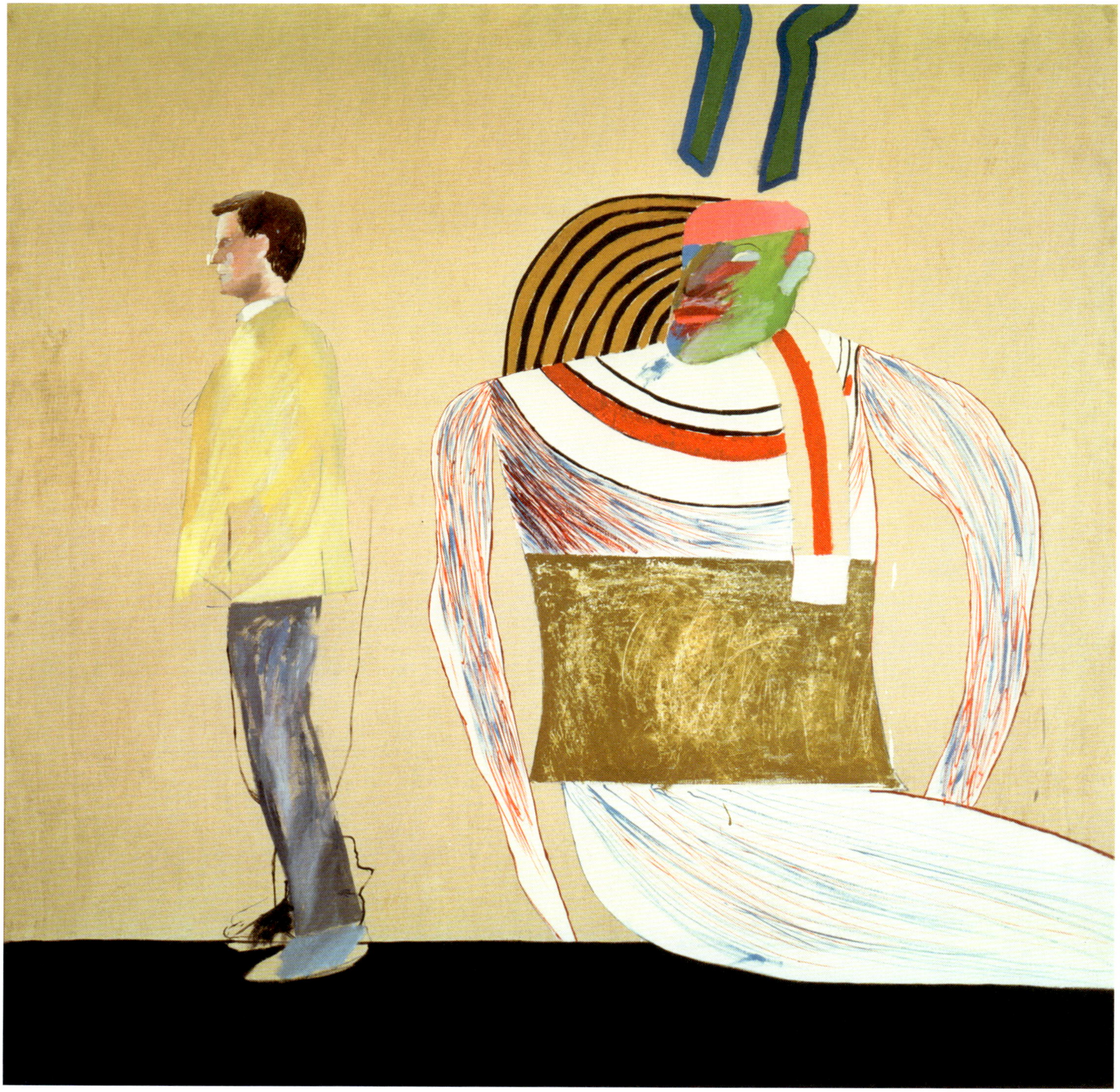

David Hockney

Man in a Museum (Or You're in the Wrong Movie), 1962
Oil on canvas
147.3 × 152.4 cm

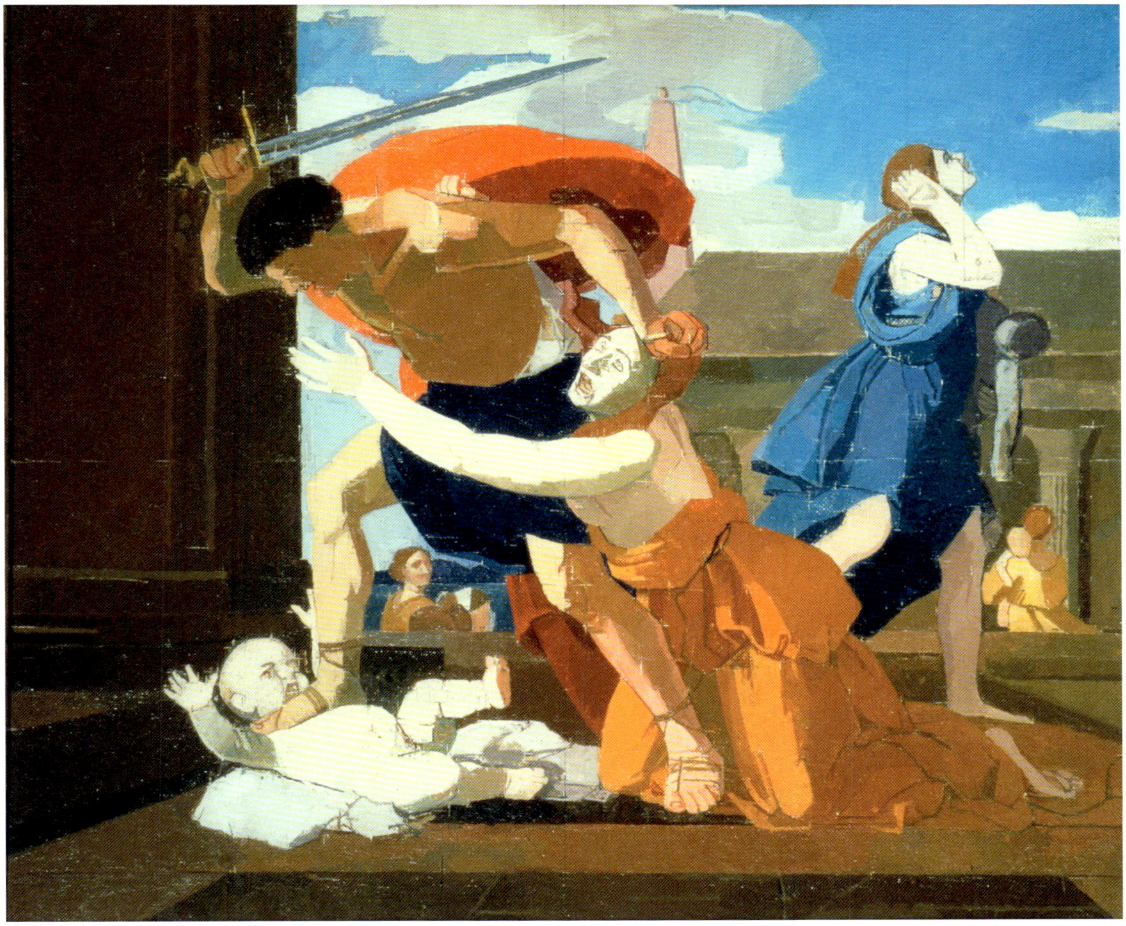

Euan Uglow

Massacre of the Innocents, 1979–81
Oil on canvas laid on panel
41.2 × 48.9 cm

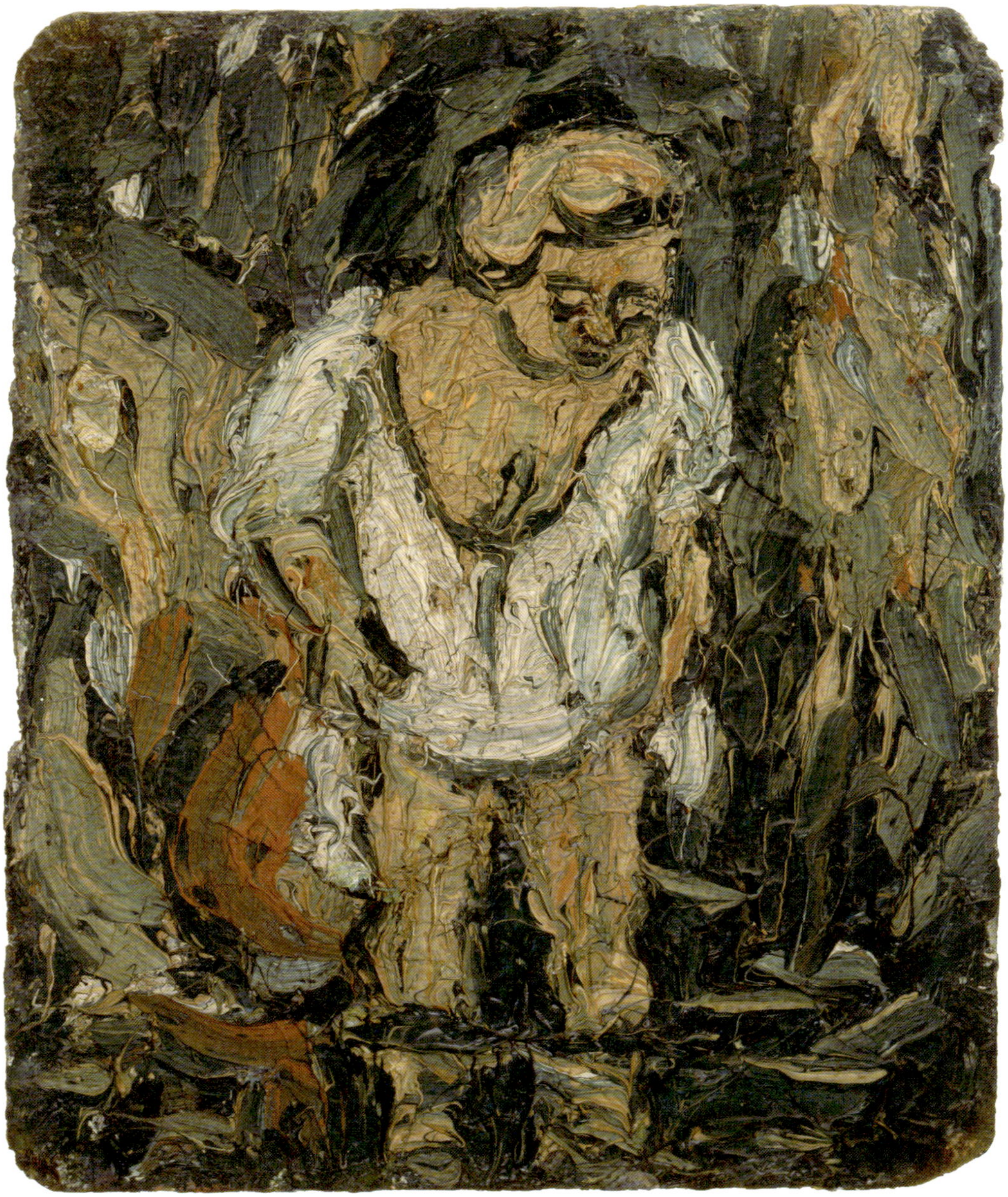

Leon Kossoff

A Woman Bathing (Study After Rembrandt), 1982
Oil on board
58.4 × 48.3 cm

Private collection

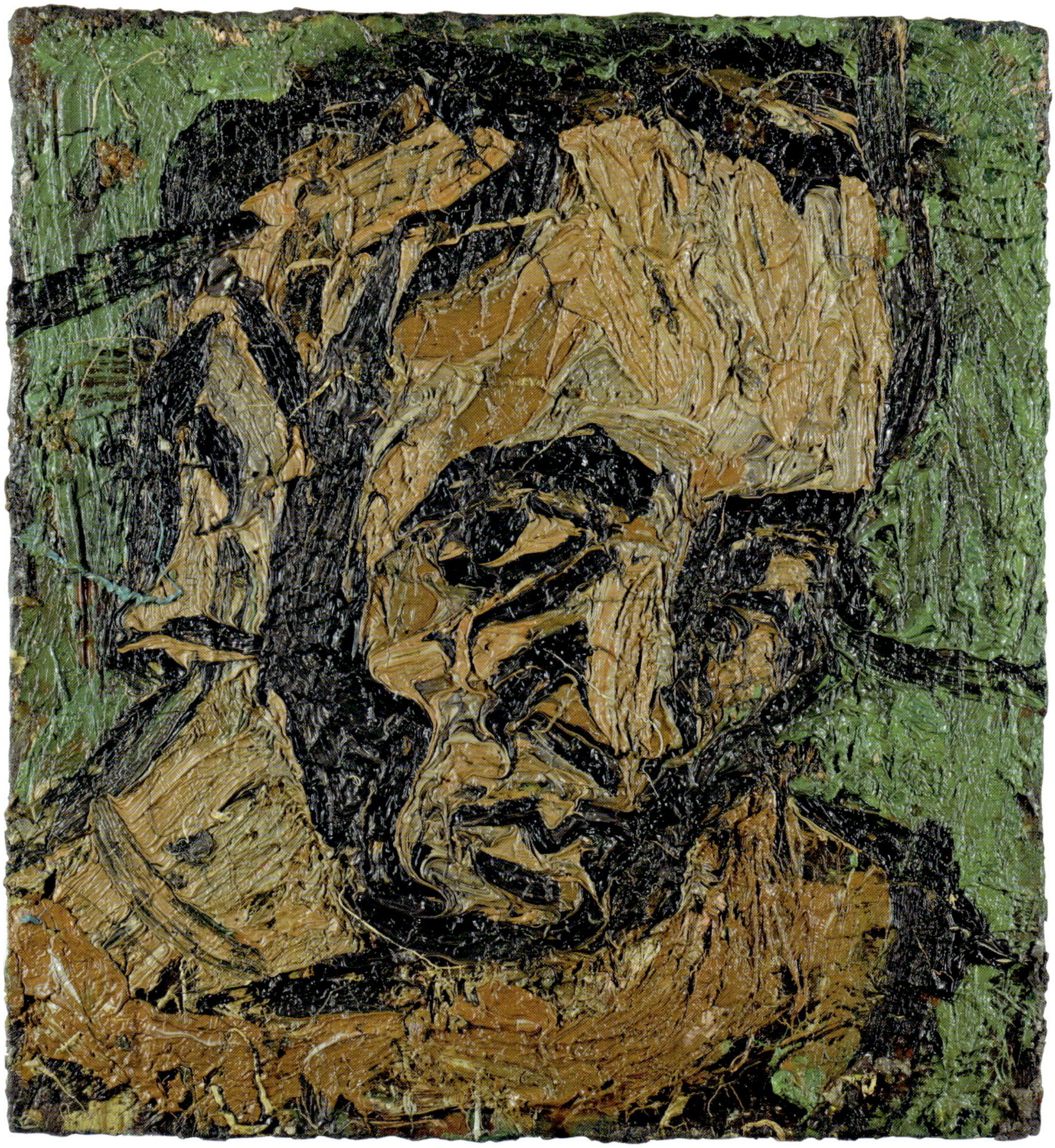

Leon Kossoff

Self Portrait II, 1972
Oil on wood
56 × 51 cm

Private collection

Richard Hamilton

Mother and Child, 1984–85
Oil on canvas
150 × 150 cm

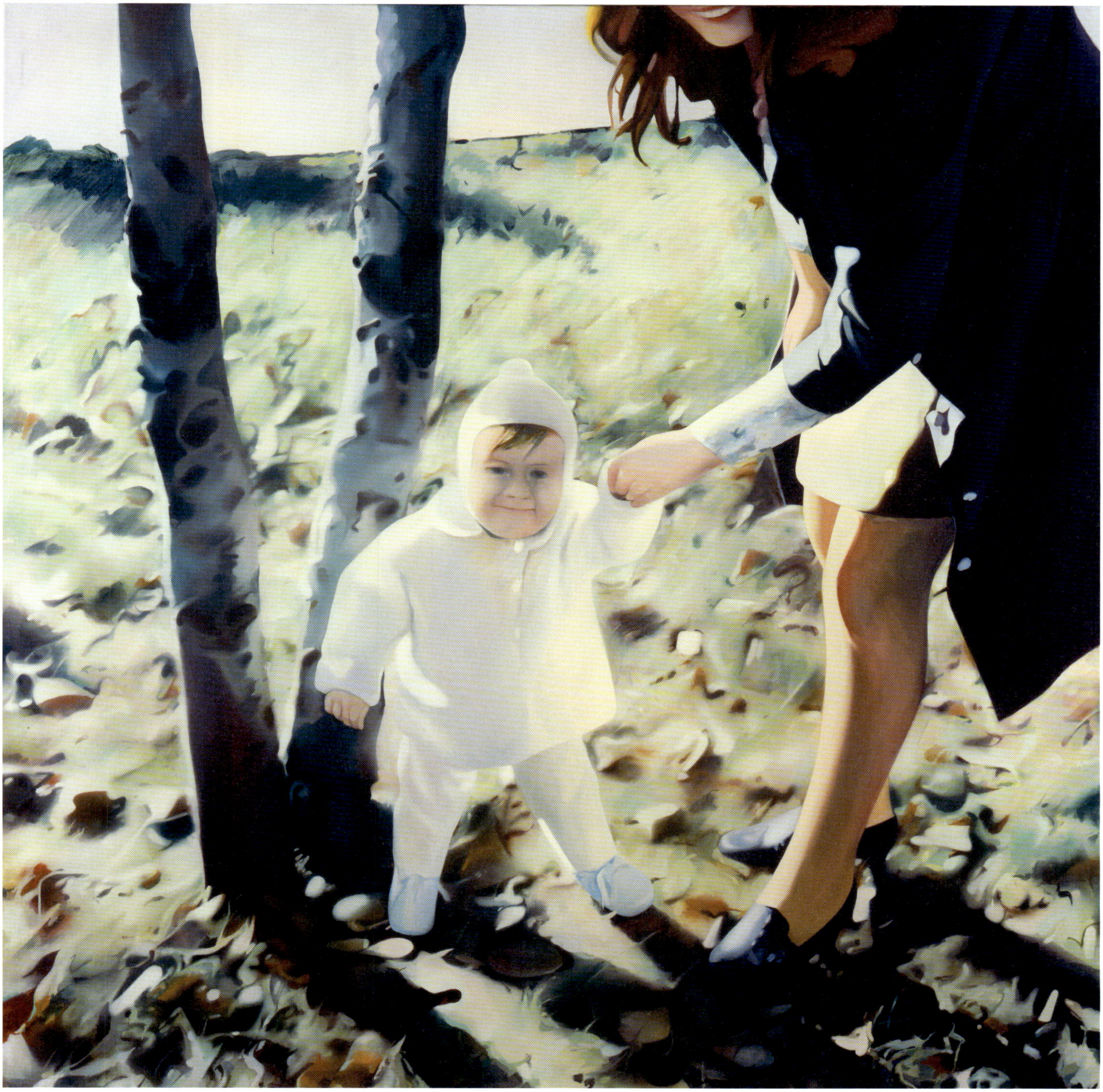

Michael Andrews

The Thames at Low Tide, 1994–95
Oil, sand, and paint residue on canvas
182.9 × 167.6 cm

Private collection

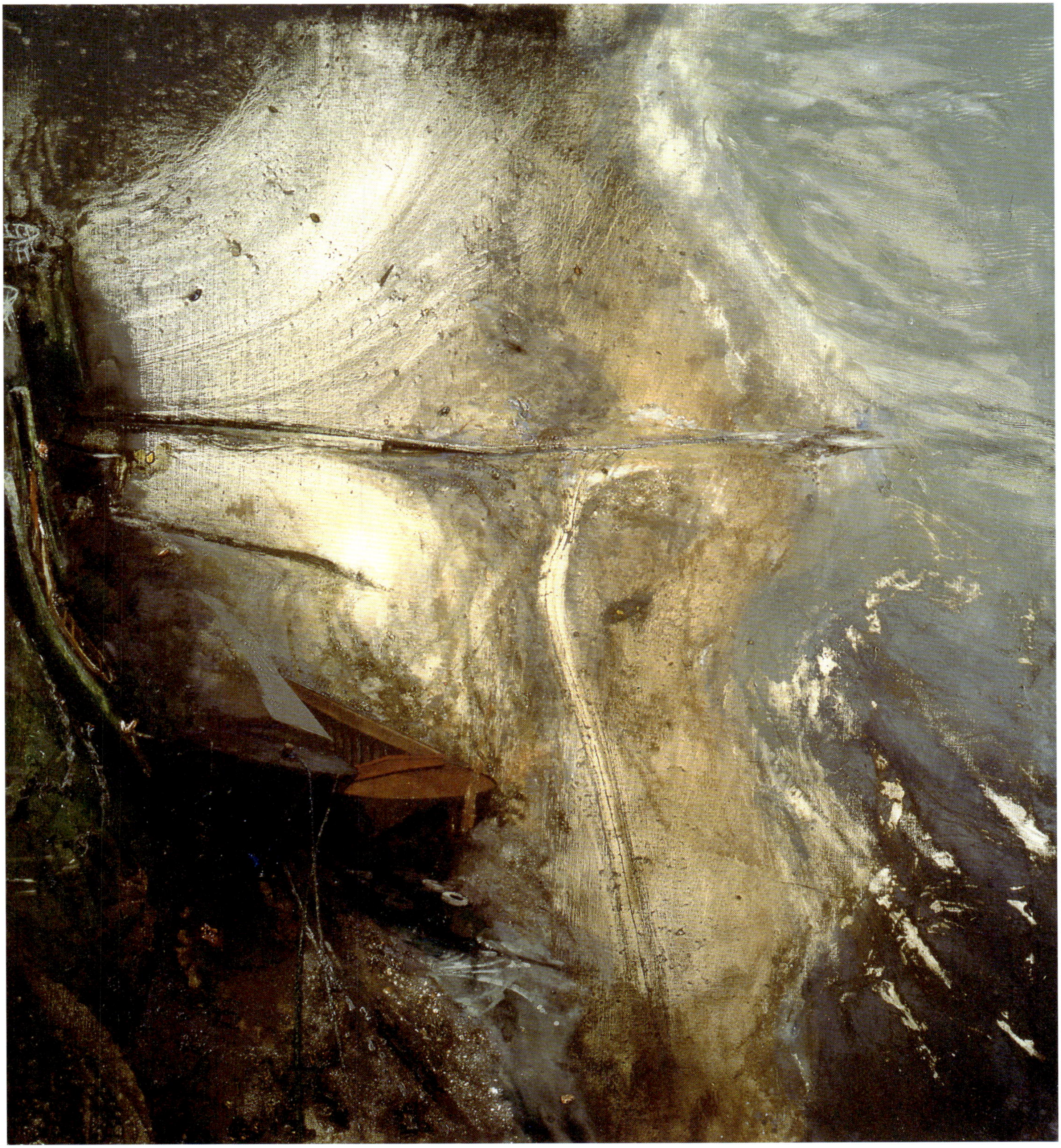

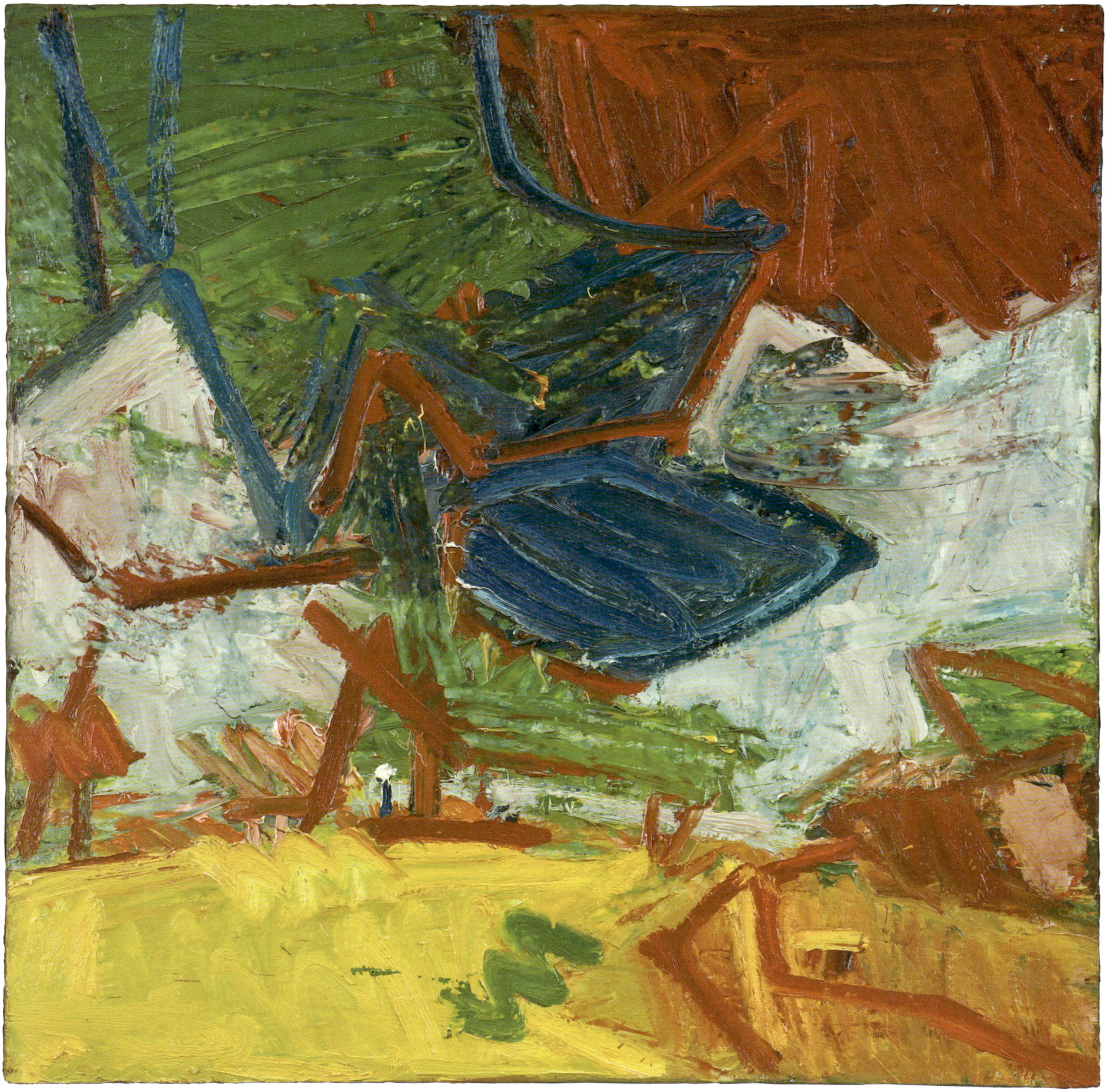

Frank Auerbach

Study of Primrose Hill, 1973–74
Oil on board
121.9 × 121.9 cm

Private collection

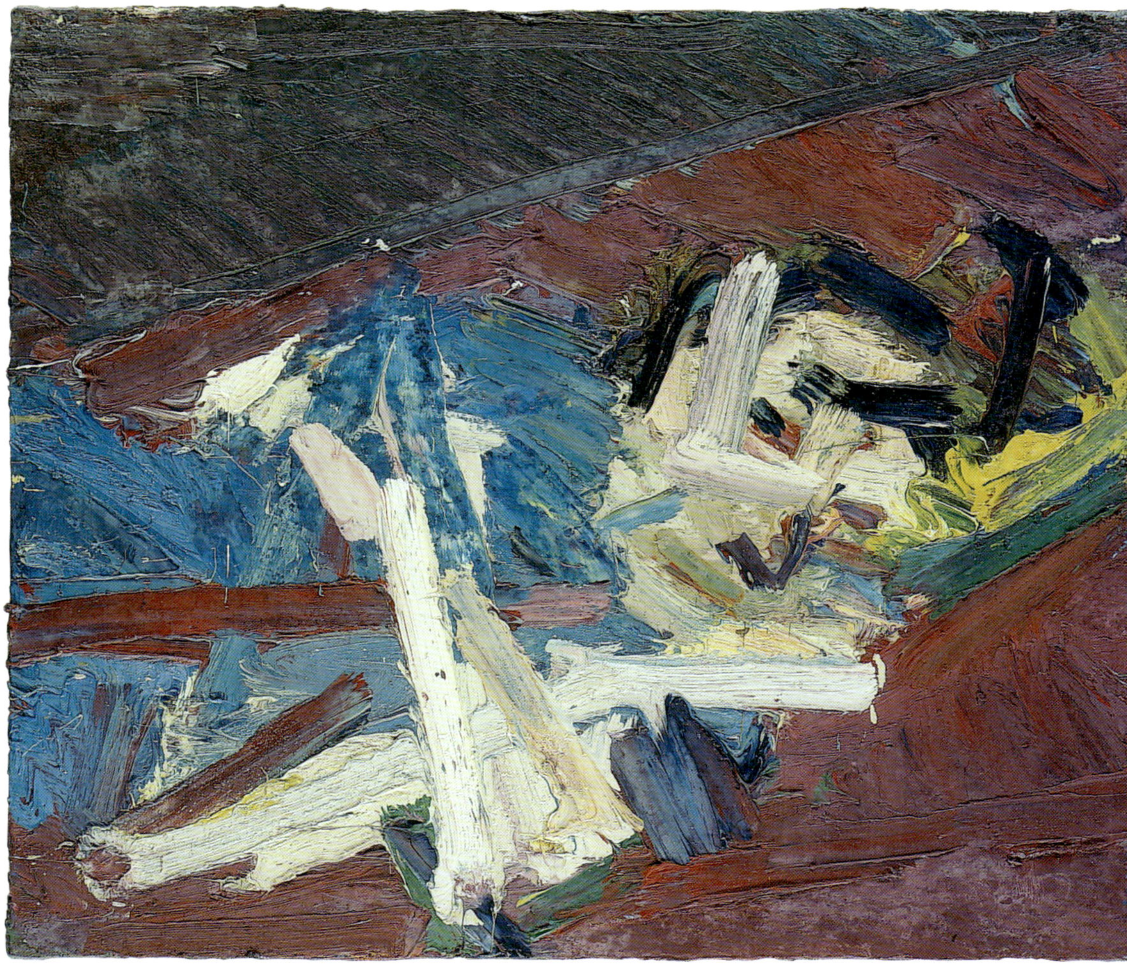

Frank Auerbach

Gerda Boehm, 1971–73
Oil on board
61 × 71.1 cm

Private collection

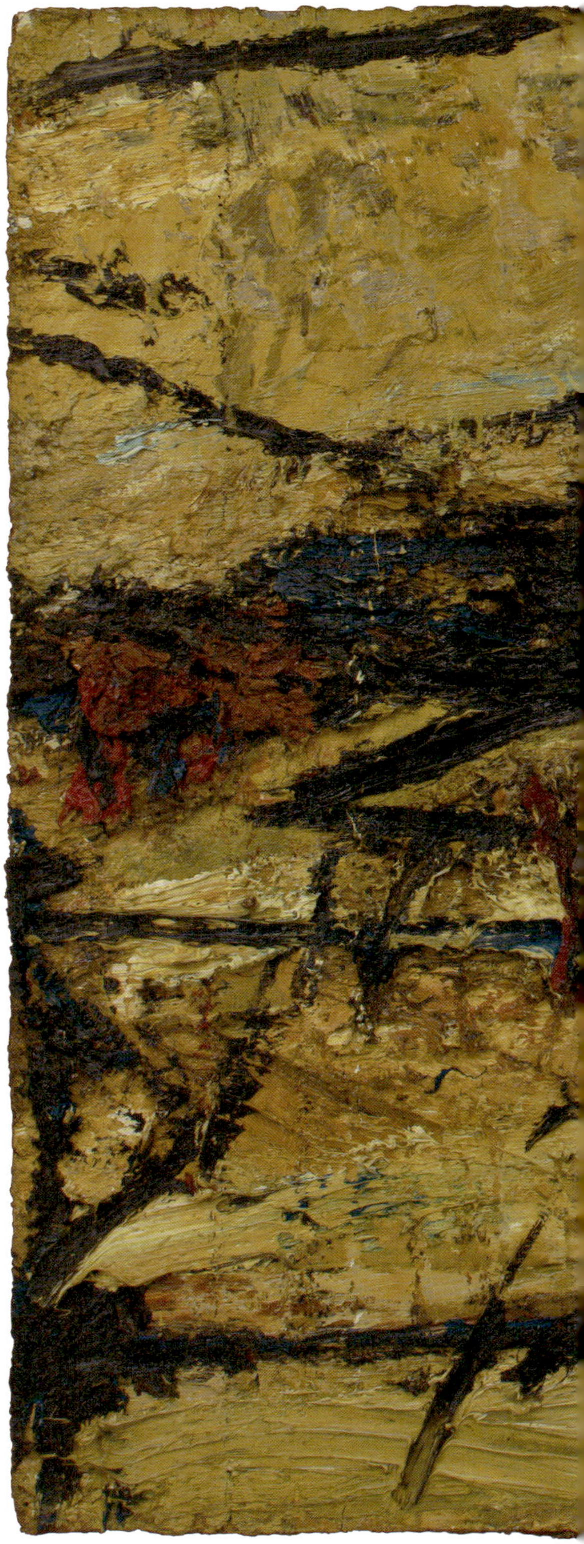

Frank Auerbach

Primrose Hill, Winter Sunshine, 1962–64
Oil on board
104.1 × 144.8 cm

Private collection

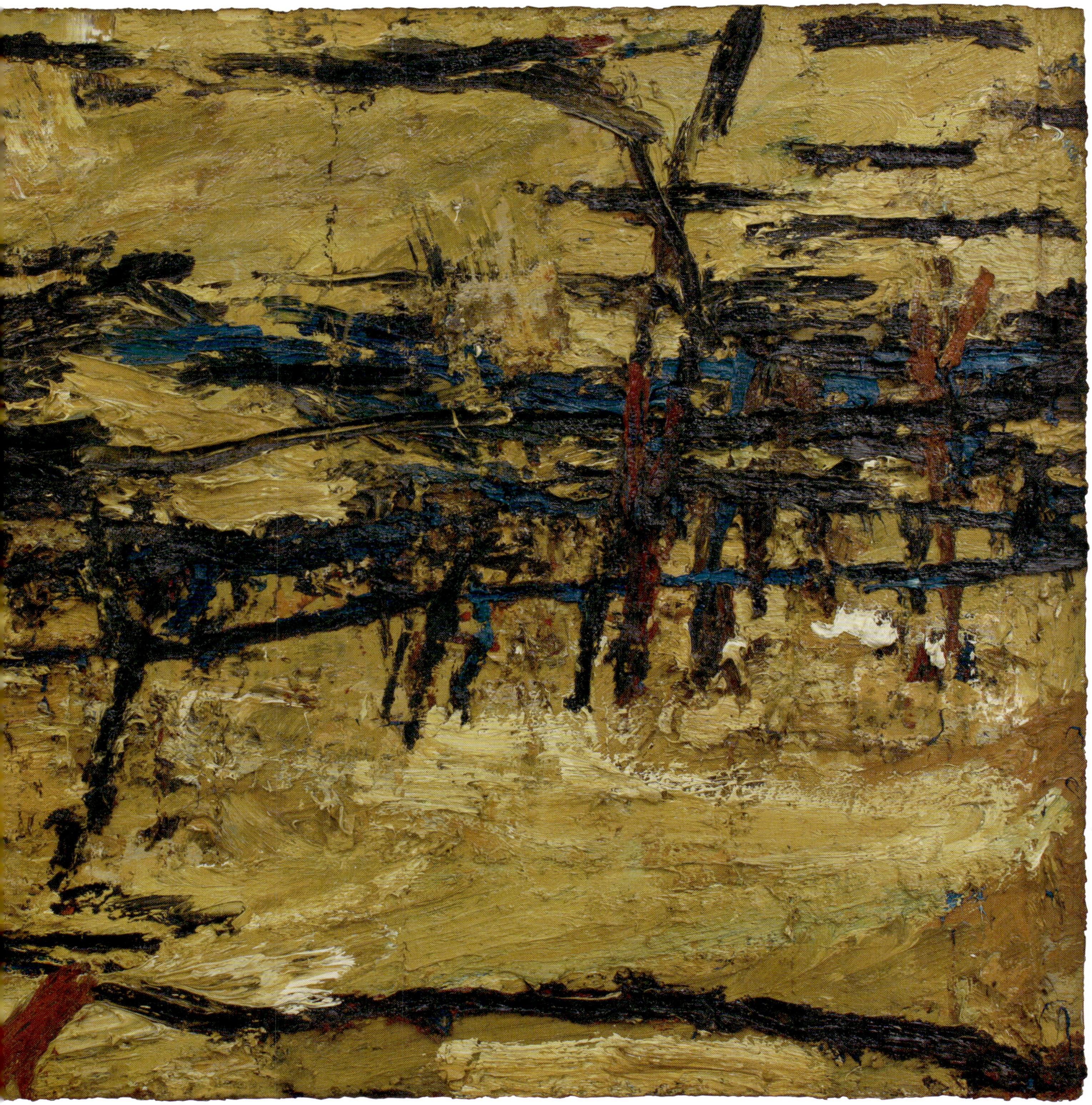

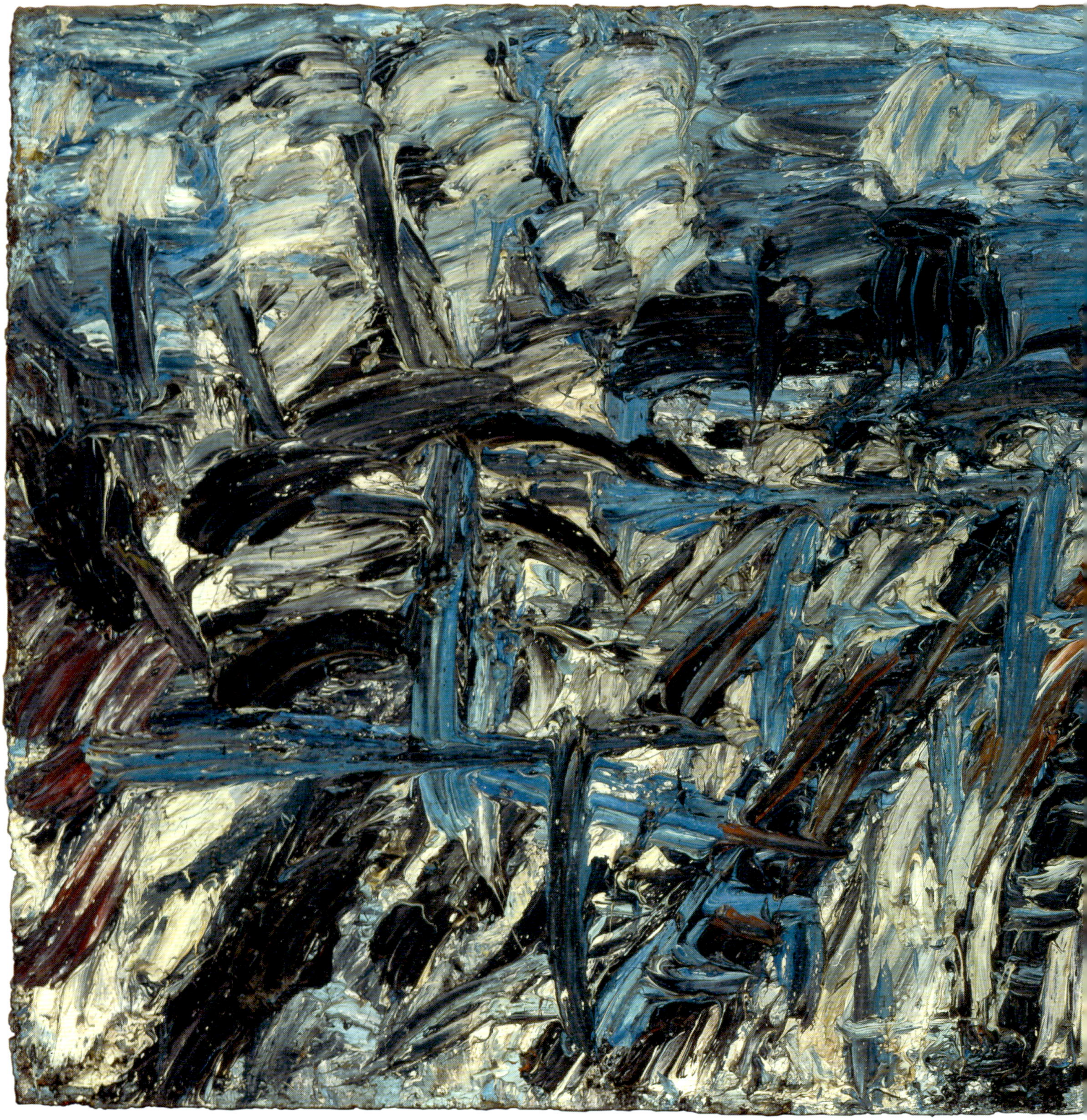

Leon Kossoff

Willesden Junction, Summer No.1, 1966
Oil on board
91.4 × 152.4 cm

Private collection

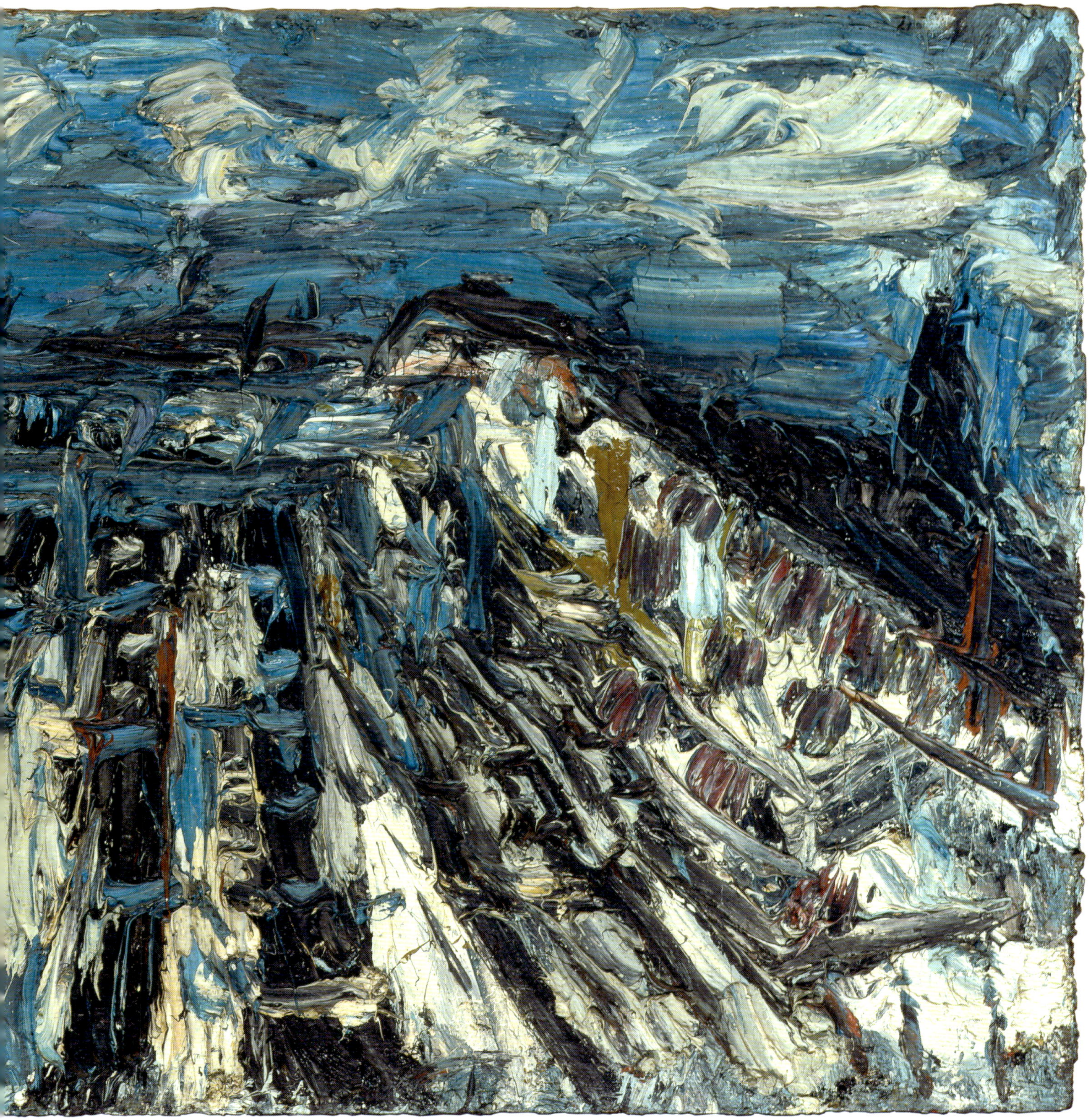

Lucian Freud

Portrait of a Woman (Portrait of Lady Anne Tree), c. 1950
Oil on canvas
44 × 34.5 cm

Devonshire Collection, Chatsworth

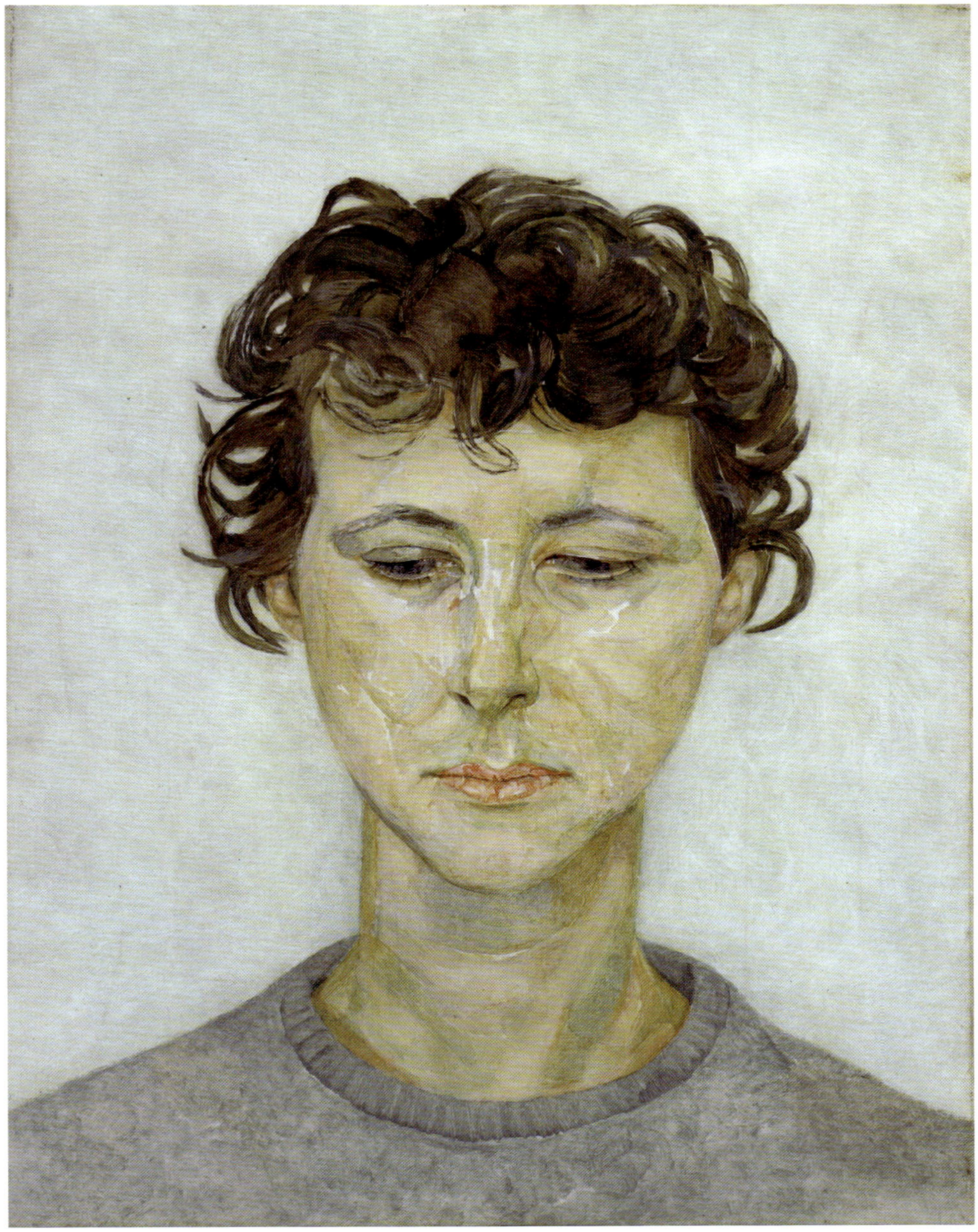

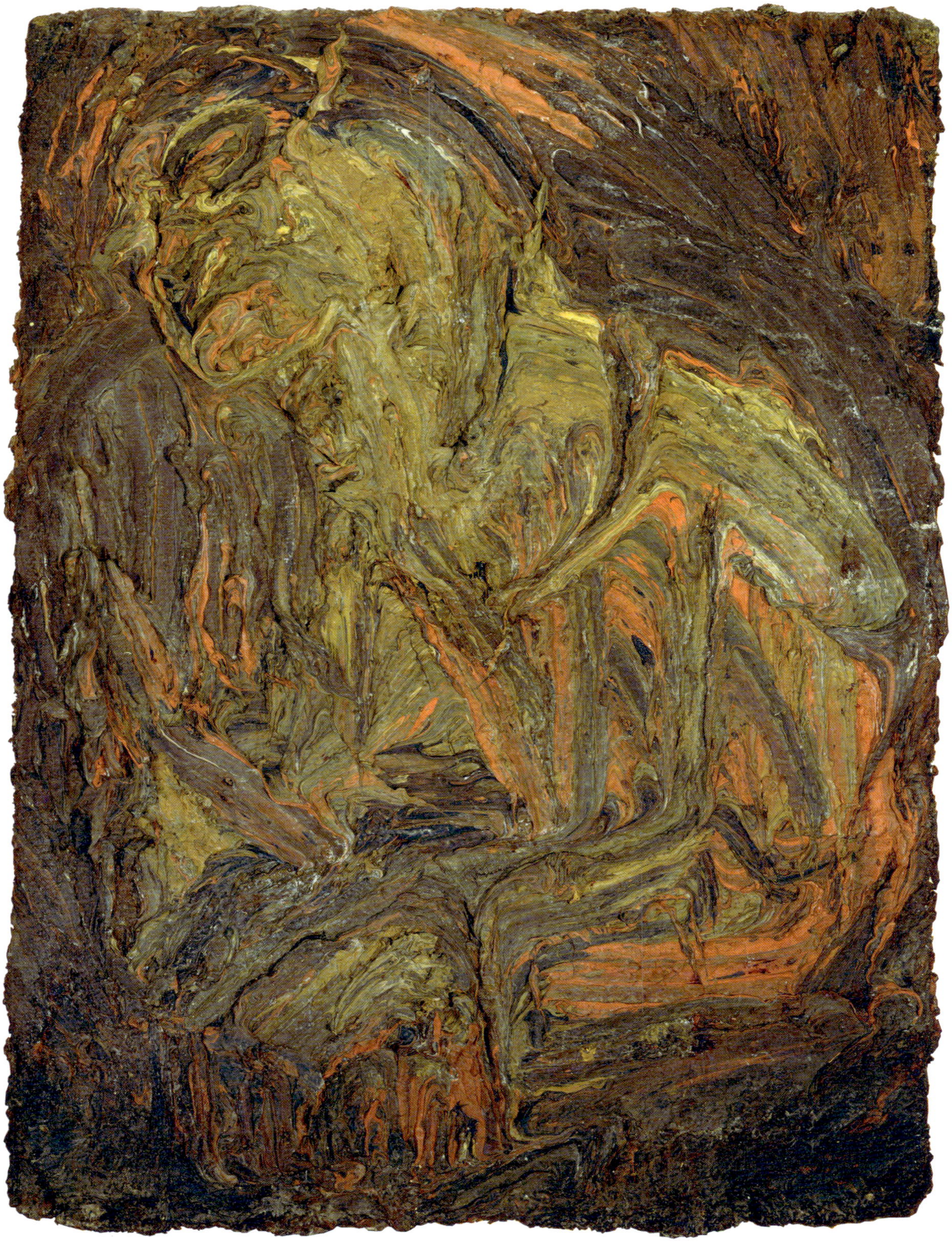

Leon Kossoff

Seated Woman No.2, 1959
Oil on board
111.8 × 83.8 cm

Private collection

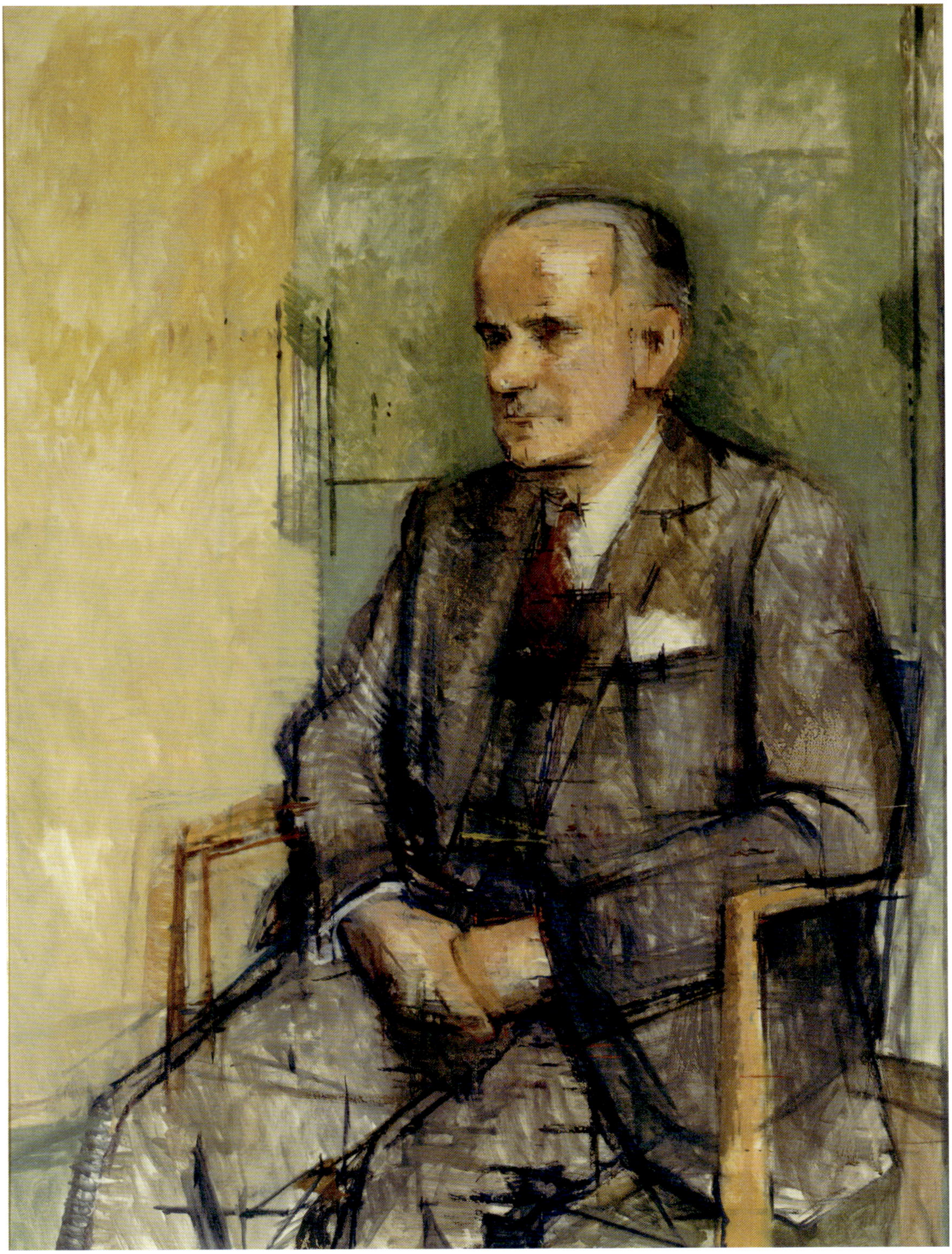

William Coldstream

Lord Ifor Evans, 1958–60
Oil on canvas
110.8 × 83.7 cm

Richard Hamilton

Respective, 1951
Oil on hardboard
91.5 × 122 cm

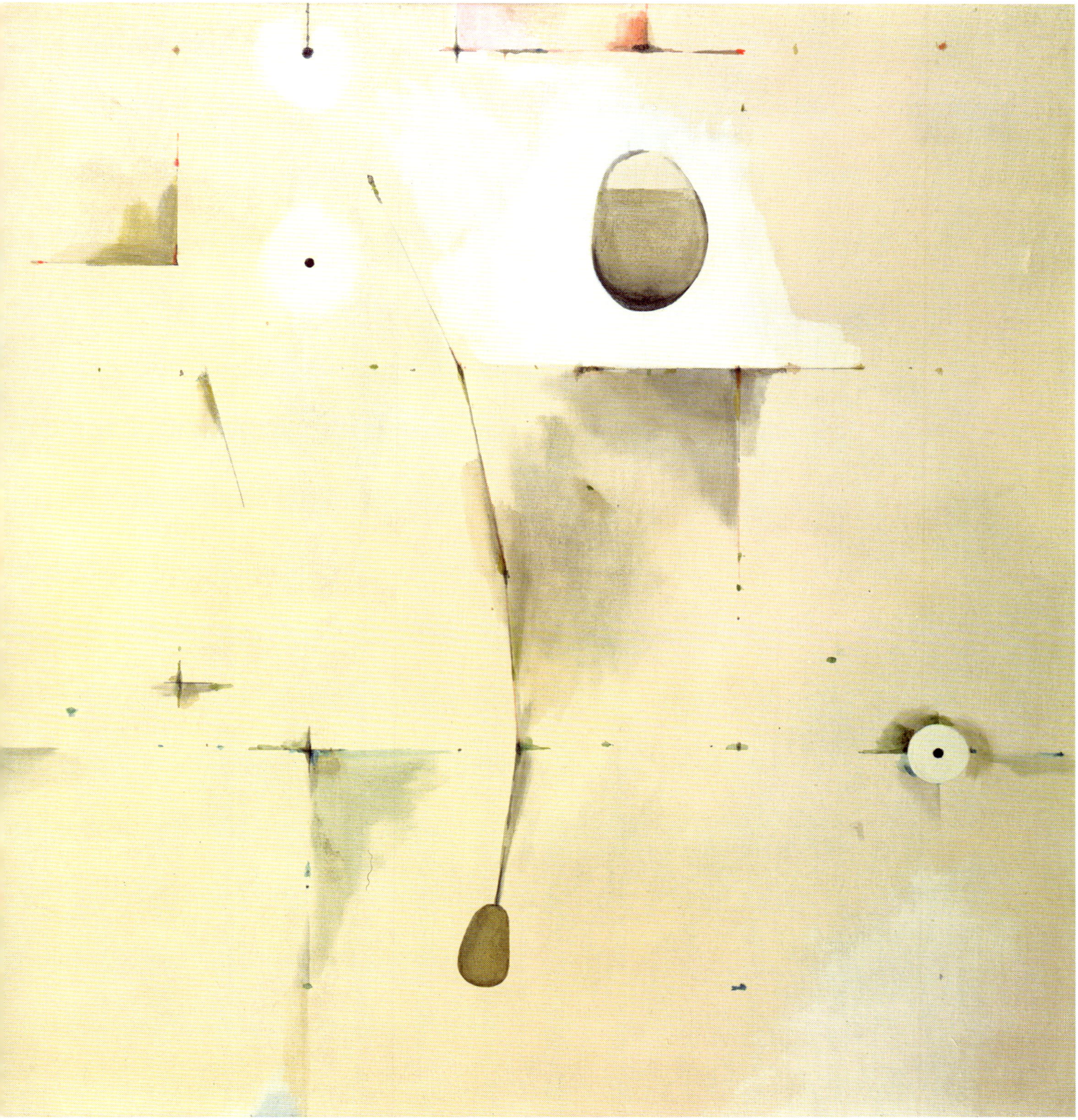

Euan Uglow

Mosque at Çiftlik Koyou, 1966
Oil on canvas
105 × 121 cm

Private collection

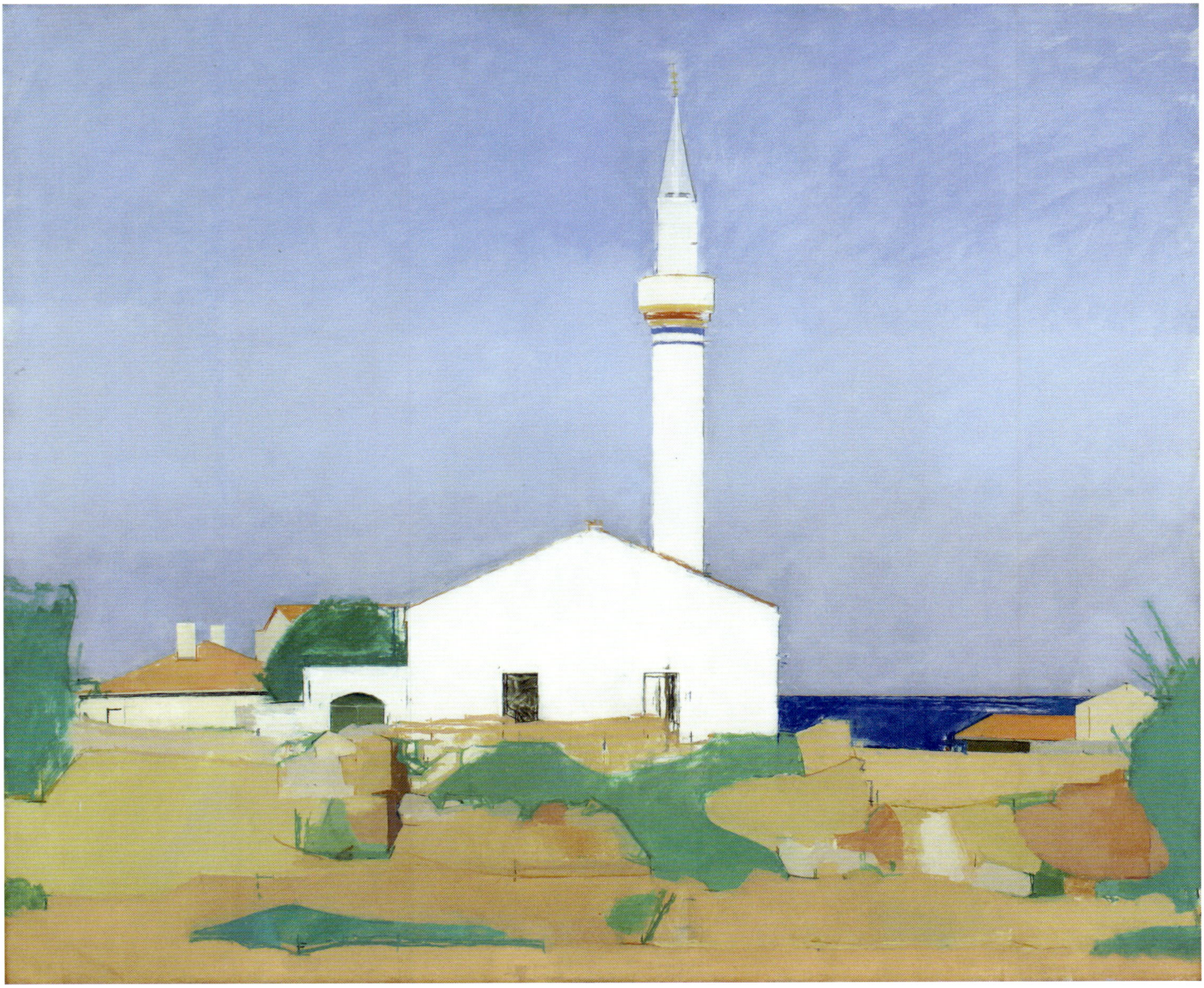

David Hockney

The Room Tarzana, 1967
Acrylic on canvas
243.8 × 243.8 cm

Private collection

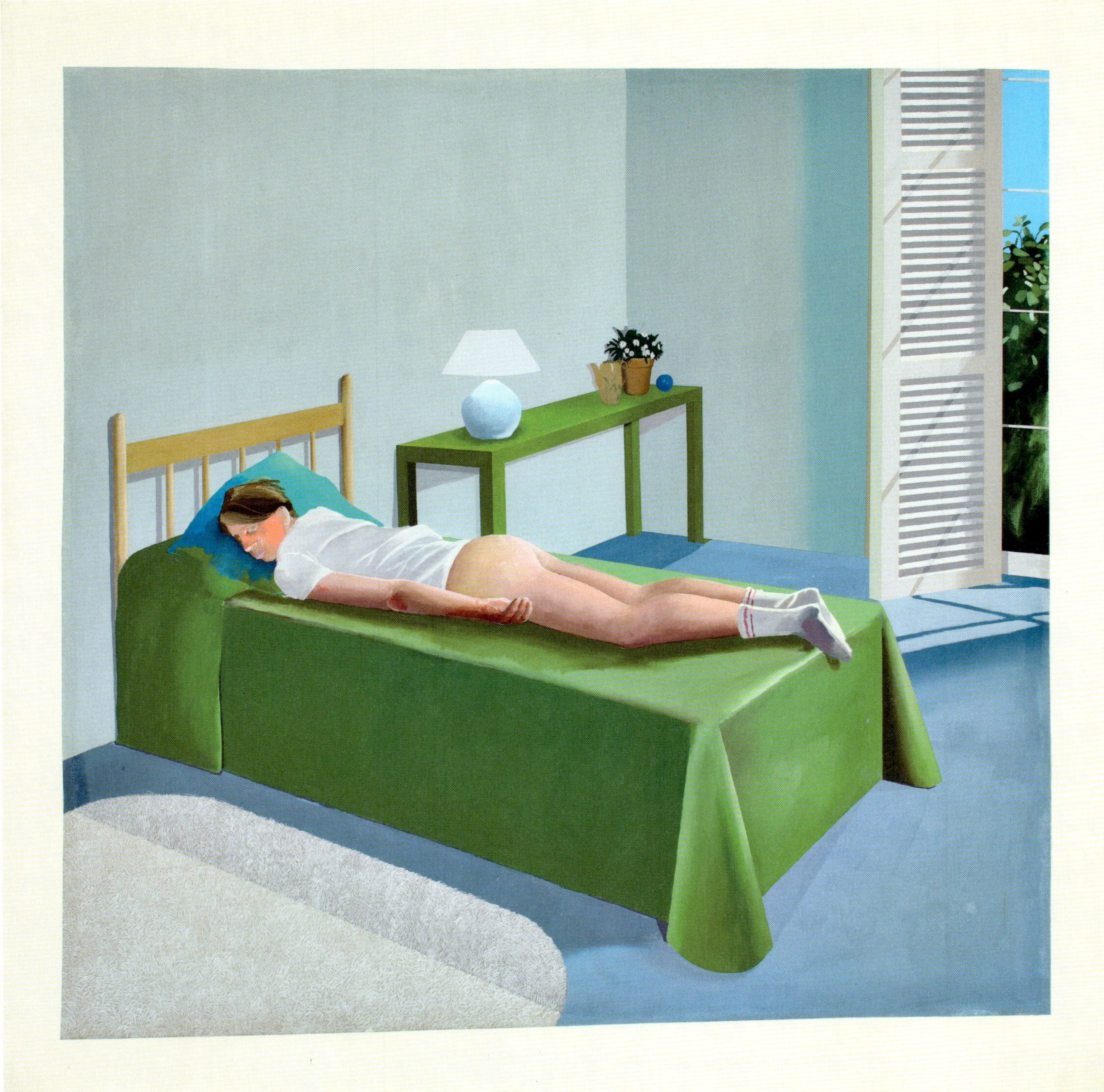

Michael Andrews

The Lord Mayor's Reception in Norwich Castle Keep, On the Eve of the Installation of the First Chancellor of the University of East Anglia, 1966–69
Oil on canvas, 213.3 × 213.3 cm

Norfolk Museums and Archaeology Service, Norwich Castle Museum and Art Gallery

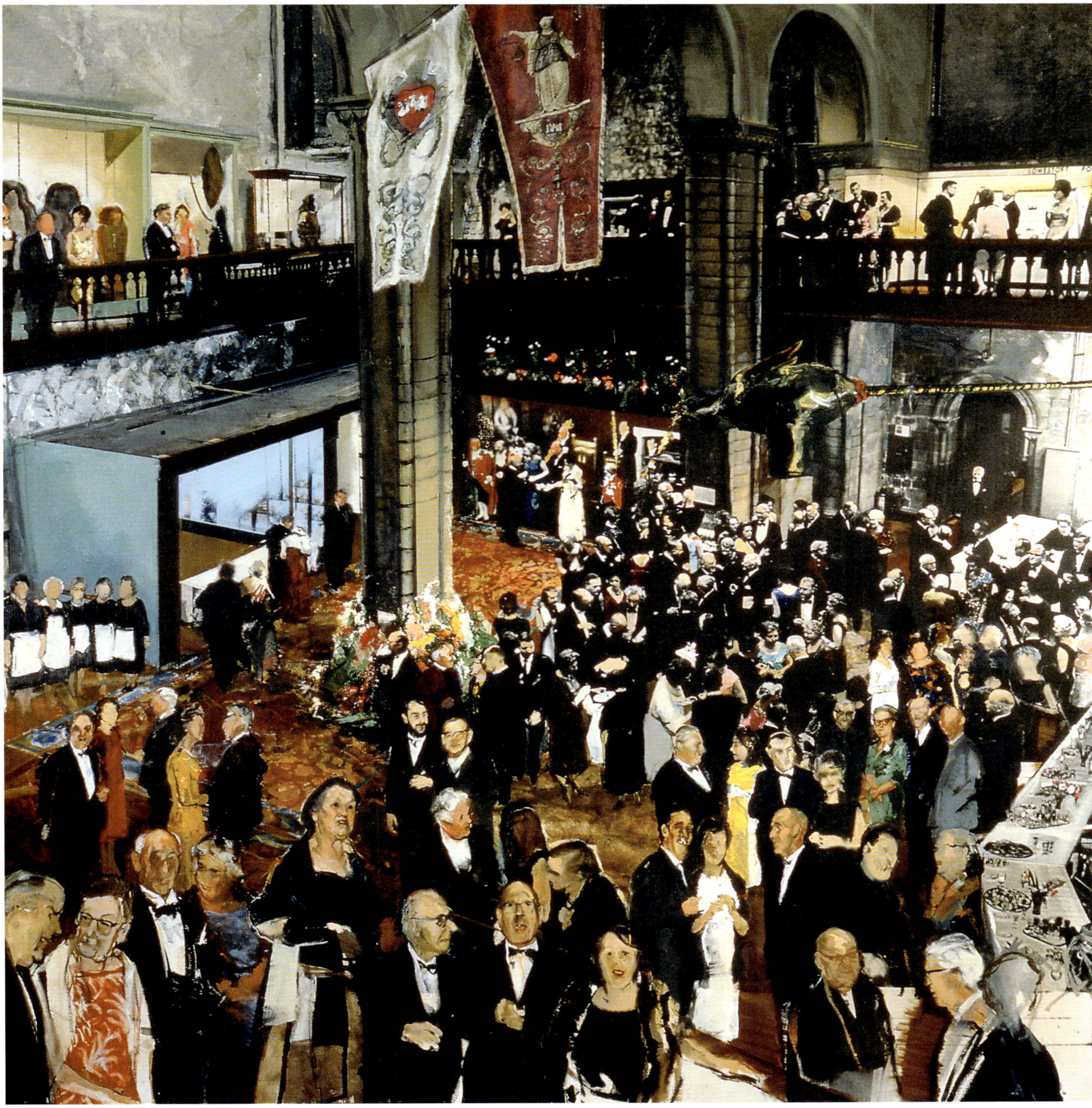

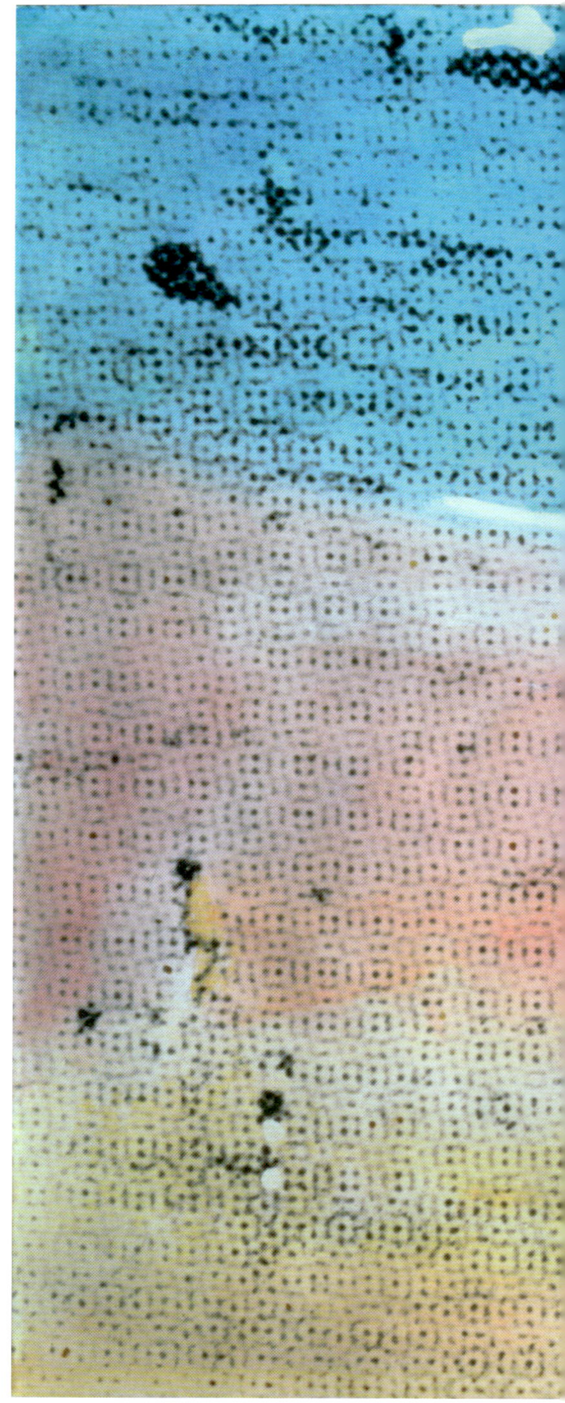

Richard Hamilton

Whitley Bay, 1965
Oil on photograph laid on panel
81 × 122 cm

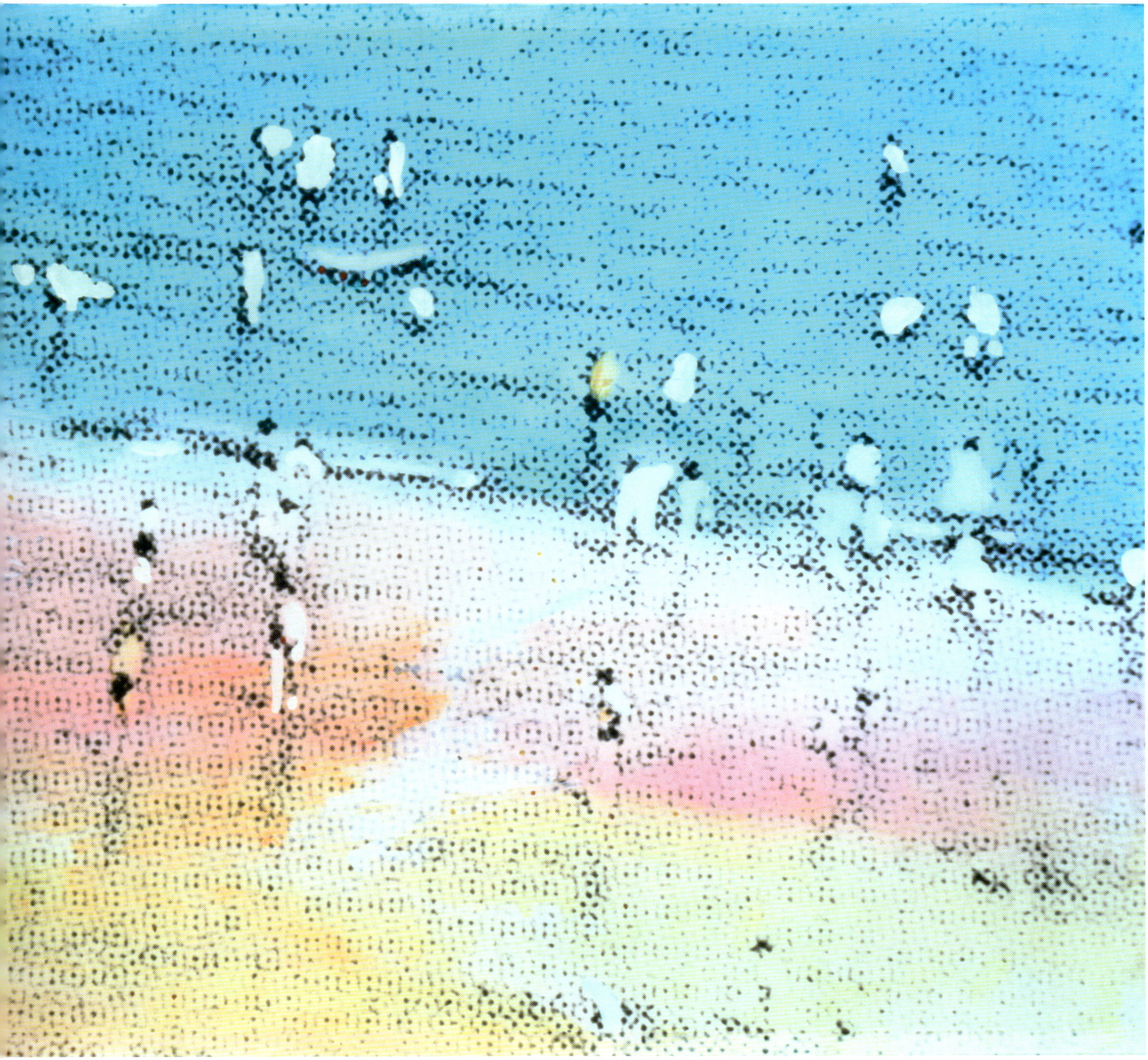

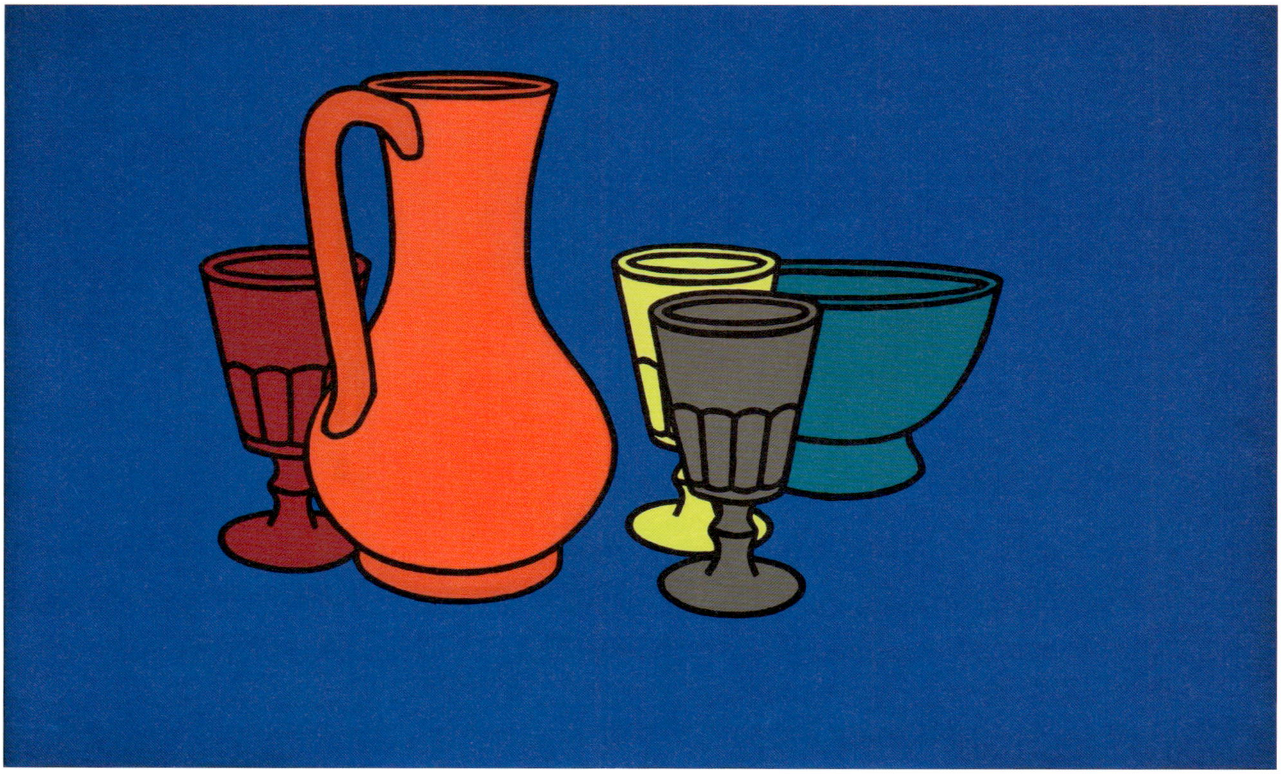

Patrick Caulfield

Coloured Still Life, 1967
Acrylic on board
56 × 89 cm

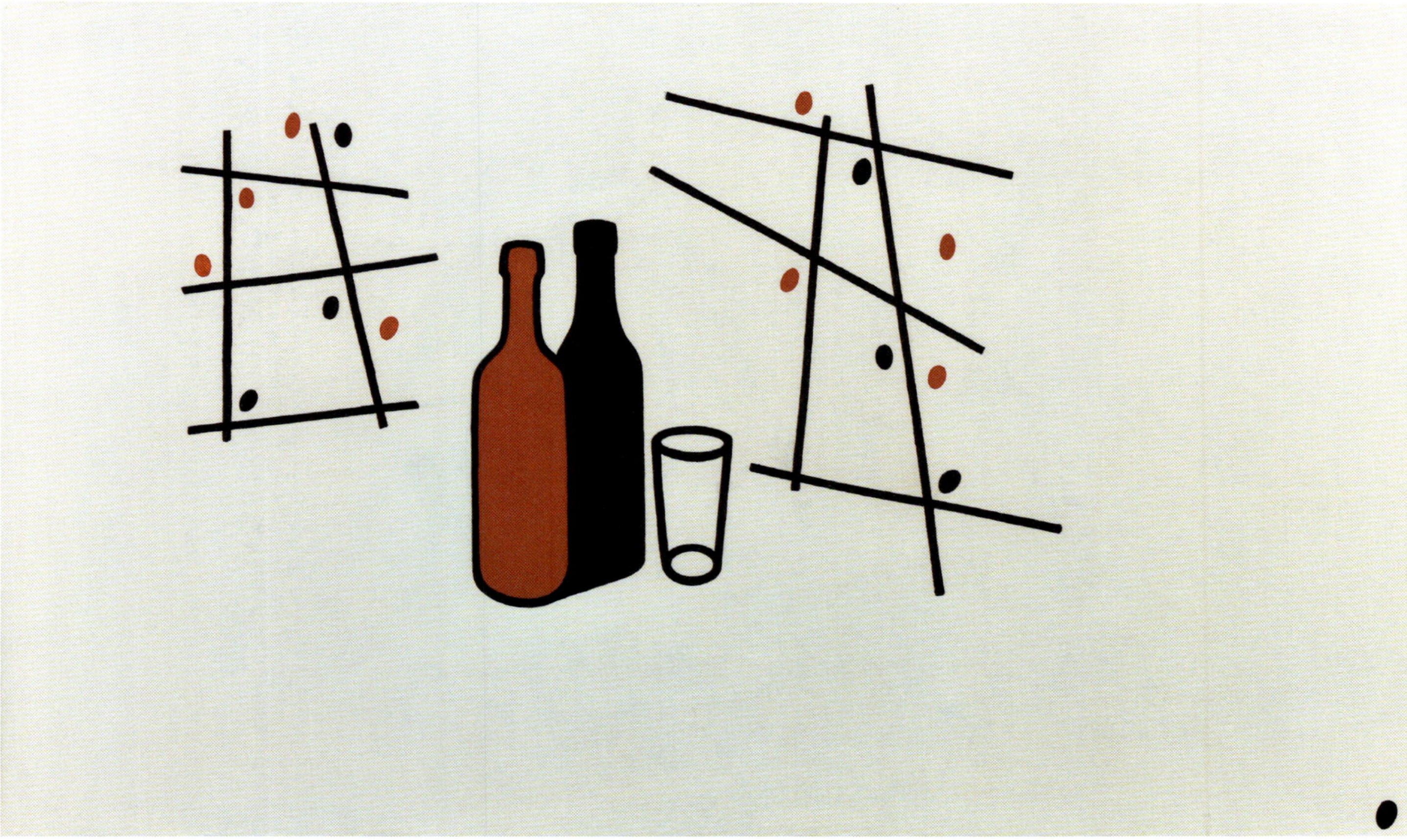

Patrick Caulfield

Red, White and Black Still Life, 1966/1984
Acrylic on canvas laid down on board
91.4 × 152.4 cm

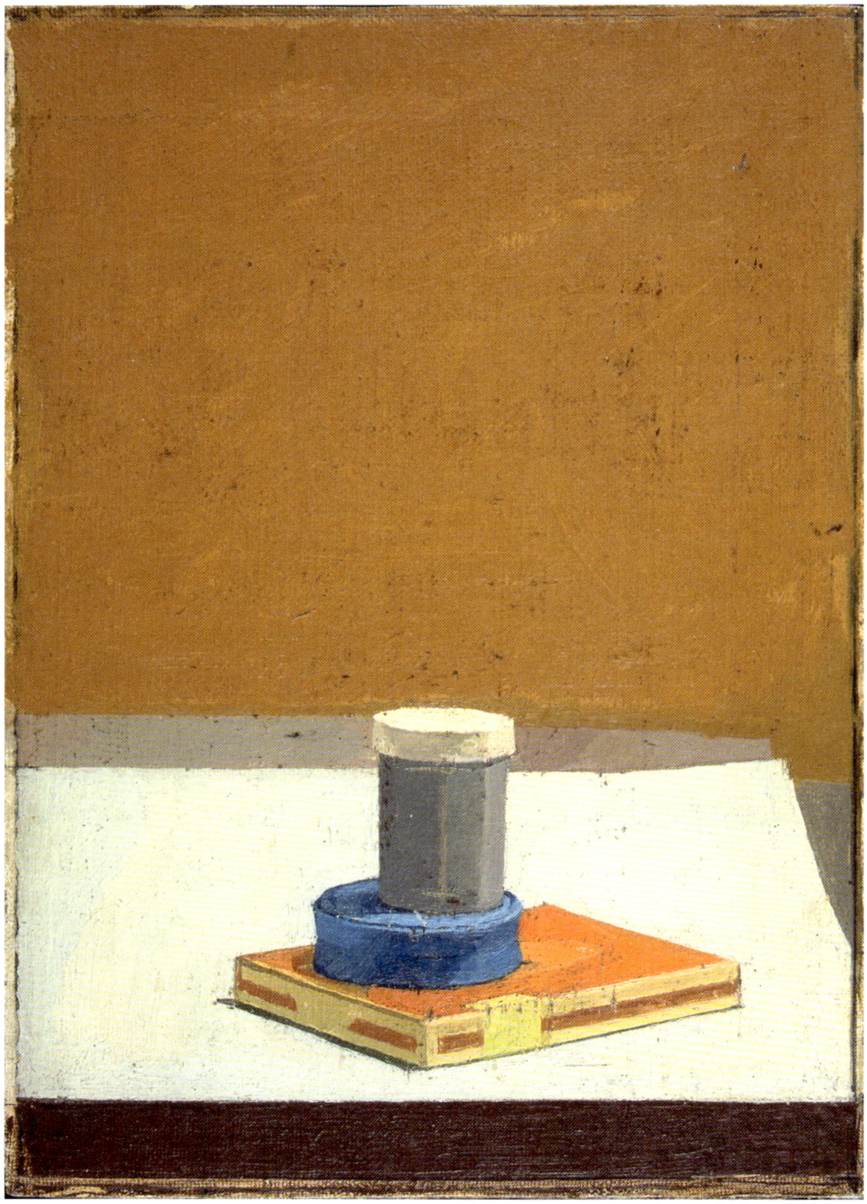

Euan Uglow

Polygons, c. 1970
Oil on canvas on board
21 × 15 cm

Private collection

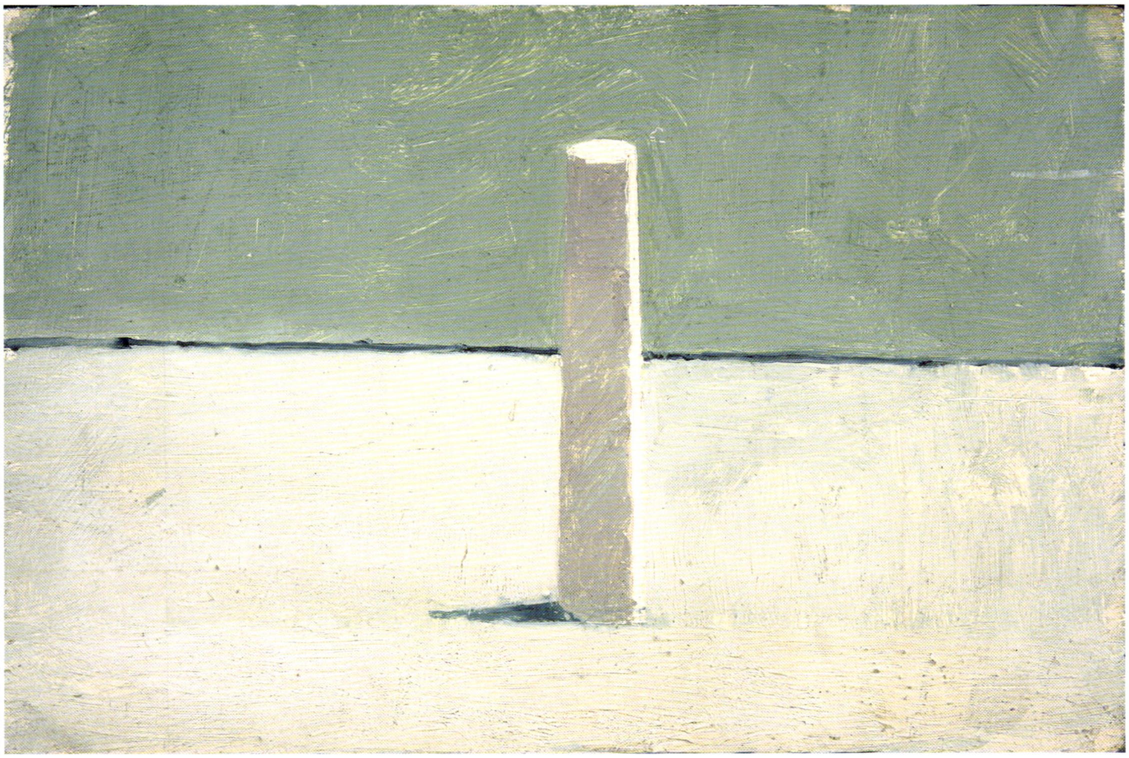

Euan Uglow

Obelisk, c. 1970
Oil on canvas
21 × 15 cm

Private collection

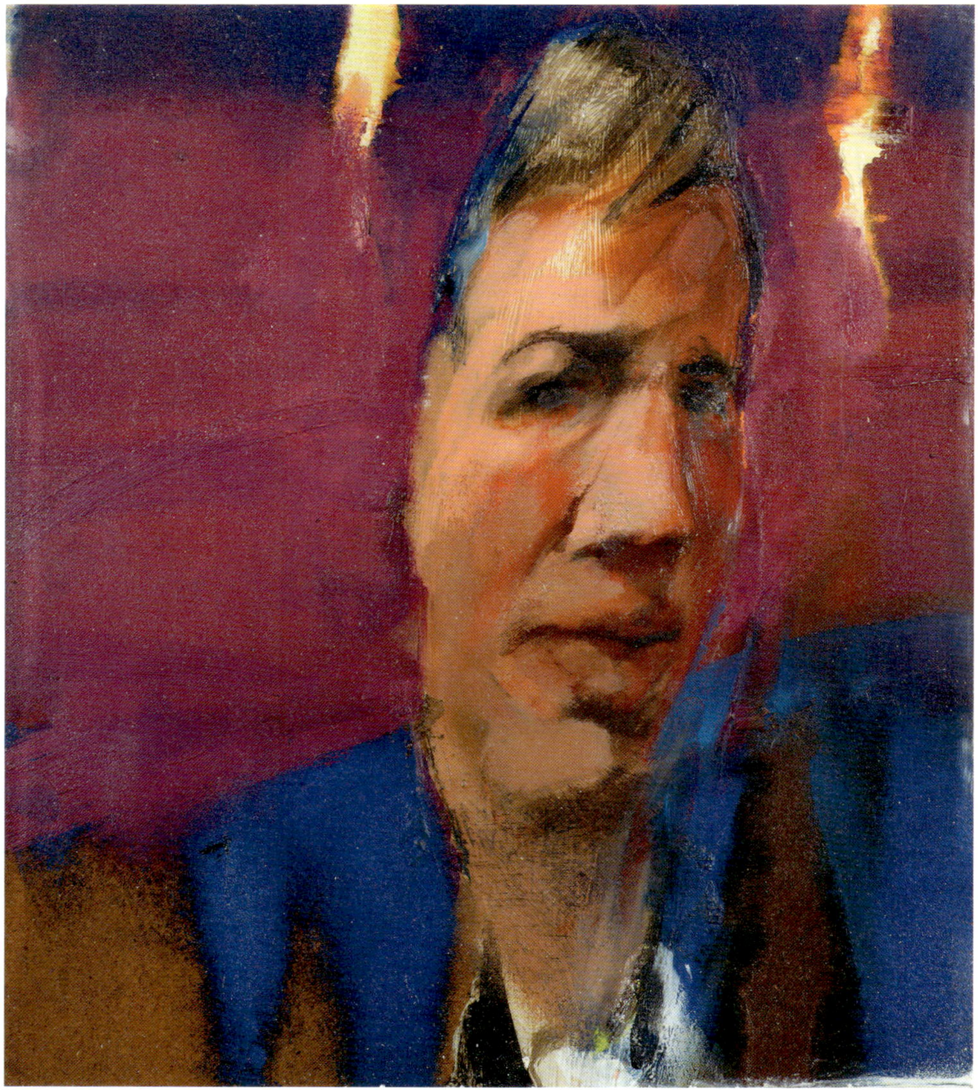

Michael Andrews

Craigie Aitchison (Study for Good and Bad at Games), 1967
Oil on board
24.9 × 21.6 cm

Private collection, courtesy of Susannah Pollen Ltd.

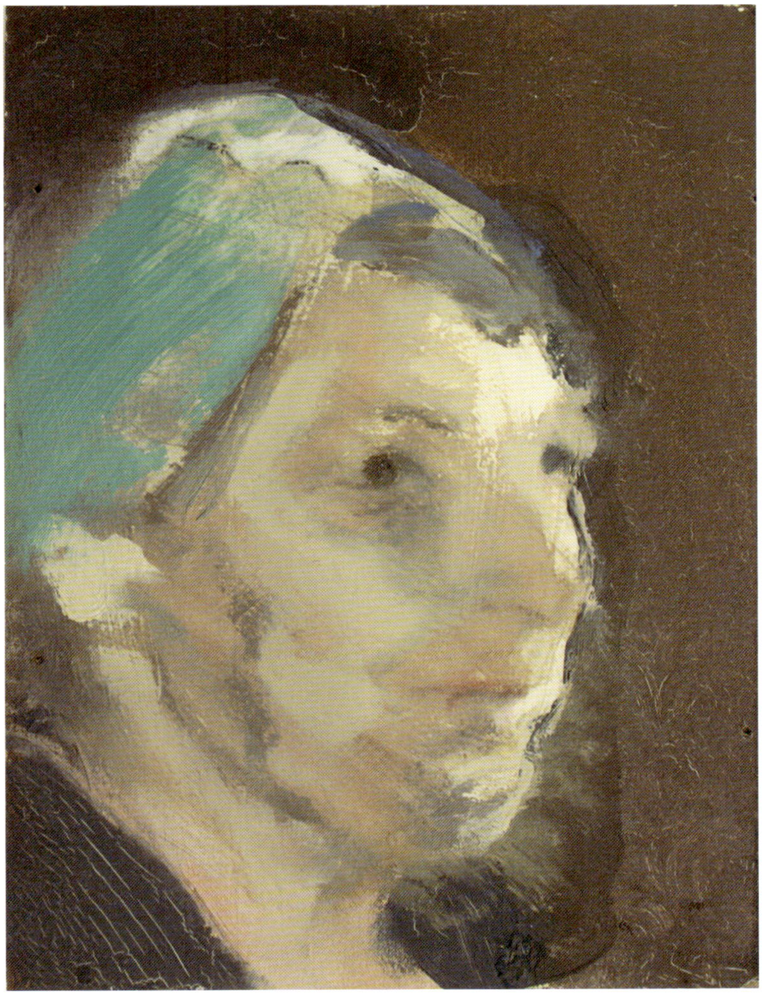

Michael Andrews

Study of a Head with a Green Turban, 1967
Oil on board
21.5 × 16.5 cm

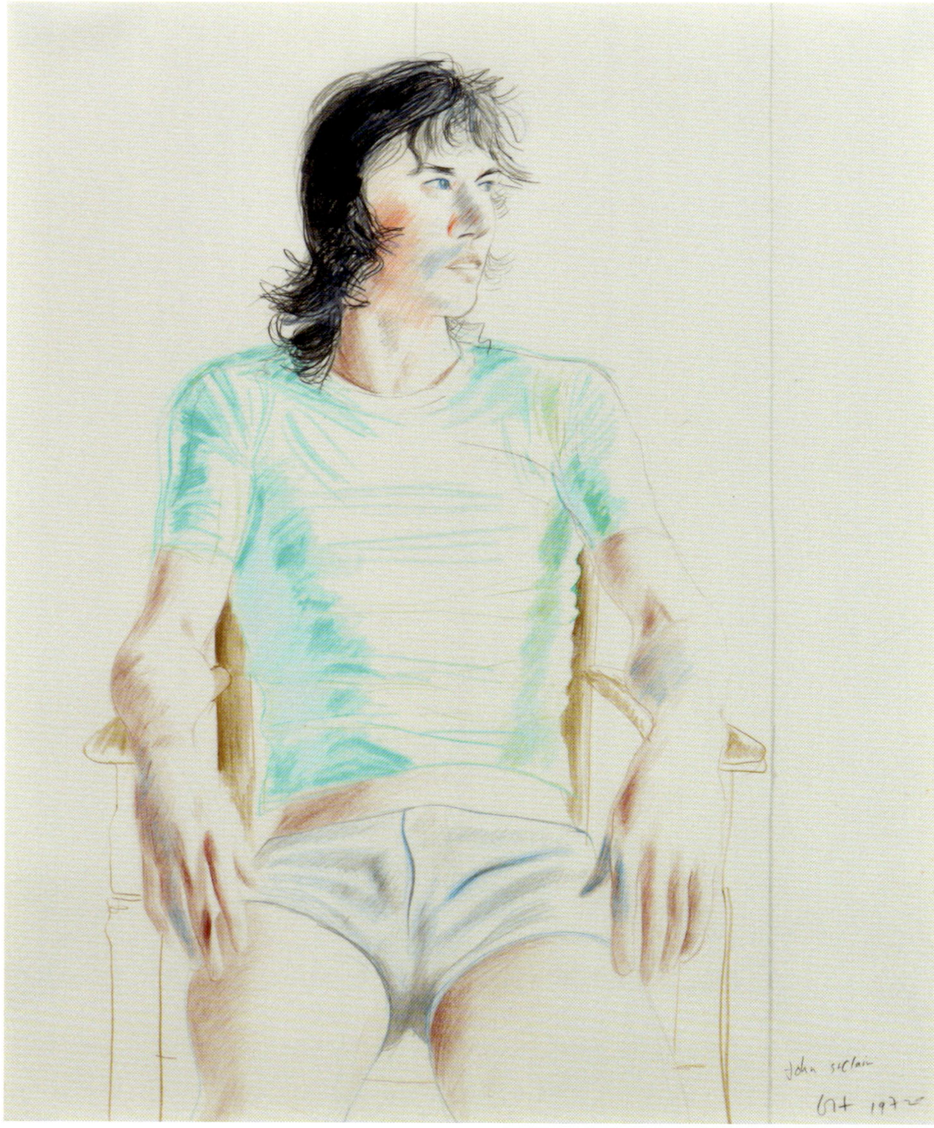

David Hockney

John St. Clair, 1972
Coloured crayon and graphite on paper
43.2 × 35.6 cm

Private collection

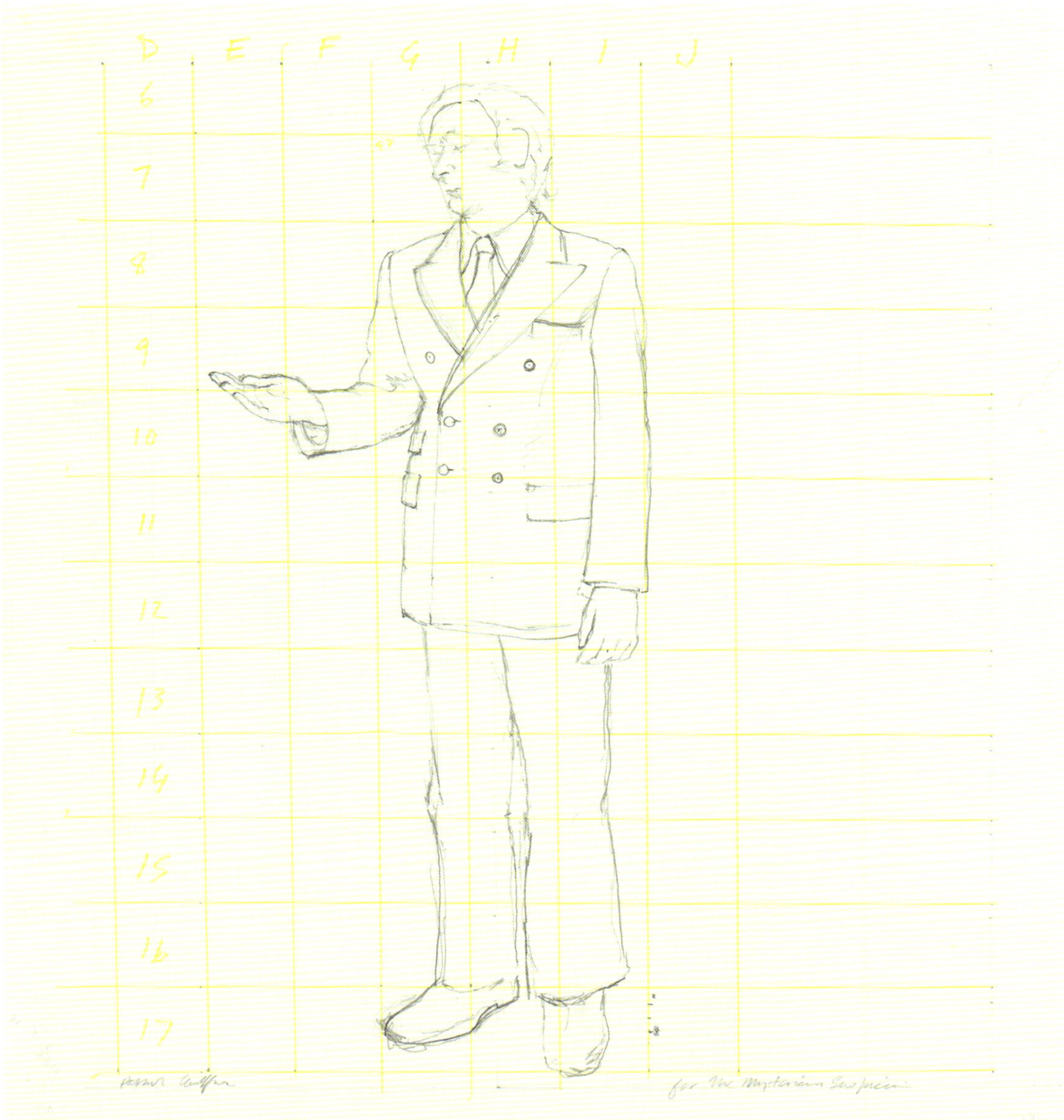

Patrick Caulfield

Study for 'The Mysterious Suspicion: After Magritte', c. 1974
Pencil and pen on paper
50.5 × 46 cm

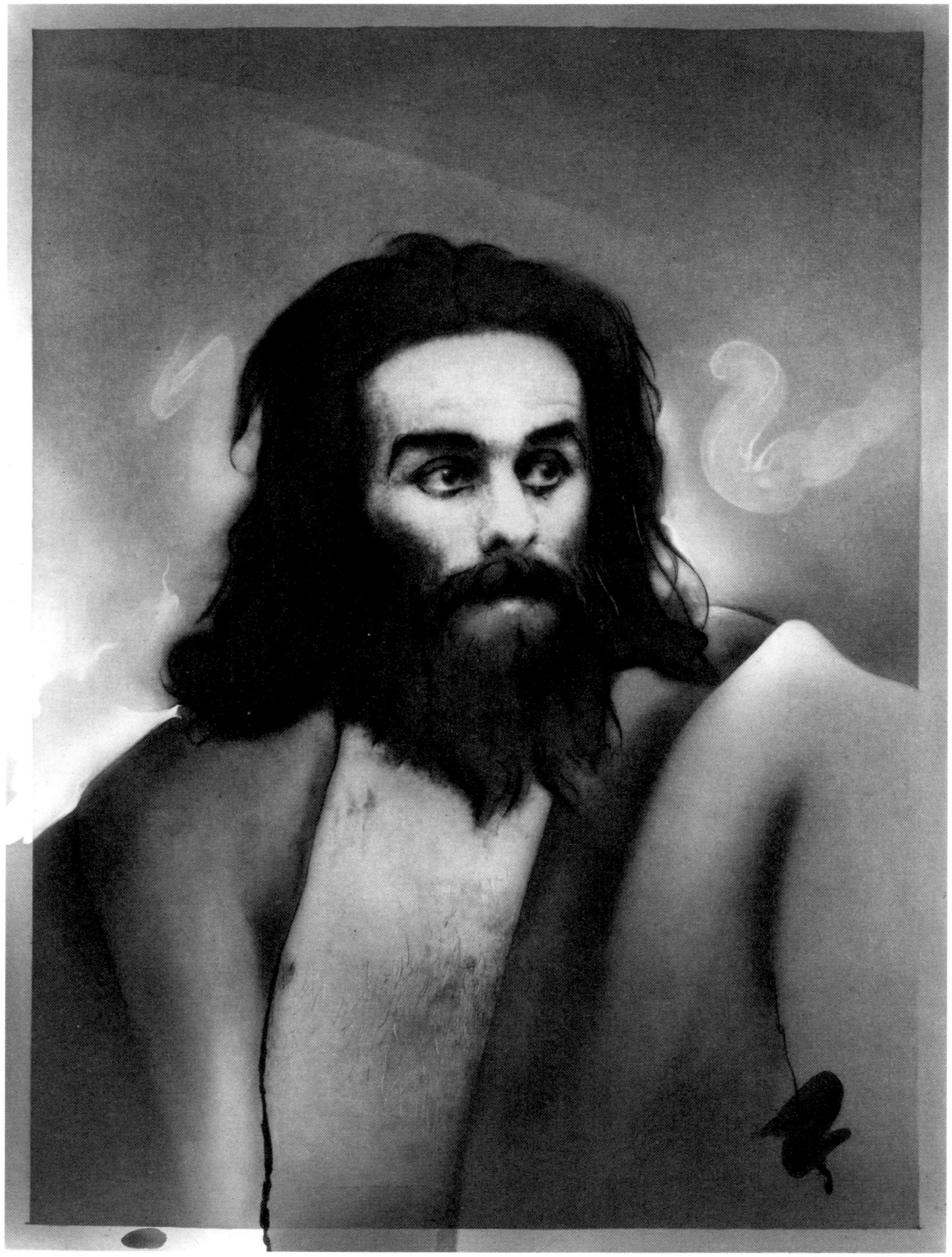

Richard Hamilton

Finn MacCool, 1983
Framed heliogravure, lift ground and spit-bite aquatint, engraving and burnisher on Rives paper, 76 × 56 cm

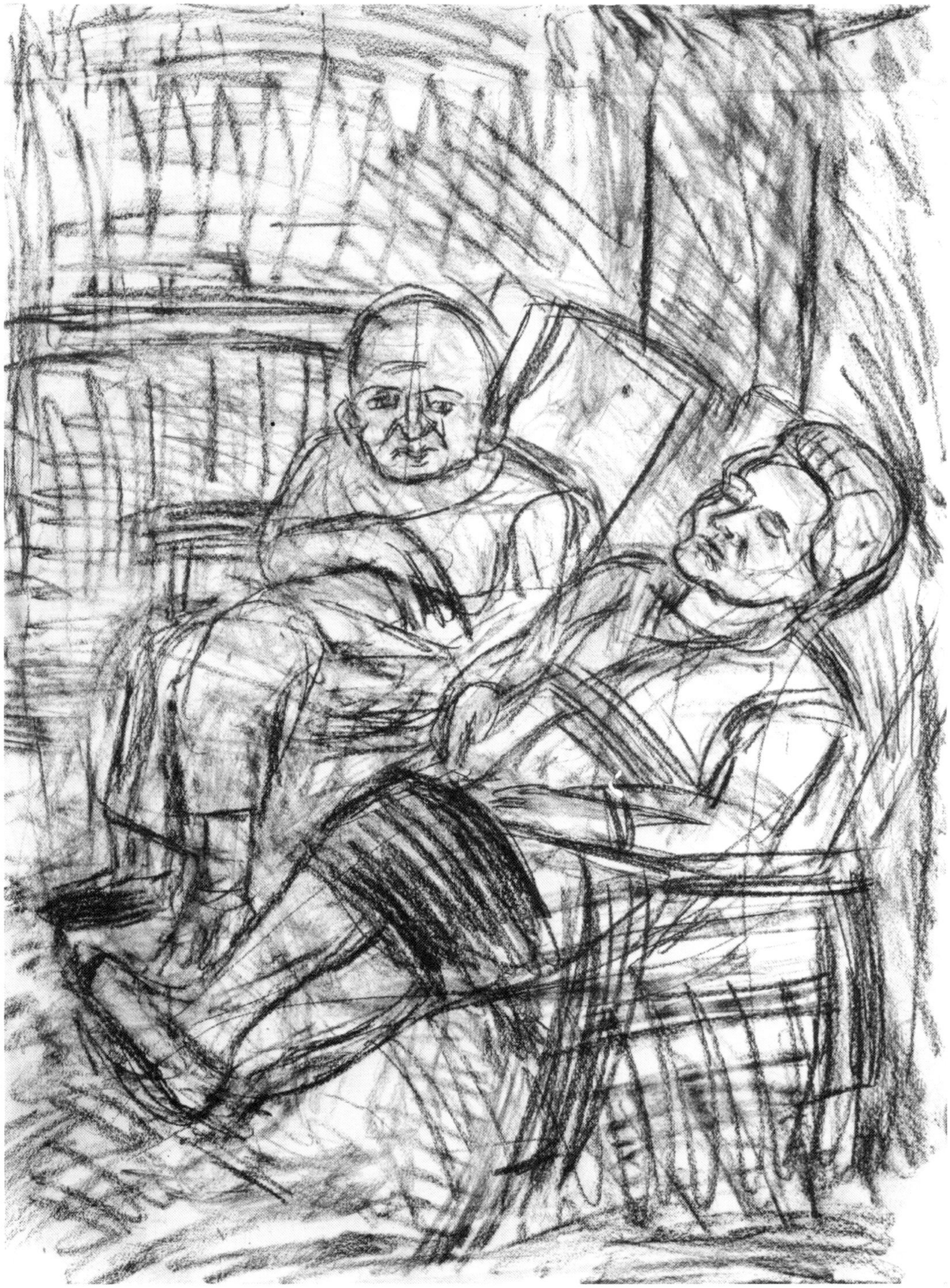

Leon Kossoff

Two Seated Figures II, 1980
Charcoal on paper
79.4 × 56.5 cm

Private collection

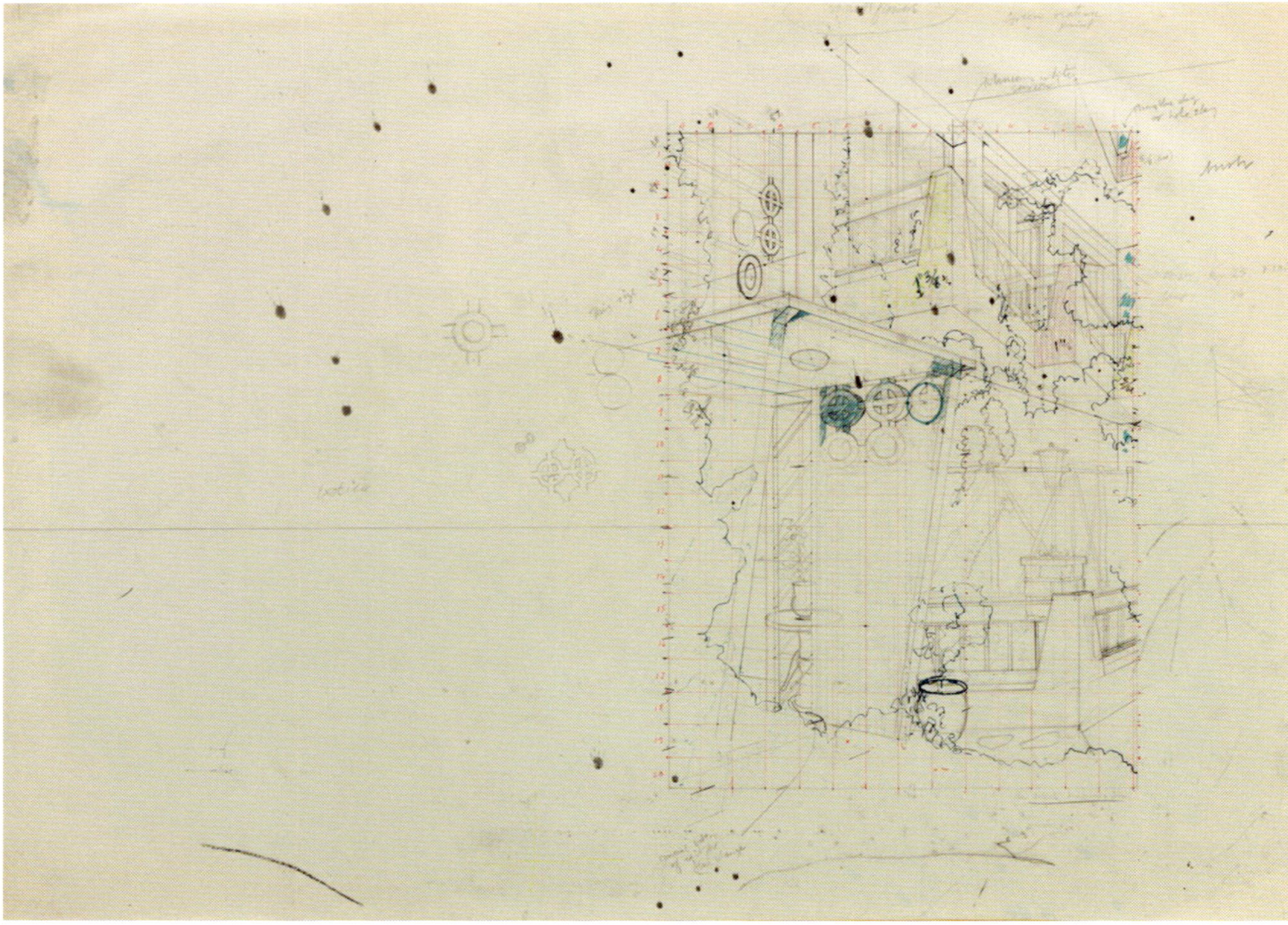

Patrick Caulfield

Study for 'Entrance', 1975
Graphite, rollerball, and coloured pen on paper
56 × 76 cm

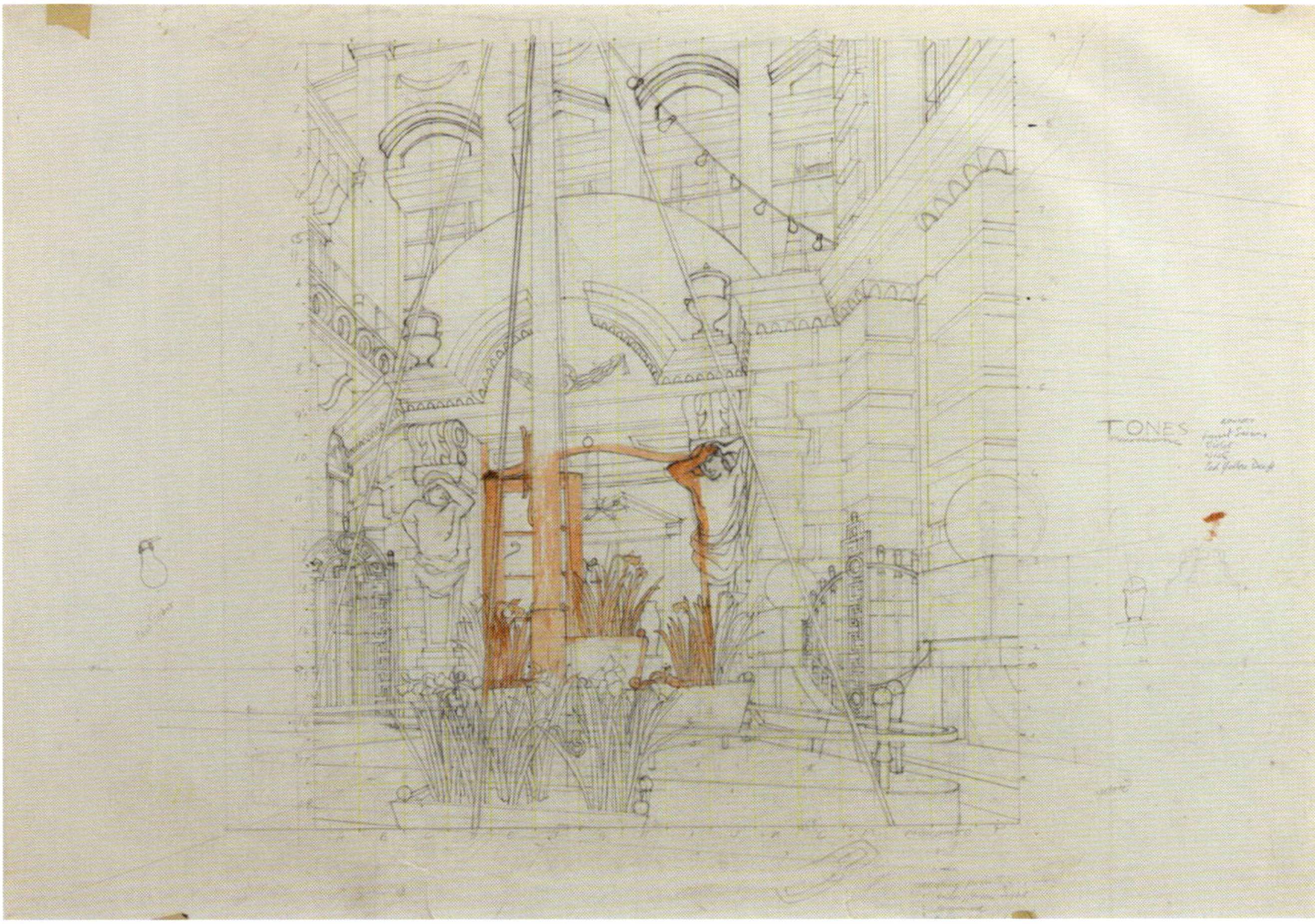

Patrick Caulfield

Study for 'Forecourt', 1975
Graphite, rollerball, and watercolour on paper
56 × 76 cm

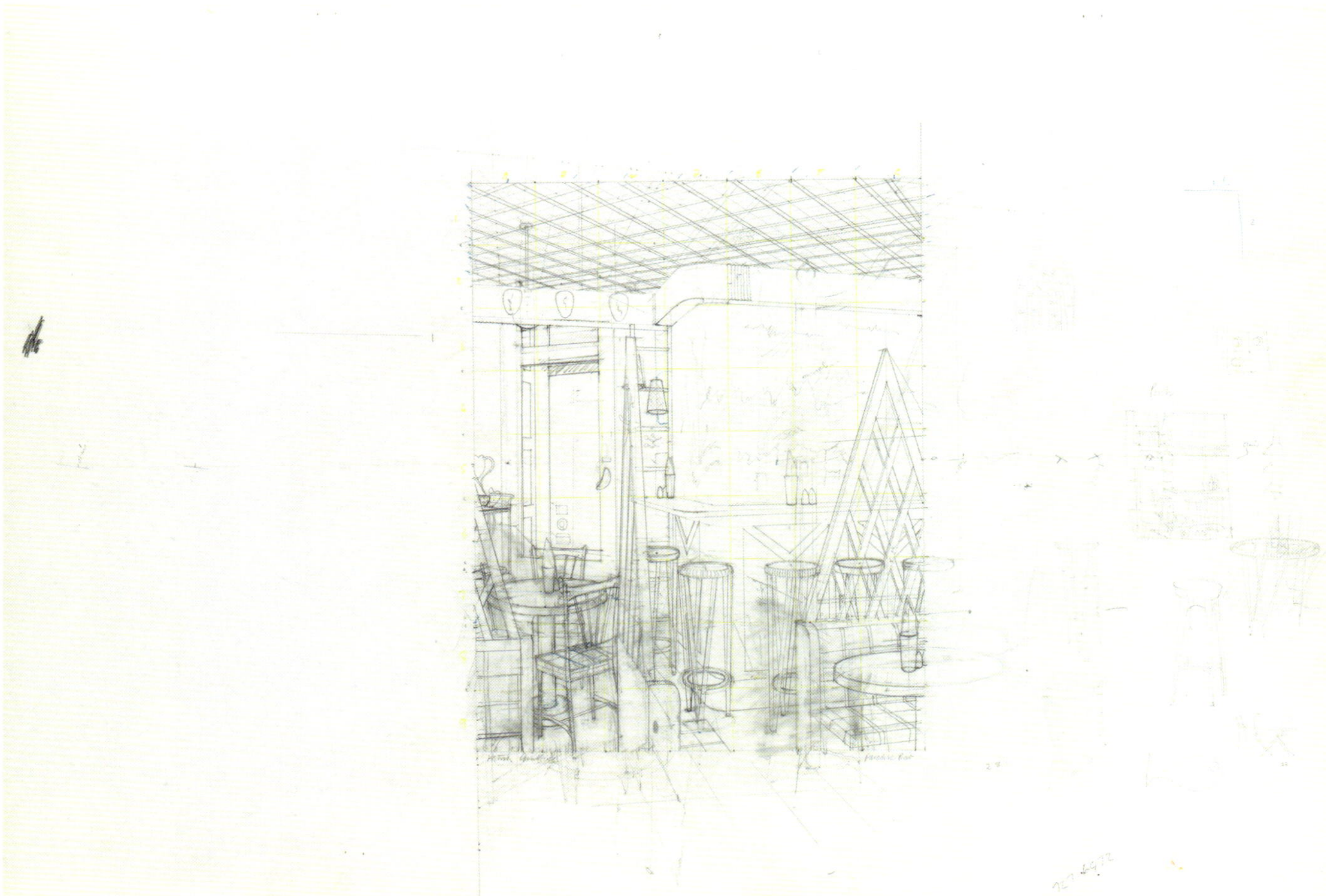

Patrick Caulfield

Study for 'Paradise Bar', c. 1974
Pencil and pen on card
54.5 × 80 cm

Painting Inside Out

Tom Hunt

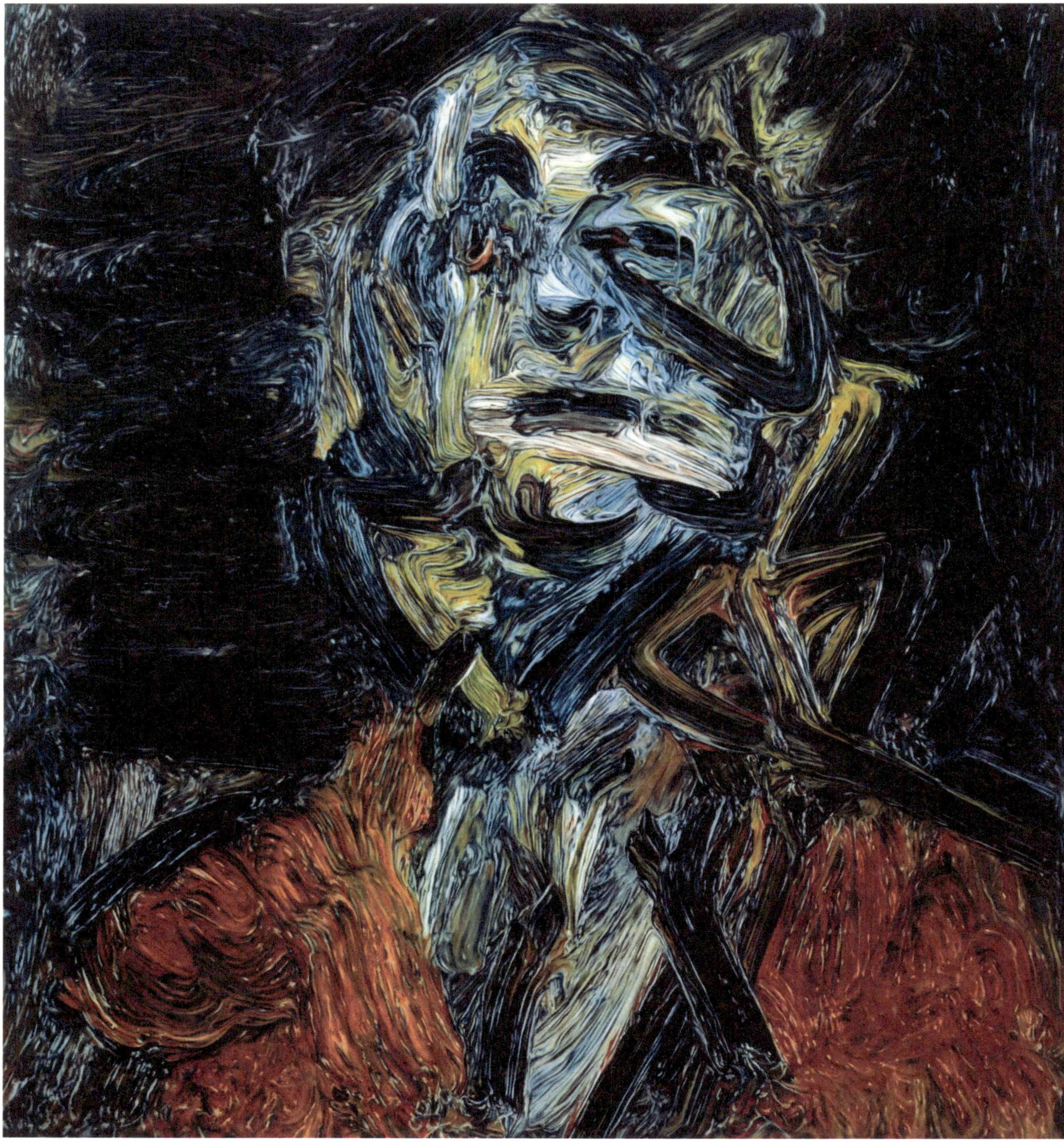

[1] Matt Price, ed., *Vitamin P2* (London, 2011).

[2] Barry Schwabsky, ed., *Vitamin P* (London, 2002).

[3] Damien Hirst, *Corpus. Drawings 1981–2006* (New York, 2006), pp. 34–35.

Given the recent deaths of Freud and Hamilton, there is poignancy in the timing of *The Mystery of Appearance*. Yet the ongoing relevance of these ten artists is evident from the impact their work continues to make, often in unexpected ways, on a generation of international artists. *Vitamin P2,* a large volume recently published by Phaidon, introduces 115 emerging artists, considered by the book's contributing writers and curators to be among the most exciting new voices in the field.[1] *Vitamin P* was published in 2002 with the same aim.[2] All of these artists—some 229—are linked by their primary medium: paint. While none of those in this exhibition is featured, their attitudes, whether in the handling of paint, the approach to subject matter, or the combination of the abstract with the figurative, is suggested across the pages of both books.

One might recall Freud in the stark nakedness and domestic surrealism of Ellen Altfest's paintings, while Dana Schutz's use of colour is reminiscent of early Hockney. Elsewhere, Varda Civano's corporeal surfaces bring to mind Kossoff, just as a Cecily Brown seems to occupy a space between de Kooning and Auerbach, and Adrian Ghenie's sinister tableaux appear indubitably after-Bacon. The fusion of media, art, and politics in Wilhelm Sasnal can perhaps be traced to Hamilton, and the veiled light and low-flying plane perspective in Dirk Skreber's scenes evoke an atmosphere we have encountered in Andrews' Lights series, while Zhang Enli observes figures and objects in isolation with a similar exacting purity as Uglow.

The emphasis on a formal rather than social reading of the work above and in the discussion below is based on a desire to investigate this relationship between the appearing and the appearance of a painting. While Catherine Lampert's essay draws on her friendship with the artists to construct a vivid sense of their histories and the context of their emergence, this essay proposes fresh trajectories against the grain of generational or categorical groupings and focuses instead on the canvas.

Furthermore, despite their often discussed admiration for Rembrandt, Poussin, Velázquez, et al, the artists in *The Mystery of Appearance* are wary of simplistic attributions of influence. In turn, we should be mindful of insisting connections in the other direction. Partly there is a danger of relegating the work of the older generation to a cultural artefact, but also because the works, which have been produced over careers of fifty and sixty years, are remarkably diverse. But for his inimitable eye, it would be hard to connect the draughtsman in Freud's schematic early portraits with the moulder of his late nudes.

Equally, it can seem a long way from Caulfield to Kossoff, from Bacon to Uglow, Freud to Hamilton, and suggestions of further links cannot be categorised by a generational, national or stylistic yardstick. In many ways the aim of the exhibition is to show how unrestricted the influence of these artists appears to be, one that is not confined to parochial, vaguely pejorative terms like "London School" or "modernist realism," nor necessarily even to painting.

For example, consider the play of influence between a painter and an artist whose best known work is three-dimensional. The former is known for his visions of the tormented human soul and the latter for ironised interpretations of existential dread embodied in dead animals. In one, the spectre of death hovers immovably and in the other it is a cold, hard fact. Both set these scenes of being and nothingness within cages. For Bacon, they are metaphors for the imprisoned self locked in and isolated from comfort, while Damien Hirst's formaldehyde tanks represent an apparatus for optimum viewing. The tension in Hirst's exploration of Bacon's thematic comes from its three-dimensional literalisation. He describes "the horror" in Bacon's painting as "biological," "like touching something," and admires the process involved in achieving this effect: "Painting's got a better process of time [than photography] . . . To work and work and work like that, eventually only to create a glimpse of something, is a great thing to do."[3]

Opposite: Glenn Brown, *The Day the World Turned Auerbach,* 1991.

[4] Michael Andrews, "Notes and Preoccupations," *X: A Quarterly Review,* Volume One, no. 2, March 1960.

[5] Peter Doig, "Peter Doig and Chris Ofili in Conversation," *Peter Doig,* ex. cat., Tate (London, 2008), p. 121.

[6] Francis Bacon, Sylvester interviews, (London, 1980).

Painting as mystery

In many ways, the blizzard of colour and nocturnal appearances in Peter Doig's paintings suggest a more straightforward formal connection, both to Bacon but also to Andrews. Key to this might be their expansion of a world implied by a photographic source. There seems to be a particular meeting point between Andrews and Doig in works like *Deer Park,* 1962, and *Gasthof Zur Muldentalsperre,* 2000–02; *The Sun Reflected in the River,* 1977, and *Pelican Island,* 2006; *The Thames at Low Tide,* 1994–95, and *Jetty,* 1994. In these paintings the viewer is presented with habitable environments, and yet in each they are visions that feel closer to the field of the subconscious than grounded reality. Through the interplay of abstract washes of colour and concrete, recognisably human figures and man-made objects, these works question the nature of realism and offer what Andrews describes as "a palpable presence of apparent reality,"[4] and Doig characterises as ". . . searching for a way to make pure painting. Painting should evolve into a type of abstraction; it should slowly dissipate into something else through time, through working, seeing things through."[5]

There is an enigmatic current in these artists' work and in the context of this exhibition an intriguing comparison between three visions of a single figure emerging from, or in the case of the Bacon, disappearing into, curtains and darkness. Bacon's *Study from the Human Body,* 1949, Andrews' *Portrait of Tim Behrens,* 1962, and Doig's *Untitled (Jungle Painting),* 2007, each "catch" both the metaphor and the literal representation of "the mystery of appearance within the mystery of the making."[6] These are exceptionally flat, frontal paintings with no discernible depth of field for the viewer to anchor themselves, yet their subject is transition. They are about a figure moving between spaces, between this position here and that position there. This paradox of a space that we are required to read into the picture but cannot see is central to their subversion of verisimilitude.

Below left: Francis Bacon, *Study from the Human Body,* 1949. National Gallery of Victoria, Melbourne.

Below right: Michael Andrews, *Portrait of Tim Behrens,* 1962. Museo Thyssen-Bornemisza, Madrid.

Opposite: Peter Doig, *Untitled (Jungle Painting),* 2007.

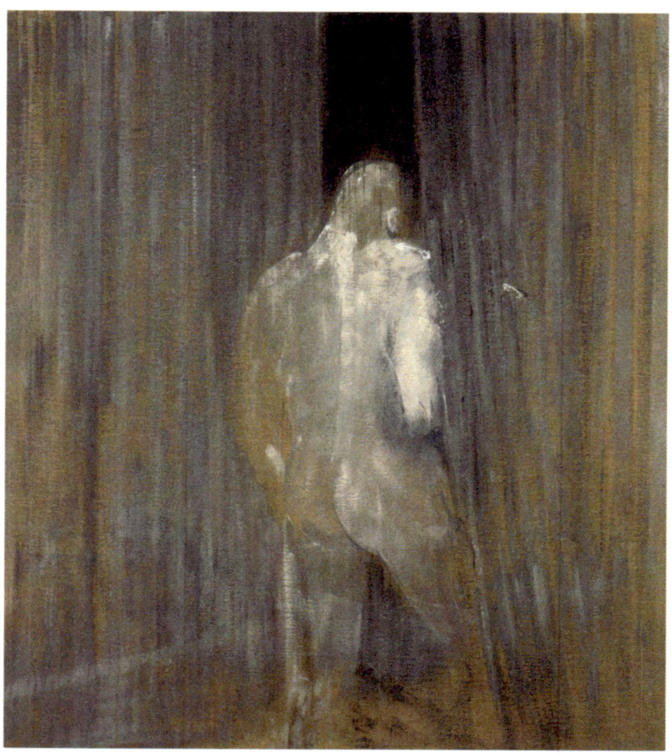

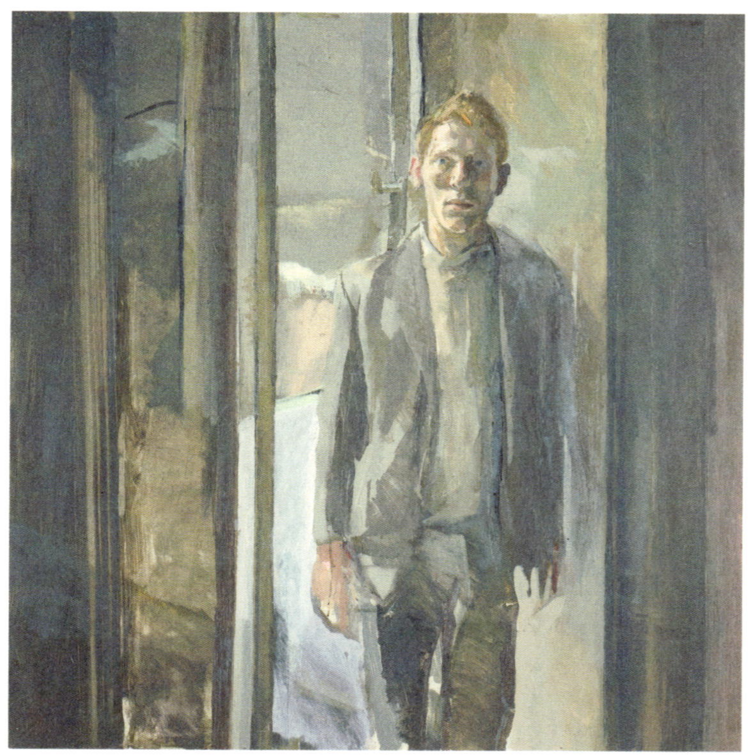

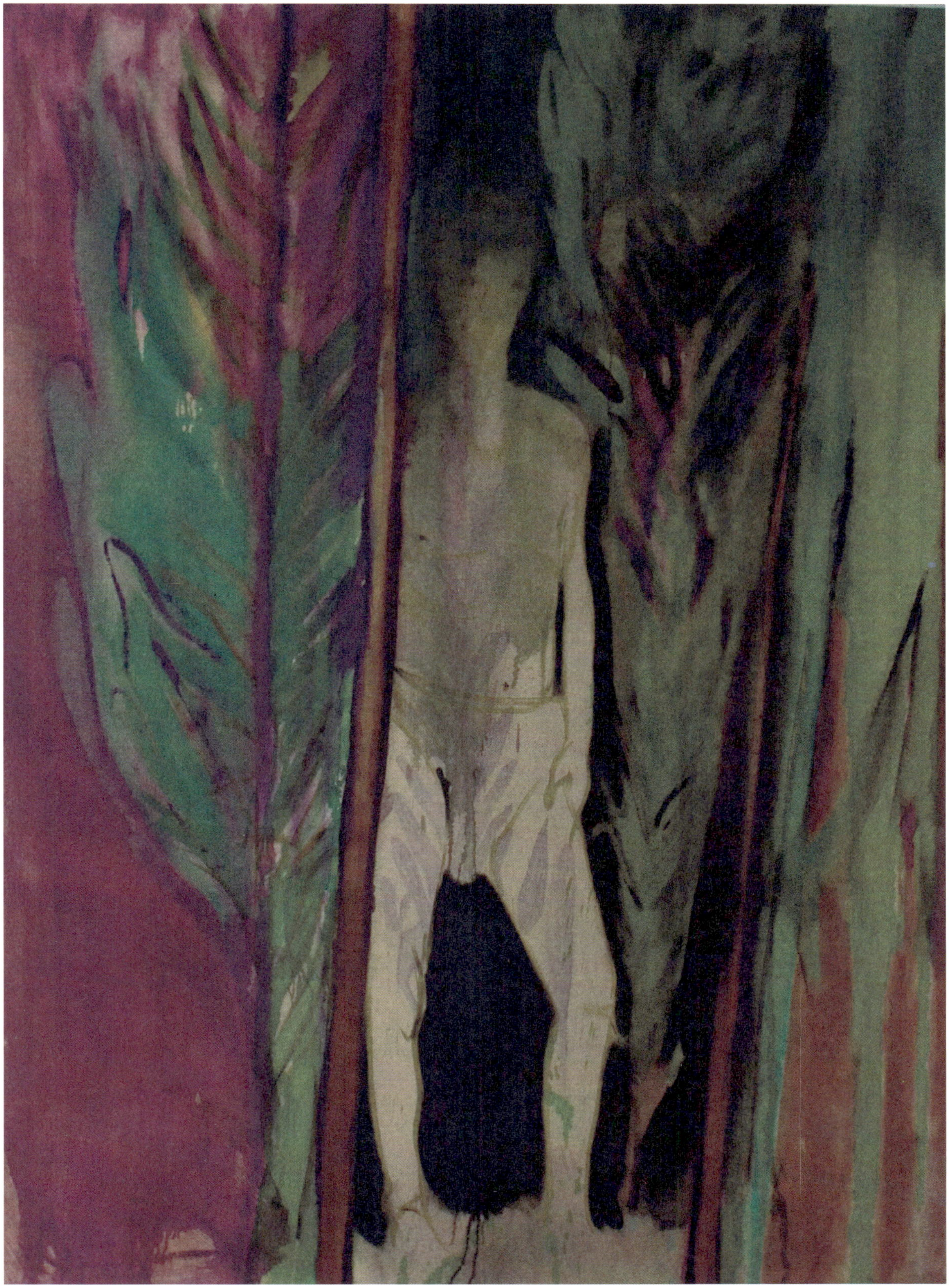

[7] Michael Andrews, in conversation with William Feaver 1993, quoted William Feaver, *Michael Andrews: The Thames Paintings* (London, 1998), p. 22.

[8] Euan Uglow, "Snatches of Conversation," reproduced in *Euan Uglow* (London, 2003), p. 7, courtesy of *The Artist's and Illustrator's Magazine*, based on three conversations between Euan Uglow and Andrew Lambirth.

[9] Colin St. John Wilson alludes to Coldstream's "contention that he was making a discovery not an invention," Colin St. John Wilson, *The Artist at Work: On the Working Methods of William Coldstream and Michael Andrews* (Surrey, 1999), p. 33.

[10] Michel Leiris, *Francis Bacon, face et profil* (Paris, Munich, and Milan, 1983), trans. *John Weightman as Francis Bacon: Full Face and in Profile* (Oxford, 1983).

[11] Jake Auerbach, *Lucian Freud: Portraits*, Jake Auerbach Films Ltd, 2005.

There are two appearances forming in these paintings: one is the figure and the other is the painting. Loose brushwork, areas of unpainted canvas, portions of colour that without the solitary upright figure would appear abstract and obscurely seductive. As emphasized by Andrews' note to self, these are works about the arrival of an artwork, the making and the realising of itself as a thing in and of itself. "Must actually find excitement in the flow of time—not in its important moments. Accept the flow and flux of things through the mind, the continual change, disappearance, and reappearance. Accept it, let it happen."[7]

Painting as process

Using different and changing methods, the artists in *The Mystery of Appearance* strive towards an ending that is perpetually put-off. When Uglow was asked why he left the measuring marks on the "final" canvas, he replied, "how can you lose those marks when the next second you may need them. I don't really finish a painting, it stops."[8] Likewise Coldstream left in his notations as though the inner architecture of the picture could have gone on being constructed for years.

Many of them return to the same subject—a sitter, a postcard, a scene—on numerous occasions, and in Andrews, Auerbach, Coldstream, Freud, and Kossoff this returning and revising also takes place upon the same canvas which over time becomes a depository of gestures, a palimpsest. The experience of sitting for them over many months for a single picture is often remarked upon, and Catherine Lampert herself has sat for Auerbach once a week for the last thirty-three years. Coldstream spoke of the resulting paintings as discoveries rather than inventions[9] while Freud demands "an equivalence" between his painting and his subject. The attention he lavishes on both is not directed towards achieving a photo-realist product but a "fragment of nature"[10] based as much on the intelligible as well as the observable. There is a moment in Jake Auerbach's film portrait when the Duchess of Devonshire describes thinking how much more alike she looks to her portrait, *Woman in a White Shirt*, 1956–57, than when it was painted fifty years before.[11]

The iterative quality in many of Hamilton's works is premised on deliberately altering the complexion of an original image and then creating a sequence of further variations from this second-type derivative. Each of

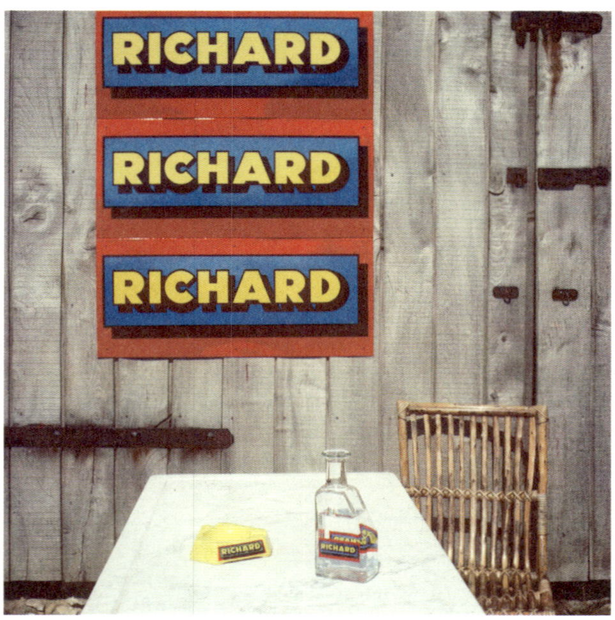

Below left: Richard Hamilton, *Sign*, 1975, *Carafe*, 1978, and *Ashtray*, 1979.

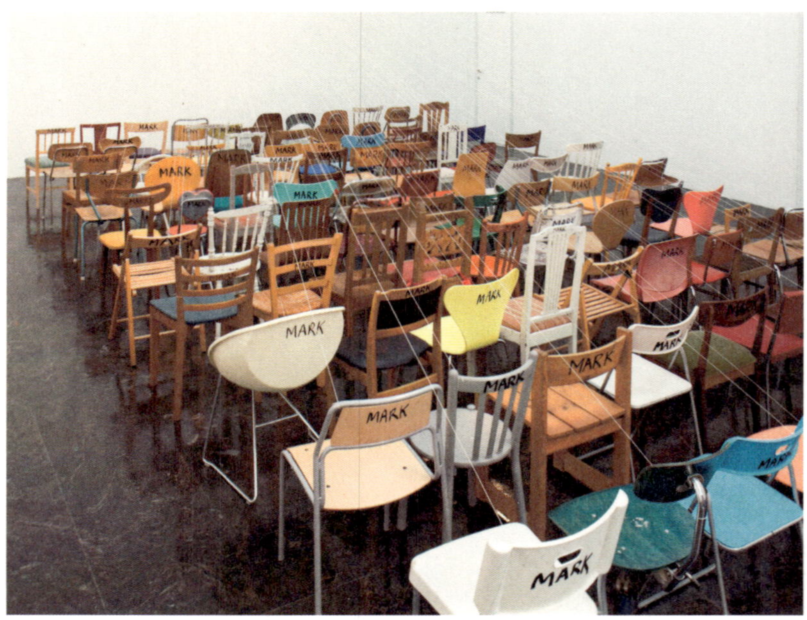

Below right: Mark Wallinger, *According to Mark*, 2010.

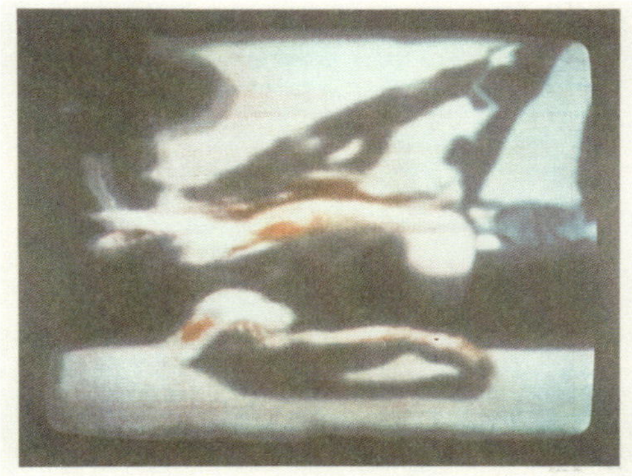

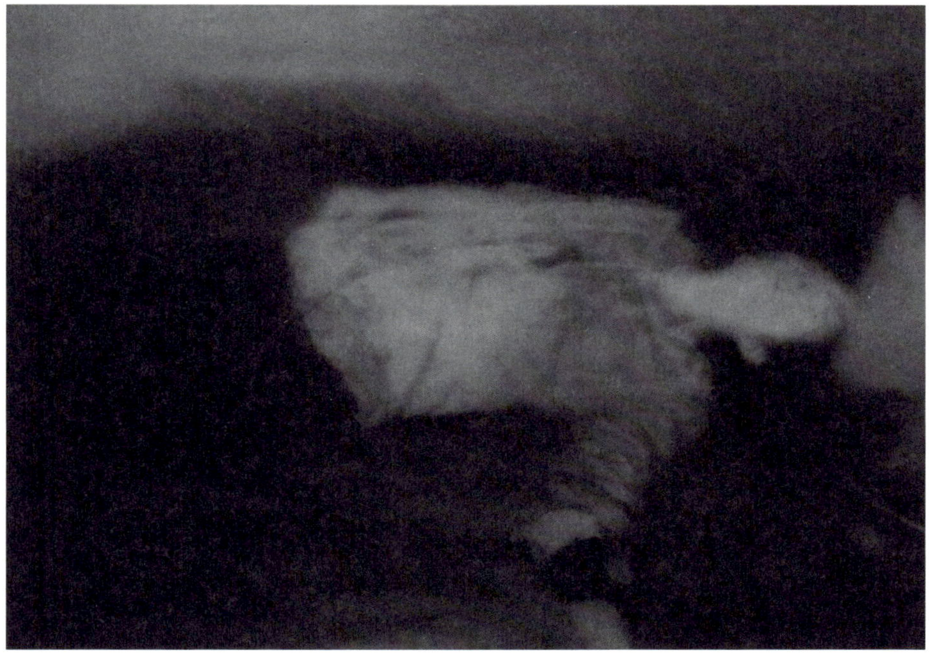

[12] For further discussion of the relationship between Hamilton and Richter, see Catherine Lampert and Lynda Morris, *Pictures of Pictures*, Arnolfini/Norwich Gallery, 1999.

Above left: Richard Hamilton, *Kent State,* 1970. Tate, London.

Above right: Gerhard Richter, *Man Shot Down 2,* 1988. Museum of Modern Art, New York.

The Solomon R. Guggenheim, 1965-66, pictures is differentiated solely by colour, which runs from white to Neapolitan to metalflake and gold, and the re-processing of *I'm dreaming of a white Christmas,* 1967-68, turns it into *I'm dreaming of a black Christmas,* 1971, and curiously returns it to a closer approximation of the original.

In *Interior I,* 1964, which is based on a black and white publicity still, a woman stands in an apartment surrounded by a desk and some lamps. Hamilton has added paint to accentuate certain elements and introduced others by invention. In version *II,* the desk has gone and a painting within the painting that appeared in version *I* has been replaced by a colour television screen. This game of ciphers and substitutes plays throughout Hamilton's oeuvre. Of a younger generation, Mark Wallinger's work seems to share particular traits, certainly a political bent, but also a knowing humour. In *Self-Portrait (Tahoma),* 2008, *Mark,* 2010, and *According to Mark,* 2010, there appears to be a direct continuation of Hamilton's witty play on identity politics in works like *Sign,* 1975, *Carafe,* 1978, and *Ashtray,* 1979.

Usually understood as a cerebral dissector of political and social mores, Hamilton's work is also often tender. He shares this quality with Gerhard Richter, whose painted games of hide and seek have yielded to something more open and affecting. The artists are known to have admired each other and at the beginning of their careers, despite their infatuation with paint, both looked to Duchamp as an avatar.[12]

Hamilton and Richter share the method of nurturing a painting from a photograph and there is considerable overlap in their subject matter over the years: nudes, flower paintings, seascapes, etc. These choices are clearly prompted by their mutual fascination with art historical traditions but most interesting is the similarity in the formal and emotional register of their approach. Hamilton's *Kent State,* 1970, shows the horizontal body of a Vietnam War demonstrator. The image is imprecise but unequivocal: this is the body of a dead man. Likewise from Richter's Baader-Meinhof series, *Man Shot Down I* and *2,* 1988, show a blurry figure, supine on the floor and positioned from right to left across the canvas. Again, he is clearly dead. The flat plane of the bodies and the outstretched arms in both works recall the

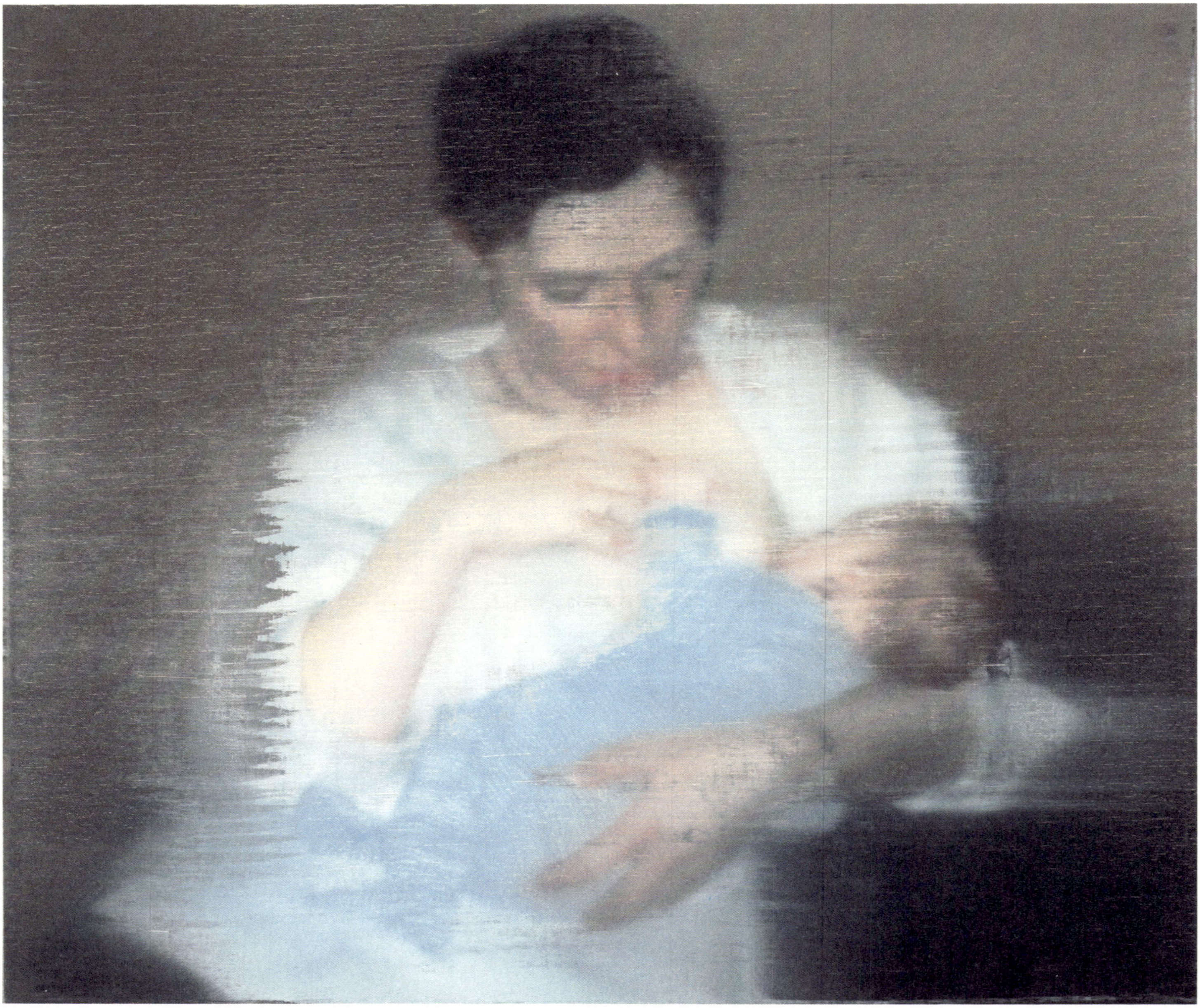

Above: Gerhard Richter, *S. with Child,* 1995. Hamburger Kunsthalle, Germany

Opposite: Per Kirkeby, *Erdbrben,* 1983. Carnegie Museum of Art, Pittsburgh.

[13] Al Alvarez, "Life with Kossoff," *Leon Kossoff: From the Early Years, 1957–1967* (New York, 2009), p. 12.

[14] Ibid., p. 11.

[15] Ibid.

extraordinarily intense *The Body of the Dead Christ in the Tomb,* 1520–22, by Holbein.

In their treatment of the most famous of all western pictorial genres, the mother and child, they again adopt similar techniques. Unusually, Hamilton's version from 1984–85 shows the pair standing up, happily posing for a camera. In *S. with Child,* 1995, Richter paints the mother cupping her baby in more conventional fashion, though rather than facing outwards or looking into its mother's eyes, this baby is turned in to the mother's breast. In both artists' accounts there is a sense of elemental intimacy enfolding the scene which must partly come from the warmth of the original photos but is fully achieved by the unfocused gauze which separates the viewer from the pair.

Painting as presence

Potential links between artists are also to be found on a haptic level, beyond questions of subject matter and directed at a picture's content. Not so much its meaning but literally what it is made of. Early in their careers Auerbach and Kossoff made famously heavy paintings, works weighed down by the sheer volume of paint piled on to them. Such is the mass of material that the image can sometimes break down into illegibility until the hook of a nose or the slopes of an eye emerge and you are able to put the face together from there. In an essay written about Kossoff's *Seated Woman No.2,* 1959, Al Alvarez describes how the painting "became a living presence . . . a presence that was somehow in flux,"[13] just as when looking at the painting "the figure emerged from the impasto."[14] This double effect, of on the one hand the paint seeming to "accrete, layer by layer, like a geological formation,"[15] and on the other, of a presence depicted within the painting, carved out and alive, is a lovely tautology inherent in Kossoff's best work. It represents the duality of geological and human time in his paintings and comes from his attention to Bomberg's quest for "the spirit in the mass."

The Danish "nature" painter Per Kirkeby noticed this in Kossoff, and spoke of there being "... something landslide like in them, even

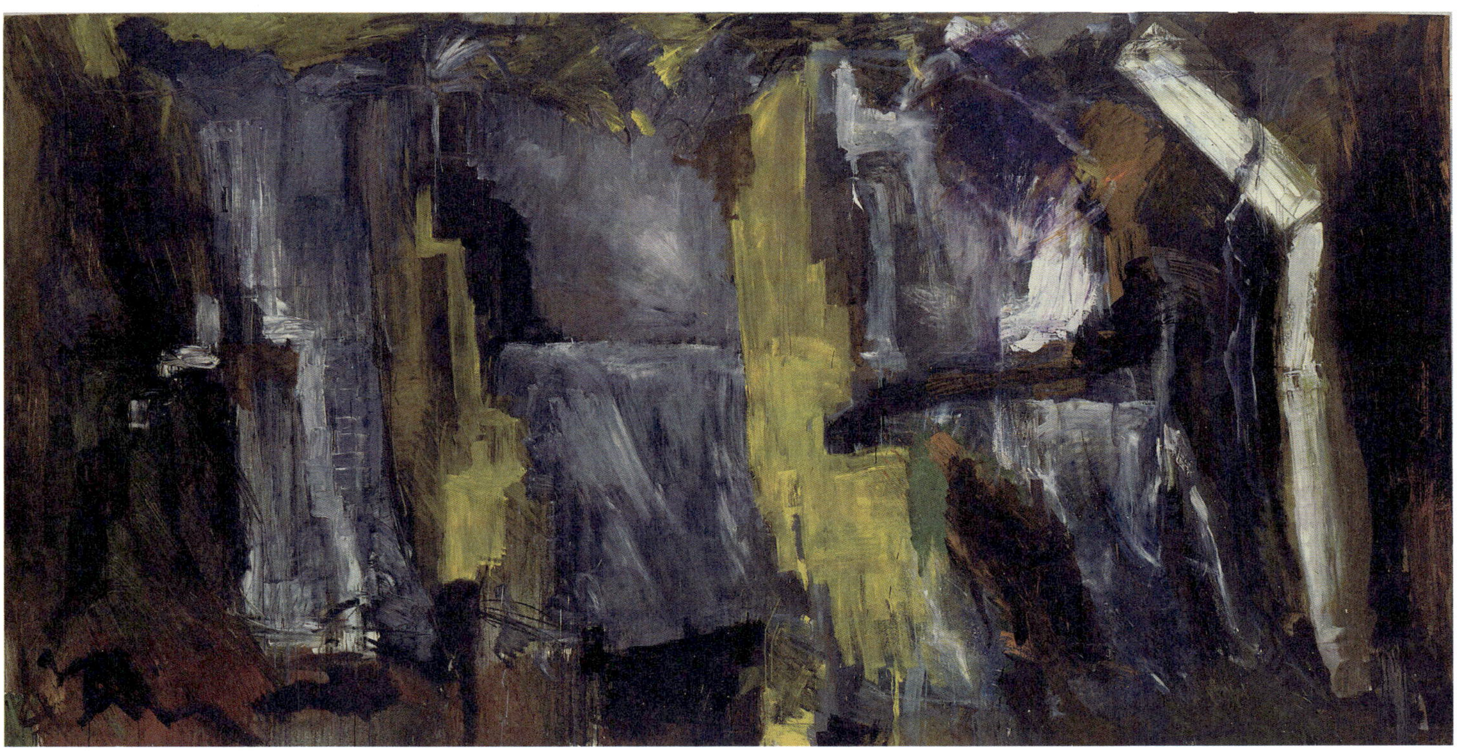

[16] Per Kirkeby, quoted in interview with Poul Erik Tøjner, "You can look at it and you have no choice but to go into it," *Leon Kossoff: Selected paintings: 1956–2000*, exh. cat., Louisiana Museum of Modern Art (Copenhagen, 2004), p. 10.

[17] Ibid., p. 11.

[18] Leon Kossoff, reply to a letter from John Berger, *The Shape of a Pocket.*

[19] Glenn Brown quoted in the *Independent*, February 2009 .

[20] Ibid.

[21] Brown quoted in Rochelle Steiner, "Interview with Glenn Brown," *Glenn Brown*, exh. cat., Serpentine (London, 2004), p. 98.

[22] Marco Livingstone, *David Hockney* (London, 1996), p. 56.

[23] Elizabeth Peyton in conversation with David Shapiro, "Talks with David Shapiro," theblowup.com.

[24] Livingstone, *Patrick Caulfield Paintings (London, 2005)*, p. 9.

the colour can be about to fall off. That's the universal feature of his portraits, despite their individuality; the painting drags something bigger along with it. Kossoff looks at the model, but the painting takes it over."[16]

Kirkeby's own paintings, largely abstract interpretations of the great outdoors, are similarly obsessed with slow-time, with matter, and what he sees in Kossoff as a liberation from intention; "the picture decides,"[17] he says. Kossoff catches this in his own formulation: "'Thereness' follows nothingness. It is impossible to premeditate."[18]

Glenn Brown's fastidious Auerbach "copies" are much further away in sensibility. Reproduced in a catalogue, Brown's *The Day The World Turned Auerbach,* 1991, could almost be mistaken for an Auerbach such is his control of paint, yet in the flesh one is instantly struck by the flatness of the surface and its virtuoso rather than expressive application.

The notion of inspiration is elusive but Brown speaks of the relationship his paintings have to Auerbachs, El Grecos, Rembrandts, and Fragonards as coming "from real life,"[19] ". . . Like a painter going out and painting the landscape and the buildings, these paintings that I use do already exist and they are part of my life."[20]

In the case of Auerbach, whose work Brown has returned to more than any other, this affinity is understood as wonder at the vitality of his paintings and their evidence of a physical encounter between artist and canvas: "To me, his work epitomises existentialism through his depiction of the isolated, tortured figure. His brush marks really grab the canvas."[21]

Painting as artifice

In many ways Caulfield and Hockney seem the most autobiographical painters in the exhibition. Their work is the least obviously realist but their subjects are based on experiences that expose the personalities of the artists in sincere and moving ways. Hockney has painted people he knows intimately just as Auerbach, Bacon, Freud, and Kossoff have done, but in his early work particularly, there is an immediacy to the images that is about desire in a way the others' pictures are not. Marco Livingstone identifies the equation of the visual to truth of feeling as a conceptual strategy: "In the shower pictures, the water is blatantly unreal but it corresponds to the way in which we experience a moment of gravity. Image is thus strongly conceptual in its basis: it arises from what we think we know rather than simply what we see."[22]

So too in Peyton's portraits of Pete Doherty, Jarvis Cocker, Catherine Deneuve and Francois Truffaut, et al. The brief, expressive lines, exaggerated colours and celebrity of the subjects coat these visions in fantasy. They are not authentic in the sense of objectively accurate but they, like Hockney's pictures from California, are images whose psychology is just as real. She is evidently attracted to the savvy guilelessness in Hockney's portraits. "I love that in the seventies, in the time of high dry conceptualism, he was doing portraits, and he was really rendering them. And he believed in it too." And why did he believe in it? "Because he believed in humanity, and humanism, and people—and he also looked fantastic. He was so aware of his image. He became a blonde pretty young, and had more fun, he just had a lot of glamour to him. And he paints things he loves."[23]

Caulfield's interiors and still lifes are similar in their heightening of the particular and their prioritising of the personal. The description of forms in *Coloured Still Life,* 1967, *Stained Glass Window,* 1967 and *Dining Recess*, 1972, like Gary Hume's Doors from the 1990s and *Yellow Window,* 2002, is so reduced as to verge on the abstract, yet their insistent literalism, despite this, lends them "a mysterious charge,"[24] prompted perhaps by latent associations of religion and friendship.

One is aware of the role of memory as the driving impetus behind the images but also as subject matter. There is something in them of the parlour game where you are presented with a tray full of objects—thimbles, scissors, nut

[25] Francis Bacon, Sylvester interviews (London, 1980).

crackers, napkin rings—which is then taken away and you have to recall as many of the items on the tray as you can. In *Red, White and Black Still Life,* 1966/1984, this is given a philosophical dimension. In its first incarnation there were two bottles, but as Catherine Lampert mentions, when Caulfield returned to it, the second bottle had merged into the first, becoming its shadow. The reduced circumstances are surely a metaphor for time on the march.

The passing of time plays its part in our understanding of the way the paintings in this exhibition have emerged, whether from memories, from repeated encounters with a subject or from a photograph, through the examination of mortality in the works themselves, but inevitably also in the audience's knowledge that ten artists are now three. However, the pertinence of *The Mystery of Appearance* extends to a new generation of Eastern European painters for whom these artists are guiding lights, in a large number of young British painters with the desire and ambition to make work about "real life," in members of the immediate circle such as Freud's former studio assistant, the painter and photographer David Dawson, as well as Jenny Saville, Celia Paul, Paula Rego, Keith Coventry, and John Currin. But just as timely and persuasive there is the astonishing quality and freshness of Auerbach, Hockney and Kossoff's recent paintings. For Auerbach and Kossoff the subjects are as ever the faces and landscapes that are near them, and for Hockney his native Yorkshire woodland. Seemingly, they remain engrossed by the painter's problem: "How can this thing be made so that you catch the mystery of appearance within the mystery of the making?"[25]

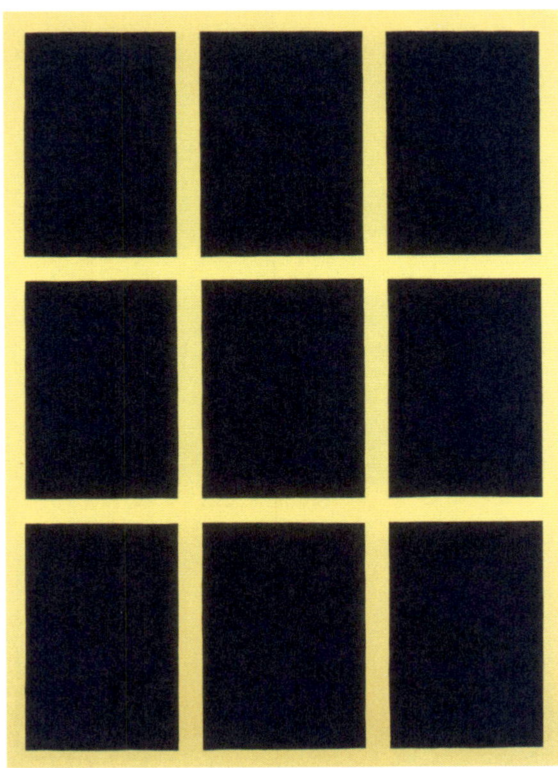

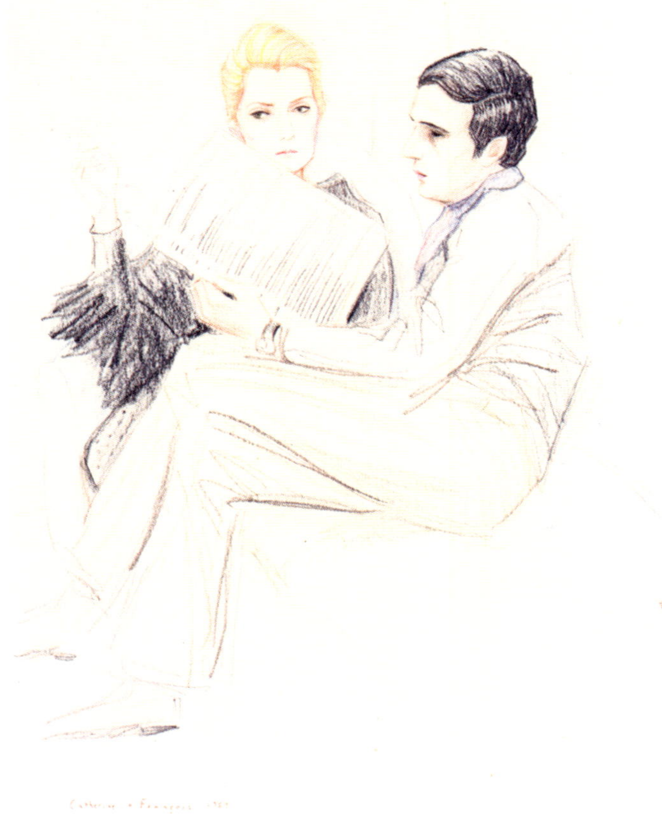

Above: Gary Hume, *Yellow Window,* 2002.

Right: Elizbeth Peyton, *Catherine Deneuve and François Truffaut,* 2005.

The Mystery of Appearance:
List of Works

Michael Andrews

The Thames at Low Tide, 1994–95
Oil, sand, and paint residue on canvas
182.9 × 167.6 cm
Private collection

The Lord Mayor's Reception in Norwich Castle Keep, On the Eve of the Installation of the First Chancellor of the University of East Anglia, 1966–69
Oil on canvas, 213.3 × 213.3 cm
Norfolk Museums and Archaeology Service, Norwich Castle Museum and Art Gallery

Craigie Aitchison (Study for Good and Bad at Games), 1967
Oil on board, 24.9 × 21.6 cm
Private collection, courtesy of Susannah Pollen Ltd.

Study of a Head with a Green Turban, 1967
Oil on board
21.5 × 16.5 cm
Pallant House Gallery

Frank Auerbach

Reclining Figure, 1972
Oil on board
38.1 × 40.6 cm
Private collection, NY

Study of Primrose Hill, 1973–74
Oil on board
121.9 × 121.9 cm
Private collection

Gerda Boehm, 1971–73
Oil on board
61 × 71.1 cm
Private collection

Primrose Hill, Winter Sunshine, 1962–64
Oil on board
104.1 × 144.8 cm
Private collection

Francis Bacon

Pope I—Study after Pope Innocent X by Velázquez, 1951
Oil on canvas
197.8 × 137.4 cm
Aberdeen Art Gallery and Museums Collections

Patrick Caulfield

Coloured Still Life, 1967
Acrylic on board
56 × 89 cm
Pallant House Gallery

Red, White and Black Still Life, 1966/1984
Acrylic on canvas laid down on board
91.4 × 152.4 cm
Pauline Caulfield

Study for 'The Mysterious Suspicion: After Magritte', c. 1974
Pencil and pen on paper, 50.5 × 46 cm
Waddington Custot Galleries

Study for 'Entrance', 1975
Graphite, rollerball, and coloured pen on paper, 56 × 76 cm
Pauline Caulfield

Study for 'Forecourt', 1975
Graphite, rollerball, and watercolour on paper
56 × 76 cm
Pauline Caulfield

Study for 'Paradise Bar', c. 1974
Pencil and pen on card
54.5 × 80 cm
Waddington Custot Galleries

William Coldstream

Seated Nude, 1972–73
Oil on canvas
110.6 × 61.4 cm
Private collection

Lord Ifor Evans, 1958–60
Oil on canvas
110.8 × 83.7 cm
UCL Art Museum, University College London

Lucian Freud

Francis Bacon (Study), 1951
Pencil and charcoal on paper
54.7 × 42 cm
Private collection

Girl on a Turkish Sofa, 1966
Oil on canvas
26.7 × 34.9 cm
Private collection

Portrait of a Woman (Portrait of Lady Ann Tree), c. 1950
Oil on canvas, 44 × 34.5 cm
Devonshire Collection, Chatsworth

Richard Hamilton

reNude Study, 1954
Pencil and watercolour on paper
37 × 22.7 cm
Herbert Art Gallery & Museum, Coventry

Study for reNude, 1953
Pencil and watercolour on paper
53 × 33.6 cm
Pallant House Gallery

Mother and Child, 1984–85
Oil on canvas
150 × 150 cm
Katherine and Keith L. Sachs

Respective, 1951
Oil on hardboard
91.5 × 122 cm
Pallant House Gallery

Whitley Bay, 1965
Oil on photograph laid on panel
81 × 122 cm
Birimingham Museums and Art Gallery Collection

Finn MacCool, 1983
Framed heliogravure, lift ground and spit-bite aquatint, engraving, and burnisher on Rives paper, 76 × 56 cm
Alan Cristea Gallery

David Hockney

Man in a Museum (Or You're in the Wrong Movie), 1962
Oil on canvas, 147.3 × 152.4 cm
British Council Collection

The Room Tarzana, 1967
Acrylic on canvas
243.8 × 243.8 cm
Private collection

John St. Clair, 1972
Coloured crayon, and graphite on paper
43.2 × 35.6 cm
Private collection

Leon Kossoff

Nude (Autumn Morning), 1971
Oil on board
81 × 111 cm
Private collection

A Woman Bathing (Study After Rembrandt), 1982
Oil on board
58.4 × 48.3 cm
Private collection

Leon Kossoff

Self Portrait II, 1972
Oil on wood
56 × 51 cm
Private collection

Willesden Junction, Summer No.1, 1966
Oil on board, 91.4 × 152.4 cm
Private collection

Seated Woman No.2, 1959
Oil on board
111.8 × 83.8 cm
Private collection

Two Seated Figures II, 1980
Charcoal on paper
56.5 × 79.4 cm
Private collection

Euan Uglow

Nude, Lady C, 1959–60
Oil on canvas
75 × 101.5 cm
John and Julia Scott

Massacre of the Innocents, 1979–81
Oil on canvas laid on panel
41.2 × 48.9 cm
Sharon Nassauer

Mosque at Çiftlik Koyou, 1966
Oil on canvas
105 × 121 cm
Private collection

Polygons, c. 1970
Oil on canvas on board
21 × 15 cm
Private collection

Obelisk, c. 1970
Oil on canvas
21 × 15 cm
Private collection

Illustration Credits

Page 8: © Michael Pergolani. Courtesy Catherine Lambert.
Page 11 [right]: © The National Gallery, London.
Page 11 [below left]: © The Estate of Francis Bacon, All rights reserved, DACS 2011. Photo: Prudence Cuming Associates Limited.
Page 11 [below right]: © The Estate of Francis Bacon, All rights reserved, DACS 2011. Courtesy Collezione Maramotti.
Page 12 / frontispiece: Private collection. © The Lewinski Archive at Chatsworth / The Bridgeman Art Library.
Page 15 [below]: © The Roland Penrose Collection. All rights reserved. Unknown photographer. Courtesy of Roland Penrose Estate, England 2011.
Page 15 [below right] © The Estate of Sir William Coldstream. All Rights Reserved 2010 / Bridgeman Art Library. Courtesy Tate, London.
Page 17 [above left]: D'Arcy Wentworth Thompson, *On Growth and Form,* 1917, Abridged Edition (1961), Cambridge University Press.
Page 17 [above right]: © The Estate of Francis Bacon, All rights reserved, DACS 2011. Courtesy David Plante.
Page 18: © The Times / NI Syndication. Courtesy Catherine Lampert.
Page 21: © The Estate of Francis Bacon, All rights reserved, DACS 2011. Photo: Hugo Maertens.
Page 22: © Estate of Harry Diamond. Courtesy Catherine Lampert.
Page 24 [left]: © Lord O'Neill; Fionn Morgan – The Estate of Ann Flemin. Courtesy Catherine Lampert.
Page 24 [right]: Private collection. © The Lucian Freud Archive / The Bridgeman Art Library.
Page 25: © The Estate of Bruce Bernard. Courtesy Virginia Verran.
Page 26 / frontispiece: Private collection. © The Lewinski Archive at Chatsworth / The Bridgeman Art Library.
Page 28: © S.S. Walia. Courtesy Catherine Lampert.
Page 30 [below left]: © Leon Kossoff
Page 30 [below right]: © Frank Auerbach.
Page 32: Courtesy Whitechapel Gallery, Whitechapel Gallery Archive. Photo: Sam Lambert.
Page 33: © The Estate of Richard Hamilton. All rights reserved, DACS 2011.
Page 34 / frontispiece: Private collection. Courtesy The Lewinski Archive at Chatsworth / The Bridgeman Art Library.
Page 36: © The Estate of Richard Hamilton. All rights reserved, DACS 2011. Courtesy Kunsthalle, Tubingen, Germany / The Bridgeman Art Library.
Page 38 [below left]: © Succession Giacometti / ADAGP, Paris and DACS, London 2011. Courtesy Tate, London, 2011.
Page 38 [below right]: Philadelphia Museum of Art, Pennsylvania, PA, USA/ The Louise and Walter Arensberg Collection, 1950 / The Bridgeman Art Library © Succession Marcel Duchamp / ADAGP, Paris and DACS, London 2011.
Page 39: © Graham Keen.
Page 41 [below]: © Tate, London.
Page 42 / frontispiece: Private collection. © The Lewinski Archive at Chatsworth / The Bridgeman Art Library.
Page 44: © David Hockney.
Page 45: © David Hockney.
Page 46: © The John Deakin Archive. Courtesy Ben Tufnell.
Page 48 [above left]: © Robert Mason.
Page 48 [above right]: © The Estate of Bruce Bernard. Courtesy Virginia Verran.
Page 49: © The Estate of Michael Andrews / James Hyman Fine Art, London. Courtesy Tate, London.
Page 50: © The Estate of Patrick Caulfield. All rights reserved, DACS 2011. Courtesy Virginia Museum of Fine Arts, Richmond. Sydney and Frances Lewis Contemporary Art Fund. Photo: Katherine Wetzel © Virginia Museum of Fine Arts.
Page 51 [above]: © The Estate of Patrick Caulfield. All rights reserved, DACS 2011. Courtesy Tate, London 2011.
Page 51 [right]: © The Estate of Patrick Caulfield. All rights reserved, DACS 2011. Private collection. Photo: Prudence Cuming Associates, London.
Page 52 / frontispiece: Private collection. © The Lewinski Archive at Chatsworth / The Bridgeman Art Library.
Page 52 / frontispiece: Private collection. © The Lewinski Archive at Chatsworth / The Bridgeman Art Library.
Page 56 [above]: © The Artist.
Page 56 [right]: Musée Conde, Chantilly, France/ Giraudon/ The Bridgeman Art Library.
Page 57 [above left]: © The Estate of Euan Uglow.
Page 57 [above right]: Courtesy Catherine Lampert.
Page 58: © The Lucian Freud Archive.
Page 61: © The Lucian Freud Archive. Image © Christie's Images Limited.
Page 62: © The Estate of Richard Hamilton. Courtesy Herbert Art Gallery and Museum, Coventry.
Page 63: © The Estate of Richard Hamilton. Pallant House Gallery, Chichester (Wilson loan, 2006).
Page 64: © Frank Auerbach.
Page 65: © Leon Kossoff.
Page 67: © The Estate of Sir William Coldstream.
Page 68: © The Lucian Freud Archive / The Bridgeman Art Library.
Page 69: © The Estate of Euan Uglow.
Page 71: Aberdeen Art Gallery and Museums Collections.
Page 72: © David Hockney.
Page 73: © The Estate of Euan Uglow. Image courtesy of Browse and Darby.
Page 74: © Leon Kossoff.
Page 75: © Leon Kossoff. Image courtesy Sotheby's.
Page 77: © The Estate of Richard Hamilton.
Page 79: © The Estate of Michael Andrews / James Hyman Fine Art, London.
Page 80: © Frank Auerbach.
Page 81: © Frank Auerbach.
Page 83 and cover: © Frank Auerbach. Photo: Peter Mallet.
Page 84–85: © Leon Kossoff.
Page 87: © The Lucian Freud Archive / The Bridgeman Art Library. Courtesy Devonshire Collection, Chatsworth.
Page 88: © Leon Kossoff.
Page 89: © The Estate of Sir William Coldstream. Courtesy UCL Art Museum, University College London.
Page 90–91: © The Estate of Richard Hamilton. All rights reserved, DACS 2011. Courtesy Pallant House Gallery, Chichester, UK / Wilson Loan / The Bridgeman Art Library.
Page 93: © The Estate of Euan Uglow.
Page 95: © David Hockney. Photo: Peter Mallet.
Page 97: © The Estate of Michael Andrews / James Hyman Fine Art, London. Courtesy Norfolk Museums and Archaeology Service, Norwich Castle Museum and Art Gallery.
Page 98–99: © The Estate of Richard Hamilton. All rights reserved, DACS 2011.
Page 100: © The Estate of Patrick Caulfield. All rights reserved, DACS 2011. Courtesy Pallant House Gallery, Chichester, UK.
Page 101: © The Estate of Patrick Caulfield. All rights reserved, DACS 2011. Photo: Peter Mallet.
Page 102: © The Estate of Euan Uglow. Courtesy Catherine Lampert.
Page 103: © The Estate of Euan Uglow. Courtesy Catherine Lampert.
Page 104: © The Estate of Michael Andrews / James Hyman Fine Art, London.
Page 105: © The Estate of Michael Andrews / James Hyman Fine Art, London. Courtesy Pallant House Gallery, Chichester, UK.
Page 106: © David Hockney. Photo: Peter Mallet.
Page 107: © The Estate of Patrick Caulfield. All rights reserved, DACS 2011. Courtesy Waddington Custot Galleries.
Page 108: © The Estate of Richard Hamilton. All rights reserved, DACS 2011. Courtesy Alan Cristea Gallery.
Page 109: © Leon Kossoff.
Page 110: © The Estate of Patrick Caulfield. All rights reserved, DACS 2011. Photo: Peter Mallet.
Page 111: © The Estate of Patrick Caulfield. All rights reserved, DACS 2011. Photo: Peter Mallet.
Page 112: © The Estate of Patrick Caulfield. All rights reserved, DACS 2011. Courtesy Waddington Custot Galleries.
Page 114: © Glenn Brown 2011.
Page 116 [left]: © The Estate of Francis Bacon, All rights reserved, DACS 2011. Photo: Hugo Maertens.
Page 116 [right]: © The Estate of Michael Andrews / Courtesy James Hyman Fine Art, London. Photo © Museo Thyssen-Bornemisza, Madrid.
Page 117: © The artist. Courtesy the artist and Gavin Brown's Enterprise. Photo: Thomas Müller.
Page 118 [left]: © The Estate of Richard Hamilton. All rights reserved, DACS 2011. Courtesy Rita Donagh.
Page 118 [right]: © The artist. Courtesy Anthony Reynolds Gallery, London. Photo: Vegar Kleven.
Page 118 [left]: © The Estate of Richard Hamilton. All rights reserved, DACS 2011. Courtesy Tate, London, 2011.
Page 119 [right]: ©Gerhard Richter, 2011.
Page 120: © Gerhard Richter, 2011.
Page 121: © Per Kirkeby, 2011. Courtesy Carnegie Museum of Art, Pittsburgh; Purchase: gift of Mr. and Mrs. Stanley R. Gumberg.
Page 123 [left]: © The artist / White Cube. Photo: Stephen White, courtesy White Cube. Courtesy Sotheby's, New York.
Page 123 [right]: © The artist. Courtesy Sadie Coles HQ, London.

Published on the occasion
of the exhibition

The Mystery of Appearance
Conversations Between
Ten British Post-War Painters

Curated by Catherine Lampert

Haunch of Venison, London
7 December 2011–18 February 2012

Haunch of Venison
103 New Bond Street
London W1S 1ST
United Kingdom
T +44 (0)20 7495 5050
F +44 (0)20 7495 4050
london@haunchofvenison.com
www.haunchofvenison.com

Editor: Catherine Lampert
Managing Editor: Tom Hunt
Design: Matt Watkins
Picture Research: Katie Barkes
Print: Lecturis, Eindhoven

ISBN: 978-1-905620-63-0

Cover:
Frank Auerbach,
Primrose Hill, Winter Sunshine,
1962–1964.
© Frank Auerbach. Photo: Peter Mallet.

Haunch of Venison and Catherine Lampert
would like to thank:
Susan K. Anderson, Sarah Bailey, Rosalie Barkes, Ivor Braka, Adrianne Bratis, Andrew Brown, Susan Campbell, Pauline Caulfield, Alan Cristea, Celia Coke-Steel, Caroline Cuthbert, Andrew Dempsey, David Dawson, Edith Devaney, Corinne Diserens, Diana Eccles, Brendan Flynn, Andrea Fredericksen, Georgia Georgallas, Hugh Gibson, Julie Green, Matthew Hirst, James Hyman, David Juda, Marco Livingstone, Miranda Margetson, Simon Martin, Jennifer Melville, Lucy Mitchell-Innes, Andrew Moore, Felix Mottram, Richard Nagy, Janet Nathan, Sharon Nassauer, Francis Outred, Nina Pearlman, David Plante, Sussanah Pollen, Mariangela Renshaw, Richard Riley, Martin Roberts, Andrea Rose, Piers Secunda, Hannah Sorrel, Virginia Verran.

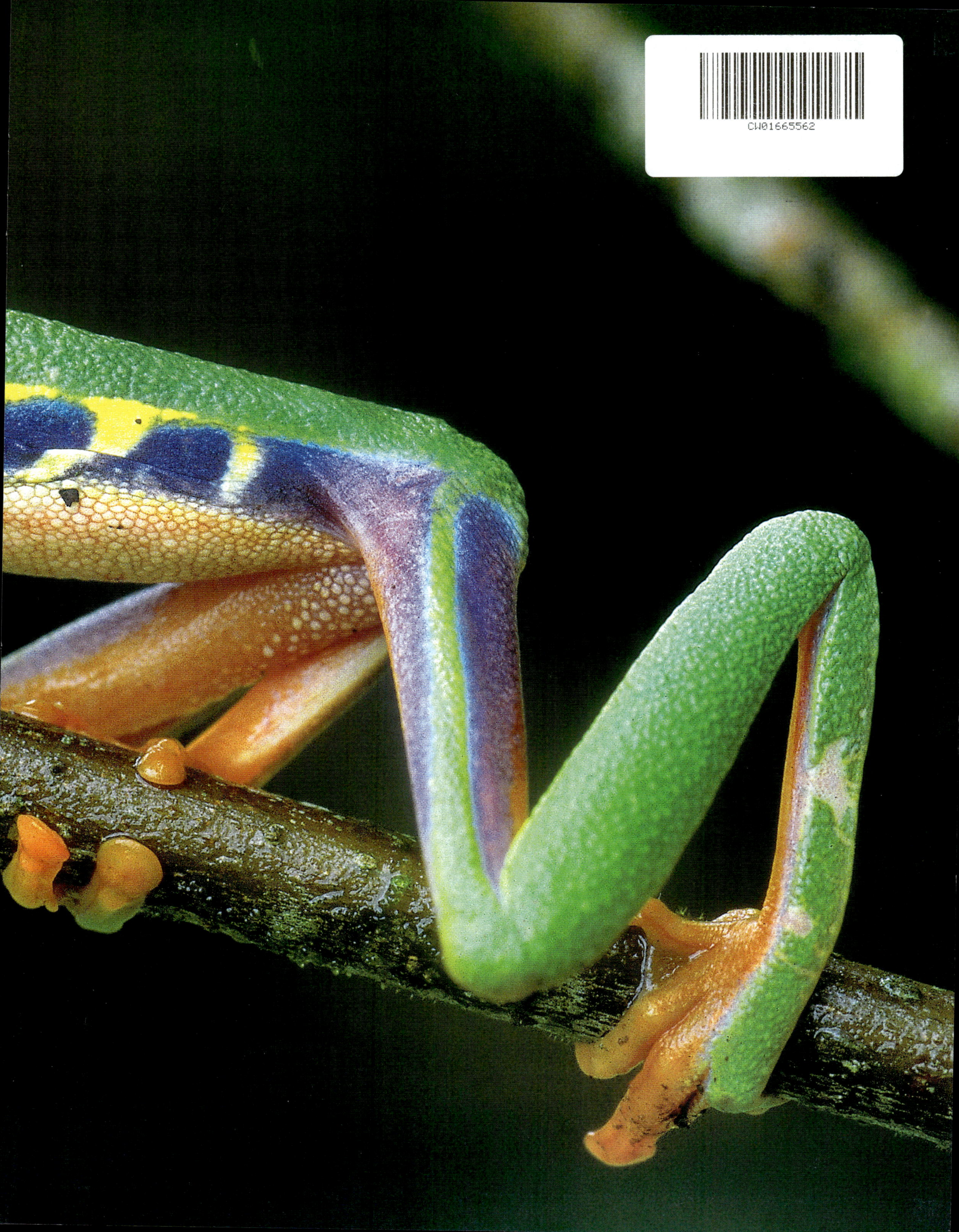

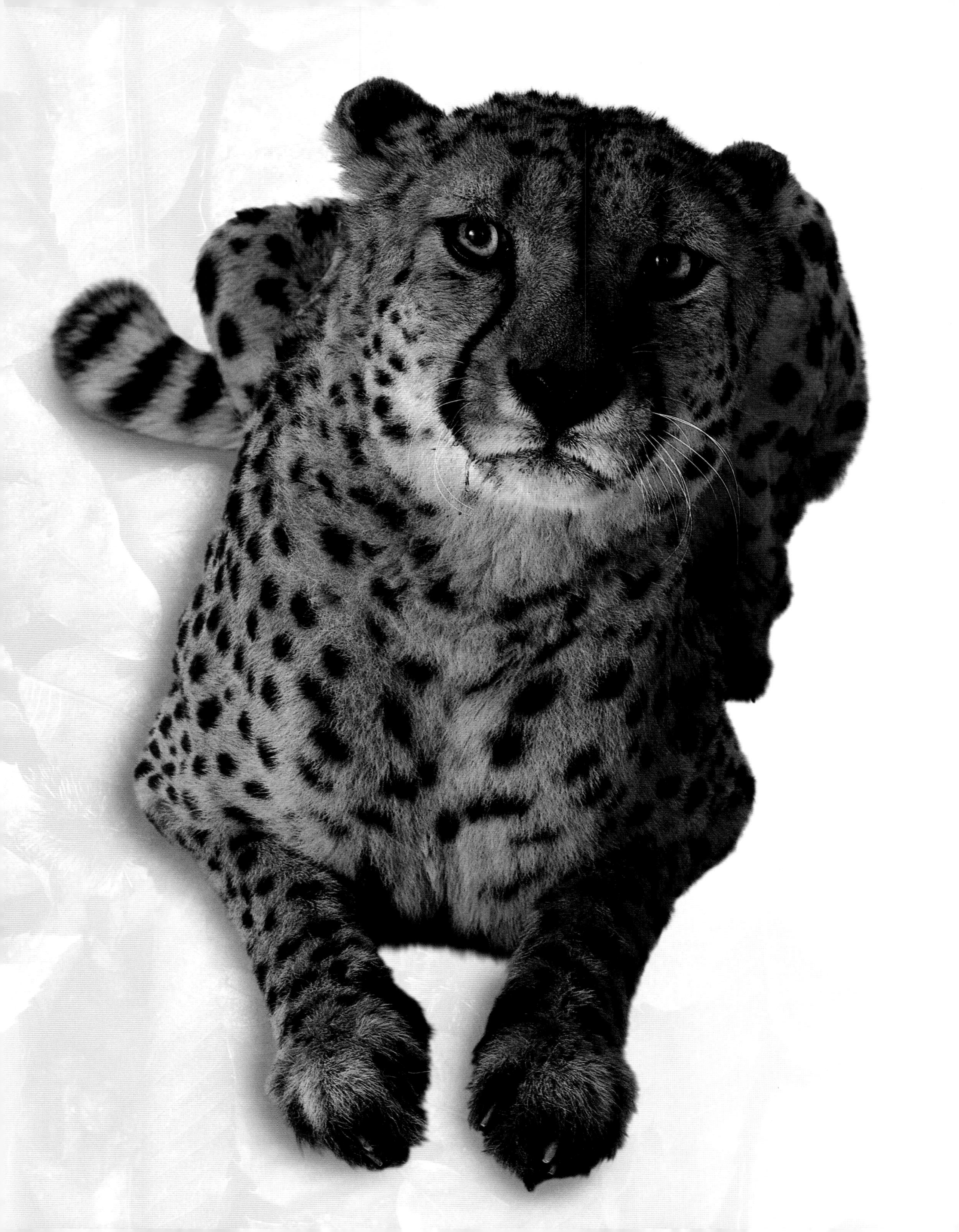

Incroyables animaux

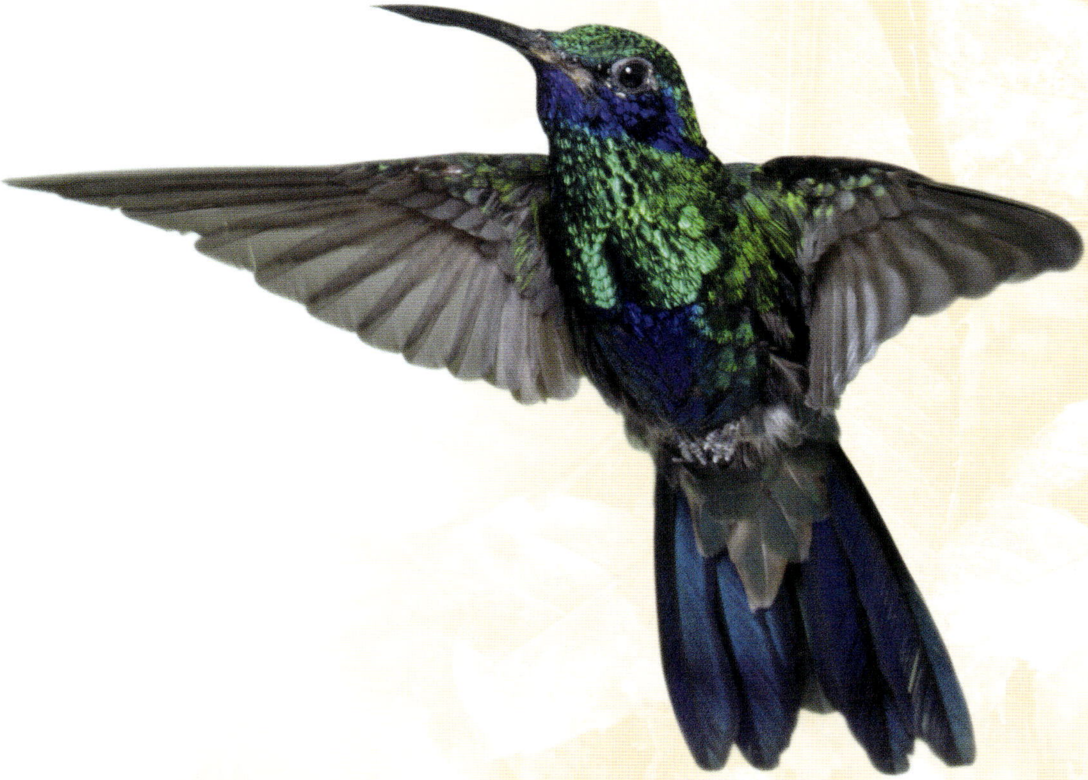

Écrit par David Burnie

Consultant : Dr Kim Dennis-Bryan

publie un livre

Maquettiste : Smiljka Surla
Éditeur senior : Fran Jones
Éditeur en chef : Linda Esposito
Directeur artistique : Diane Thistletwaite
Directeur des publications : Andrew Macintyre
Directeur du service artistique : Sophia M Tampakopoulos
Fabrication : Georgina Hayworth
Recherche iconographique : Jo Walton
Photothèque DK : Claire Bowers
Rédaction de la couverture : Mariza O'Keefe
Créateurs de la couverture : Johnny Pau, Rebecca Wright

DK Dehli
Maquettistes : Neerja Rawat, Tannishtha Chakaborty
Responsable des maquettes : Kavita Dutta
Directeur artistique : Shefali Ypadhyay

Première édition en langue anglaise en Grande-Bretagne
en 2007 par Dorling Kindersley Ltd, 80 Strand,
London WC2R 0RLA
Penguin Company

Adaptation française de Bénédicte Servignat.

Imprimé en Chine et importé par
Langue au chat,
Chaussée Romaine, 5
4190 Werbomont,
Belgique

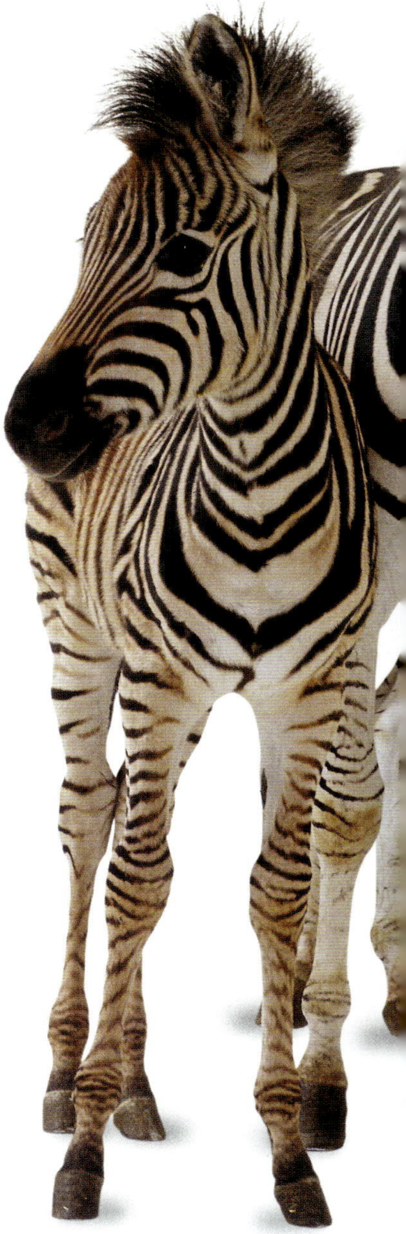

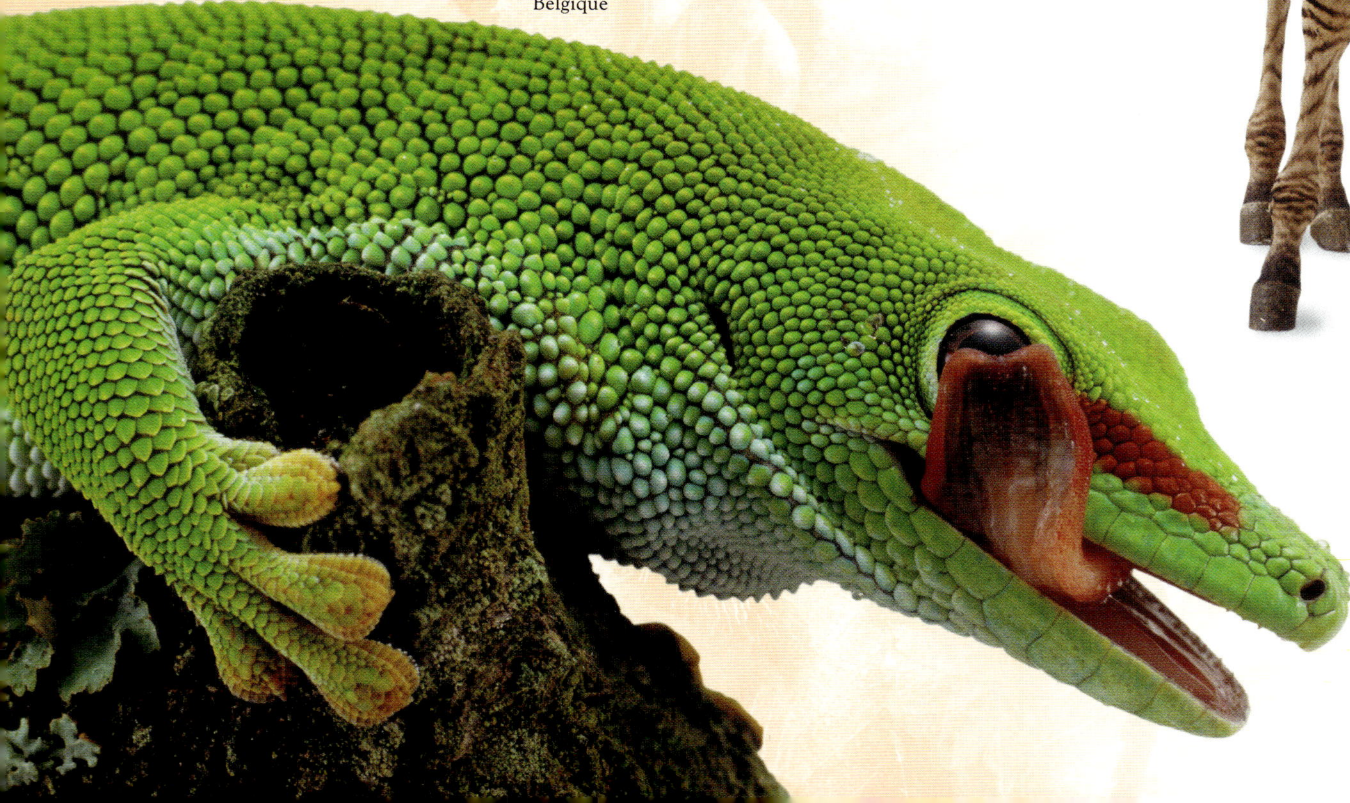

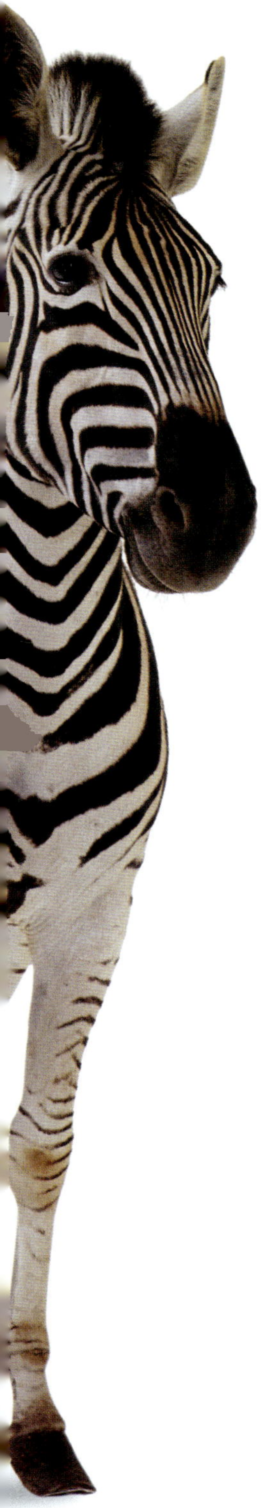
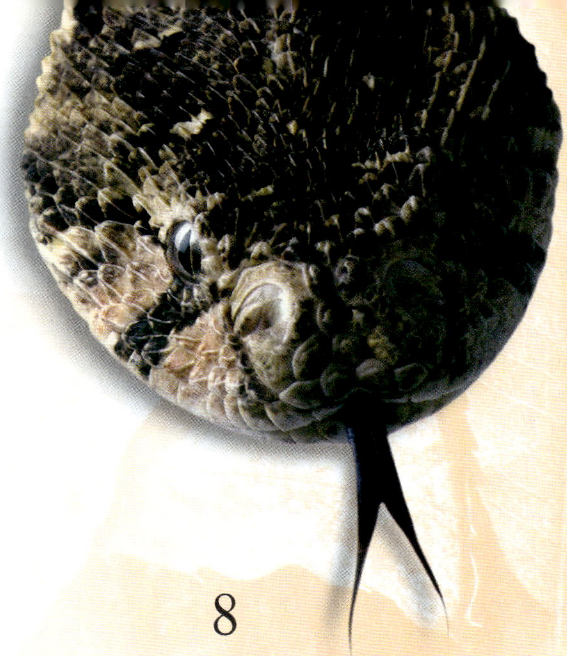

SOMMAIRE

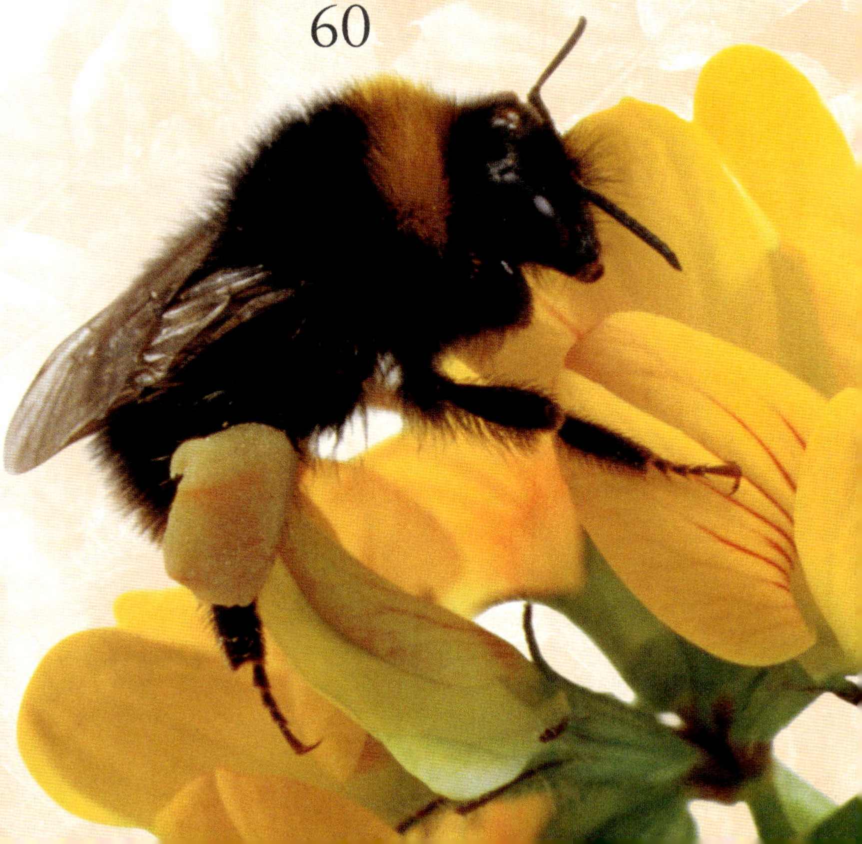

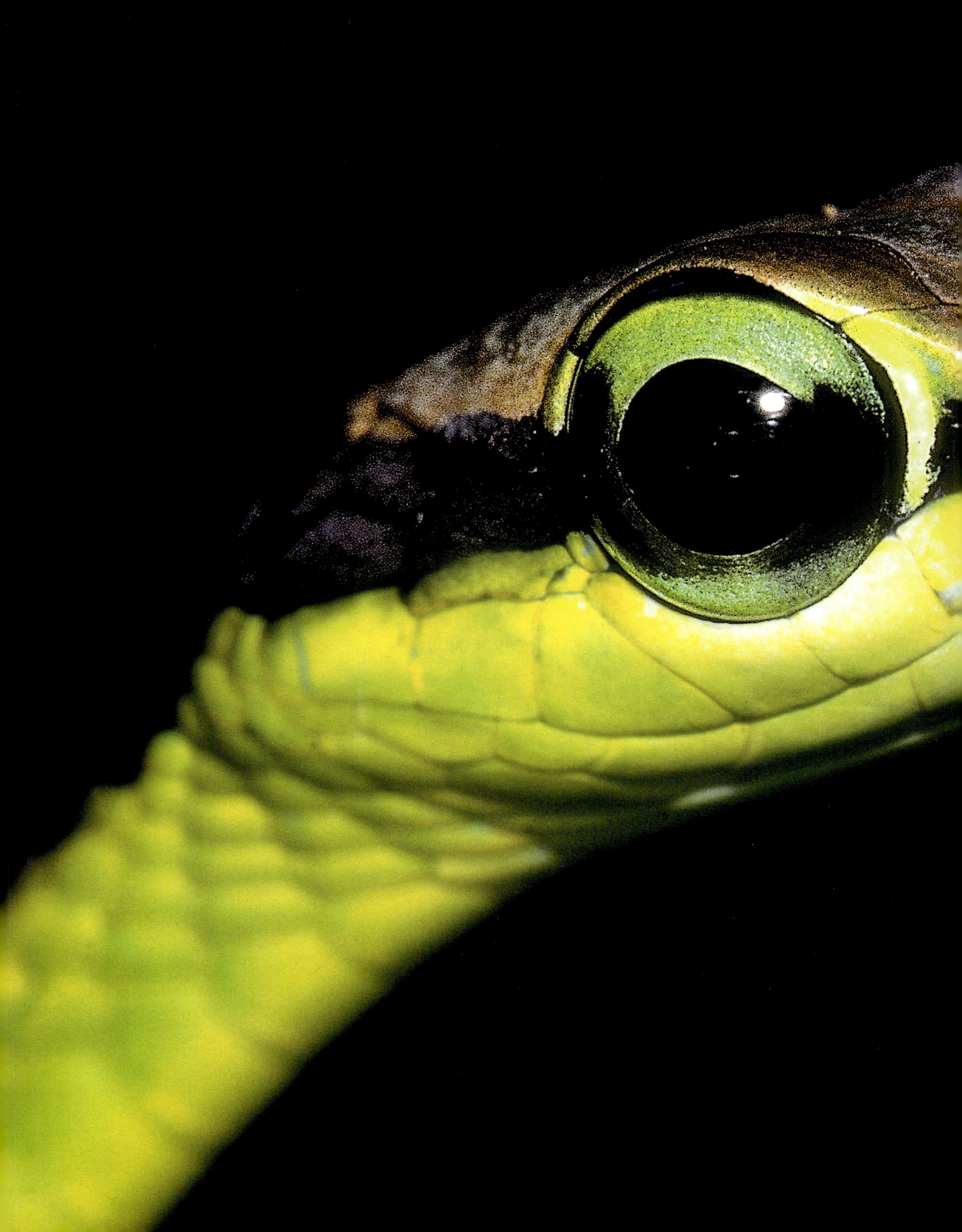

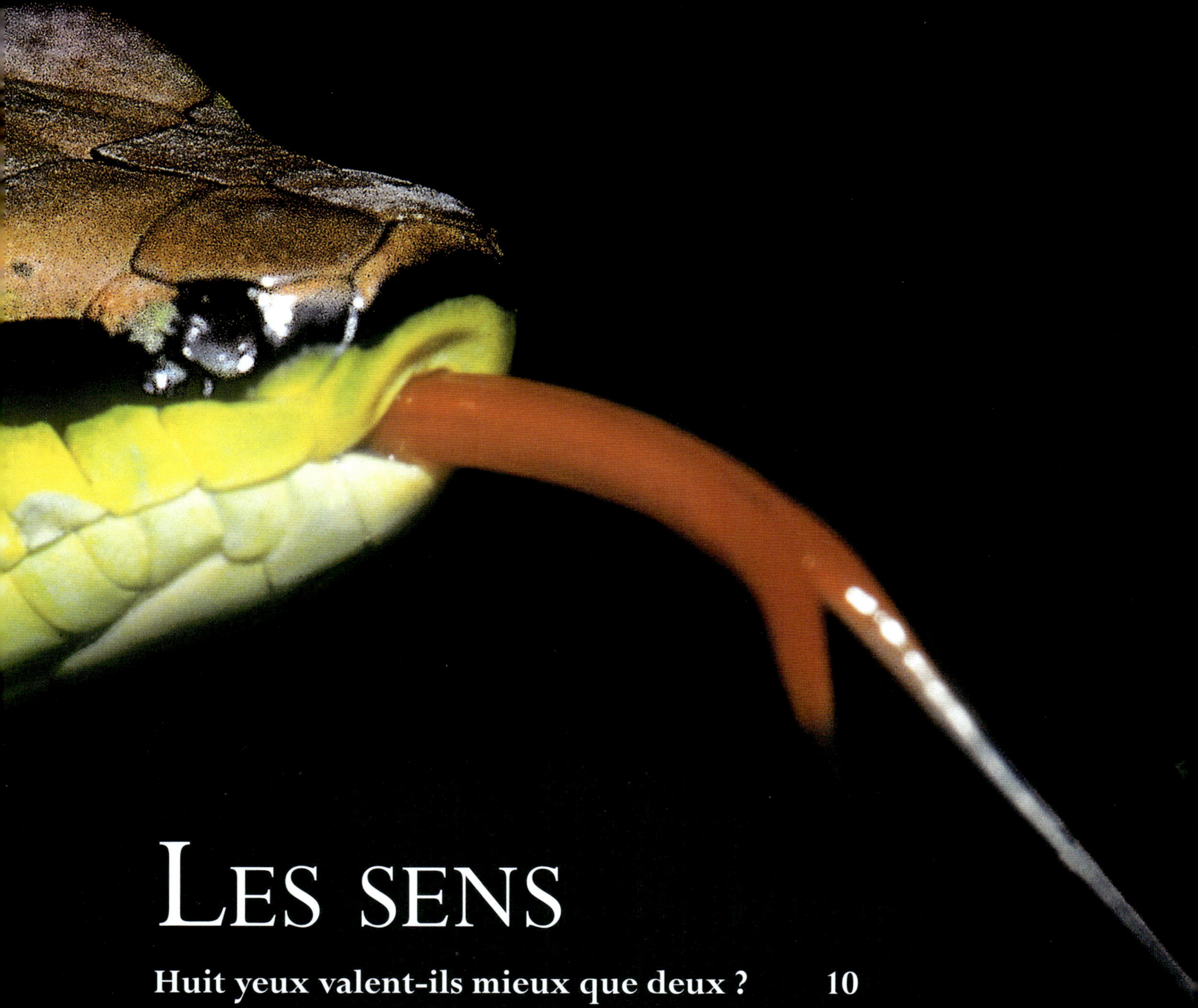

LES SENS

Huit yeux valent-ils mieux que deux ?

Pour la grande majorité des animaux, deux yeux sont largement suffisants pour trouver de la nourriture et se préserver des dangers. La position de ces yeux est importante car elle détermine la largeur du champ visuel de l'animal sans qu'il tourne la tête. Les araignées sont différentes. Elles ont jusqu'à huit yeux disposés à l'avant et de chaque côté de la tête. Chez les araignées sauteuses, les deux yeux de devant sont très grands et leur permettent de jauger les distances lorsqu'elles bondissent sur leur proie. Bien que dotées de nombreux yeux, la plupart des autres araignées sont myopes.

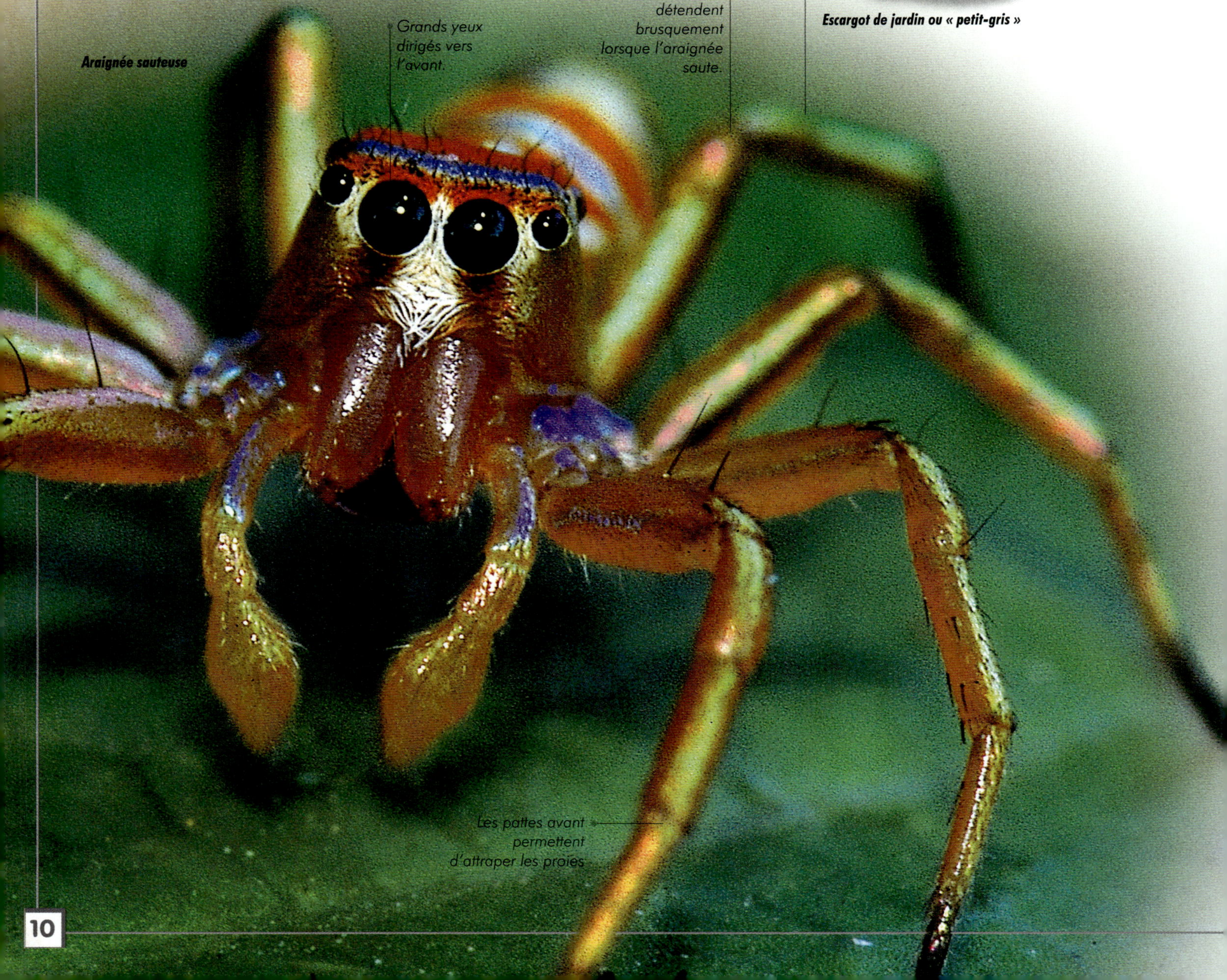

Araignée sauteuse

Q R Pourquoi les escargots ont-ils des yeux sur les tentacules?

Les escargots ont besoin de voir mais ils doivent aussi pouvoir se cacher dans leur coquille, ce que permettent les yeux à l'extrémité des tentacules. Ceux-ci, longs et fins, assurent un bon champ de vision. En cas de danger, ils peuvent se rétracter comme des petits téléscopes. L'escargot peut alors disparaître totalement dans sa coquille.

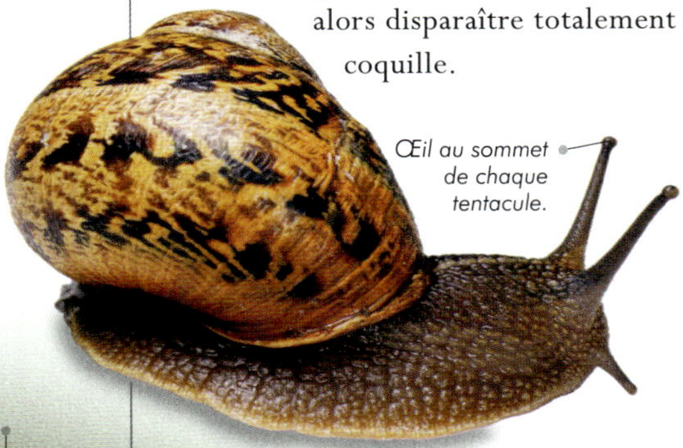

Escargot de jardin ou « petit-gris »

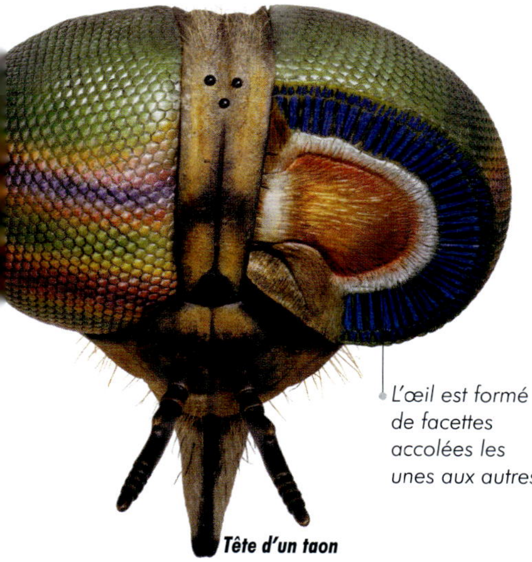

L'œil est formé de facettes accolées les unes aux autres.

Tête d'un taon

Comment fonctionnent les yeux des insectes ?

Les yeux des insectes sont très différents des nôtres. Ils sont durs et divisés en centaines, voire en milliers de petites lentilles ou facettes (appelées ommatidies). Chaque facette est comme un mini-œil, et elles fonctionnent toutes ensembles pour offrir à l'insecte une vision de son environnement. Certains d'entre eux, tels que les libellules ou les taons, ont de gros yeux protubérants. Ils peuvent voir dans toutes les directions en même temps sans bouger la tête.

Qui a la vue la plus perçante ?

Les rapaces, tels que les milans ou les aigles, ont des yeux plus petits que ceux des humains, mais leur acuité visuelle est au moins quatre fois plus grande que la nôtre. Cela signifie que, même de très haut dans le ciel, ils ont une vision excellente des petits détails ou d'une proie minuscule. Ils peuvent fondre sur une souris ou un lapereau sans que cette proie les détecte.

Qui a les plus grands yeux ?

Le calmar géant. Cet animal des profondeurs peut mesurer plus de 7 m de long avec des yeux de 50 cm de diamètre. Les calmars géants utilisent leurs énormes yeux pour chercher du poisson et d'autres animaux dans les profondeurs obscures de l'océan.

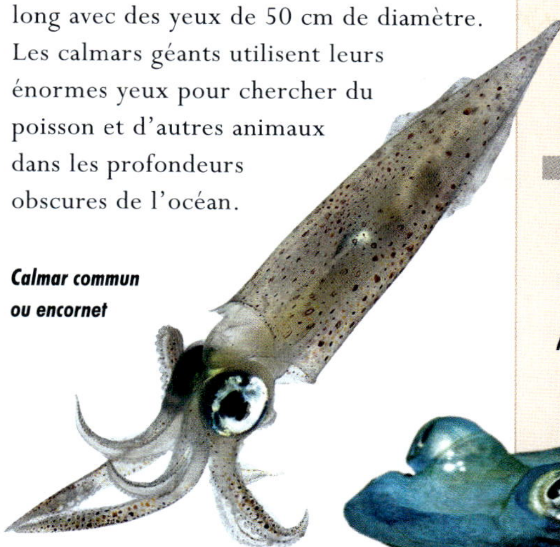

Calmar commun ou encornet

Pourquoi certains animaux ont-ils des yeux très écartés ?

Les mammifères herbivores, tels que les gazelles, doivent rester sur leur garde dans la savane. Pendant que leur tête est baissée vers le sol pour brouter, il y a toujours le risque qu'un prédateur attaque. Les yeux, placés latéralement, leur permettent de rester vigilantes. Les gazelles broutent souvent en troupeau. À tour de rôle, elles surveillent les alentours pour parer une attaque-surprise.

Plus d' infos

- Les coquilles Saint-Jacques possèdent des douzaines de petits yeux bleus autour des deux valves de leur coquille qui leur permettent de détecter les mouvements.
- Lorsque les grenouilles et les crapauds avalent, leurs yeux s'enfoncent pour aider à pousser la nourriture vers l'estomac.

Anableps

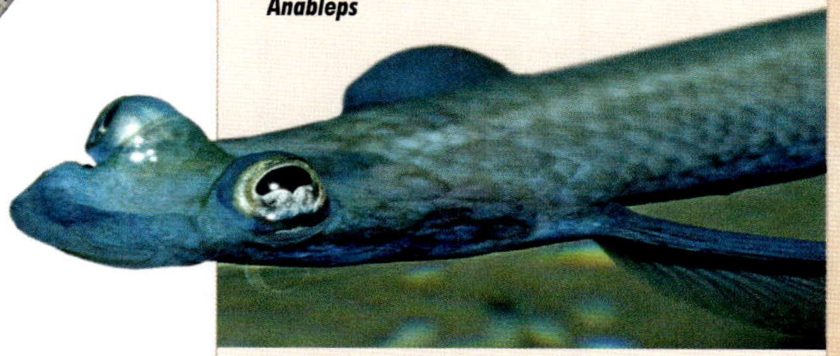

- Les anableps vivent dans les eaux de faible profondeur. Ce sont des poissons dont chaque œil est divisé en deux : une moitié qui regarde vers le bas, dans l'eau et l'autre, qui regarde vers le haut, dans l'air.

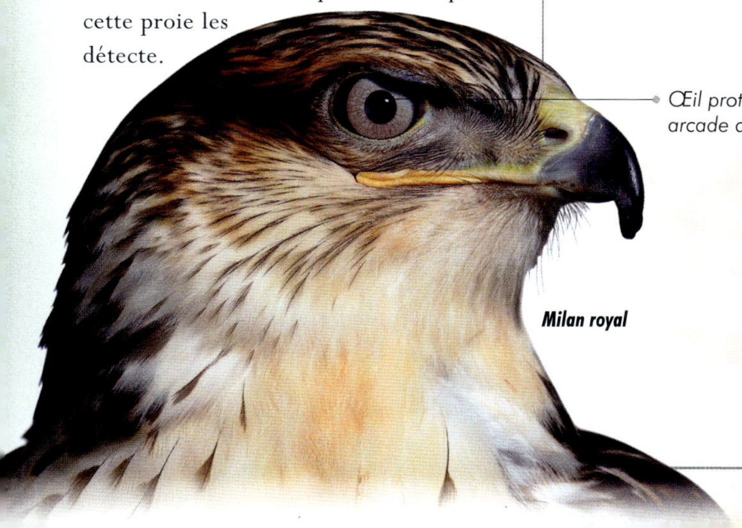

Œil protégé par une arcade de plumes.

Milan royal

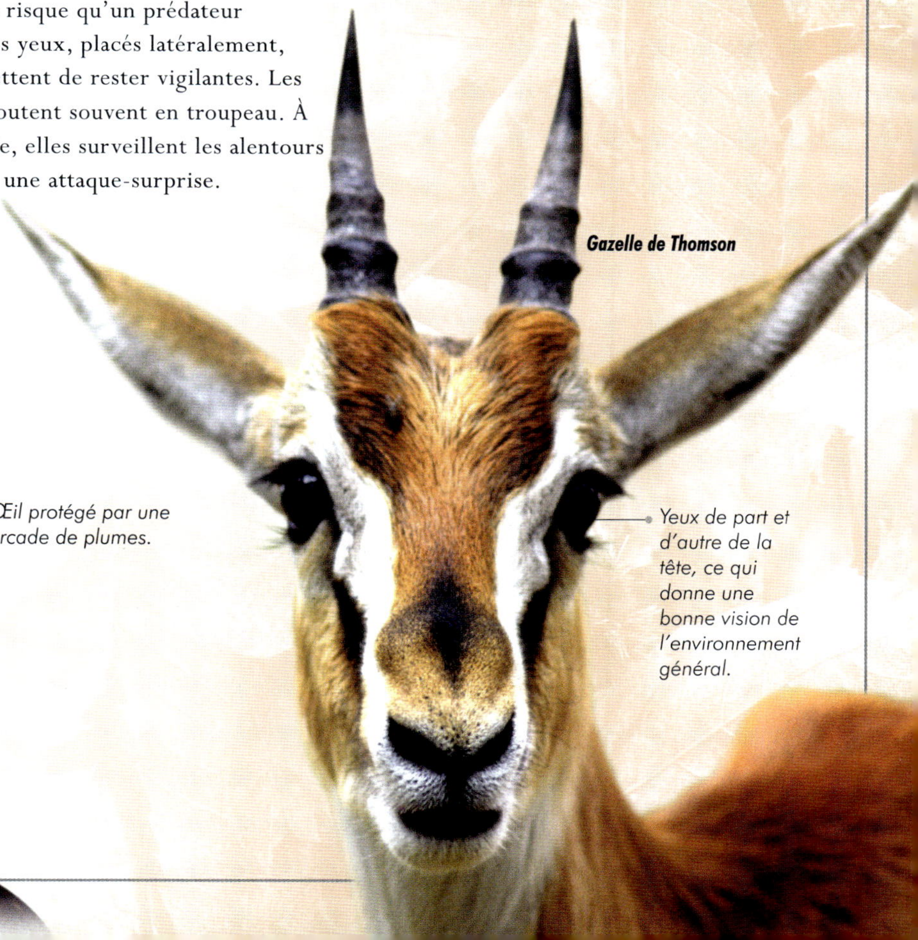

Gazelle de Thomson

Yeux de part et d'autre de la tête, ce qui donne une bonne vision de l'environnement général.

Qui voit le mieux dans le noir ?

Beaucoup d'animaux se déplacent la nuit et se servent de leurs yeux pour se diriger. Les chouettes sont incomparables pour voler sans danger au milieu des arbres. Leurs yeux sont très sensibles même quand il y a peu de lumière. Les pupilles sont très grandes. Ainsi, un maximum de lumière y pénètre. Mais les animaux nocturnes ne sont pas les seuls à vivre dans le noir. Sous terre et dans les grottes, il y a des créatures qui vivent dans l'obscurité en permanence.

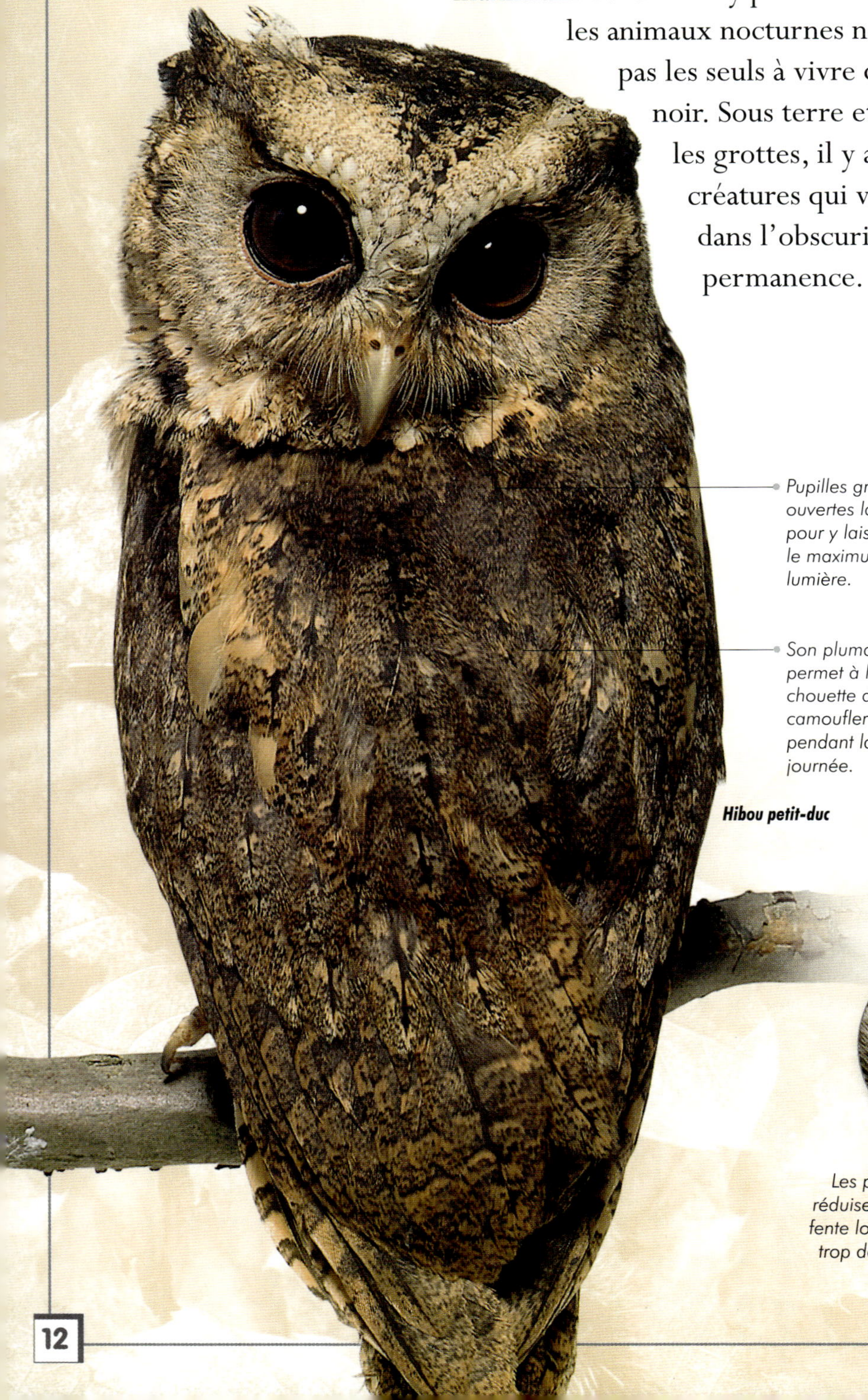

Pupilles grandes ouvertes la nuit pour y laisser entrer le maximum de lumière.

Son plumage permet à la chouette de se camoufler pendant la journée.

Hibou petit-duc

Q R Les vers de terre ont-ils des yeux ?

Non, ils n'en ont pas. À la place, ils ont des petits récepteurs sensibles à la lumière sur tout le corps, surtout sur la tête et la queue. Ces capteurs sont trop petits pour voir les choses en détail. Ils indiquent simplement au ver l'intensité lumineuse environnante. Si un ver est déterré, il utilise ses détecteurs pour s'éloigner de la lumière et se remettre à l'abri sous la terre.

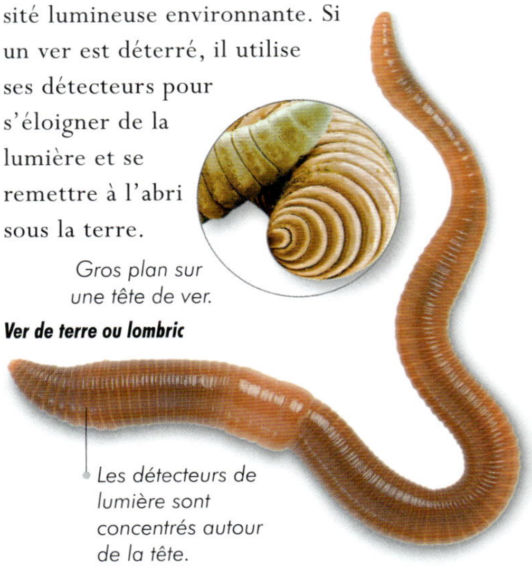

Gros plan sur une tête de ver.

Ver de terre ou lombric

Les détecteurs de lumière sont concentrés autour de la tête.

Q R Comment les yeux des chats changent-ils dans le noir ?

Au soleil, la pupille d'un chat ressemble à une fente étroite. Cela lui évite d'être ébloui, en empêchant que trop de lumière ne pénètre dans l'œil. Dans le noir, la pupille s'agrandit jusqu'à devenir ronde et laisse entrer le maximum de lumière. Grâce à cette particularité, les chats voient aussi bien le jour que la nuit.

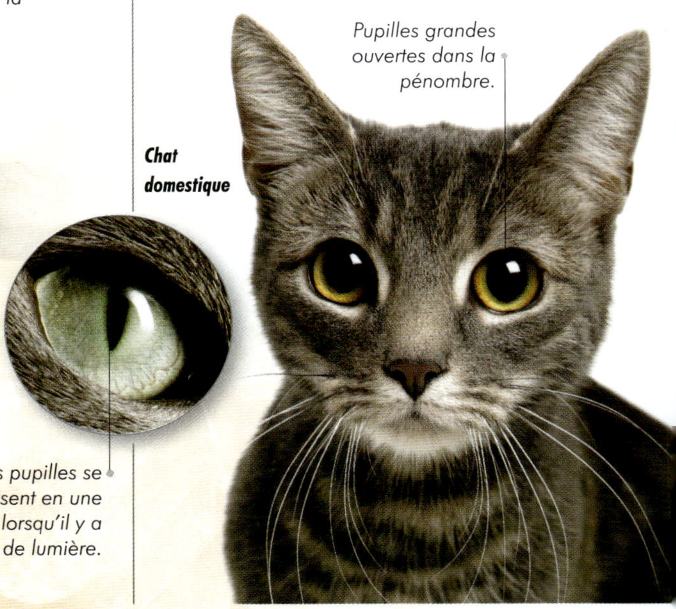

Pupilles grandes ouvertes dans la pénombre.

Chat domestique

Les pupilles se réduisent en une fente lorsqu'il y a trop de lumière.

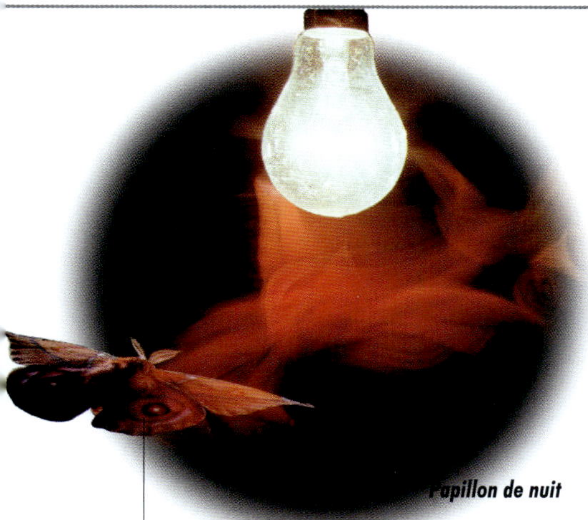

Papillon de nuit

Papillon de nuit attiré par une ampoule électrique.

Pourquoi les papillons de nuit volent-ils autour de la lumière ?

Q R Dans la nature, les papillons de nuit utilisent souvent la lune comme boussole pour se diriger. Mais s'ils volent près d'une maison, les lumières vives peuvent détériorer leur système de navigation. Le papillon tourne alors autour de la lumière jusqu'à finir dans une spirale infernale ou s'abattre sur une fenêtre.

Plus d' infos

- Les yeux des hiboux ne peuvent se mouvoir dans leurs orbites. Aussi doivent-ils tourner la tête pour regarder autour d'eux.
- Certains lézards ont une si longue langue qu'ils l' utilisent pour nettoyer leurs yeux.
- Les serpents n'ont pas de paupière, donc ils ne clignent pas des yeux. Ceux-ci restent grands ouverts même quand ils dorment.
- Le Characin aveugle, un poisson d'Amérique centrale, n'a pas d'yeux. Il s'oriente en détectant les modifications de la pression de l'eau autour de lui.

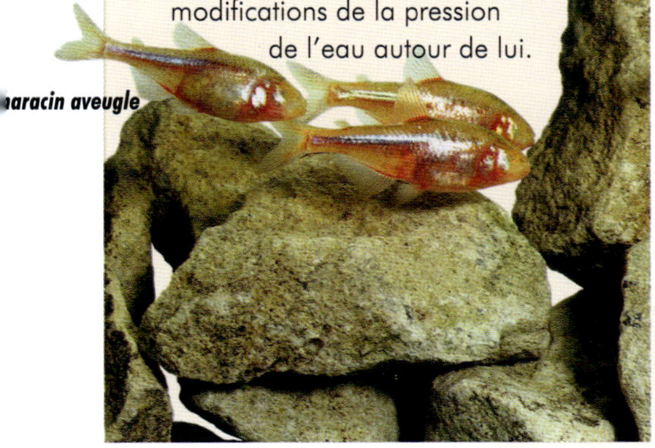

Characin aveugle

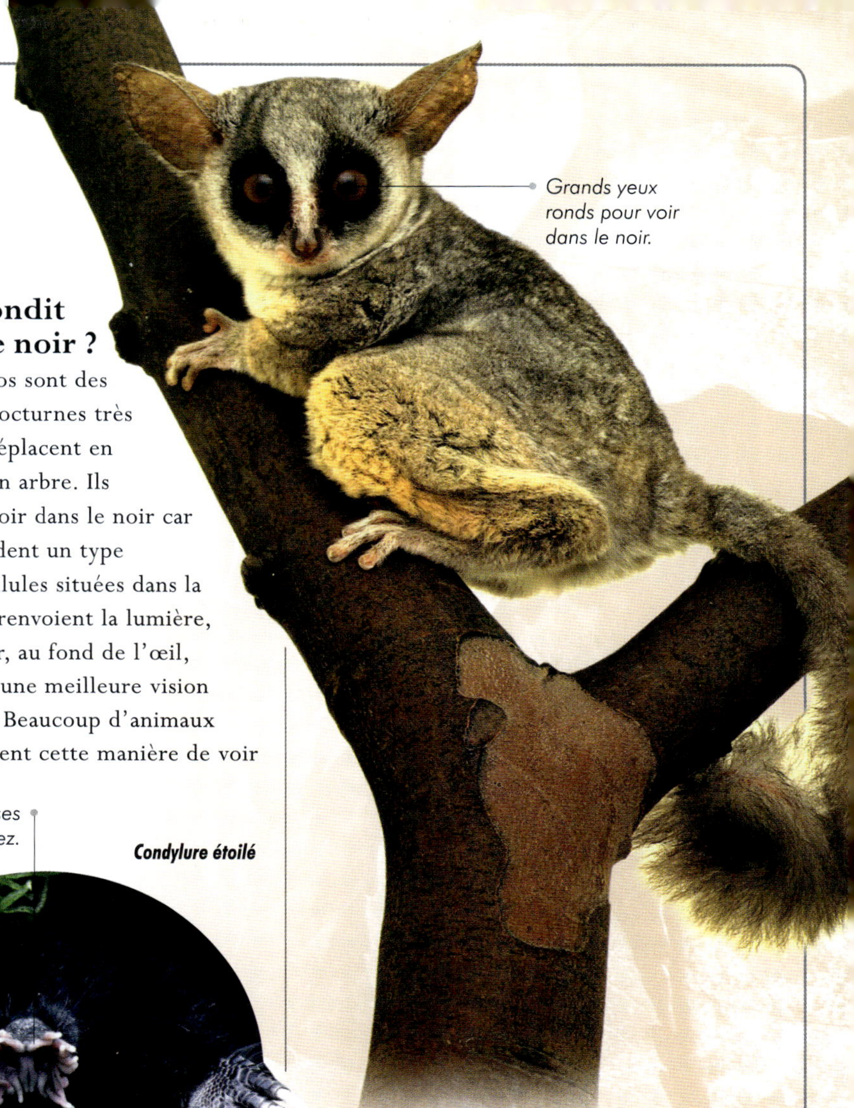

Galago

Grands yeux ronds pour voir dans le noir.

Qui bondit dans le noir ?

Q R Les galagos sont des petits primates nocturnes très agiles et qui se déplacent en sautant d'arbre en arbre. Ils peuvent se mouvoir dans le noir car leurs yeux possèdent un type particulier de cellules situées dans la rétine. Celles-ci renvoient la lumière, comme un miroir, au fond de l'œil, permettant ainsi une meilleure vision dans l'obscurité. Beaucoup d'animaux nocturnes partagent cette manière de voir dans le noir.

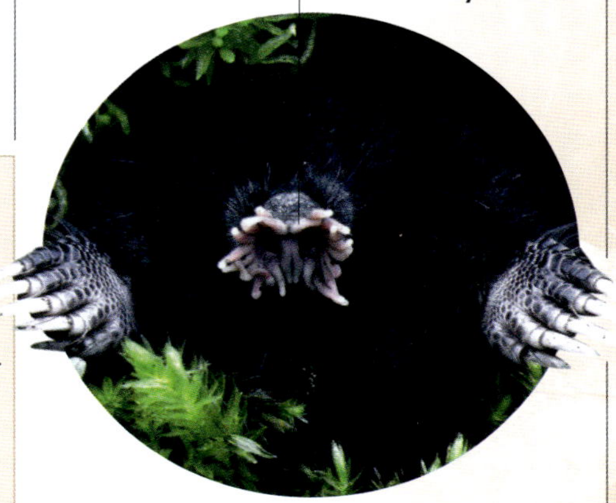

Tentacules roses sur le nez.

Condylure étoilé

Quel animal « voit » avec son nez ?

Q R Le condylure étoilé est une petite taupe qui a de tout petits yeux et qui est presque totalement aveugle. Mais sur le bout de son museau, il y a un cercle de 22 tentacules de chair rose vif. Ces tentacules peuvent bouger et fonctionnent comme de petits doigts. La taupe les utilise pour trouver son chemin et, plus important, pour trouver sa nourriture. Ces taupes passent le plus clair de leur temps dans des terriers, où « voir » avec des tentacules est plus utile que voir avec des yeux.

Qu'est-ce qui aide les serpents à voir dans le noir ?

Q R Les serpents sont spécialement équipés pour chasser la nuit. Ils ont une paire de cavités entre les yeux et les narines. Ces petites fosses contiennent des centaines de capteurs qui peuvent détecter la chaleur. Si le serpent s'approche d'un animal à sang chaud, une souris ou un lièvre, il peut localiser sa proie grâce à la chaleur qu'elle dégage.

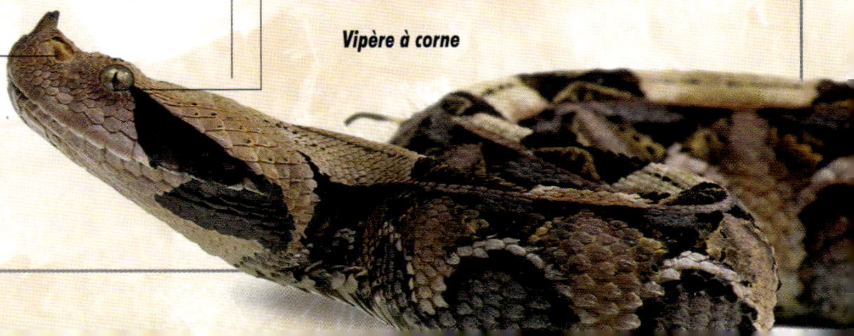

Vipère à corne

Œil avec une pupille en fente.

Fosse sensible à la chaleur située entre l'œil et la narine.

Est-ce utile d'avoir de grandes oreilles ?

L'ouïe est très importante pour beaucoup d'animaux, mais les mammifères sont les seuls à avoir des oreilles aux lobes charnus. Les oreilles des éléphants d'Afrique sont de loin les plus grandes. Elles peuvent atteindre 1,80 m de hauteur et plus de 1 m de large. Elles sont très sensibles et permettent de capter les sons produits par les autres éléphants, qui sont sur une fréquence trop basse pour les oreilles humaines. Les éléphants utilisent aussi leurs oreilles pour se rafraîchir et ils les balancent violemment s'ils ont peur ou sont en colère. Mais les oreilles n'ont pas besoin d'être grandes pour être efficaces. Beaucoup d'animaux, qui ont de petites oreilles, voire même des oreilles cachées, entendent mieux que les humains.

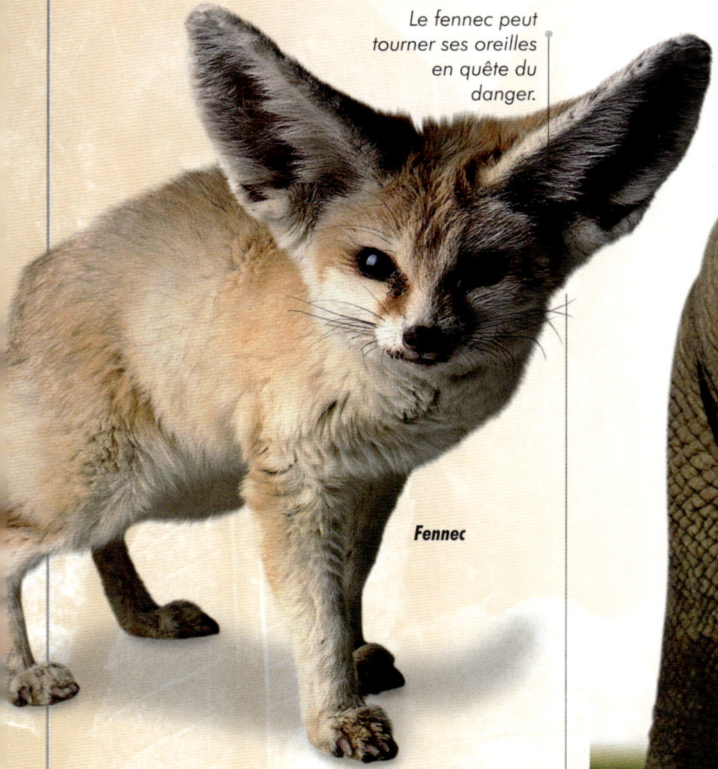

Le fennec peut tourner ses oreilles en quête du danger.

Fennec

Q/R Quel animal a la meilleure ouïe ?

Les éléphants entendent très bien les basses fréquences, mais le petit fennec entend encore mieux les sons faibles ou les hautes fréquences. Le fennec vit dans le désert du Sahara où il sort de nuit pour se nourrir d'insectes et de lézards. Ses très grandes oreilles entendent le moindre scarabée qui marche sur le sol. Elles l'aident aussi à se rafraîchir en éliminant de la chaleur corporelle.

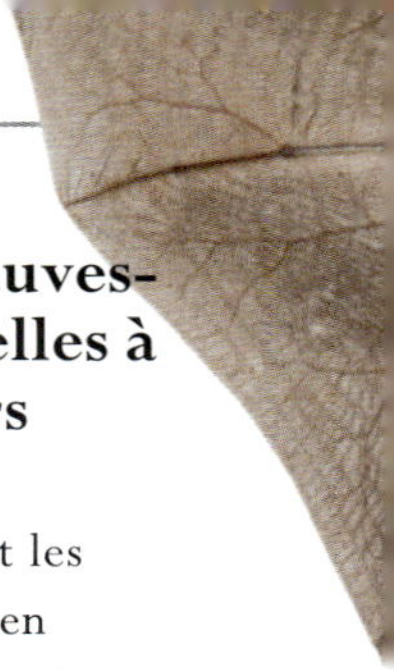

Q/R Comment les chauves-souris trouvent-elles à manger avec leurs oreilles ?

Les oreillards communs chassent les insectes la nuit. Ils les trouvent en émettant des ondes sonores. Si un insecte est proche, la chauve-souris le détecte à l'aide de son sonar qui lui renvoie son écho et la guide vers sa proie. Cette façon de se diriger est nommée écholocation. La plupart des chauves-souris insectivores utilisent ce moyen pour se nourrir.

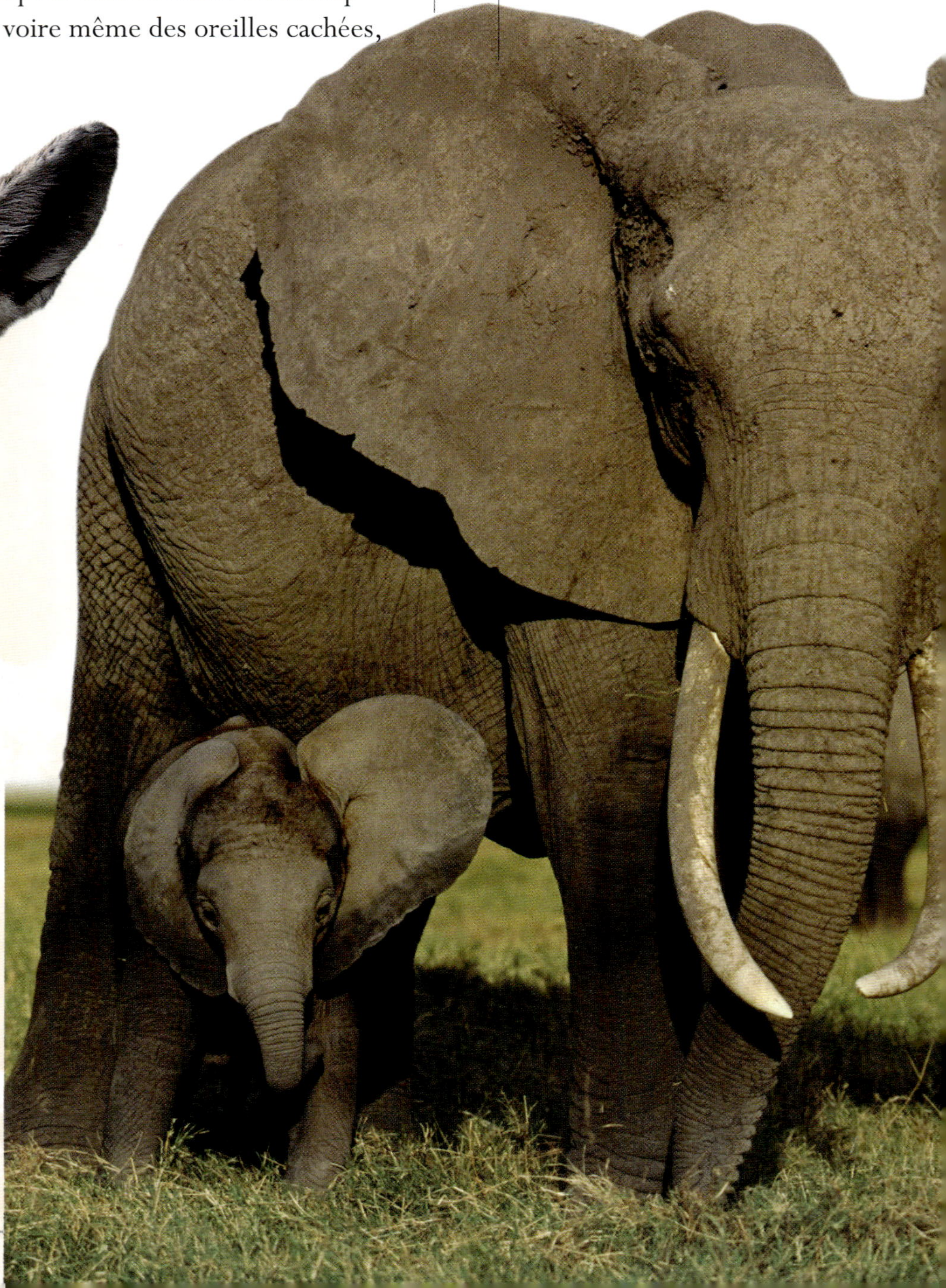

Les éléphants battent lentement leurs oreilles pour se rafraîchir, diminuant ainsi leur chaleur interne.

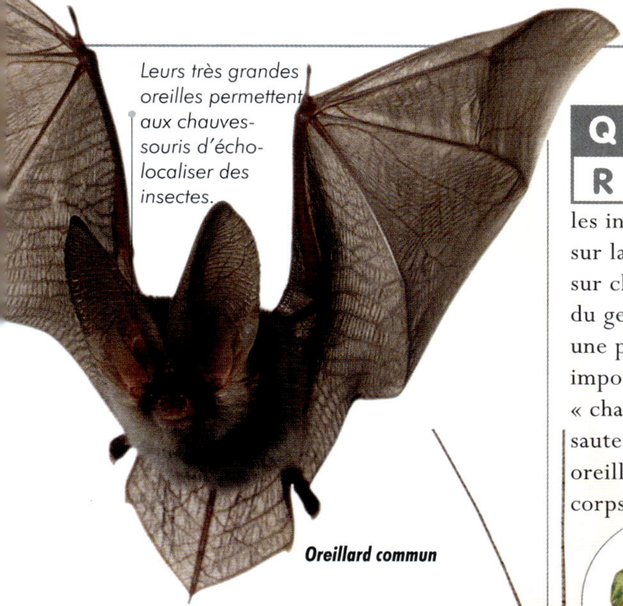

Leurs très grandes oreilles permettent aux chauves-souris d'écho-localiser des insectes.

Oreillard commun

La forme de l'oreille est unique, comme le sont les empreintes digitales des humains.

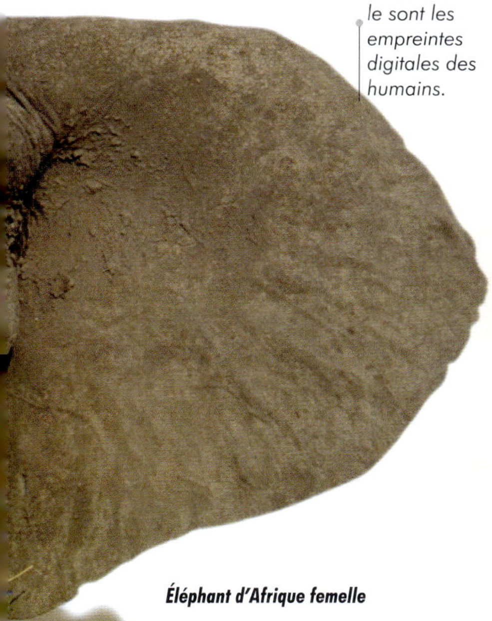

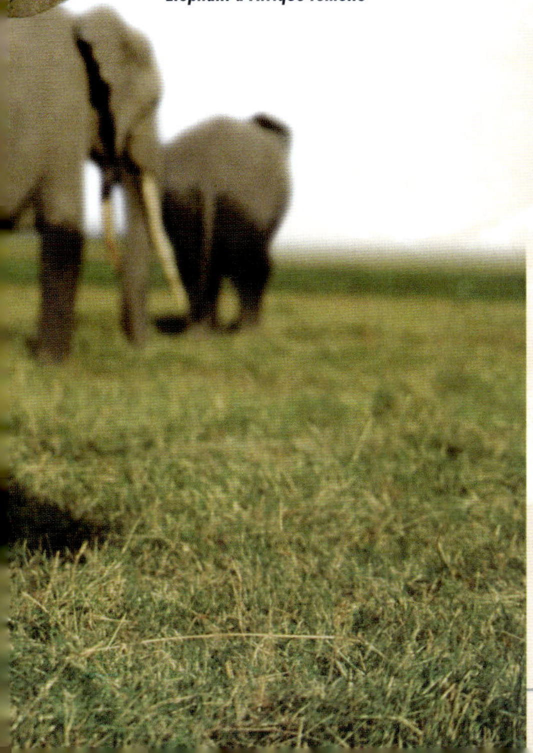

Éléphant d'Afrique femelle

Q Quel insecte a les oreilles près des genoux ?

R Contrairement aux mammifères, les insectes n'ont pas toujours les oreilles sur la tête. Les criquets ont une oreille sur chaque patte avant, juste en dessous du genou. L'oreille n'a pas de lobe, c'est une petite fente ovale. L'ouïe est importante pour les criquets car le mâle « chante » pour attirer les femelles. Les sauterelles chantent aussi, mais leurs oreilles se trouvent sur les côtés de leur corps, juste derrière leurs ailes.

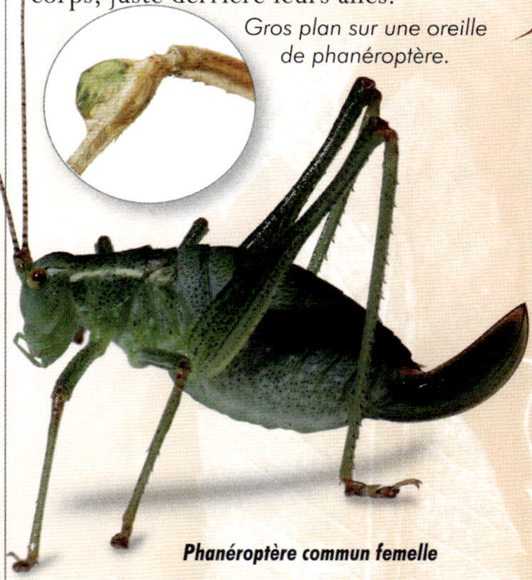

Gros plan sur une oreille de phanéroptère.

Phanéroptère commun femelle

Plus d' infos

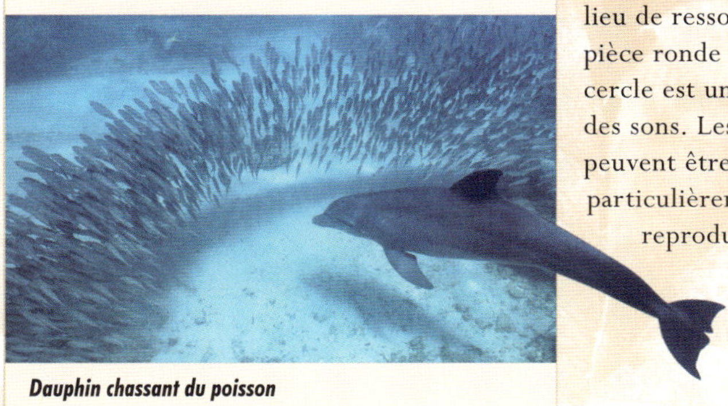

Dauphin chassant du poisson

- Les dauphins utilisent l'écholocation pour trouver leur nourriture et pour se repérer au fond de l'eau, la nuit.
- Bien que l'on ait longtemps cru que les girafes étaient muettes, les scientifiques pensent aujourd'hui qu'elles communiquent entre elles par des infrasons (graves) qui ne peuvent être entendus par l'oreille humaine.

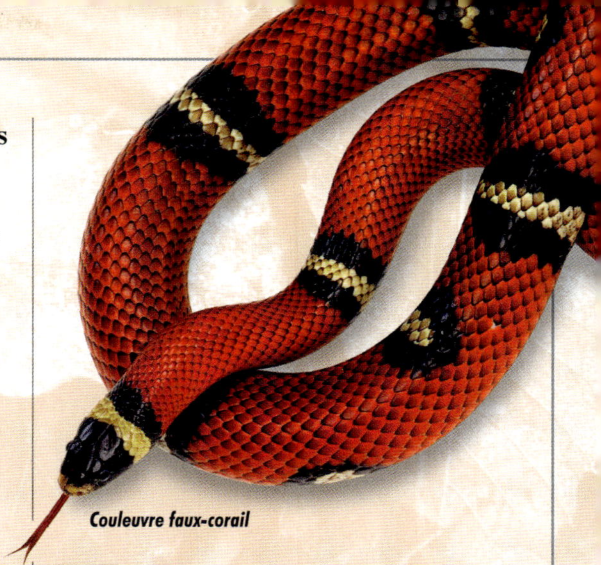

Couleuvre faux-corail

Q Est-il vrai que les serpents sont sourds ?

R Contrairement aux lézards, les serpents n'ont pas d'oreilles, mais malgré cela ils ne sont pas complètement sourds. Les scientifiques ne savent pas exactement quel est le niveau de leur ouïe, mais ils captent probablement les vibrations sonores avec leur corps et avec des capteurs situés dans leur tête. Les serpents ressentent intensément les vibrations du sol. S'ils perçoivent des pas venant dans leur direction, la plupart prendront vite la fuite.

Q Les grenouilles et les crapauds ont-ils des oreilles ?

R Oui. Si tu regardes une grenouille de près, tu verras facilement ses oreilles. Au lieu de ressortir, chacune ressemble à une pièce ronde juste derrière les yeux. Ce cercle est un tympan, il vibre au passage des sons. Les grenouilles et les crapauds peuvent être très bruyants, particulièrement au moment de la reproduction. Ils utilisent leurs oreilles pour déceler les appels et trouver un partenaire.

Tympan à la surface du corps.

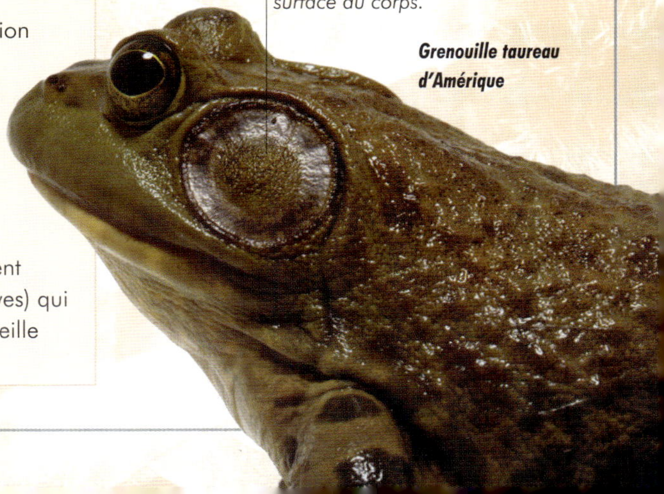

Grenouille taureau d'Amérique

Les oiseaux ont-ils un nez ?

La plupart des animaux ont le sens de l'odorat mais leur nez - ou leurs narines – ne sont pas toujours là où tu pourrais penser les trouver. Le nez des oiseaux est souvent au-dessus de leur bec ou parfois même à l'intérieur. Les albatros ont un très grand nez et un excellent odorat. Cela leur permet de repérer la nourriture flottant sur la mer, même la nuit. Peu d'oiseaux ont un odorat aussi développé qu'eux. Pour beaucoup d'animaux, un bon odorat est vital pour survivre.

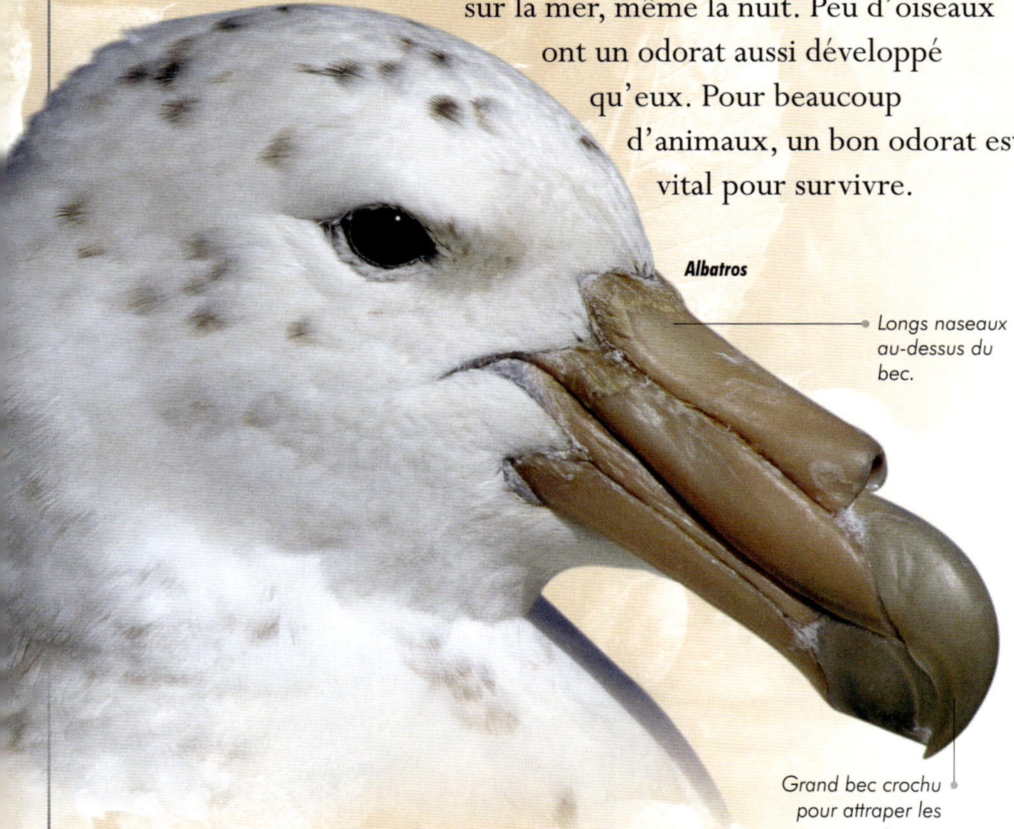

Albatros

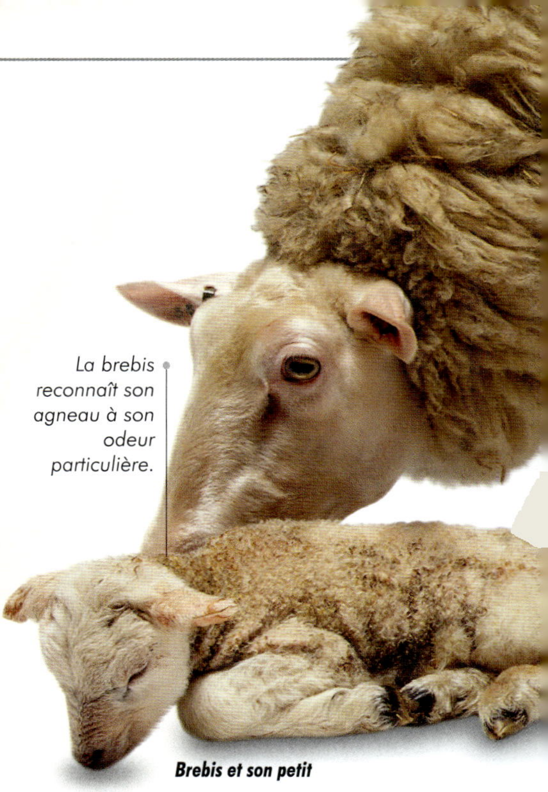

Brebis et son petit

Q R Pourquoi les brebis reniflent-elles leurs petits ?

En général, les brebis mettent bas de un à trois agneaux. Après la naissance, la mère lèche ses petits et les renifle. Ainsi, elle pourra les reconnaître à leur odeur. Si un agneau s'approche d'une brebis qui n'est pas sa mère et tente de boire son lait, celle-ci le repoussera. Beaucoup d'autres mammifères, des souris aux antilopes, utilisent leur odorat comme moyen d'identification entre eux.

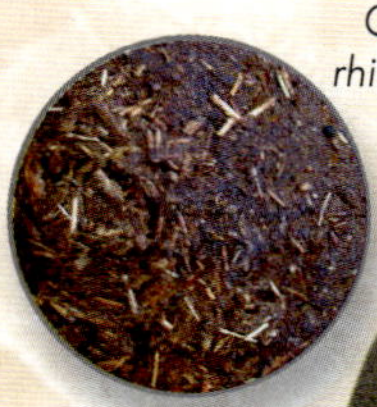
Crotte de rhinocéros.

Q R Que font les rhinocéros avec leurs crottes ?

Certains animaux enterrent leurs fèces (excréments), mais les rhinocéros font le contraire, ils les mettent en évidence. Ils les laissent en tas, qui peuvent mesurer jusqu'à 1 m de large. Un grand mâle peut faire jusqu'à 30 tas qu'il inspecte presque chaque jour. Les rhinocéros utilisent ces tas pour marquer les limites de leur territoire. Cela fonctionne bien, car ils ont une mauvaise vue mais un bon odorat.

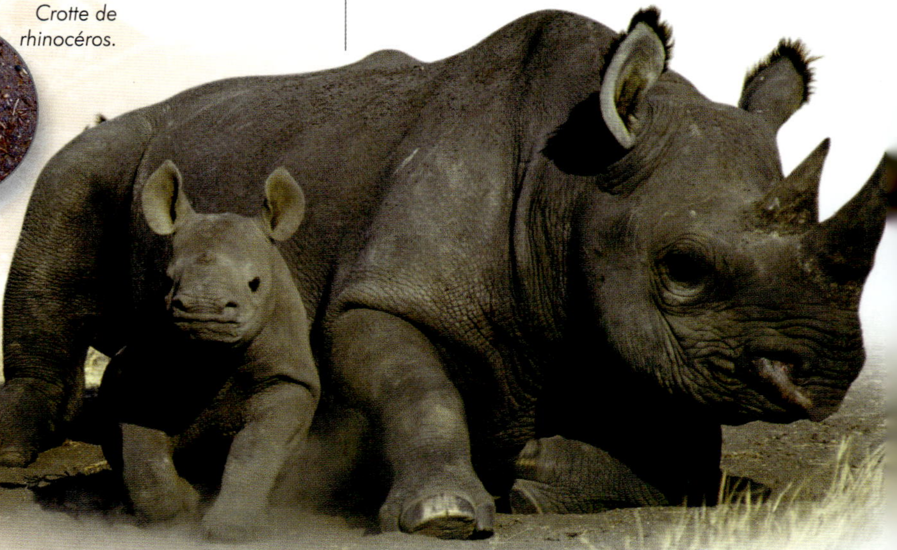
Rhinocéros femelle et son petit

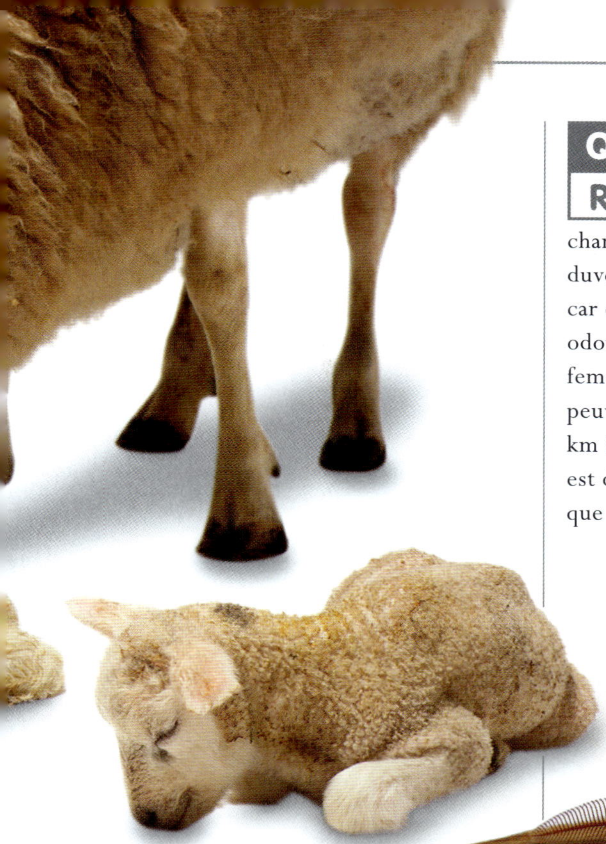

Qui a l'odorat le plus performant ?

Les papillons de nuit sont les champions de l'odorat. Leurs antennes duveteuses fonctionnent comme un nez, car elles perçoivent les particules odorantes lâchées par les papillons femelles volant dans l'air. Certains mâles peuvent sentir une femelle à plus de 10 km à la ronde. À cette distance, l'odeur est des millions de fois trop légère pour que le nez humain puisse la détecter.

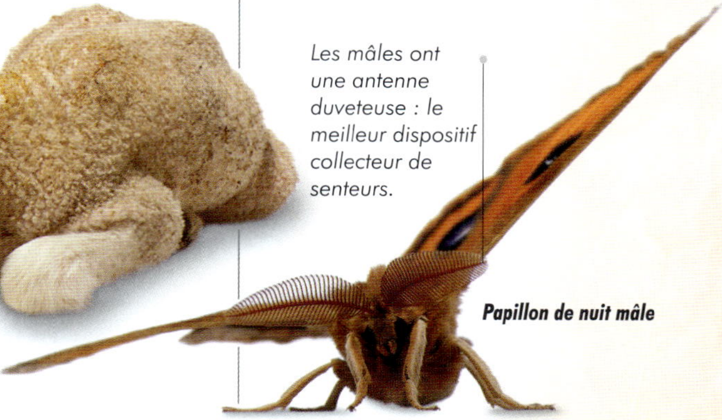

Les mâles ont une antenne duveteuse : le meilleur dispositif collecteur de senteurs.

Papillon de nuit mâle

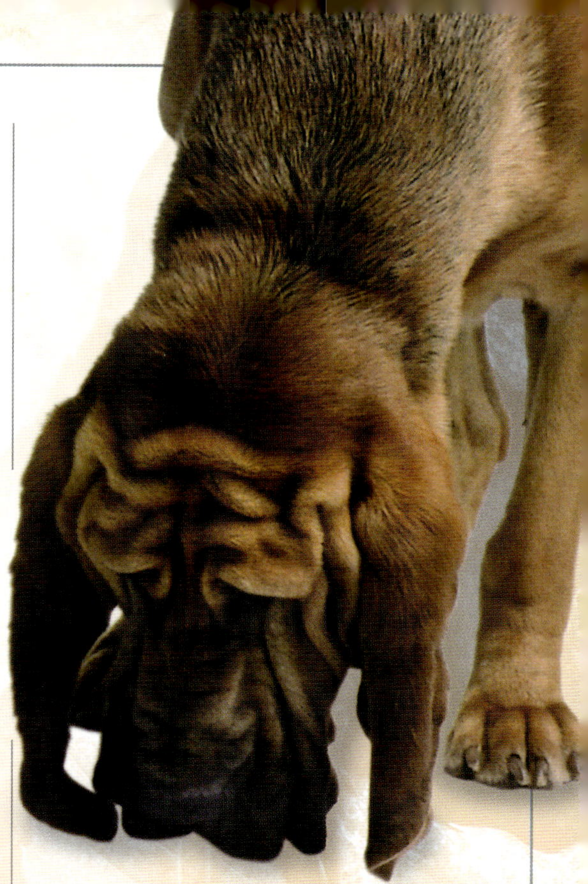

Chien de Saint-Hubert

Plus d'infos

- Les varans sentent de la même façon que les serpents, en sortant leur langue. Les plus gros varans, les dragons du Komodo, ont une langue qui peut atteindre 30 cm.
- Le kiwi est le seul oiseau dont les naseaux sont à l'extrémité du bec. Il sonde le sol humide durant la nuit, à la recherche de vers de terre et d'insectes.
- Les requins utilisent leur odorat pour localiser leur proie. Ils peuvent sentir le sang à des kilomètres de distance.

Requin dormeur taureau

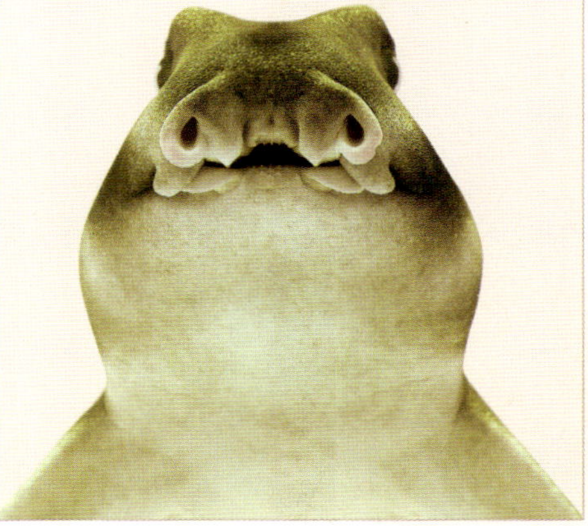

Pourquoi les serpents tirent-ils la langue ?

Plutôt que de sentir avec leur nez, les serpents utilisent leur langue. Un serpent reçoit les particules odorantes en suspension sur sa langue puis les presse dans des trous spéciaux de son palais. Les nerfs de cet orifice analysent l'odeur de la même manière qu'un nez. Si un serpent sort rapidement la langue de sa gueule, c'est que quelque chose dans l'air l'intéresse.

Qui est le meilleur détective ?

Tous les chiens ont un odorat développé, mais celui des chiens de Saint-Hubert est plus de 10 millions de fois supérieur à celui des hommes. Ils peuvent détecter l'odeur des cellules de la peau d'une personne, même si elles se sont détachées depuis plusieurs jours. Ils peuvent suivre une piste, même si la personne a traversé des foules. Les odeurs sont identifiées par des récepteurs sensoriels situés dans les fosses nasales du chien. Ces limiers peuvent ainsi aider à résoudre des enquêtes criminelles.

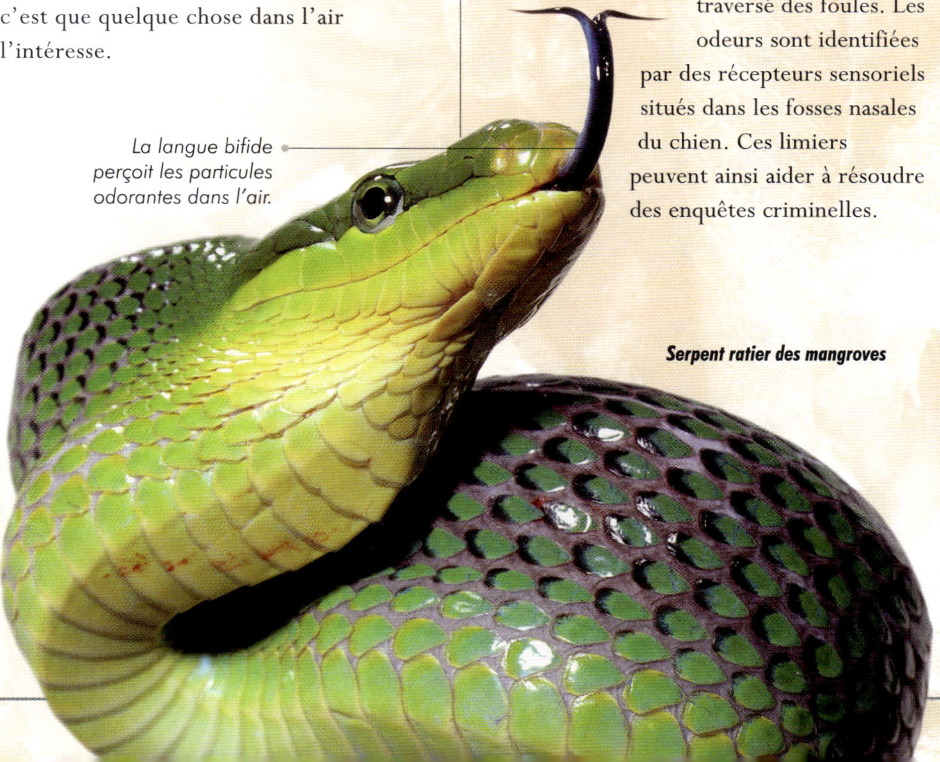

La langue bifide perçoit les particules odorantes dans l'air.

Serpent ratier des mangroves

Qui aime les boissons sucrées ?

Le goût indique aux animaux ce qui est bon à manger et ce qui pourrait être mauvais. Pour les oiseaux-mouches, une bonne nourriture doit être sucrée. Comme les abeilles, ils se nourrissent de nectar, un jus très sucré produit par les fleurs. Grâce à leur bec en forme de paille et à leur langue, ils aspirent le nectar tout en volant. Tous les animaux ne goûtent pas avec leur langue. Certains insectes goûtent avec leurs pattes. D'autres animaux se fient au toucher pour trouver leur nourriture.

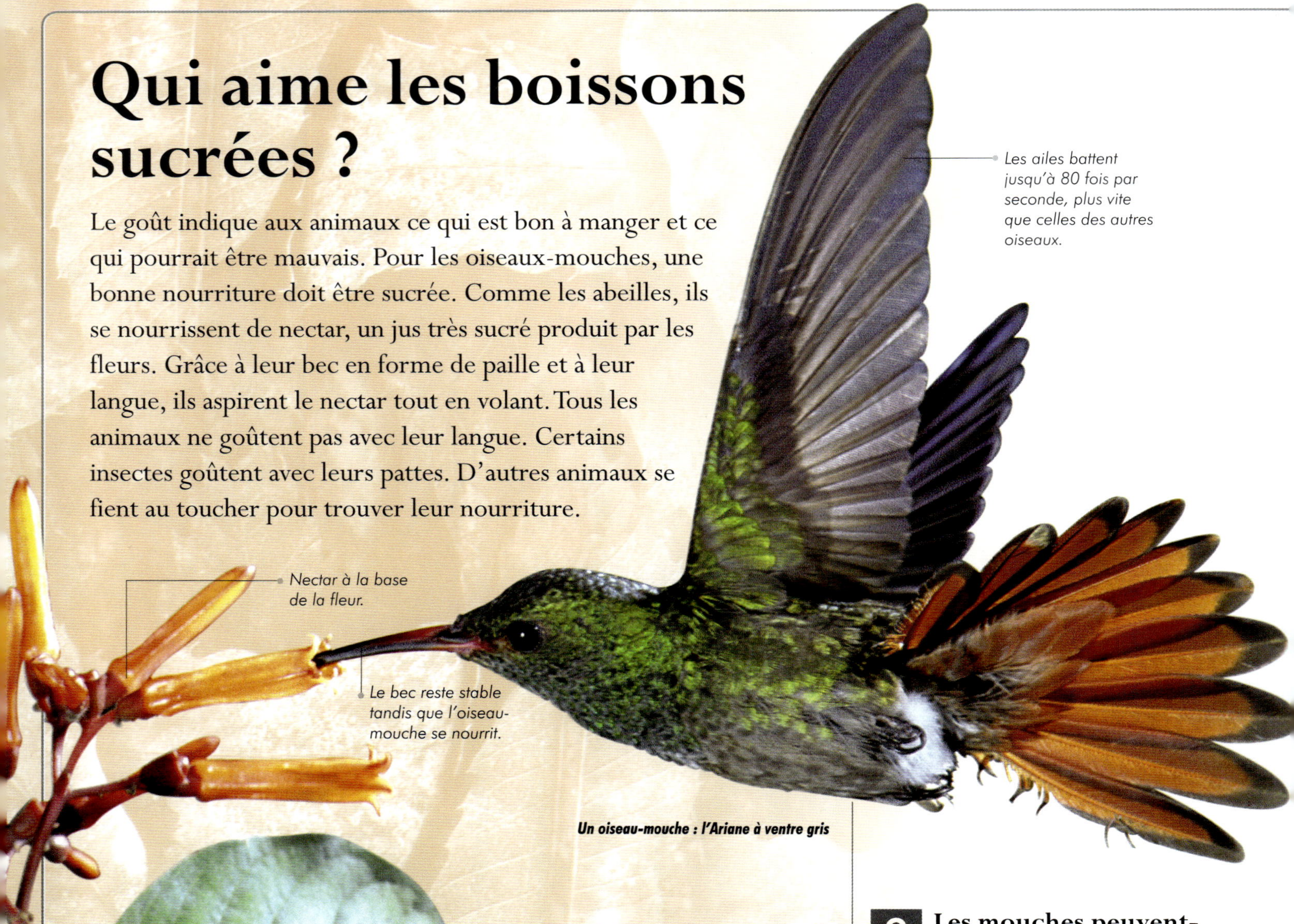

Un oiseau-mouche : l'Ariane à ventre gris

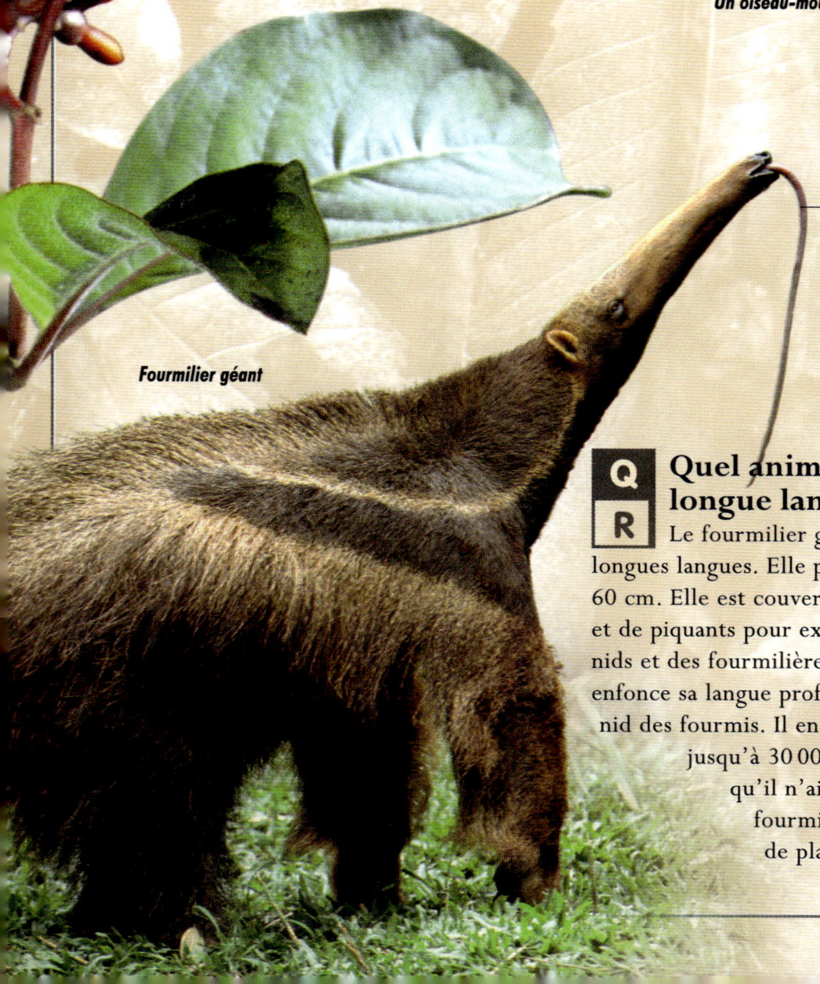

Fourmilier géant

Q R Quel animal a la plus longue langue ?

Le fourmilier géant a l'une des plus longues langues. Elle peut mesurer jusqu'à 60 cm. Elle est couverte de salive collante et de piquants pour extraire les proies des nids et des fourmilières. Le fourmilier enfonce sa langue profondément dans le nid des fourmis. Il en récupère ainsi jusqu'à 30 000 par jour. Bien qu'il n'ait pas de dents, le fourmilier se nourrit aussi de plantes tropicales.

Q R Les mouches peuvent-elles sentir avec leurs pattes ?

Oui, elles le peuvent, ainsi que d'autres insectes tels que les papillons. Cette façon de sentir leur permet de gagner beaucoup de temps, car elle leur indique s'ils sont sur de la nourriture dès leur atterrissage. Si les mouches sentent quelque chose de sucré, elles le ramassent avec leur langue qui fonctionne comme une éponge.

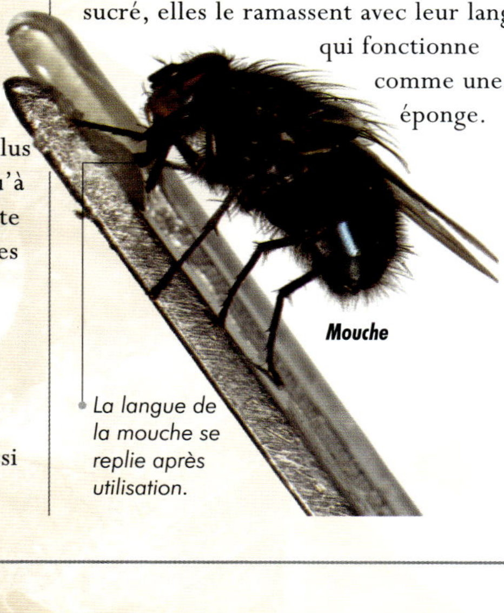

Mouche

Q R Quel animal a les plus longues antennes ?

Si un homard survit jusqu'à un âge avancé, ses antennes peuvent atteindre jusqu'à 1 mètre de long. Celles-ci « sentent » aussi bien qu'elles « touchent ». Elles grandissent chaque fois que le homard mue. Si elles se brisent lors d'un accident ou d'un combat, elles repousseront. Mais cela prendra du temps pour qu'elles retrouvent leur taille initiale.

Les homards ont deux paires d'antennes, une longue et une courte.

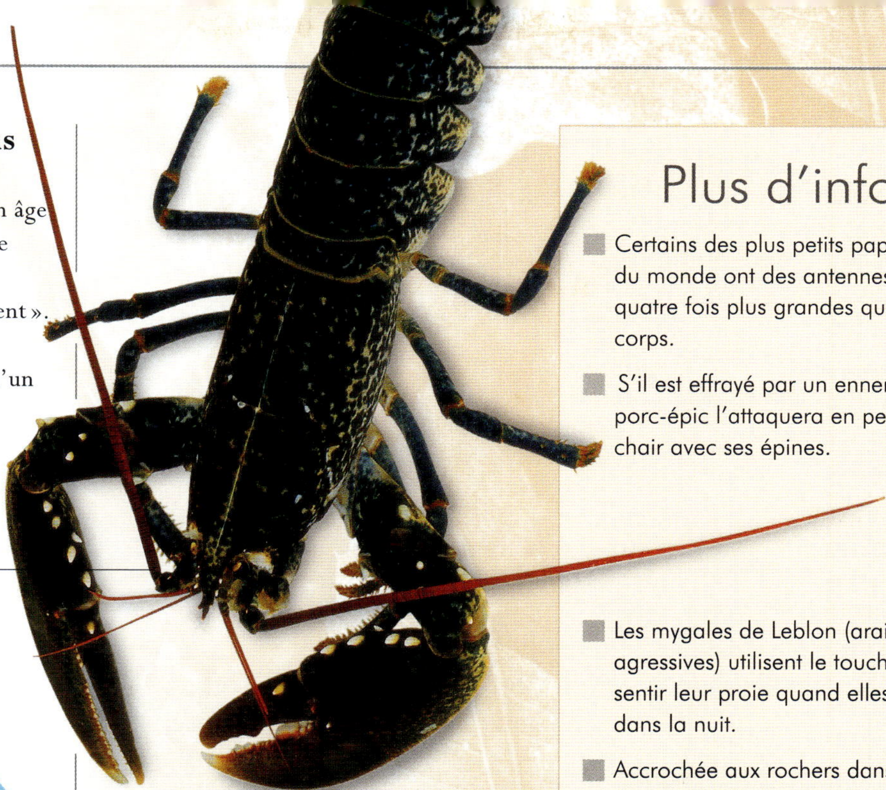

Homard

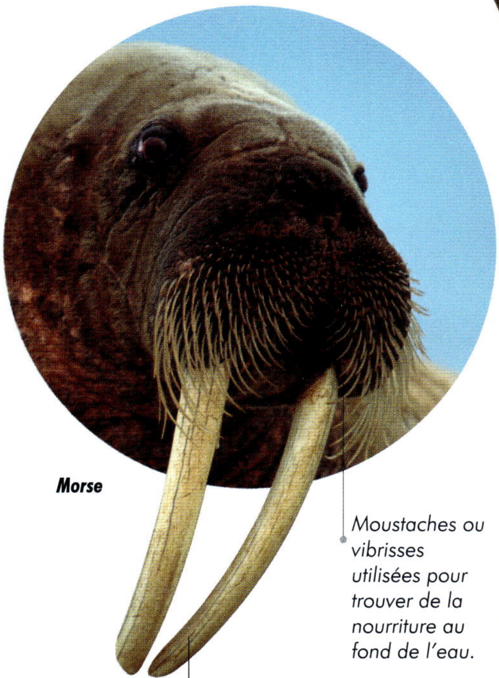

Morse

Moustaches ou vibrisses utilisées pour trouver de la nourriture au fond de l'eau.

Le morse peut utiliser ses défenses pour se hisser sur la glace.

Q R Pourquoi les morses ont-ils des moustaches ?

Contrairement aux phoques, les morses plongent jusqu'au fond de la mer pour se nourrir. Ils attrapent de nombreux petits animaux mais aiment particulièrement les vers, les concombres de mer et les coquillages comme les clams. Lorsqu'un morse se nourrit, le fond de l'eau est souvent opaque, et c'est là que les moustaches sont utiles : au lieu de chercher avec ses yeux, le morse sent avec ses moustaches. Lorsqu'il touche de la nourriture, il l'aspire en se servant de sa bouche comme d'un aspirateur pour l'avaler.

Q R Quels animaux ont le sens du toucher le plus développé au monde ?

Les rats-taupes nus vivent sous la terre et sont presque aveugles. En revanche, ils ont un sens du toucher très développé. Leur peau n'a pratiquement pas de poils, mais ils ont plusieurs dizaines de poils sensitifs sur les côtés du corps. Si un seul de ces poils est touché, le rat-taupe cherche ce qui l'a frôlé. Ces animaux vivent en groupe et se nourrissent de racines qu'ils rongent avec leurs grandes incisives.

Plus d'infos

- Certains des plus petits papillons du monde ont des antennes qui sont quatre fois plus grandes que leur corps.
- S'il est effrayé par un ennemi, le porc-épic l'attaquera en perçant sa chair avec ses épines.
- Les mygales de Leblon (araignées très agressives) utilisent le toucher pour sentir leur proie quand elles chassent dans la nuit.
- Accrochée aux rochers dans l'eau peu profonde, l'anémone de mer attend que des petites créatures touchent ses tentacules. Elle attaque alors avec des centaines de petits aiguillons.

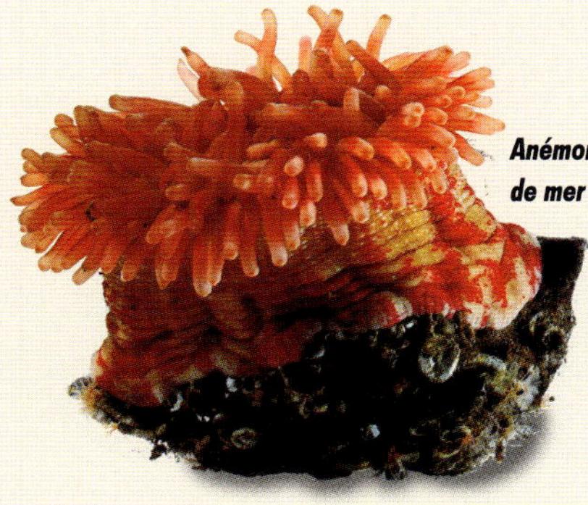

Anémone de mer

Moustaches et poils pour se repérer dans le noir.

Rats-taupes nus

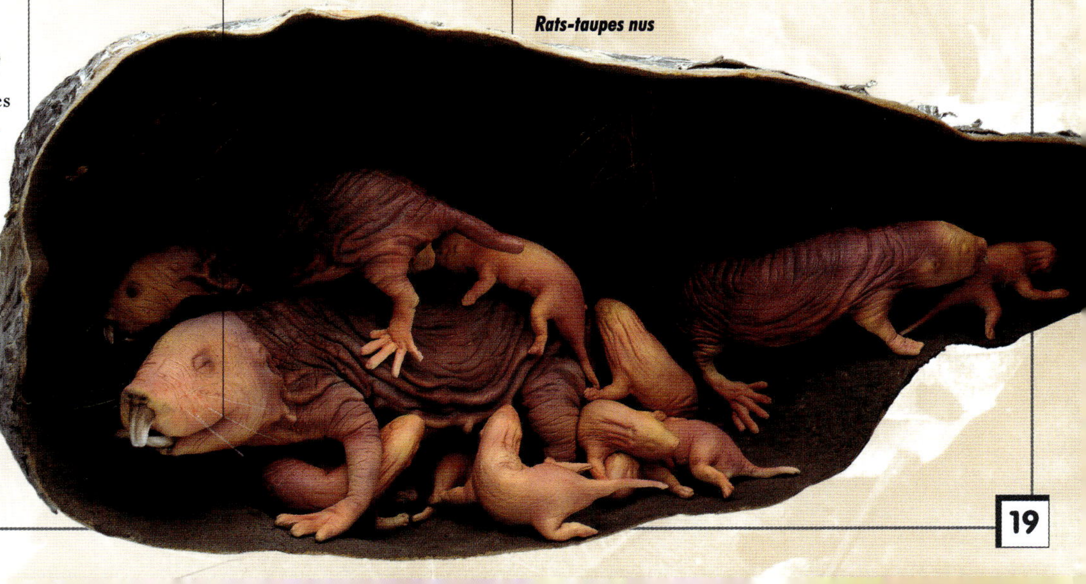

COMBATTRE POUR SURVIVRE

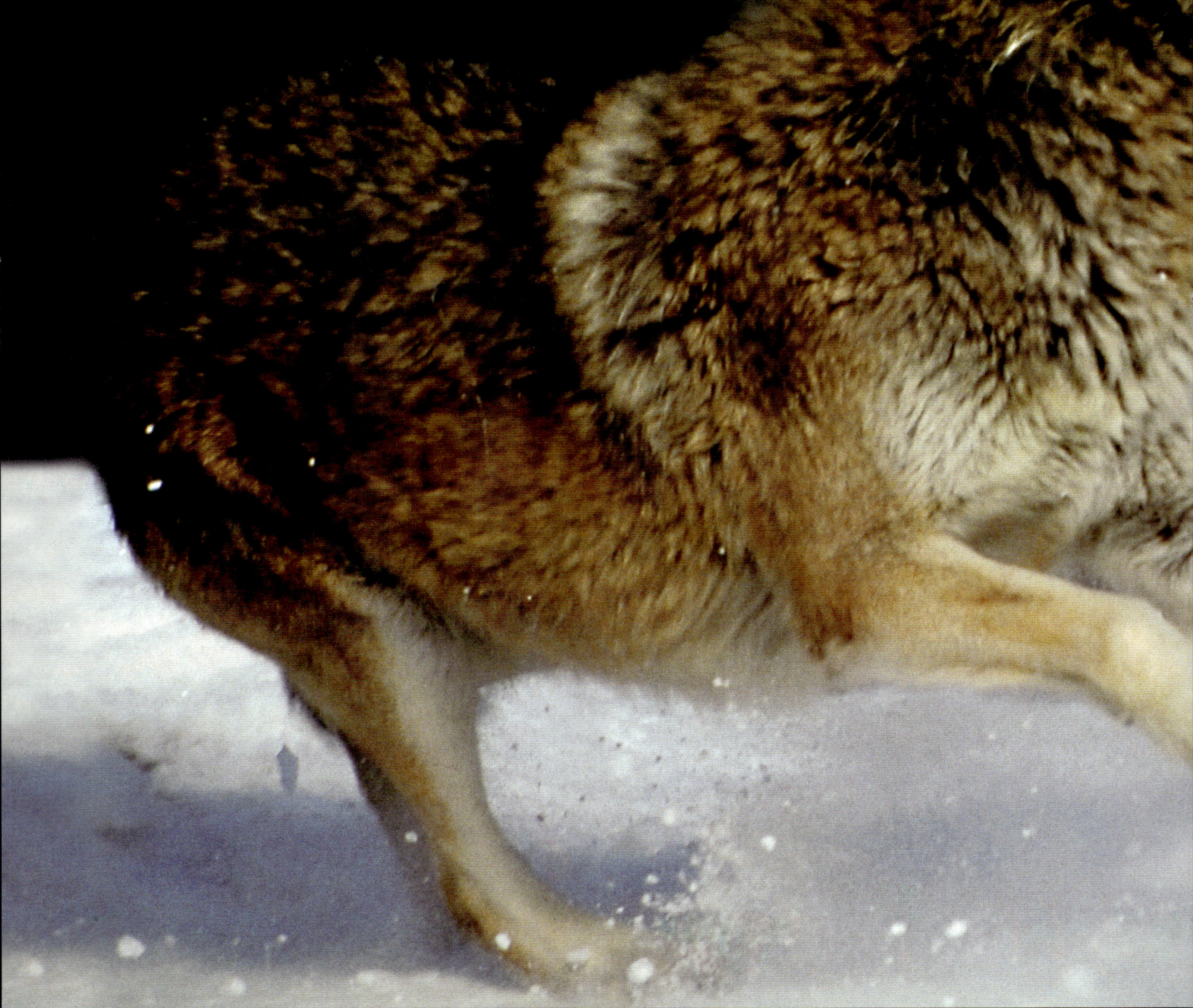

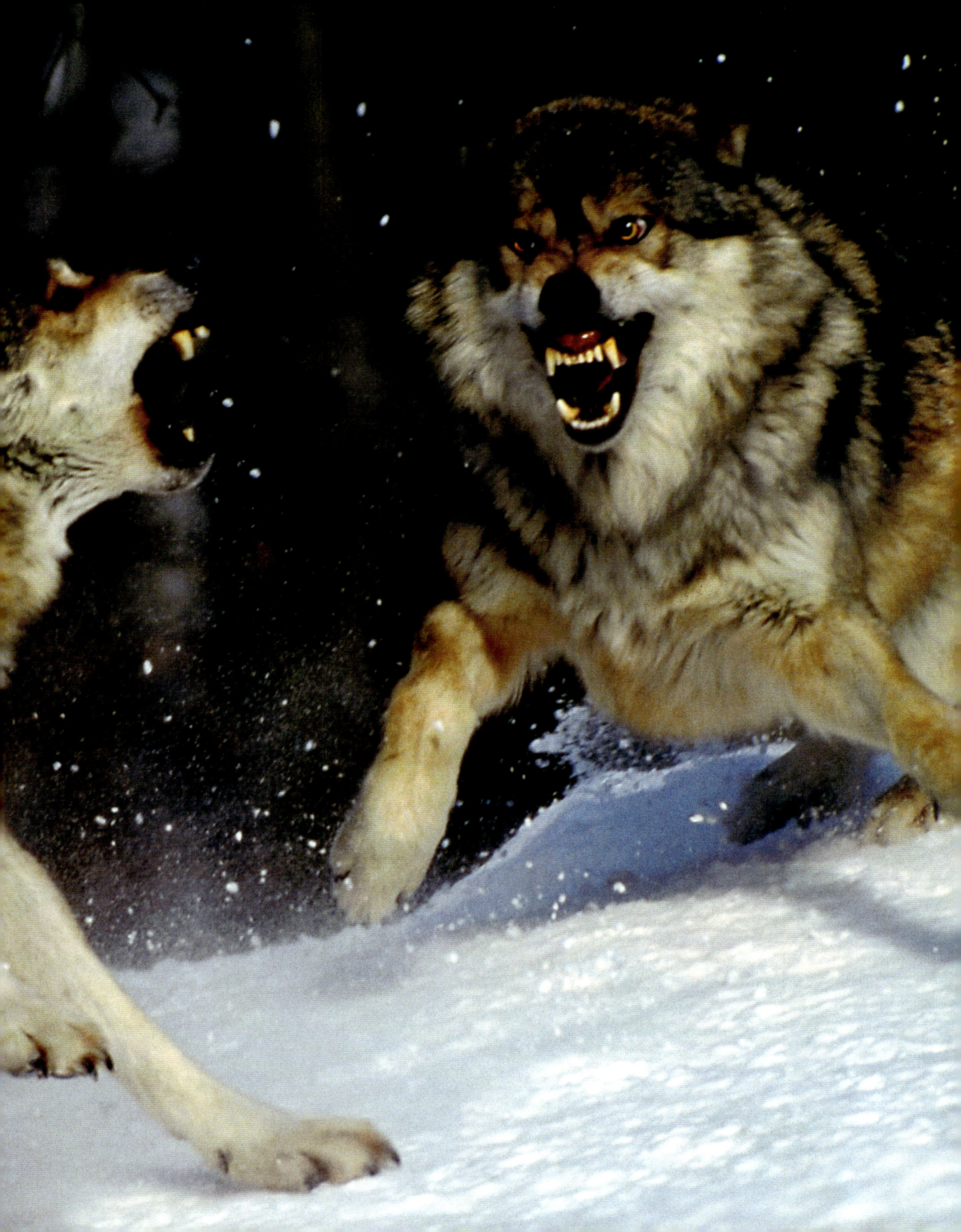

Quel est le plus grand prédateur terrestre ?

Lorsqu'il s'agit de chasser, la taille a souvent de l'importance. Parmi les grands tueurs, on trouve les ours bruns ou les grizzlis, de loin les plus grands chasseurs sur terre. Les ours bruns peuvent se tenir debout et mesurent alors 3,40 m de haut. Ils ont des dents et des griffes solides et sont incroyablement forts. Bien qu'ils restent généralement tranquilles, ils sont capables de se déplacer très rapidement à la poursuite d'une proie. Heureusement, les ours bruns se tiennent à l'écart des hommes. Mais il n'y a pas que la taille qui compte pour un prédateur, parfois les tout-petits peuvent être tout aussi redoutables.

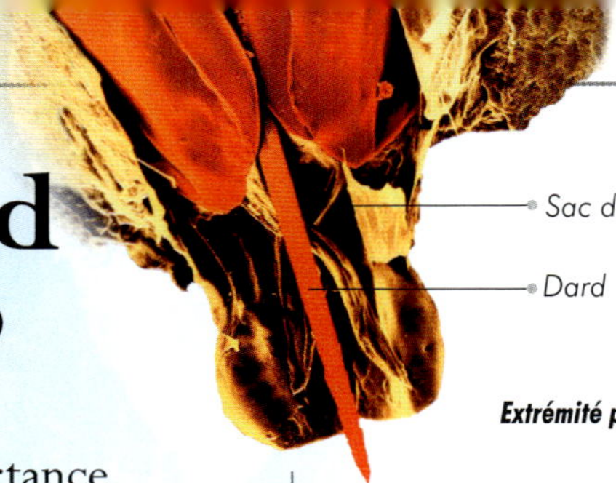

Extrémité postérieure d'une abeille

Q Les piqûres d'abeilles sont-elles mortelles ?

R Oui, elles peuvent l'être. Les abeilles ne piquent que pour se défendre. Mais leur piqûre peut se révéler mortelle si l'abeille pique la bouche ou la gorge d'un animal, par exemple. Pour la plupart des humains, une piqûre est douloureuse, mais cette sensation désagréable disparaît rapidement au fur et à mesure de la diffusion du venin dans l'organisme. Mais si l'on est allergique aux piqûres d'abeilles, la réaction peut alors être violente : difficultés pour respirer, puis, sans soins appropriés, étouffement, voire décès.

Ours bruns

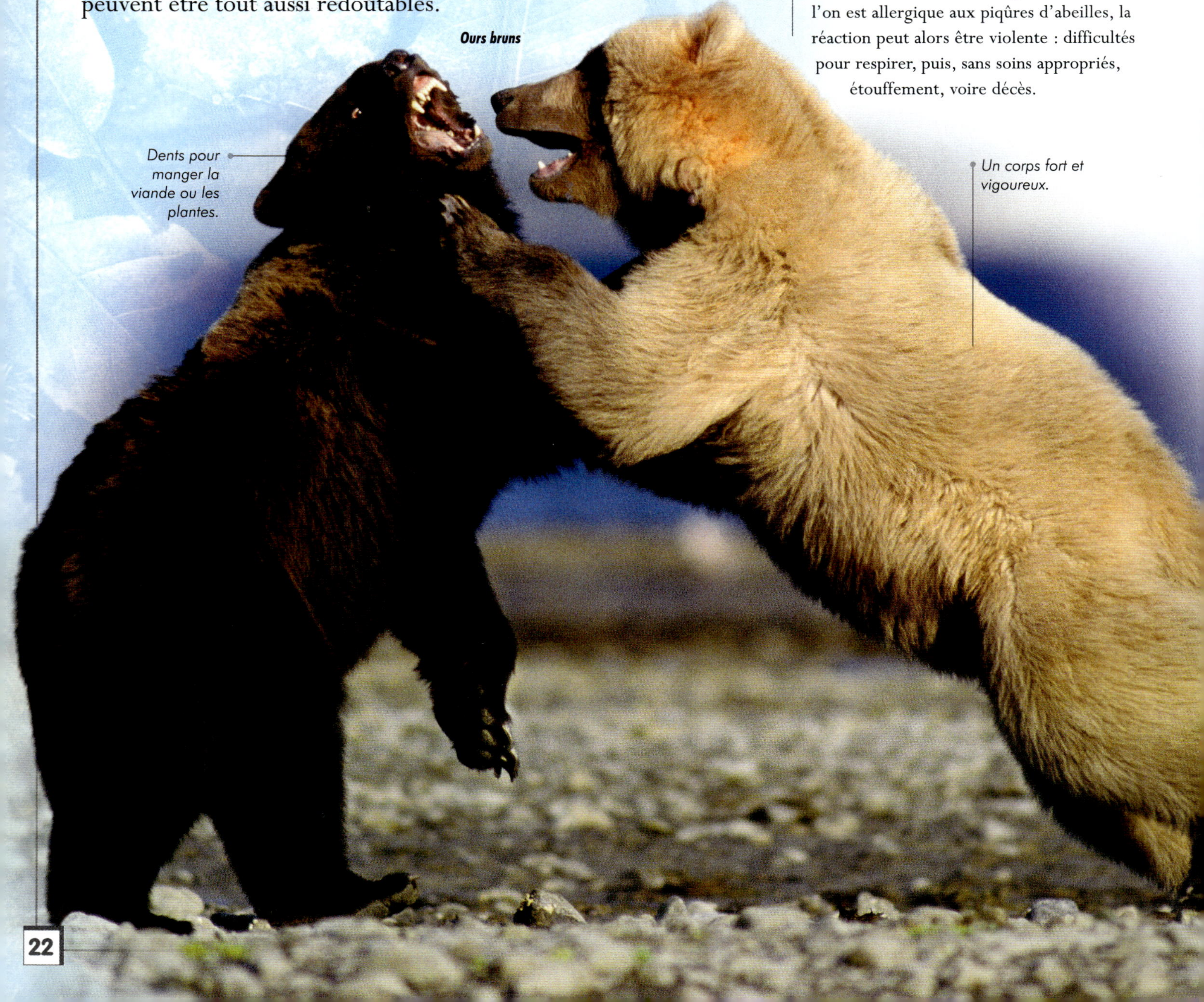

Comment une méduse tue-t-elle sa proie ?

Q

R Les cuboméduses portent un poison violent dans leurs tentacules. Elles dérivent avec les courants et enserrent leurs proies, des crevettes ou de petits poissons passant à leur portée, dans leurs tentacules venimeux. Les cuboméduses vivent dans les eaux des côtes du Nord de l'Australie. Elles peuvent être très dangereuses pour les nageurs.

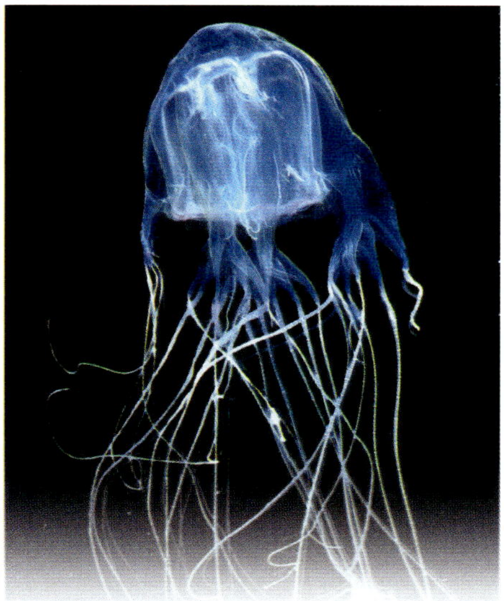

Cuboméduse

Quel est le plus gros chasseur du monde ?

Q

R Le cachalot est le plus grand prédateur du monde. Il mesure jusqu'à 20 m de long. Il plonge profondément dans les océans où il chasse les calmars géants. Contrairement aux baleines à fanons, les grands cachalots ont des dents pointues pour tuer leurs proies, qu'ils traquent en utilisant un sonar.

Cachalot

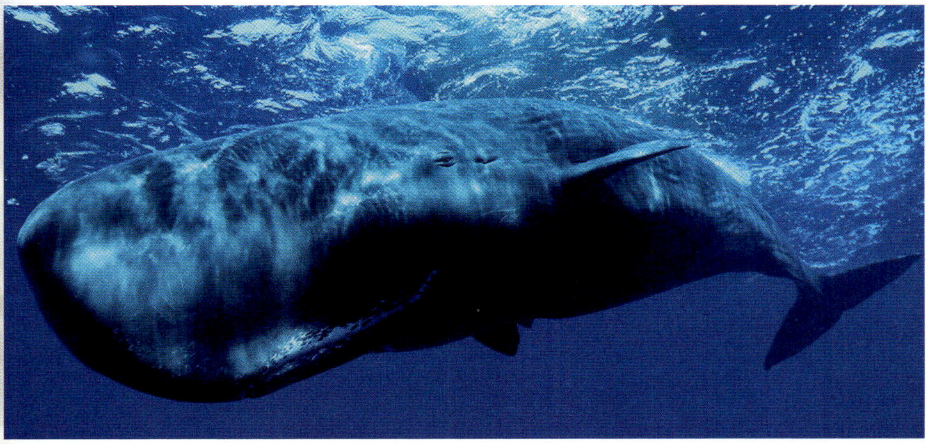

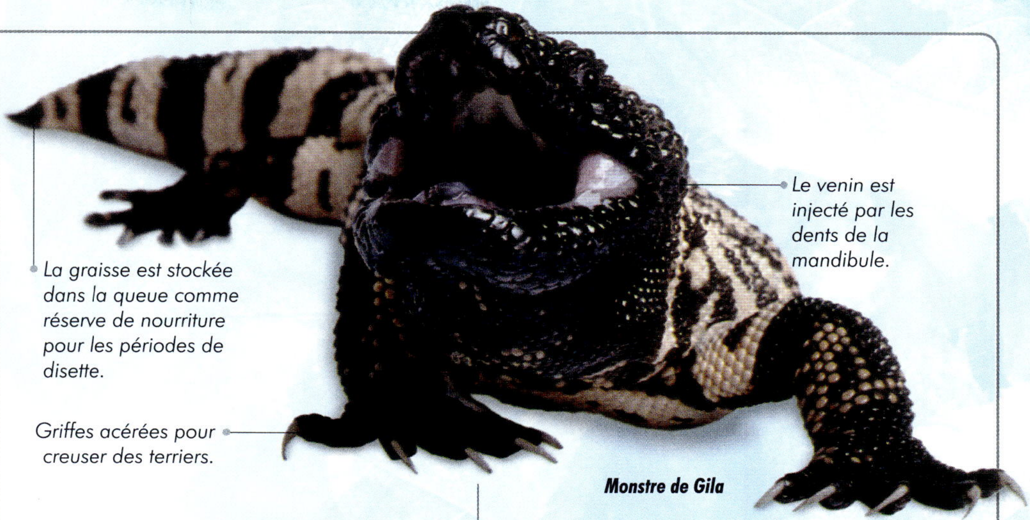

Monstre de Gila

Quel serpent a le poison le plus dangereux ?

Q

R Le serpent marin à bec que l'on trouve dans l'océan Indien est de loin le serpent le plus venimeux du monde. Sur terre, le taïpan qui vit dans les déserts d'Australie est redoutable. Une dose de son venin peut tuer 100 personnes ou 250 000 souris. Mais, parce qu'il est très craintif, il n'y a que très rarement des accidents.

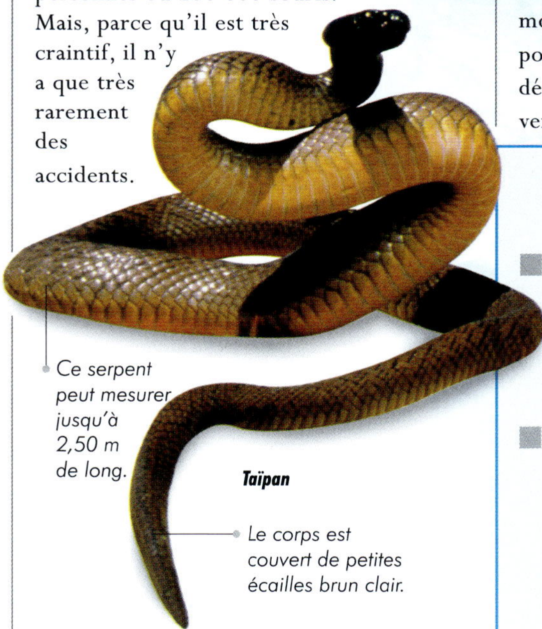

Taïpan

Les lézards sont-ils venimeux ?

Q

R Jusqu'à présent, on ne connaissait que deux lézards venimeux, le monstre de Gila et l'héloderme perlé. Ces lézards au corps massif vivent dans les déserts du centre de l'Amérique du Nord. Ils attaquent de petits animaux et les mordent en leur injectant une dose de poison. Les scientifiques ont récemment découvert que certains varans sont aussi venimeux.

Plus d' infos

- Un hippopotame attaque s'il est effrayé. Il peut couper un petit bateau en deux avec ses puissantes mâchoires et ses dents de taille imposante.
- La mouche tsé-tsé d'Afrique est l'un des insectes les plus dangereux au monde. Elle pompe le sang pour se nourrir et inocule souvent le vecteur d'une maladie mortelle appelée maladie du sommeil.

Mouche tsé-tsé

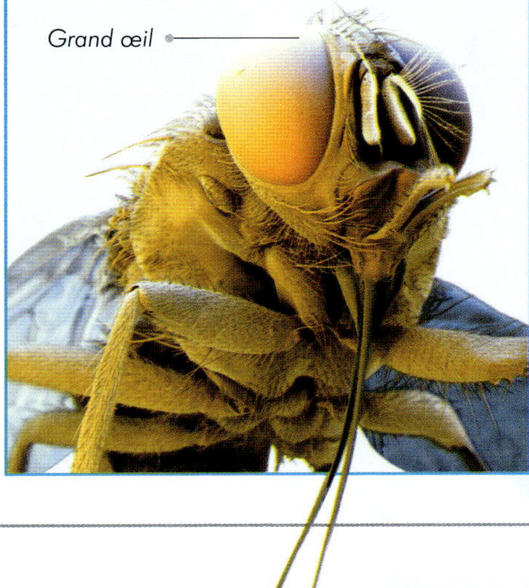

Quel animal combat le mieux ?

Pendant la saison des amours, les mâles se battent souvent entre eux pour sélectionner celui qui pourra s'accoupler. Certains utilisent leurs bois ou leurs cornes comme armes, alors que d'autres se frappent ou se mordent. Les kangourous mâles ont une autre technique. Ils se mettent debout sur leurs pattes arrière et boxent avec leurs pattes avant. Chaque mâle essaie de déstabiliser l'autre et le combat s'achève lorsque le perdant est à terre. Les combats animaux peuvent sembler violents, mais il est rare que les belligérants soient blessés. Une fois que le vainqueur a triomphé, le combat cesse et le perdant s'efface. Avec de l'expérience, il pourra peut-être vaincre la prochaine fois.

Plus d' infos

- Les crotales se battent en tournant les uns autour des autres. Ils gardent leur bouche fermée, ainsi, il n'y a pas de risque de morsure.
- Les combats entre éléphants de mer peuvent être extrêmement violents. Ils se mordent à la tête et au cou et finissent souvent couverts de sang.
- Les scorpions se battent en s'agrippant par leurs pinces. Cela les tient hors de portée du dard de leur adversaire.

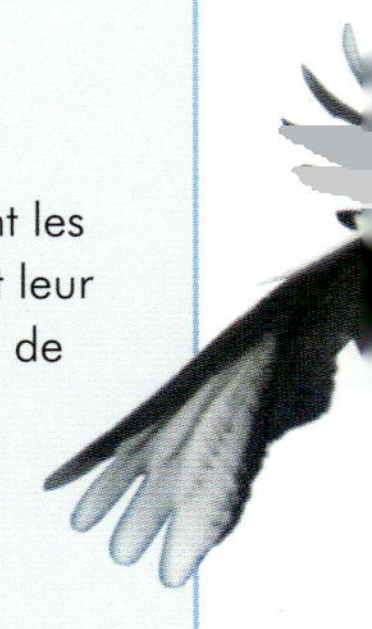

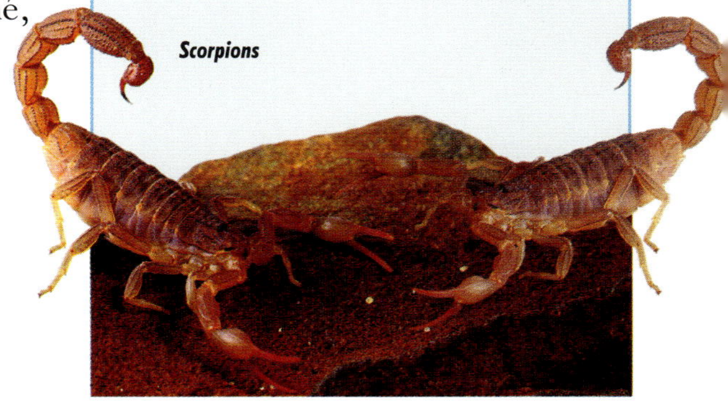

Scorpions

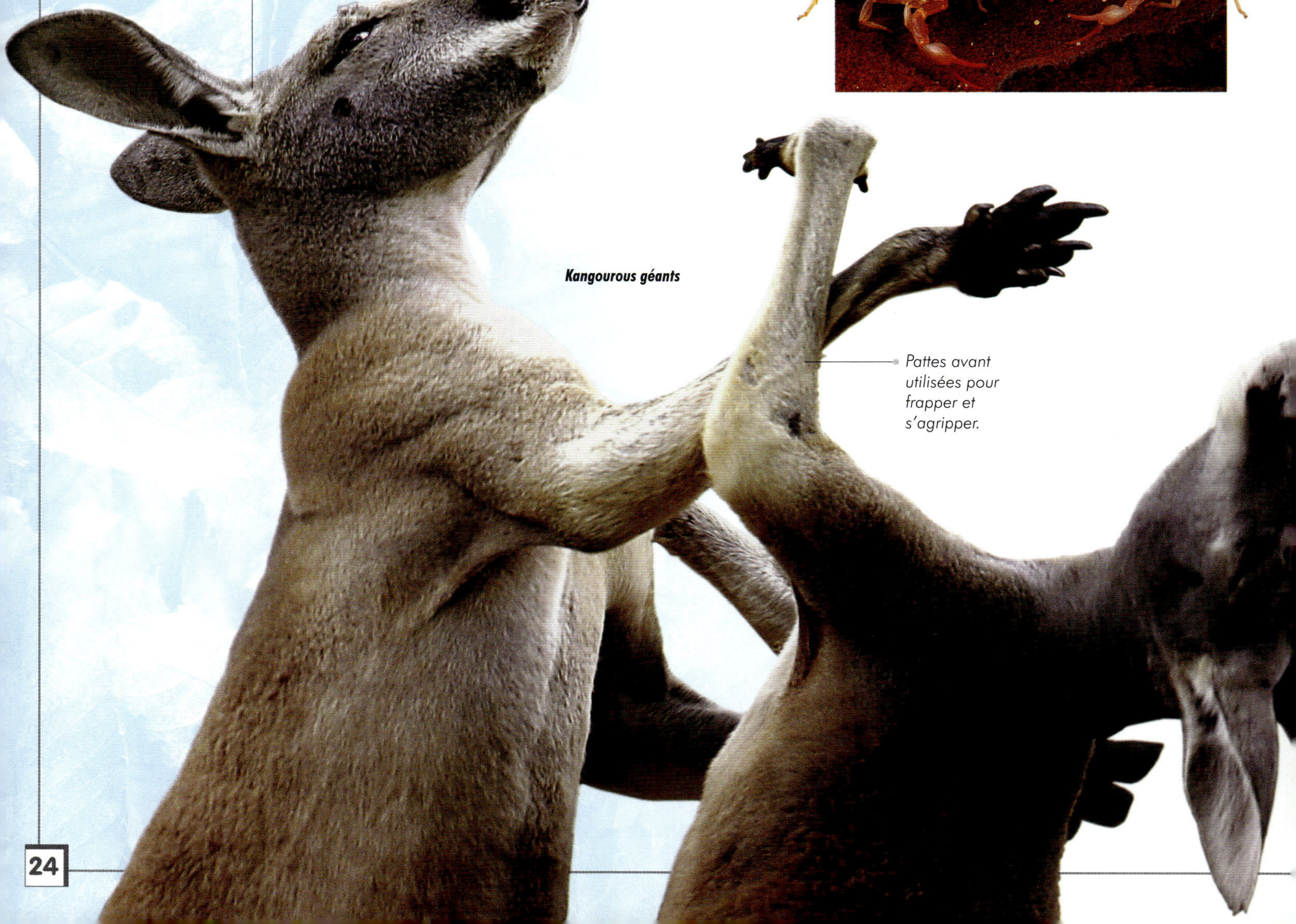

La tête est rejetée en arrière pour éviter les coups.

Kangourous géants

Pattes avant utilisées pour frapper et s'agripper.

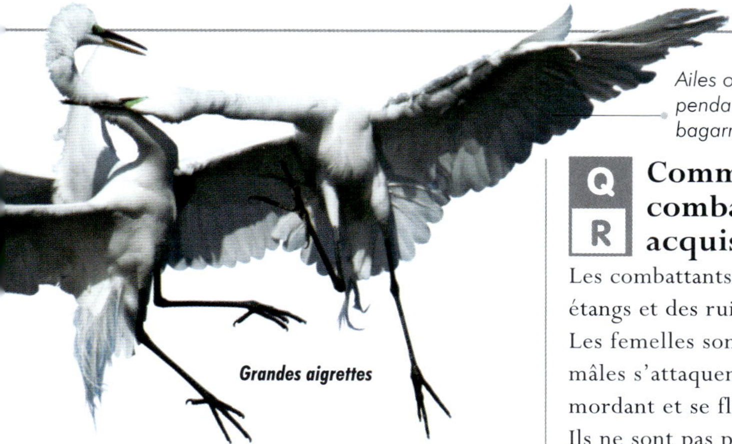

Ailes ouvertes pendant une bagarre.

Grandes aigrettes

Q R Quelle est la meilleure arme des oiseaux ?

Les oiseaux n'ont pas de dents; ils ne peuvent donc pas se mordre lorsqu'ils se battent. À la place, ils utilisent souvent leur bec. Le bec d'une grande aigrette peut mesurer plus de 25 cm de long. Il possède une pointe mortelle qui lui permet d'embrocher un poisson. Mais lorsque les aigrettes se battent, elles ne se blessent pas. Elles gardent le bec ouvert et se donnent des coups sur le cou et les ailes.

Q R Comment les poissons combattants ont-ils acquis leur nom ?

Les combattants sauvages vivent dans des étangs et des ruisseaux en Asie du Sud-Est. Les femelles sont pacifiques tandis que les mâles s'attaquent dès qu'ils se voient, se mordant et se flagellant avec leur queue. Ils ne sont pas plus longs qu'un doigt mais apparaissent plus grands en ouvrant leurs nageoires. Les combattants sont aussi des animaux domestiques appréciés mais, à cause de leur agressivité, on ne peut avoir qu'un seul mâle dans un aquarium.

Poissons combattants siamois

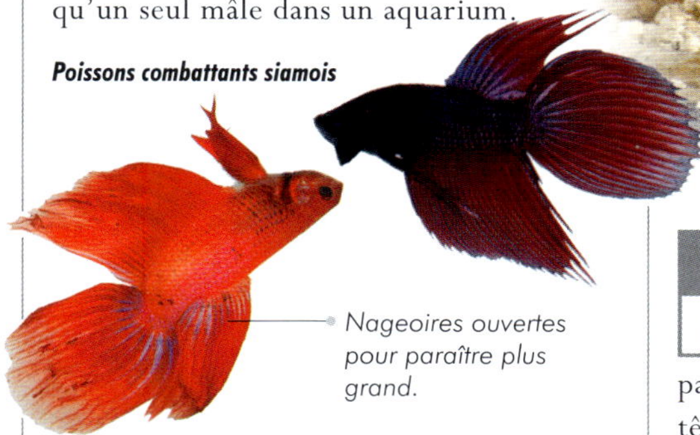

Nageoires ouvertes pour paraître plus grand.

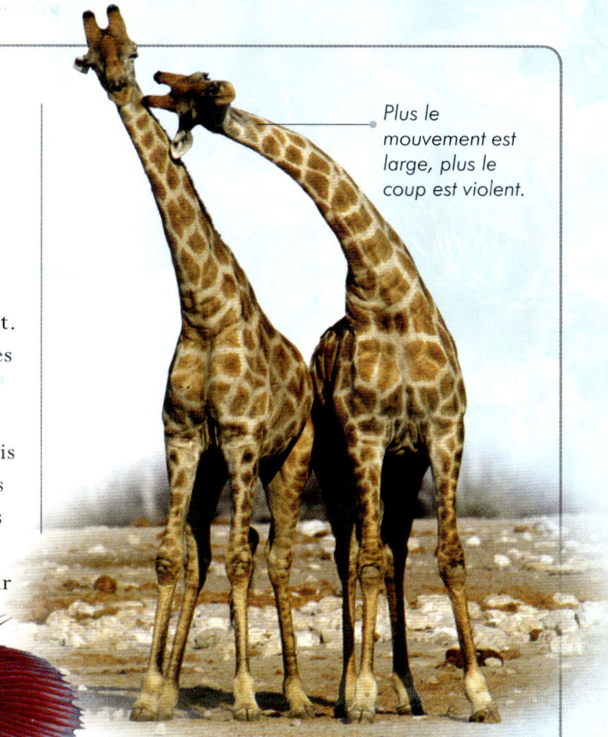

Plus le mouvement est large, plus le coup est violent.

Girafes

Q R Qui utilise sa tête pour donner des coups ?

Plutôt que de se battre avec leurs pattes, les girafes utilisent leur cou et leur tête. Une girafe s'arc-boute en pliant ses pattes, puis elle balance sa tête par-dessus ses épaules et la cogne contre le cou de son rival. Parfois le coup est si violent que l'adversaire peut être assommé.

Zèbres de Grant

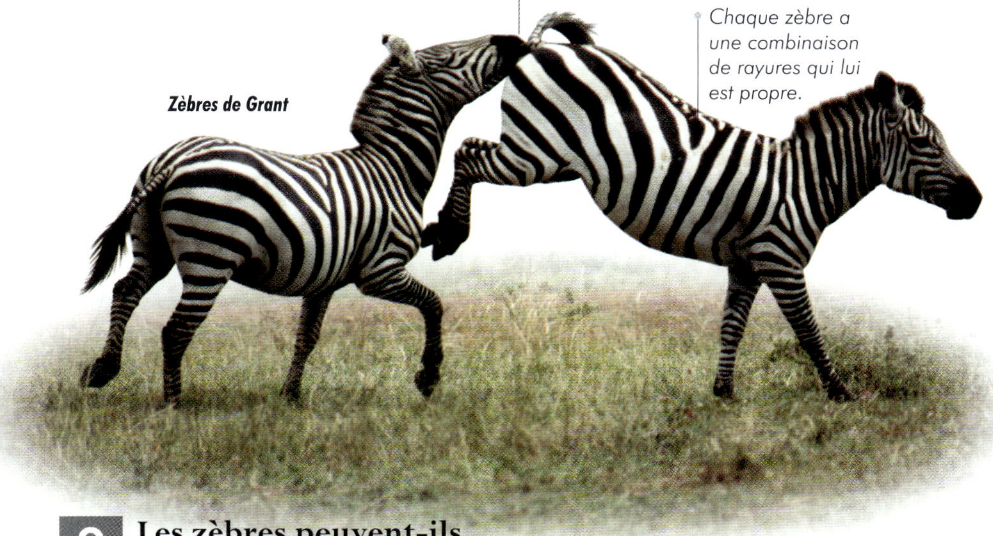

Chaque zèbre a une combinaison de rayures qui lui est propre.

Q R Les zèbres peuvent-ils se blesser avec leurs sabots ?

Lorsque les zèbres se battent, ils se mordent souvent l'un l'autre avec leurs grandes dents. Mais lorsque la bagarre devient sérieuse, ils se retournent et ruent avec leurs pattes arrière. Un coup bien ajusté touche l'adversaire au poitrail ou dans les côtes, provoquant un hématome douloureux. Si un zèbre est coincé par un prédateur et s'il ne peut pas s'enfuir, il utilise la même technique. Certains zèbres hennissent fort pendant le combat.

Q R Pourquoi les cerfs ont-ils des bois ?

Pendant la saison des amours, les mâles utilisent leurs bois pour tester leur puissance. Les rivaux sont face à face et se ruent l'un sur l'autre, entremêlant leurs bois. Ils poussent aussi fort qu'ils le peuvent jusqu'à ce que l'un des deux parvienne à repousser l'autre et à lui faire abandonner le combat. Le perdant dégage alors ses bois et s'enfuit.

Les mâles ont une nouvelle paire de bois chaque année.

Cerfs mâles

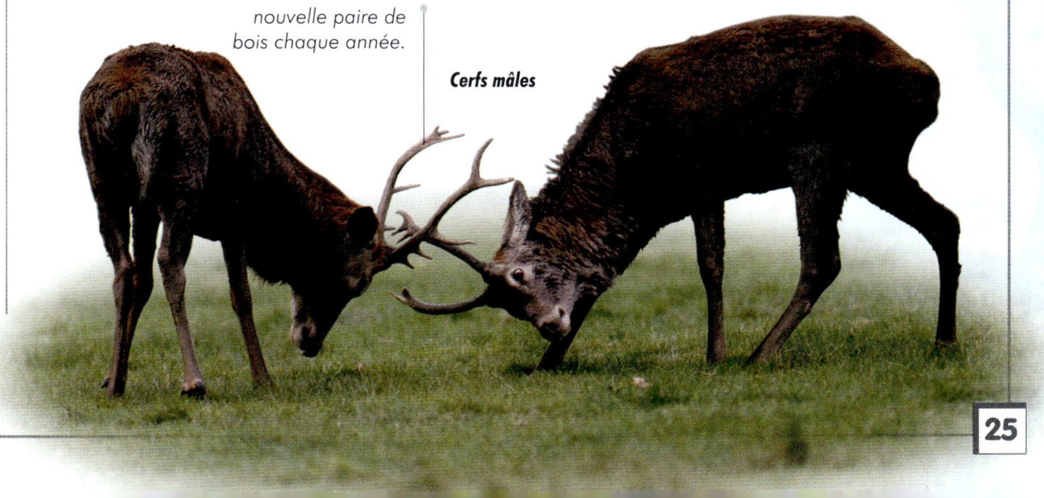

Comment un prédateur tue-t-il sa proie ?

Dans le monde animal, les chasseurs ont différentes techniques pour attraper leurs proies. Certains, comme le guépard, s'appuient sur leur vitesse et leur force. D'autres, telles les mantes religieuses, utilisent la patience. Une mante peut rester immobile des heures durant en attendant qu'un insecte s'approche. Si un insecte se pose aux alentours, la mante réagit aussitôt et s'en empare avec ses pattes avant. Elle se met à l'ingérer immédiatement, même si la victime est toujours vivante. D'autres animaux ont des méthodes plus rusées pour arriver à leurs fins.

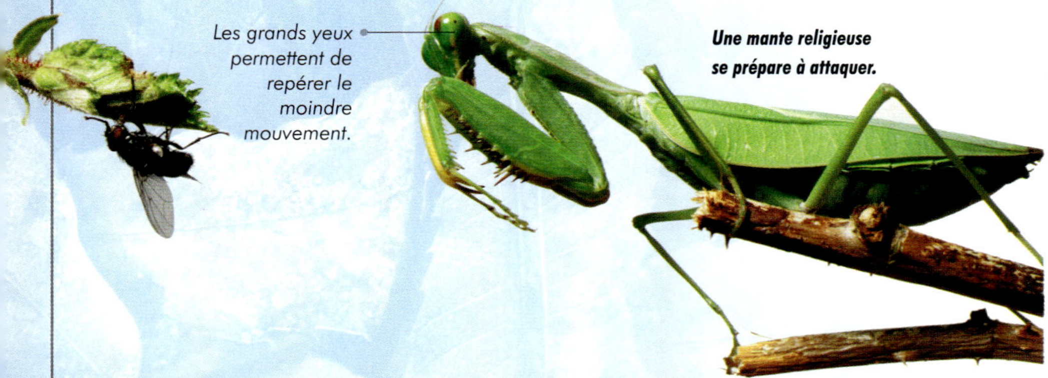

Une mante religieuse se prépare à attaquer.

La mante attrape l'insecte avec ses pattes antérieures.

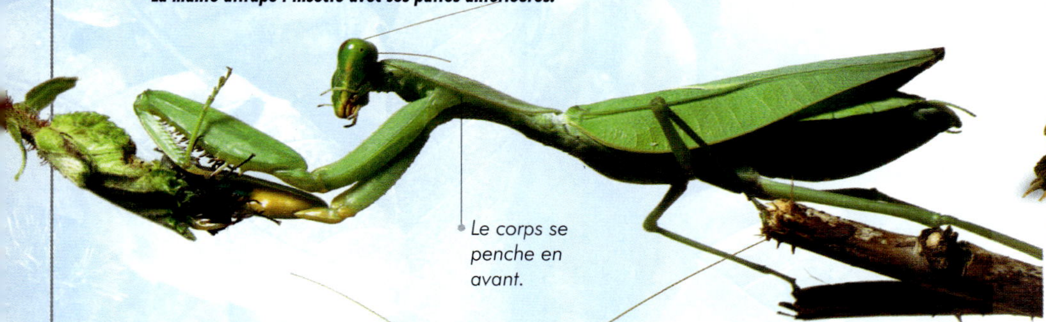

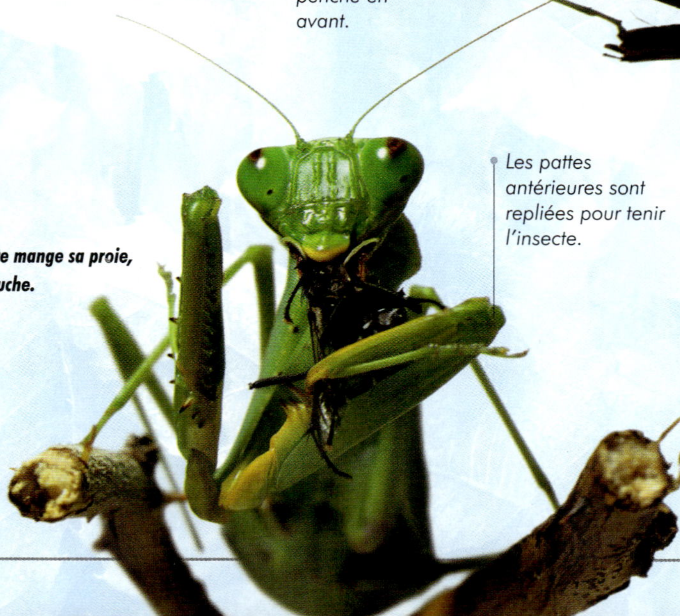

La mante mange sa proie, une mouche.

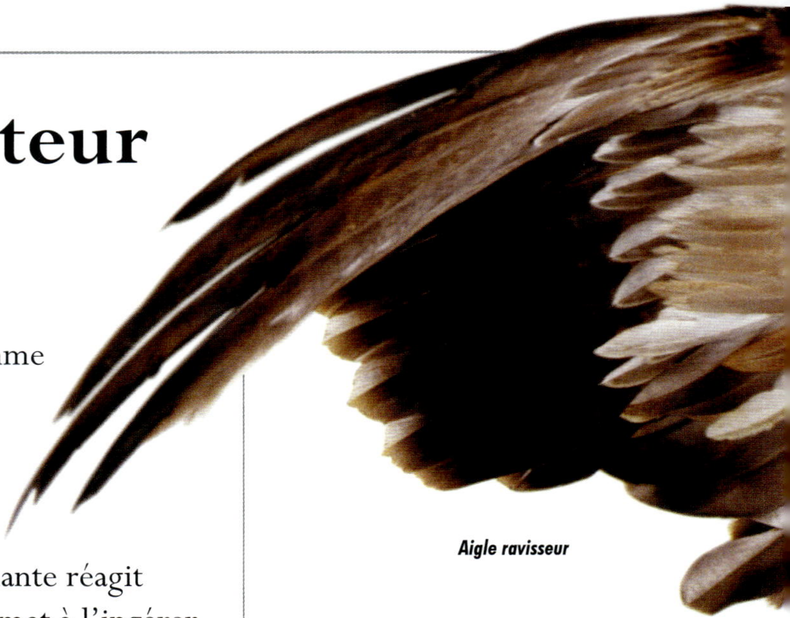

Aigle ravisseur

Q Quel est le reptile le plus retors ?

R La tortue serpentine se tapit au fond des lacs, la bouche grande ouverte. Sa langue est rose et frétille comme un ver, ce qui attire les poissons qui passent. Mais dès que l'un s'approche, la tortue ferme en un éclair ses mâchoires puissantes sur le poisson qui est le plus souvent coupé en deux. On peut reconnaître ces tortues grâce aux trois larges crêtes qui courent de la tête à la queue le long de leur carapace.

Tortue serpentine

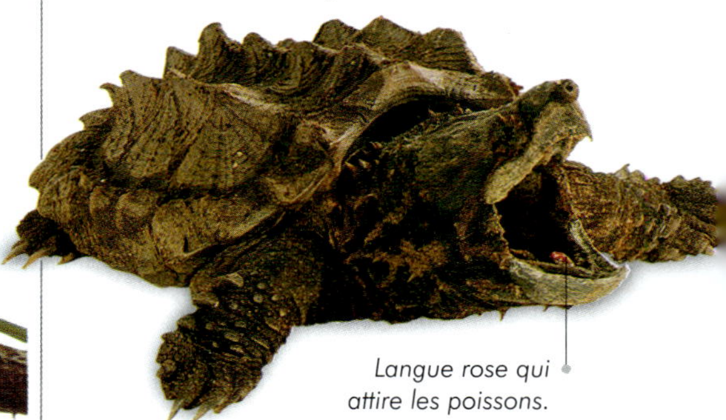

Q Quelle est l'arme secrète du guépard ?

R La réponse est simple : la vitesse. Les guépards sont les animaux terrestres les plus rapides au monde. Ils peuvent atteindre 100 km/heure pendant vingt secondes au maximum. Ils accomplissent cette performance en développant une foulée très importante, car ils ont de très longs membres et une colonne vertébrale très souple. Ils ont aussi des griffes semi-rétractiles qui leur permettent de mieux s'accrocher au sol, un peu comme les chaussures des athlètes.

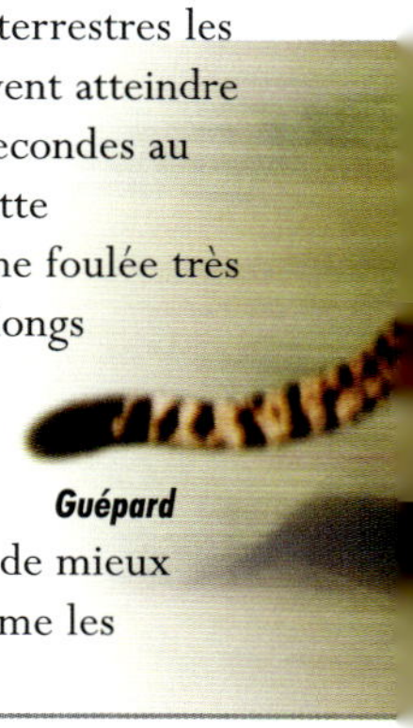

Guépard

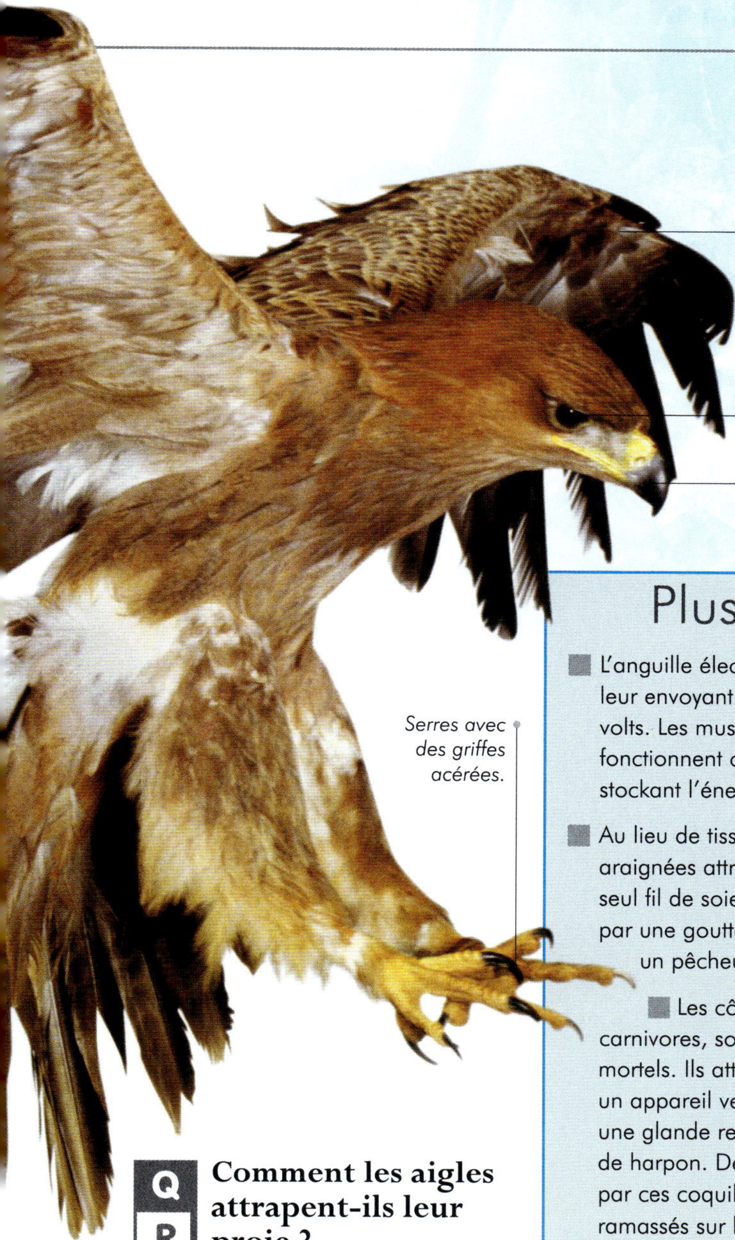

Q R Comment les aigles attrapent-ils leur proie ?

Les oiseaux de proie, tels que les aigles ou les faucons, ne chassent pas avec leur bec. Par contre, ils frappent les animaux avec leurs serres ou leurs griffes acérées. Une fois qu'ils ont tué leur proie, ils la ramènent à leur nid où ils utilisent leur bec pour la déchiqueter. Les plus petits oiseaux de proie chassent les insectes, mais les plus gros peuvent s'attaquer à des singes.

Plus d' infos

- L'anguille électrique tue les poissons en leur envoyant des décharges de 600 volts. Les muscles de l'anguille fonctionnent comme une batterie, stockant l'énergie électrique.
- Au lieu de tisser des toiles, certaines araignées attrapent les insectes avec un seul fil de soie. Elles lancent un fil retenu par une goutte de glu, un peu comme un pêcheur avec son fil de pêche.
- Les cônes, mollusques carnivores, sont magnifiques mais mortels. Ils attaquent les poissons avec un appareil venimeux, qui comprend une glande reliée à une dent en forme de harpon. Des gens sont morts, tués par ces coquillages parce qu'ils les ont ramassés sur les plages à marée basse.

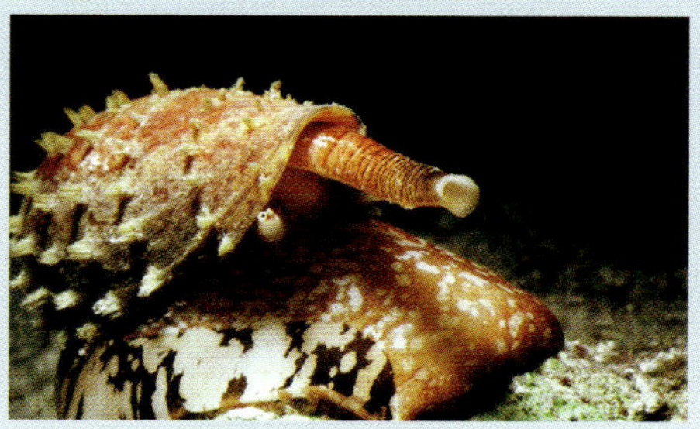

Cône

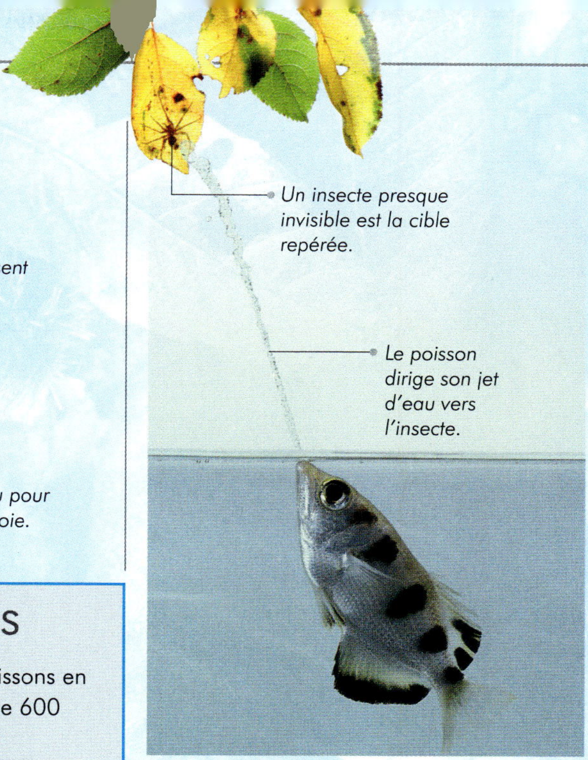

Poisson archer

Q R Quel poisson abat ses proies à distance ?

Beaucoup de poissons bondissent sur les insectes, mais le poisson archer est le seul qui les tue à distance. Il repère les insectes posés sur les plantes au bord de l'eau. Immobile,il ferme les mâchoires et vise. Il projette un jet d'eau vers l'insecte, ce qui l'assomme et le fait tomber entre ses mâchoires.

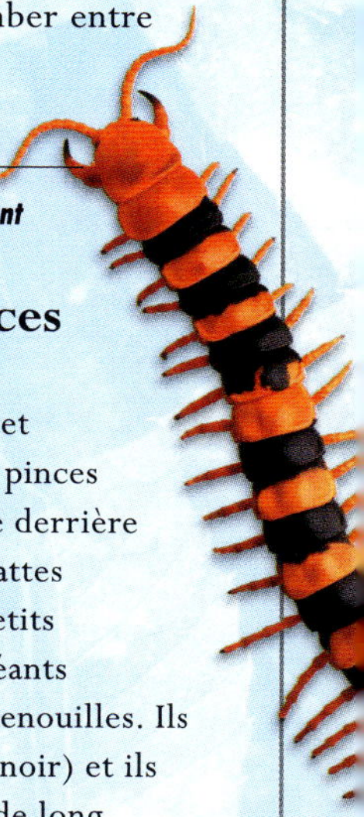

Mille-pattes géant

Q R Quel chasseur possède des pinces venimeuses ?

Les mille-pattes chassent la nuit et attaquent leurs proies avec deux pinces venimeuses qui sont situées juste derrière leur tête. La plupart des mille-pattes chassent des insectes et autres petits animaux, mais les mille-pattes géants peuvent tuer des souris et des grenouilles. Ils ont des couleurs vives (rouge et noir) et ils peuvent mesurer jusqu'à 30 cm de long.

Pourquoi les mouffettes sentent-elles mauvais ?

Avec tant de chasseurs à l'affût, les animaux doivent trouver des moyens de se protéger. La plupart d'entre eux se sauvent aussi vite qu'ils le peuvent, utilisant leurs pattes, leurs ailes ou leurs nageoires. Les mouffettes ne prennent pas toujours la fuite. Si quelque chose les inquiète, elles cambrent le dos et ébouriffent leur pelage pour le rendre effrayant. Si cela ne fonctionne pas, elles font gicler un fluide effroyablement malodorant depuis leurs glandes anales. L'odeur persiste pendant plusieurs jours et le fluide peut causer la cécité d'un animal qui le recevrait dans les yeux.

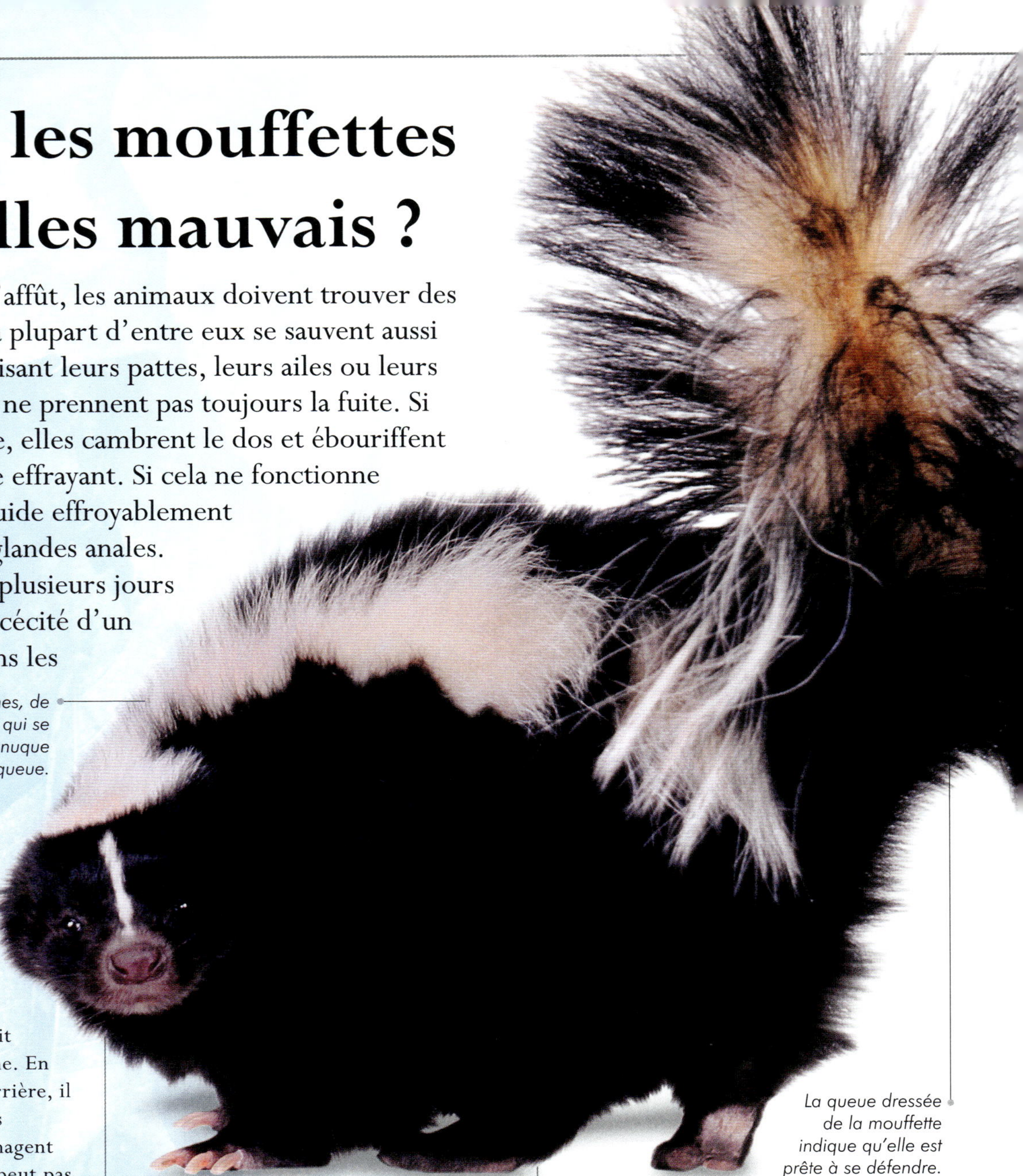

Deux bandes blanches, de la tête à la queue, qui se rejoignent sur la nuque et sur la queue.

La queue dressée de la mouffette indique qu'elle est prête à se défendre.

Mouffette rayée

Q R Quel reptile peut « courir » sur l'eau ?

Si le basilic vert est poursuivi, il plonge dans le premier point d'eau venu. C'est un lézard qui vit principalement en Amérique latine. En utilisant ses très longues pattes arrière, il court littéralement sur l'eau. Des palmures entre chaque orteil ménagent une large surface sur l'eau. Il ne peut pas courir ainsi très longtemps sans couler, mais cette fuite extraordinaire suffit souvent à le sauver.

Basilic vert

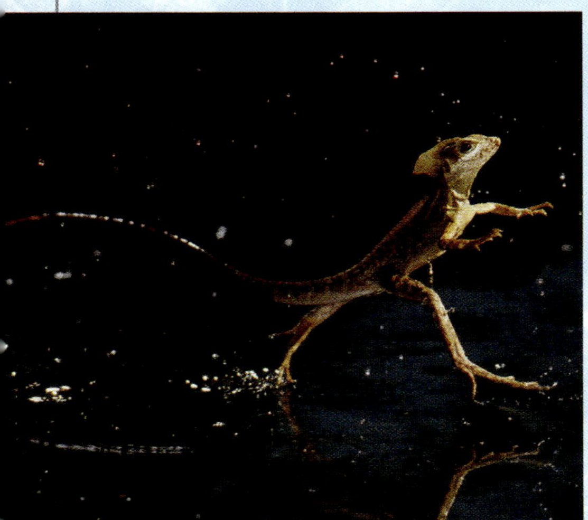

Q R Quel est l'animal le plus rapide à la détente ?

Les lièvres n'ont qu'un moyen de se protéger : ils fuient aussi vite qu'ils le peuvent. Ils ont une très bonne vue, ce qui leur permet de commencer à courir alors que le prédateur est encore loin. Plutôt que de courir en ligne droite, ils font des zigzags à travers champs. Cette technique rend leur capture plus difficile.

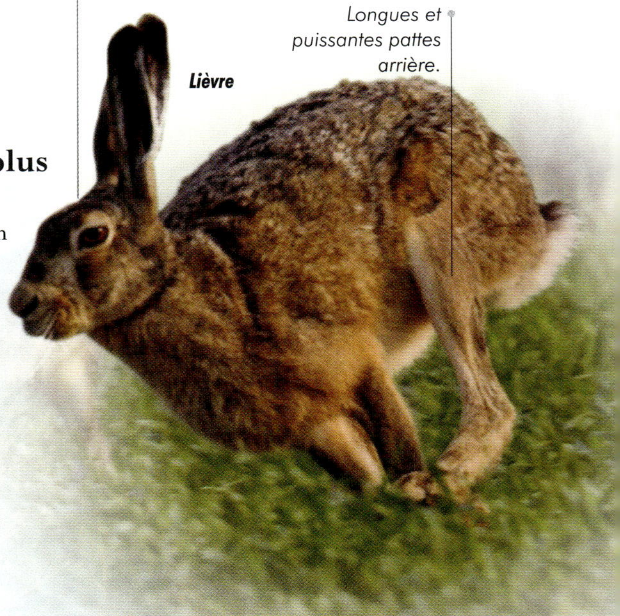

Lièvre

Longues et puissantes pattes arrière.

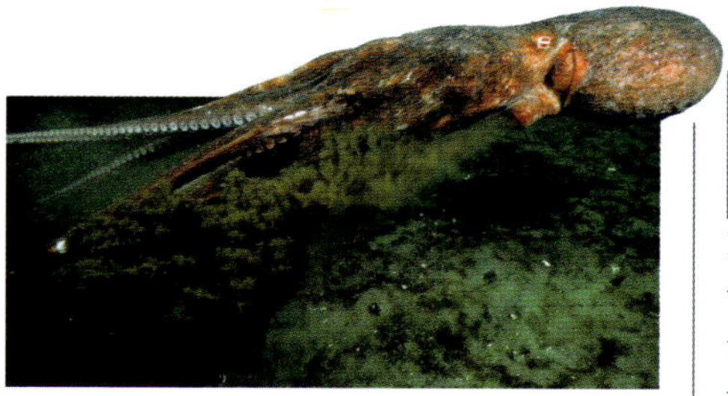

Pieuvre

Qui disparaît dans un nuage d'encre ?

Les pieuvres peuvent le faire. Elles expulsent un liquide semblable à de l'encre, et, refoulant l'eau de mer par un siphon, elles se propulsent vers l'arrière pour échapper à leur poursuivant. Pendant ce temps, le prédateur est aveuglé par le nuage d'encre.

Quel animal peut s'échapper en creusant la terre ?

Beaucoup d'animaux creusent des terriers, mais peu battent l'Oryctérope de vitesse. S'il est pourchassé, cet animal, qui ressemble un peu à un cochon, creuse furieusement avec ses griffes. Si le sol est meuble, il va vite disparaître sous la surface du sol. Lorsqu'il est effrayé, il peut aussi rouler sur le dos et tenter de se défendre avec ses griffes.

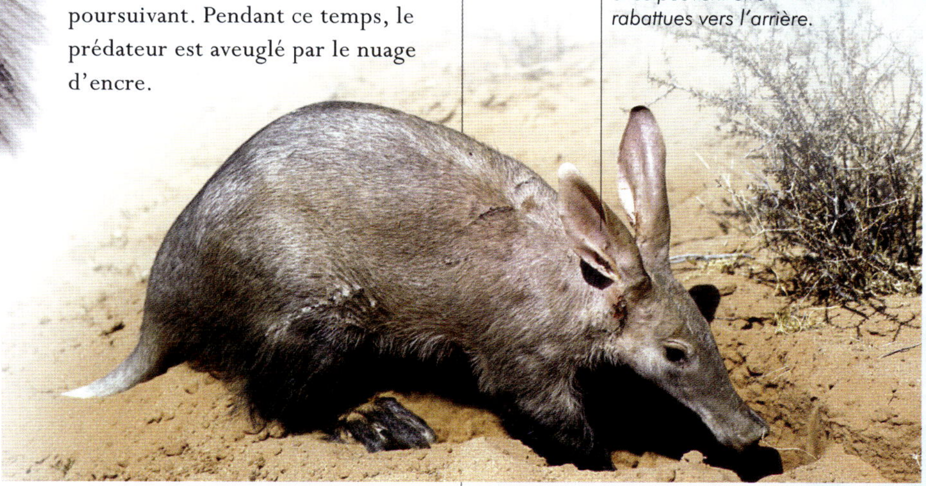

Oryctérope

Qui se met en boule ?

Plutôt que de courir loin du danger, le glomeris, un mille-pattes, choisit de s'enrouler sur lui-même. Il est alors protégé par sa carapace solide ; sa tête et ses pattes sont à l'abri. Il reste ainsi tant que le danger ne s'est pas éloigné. D'autres animaux ont cette capacité, tels que les hérissons, les cloportes ou les tatous à neuf bandes qui se recroquevillent en boules solides couvertes de plaques osseuses articulées.

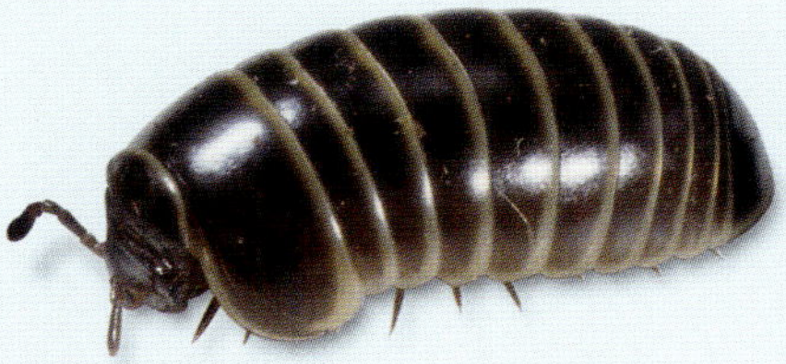

1 Le mille-pattes a rapproché les plaques de sa carapace, ce qui lui permet de se transformer en boule s'il sent un danger.

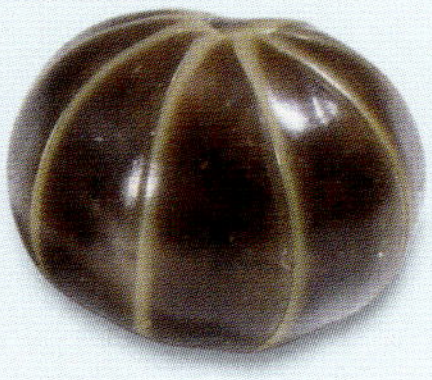

2 Il rentre totalement son corps dans cette boule impénétrable.

3 Lorsque le danger a disparu, le mille-pattes peut à nouveau se déployer.

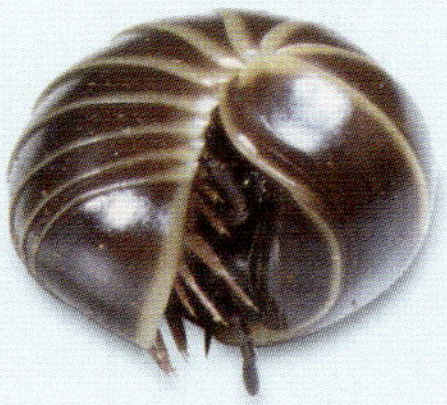

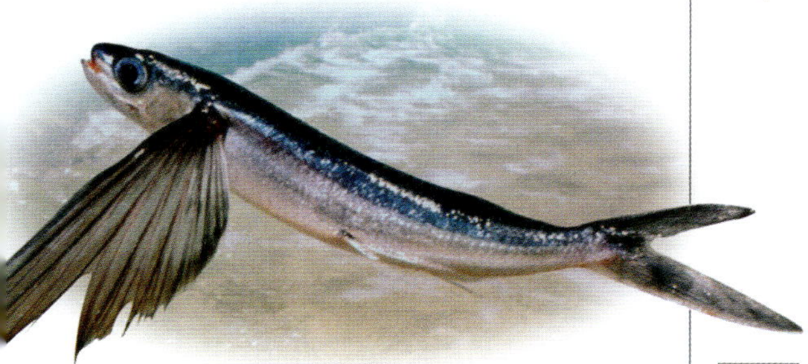

Exocet

Quel poisson peut planer dans l'air ?

Pour les poissons volants, ce n'est pas un problème. S'ils sont chassés, ils jaillissent à travers les flots et planent dans l'air grâce à leurs nageoires étalées. Certains poissons volants traînent leur queue dans l'eau et l'utilisent comme l'hélice d'un moteur. Ils jaillissent de l'eau et peuvent alors parcourir jusqu'à 400 m « à l'air libre », laissant leurs prédateurs loin derrière eux.

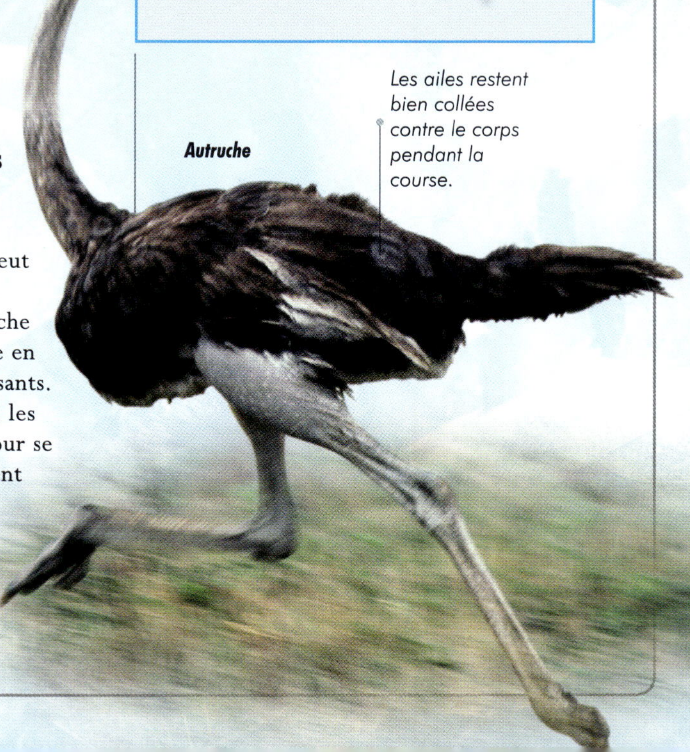

Autruche

Qui court le plus vite sur deux pattes ?

L'autruche - un oiseau qui ne peut pas voler - est le bipède le plus rapide à la course. Si une autruche est aculée, elle peut se défendre en donnant des coups de pied puissants. Mais si elles ont le champ libre, les autruches choisissent la fuite pour se protéger. Leurs pieds ressemblent à des sabots pourvus de deux doigts, et les muscles élastiques de leurs jambes leur permettent d'atteindre une vitesse de pointe de 70 km/heure.

Camouflage et couleur

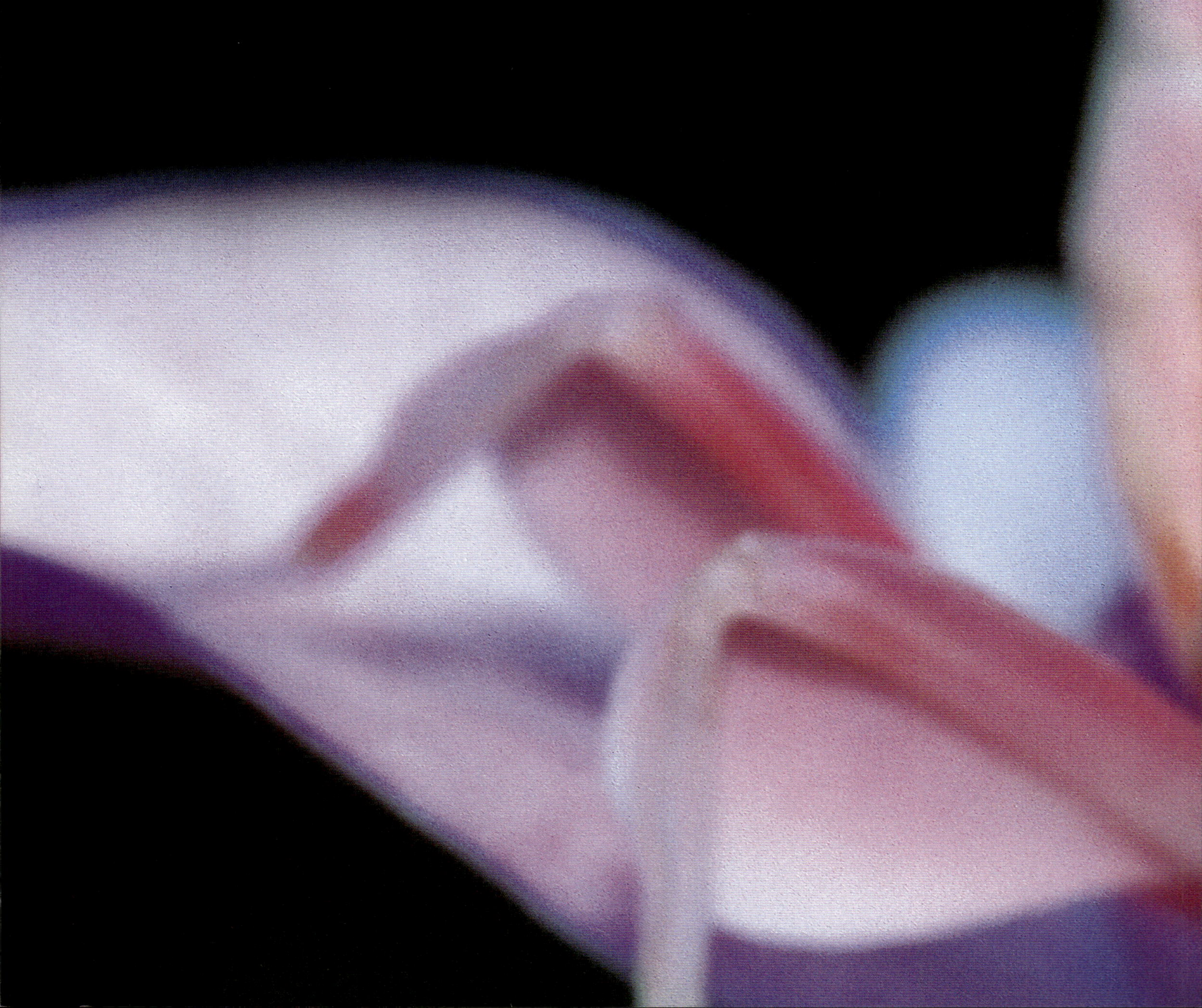

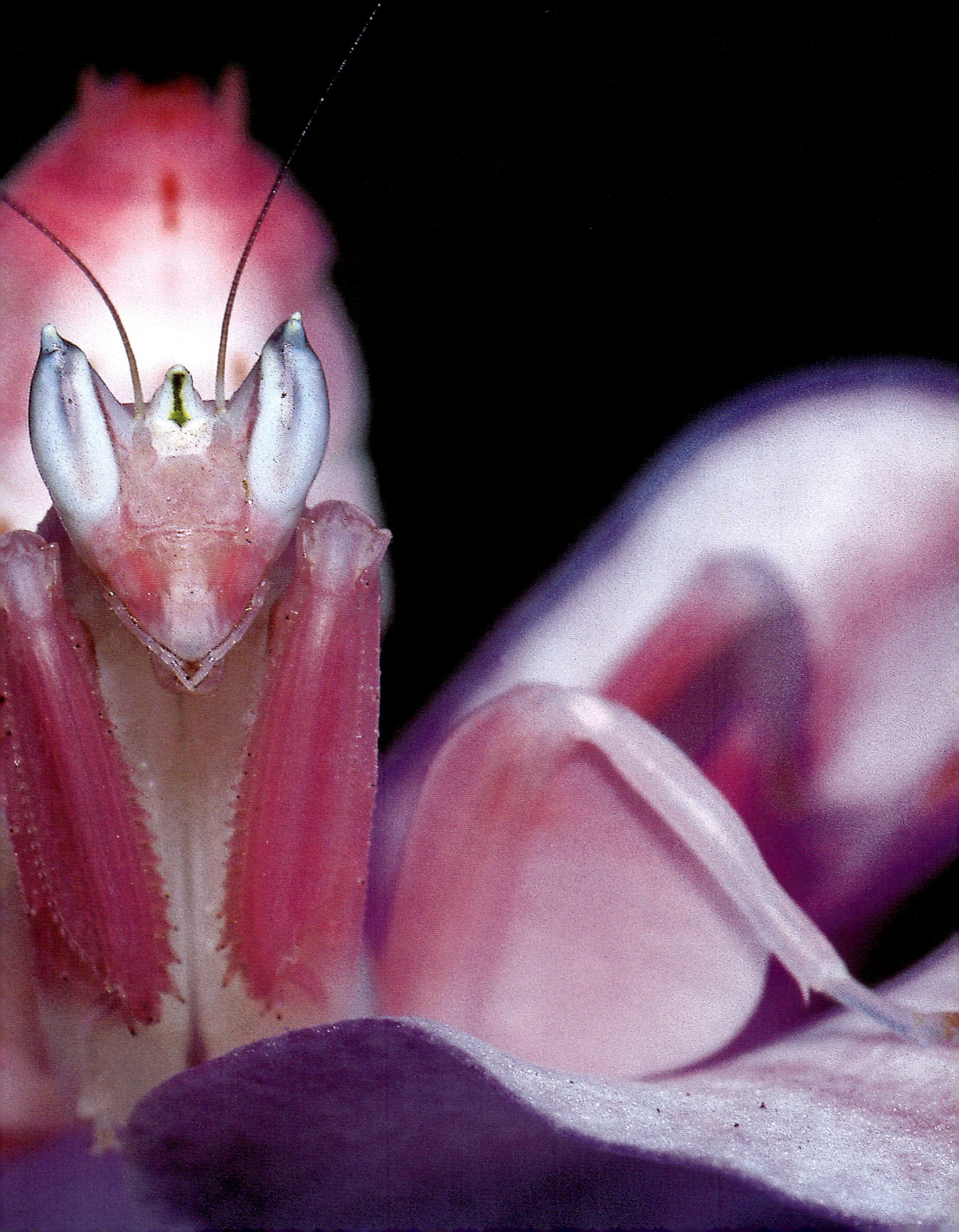

Pourquoi les tigres ont-ils des rayures ?

Beaucoup d'animaux ont des dessins et des couleurs qui les rendent difficiles à voir. Beaucoup se servent de leur camouflage pour se cacher des prédateurs, mais certains chasseurs, comme les tigres, ont besoin eux-mêmes de camouflage. Les tigres sont discrets, leurs rayures les aident à passer inaperçus à travers la forêt tropicale ou les hautes herbes. Cela leur permet de s'approcher au plus près de leur proie et de lancer des attaques-surprises mortelles.

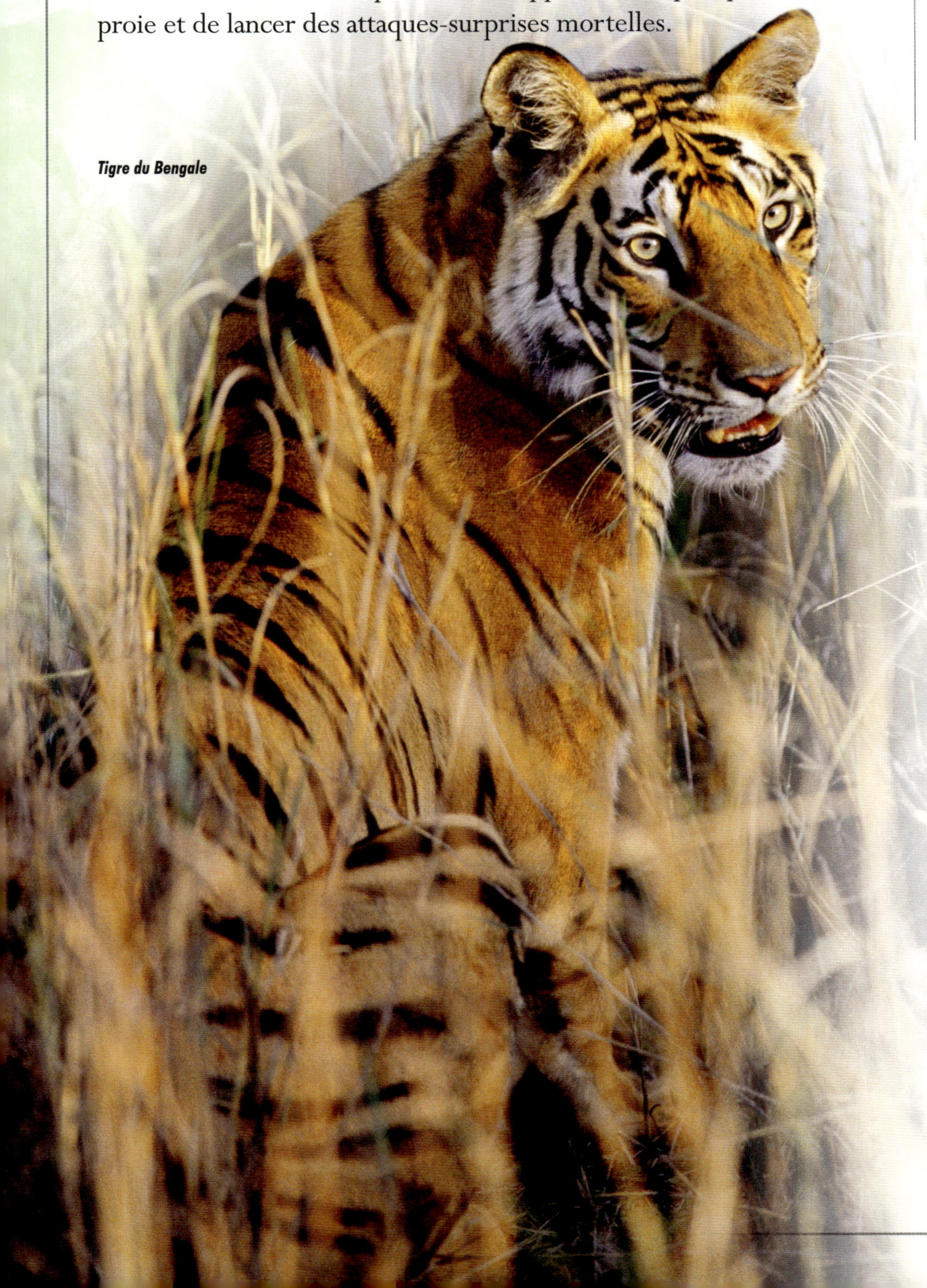

Tigre du Bengale

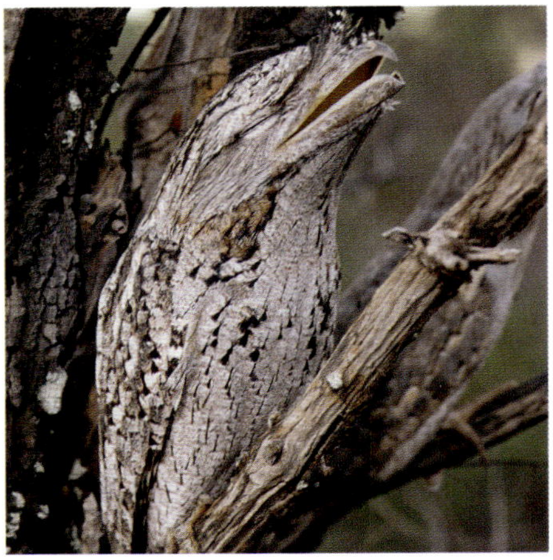

Podarge gris

Q Quel oiseau ressemble à un bout de bois ?

R Le Podarge gris, oiseau d'Australie, est l'un des oiseaux qui a le meilleur camouflage au monde. Il chasse de petits animaux la nuit et passe ses journées à dormir dans les arbres. Durant la journée, il est quasiment impossible de le voir. Il se perche en hauteur et ses plumes le font ressembler à une branche morte. De plus, il reste parfaitement immobile et ne s'envole pas.

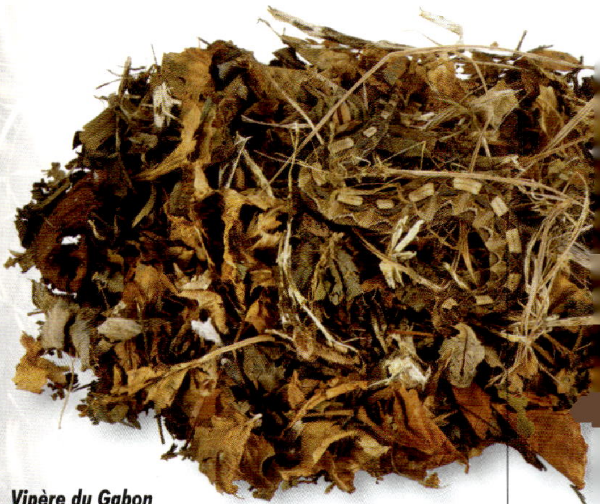

Vipère du Gabon

Q Qui se cache dans les feuilles mortes ?

R La vipère du Gabon est armée de crochets mortels. Lorsqu'elle est au milieu de feuilles mortes, son camouflage lui permet de disparaître totalement. La vipère du Gabon chasse à l'affût sur le sol. Si une proie s'approche, elle bondit immédiatement. Cette vipère est très dangereuse et agressive, son venin est mortel pour les hommes.

Q Quel est le déguisement le plus bizarre ?

R Il est difficile d'imaginer vouloir se nourrir de guano (crottes des oiseaux). C'est pourquoi certaines araignées et certaines chenilles se déguisent en déjections d'oiseau. Elles ont un corps gris et blanc et restent posées sur les feuilles des arbres, exactement comme une crotte. Les araignées replient leurs pattes tandis que les chenilles s'incurvent.

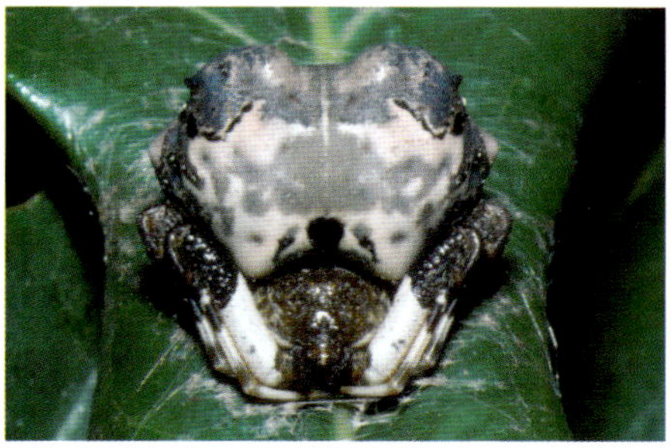

Celaenia, araignée qui mime du guano d'oiseau

Q Qui ressemble à une algue en mouvement ?

R Beaucoup de poissons utilisent le camouflage, mais le dragon de mer a un déguisement intelligent. C'est un hippocampe feuillu. Pour se camoufler, il a des appendices en forme de feuilles, qui imitent en fait les feuilles des sargasses, des algues brunes, fréquentes dans son milieu. Il nage en se tenant droit, mais ses petites nageoires en font un des poissons les plus lents. Ces dragons vivent au large des côtes sud de l'Australie, près des rochers recouverts d'algues. Si un dragon de mer feuillu est jeté sur la grève, ses appendices en forme de feuilles se désagrègent rapidement.

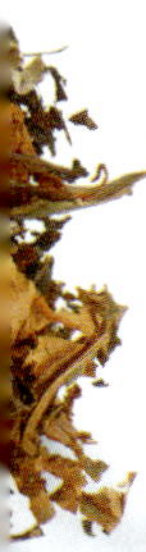

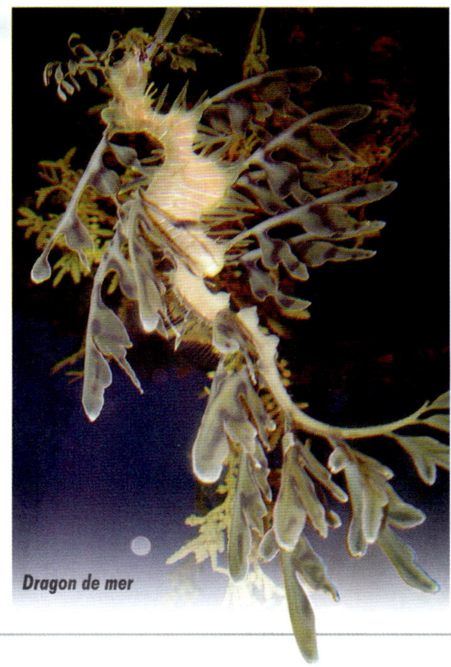

Dragon de mer

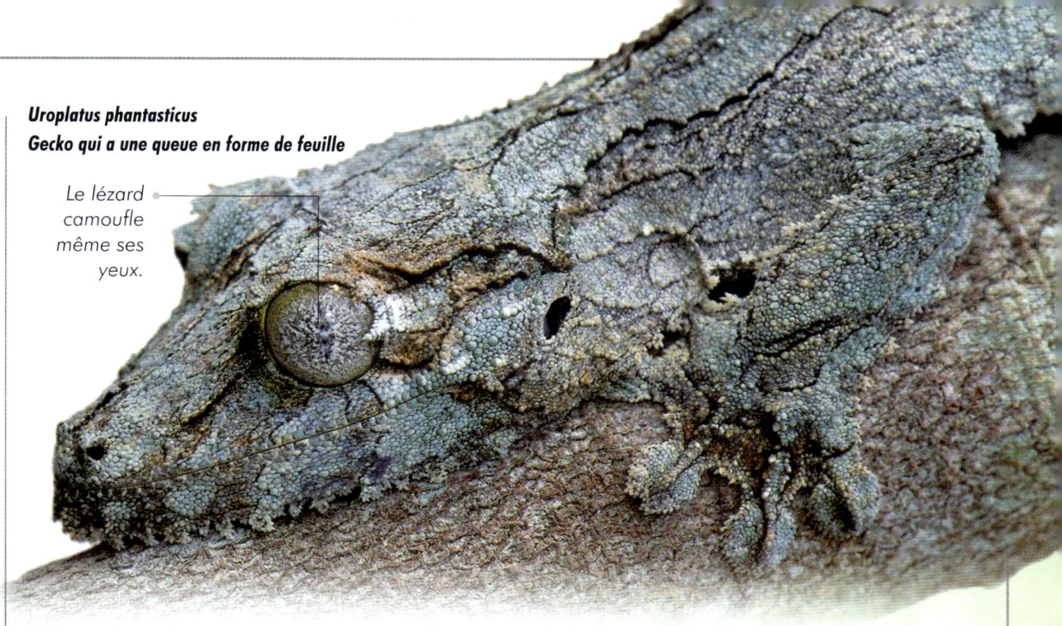

Uroplatus phantasticus
Gecko qui a une queue en forme de feuille

Le lézard camoufle même ses yeux.

Quand un papillon ressemble-t-il à une feuille ?

Les feuilles mortes jonchent souvent le sol, on ne les regarde même pas. Mais parfois, elles ne sont pas ce qu'elles semblent être. Le papillon-feuille appelé *Kallima inachus* vit en Asie du Sud-Est. Il imite les feuilles mortes pour éviter d'être vu. Beaucoup d'autres insectes comme les phalènes (papillons de nuit) et les phyllies (phasmes en forme de feuille) utilisent le même artifice pour se cacher.

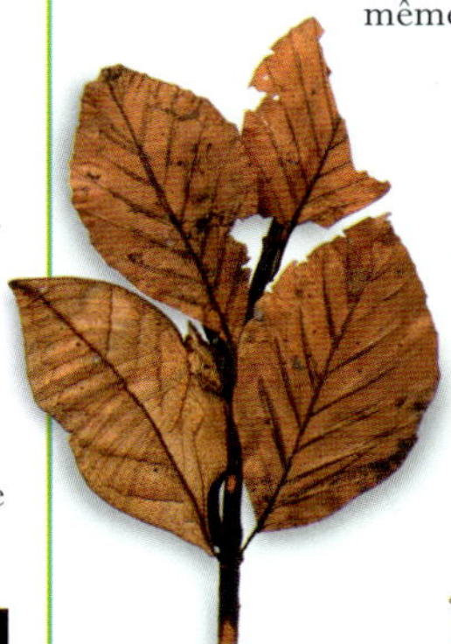

1 *Le Kallima est posé parmi des feuilles mortes. Le magnifique camouflage de ses ailes le rend invisible.*

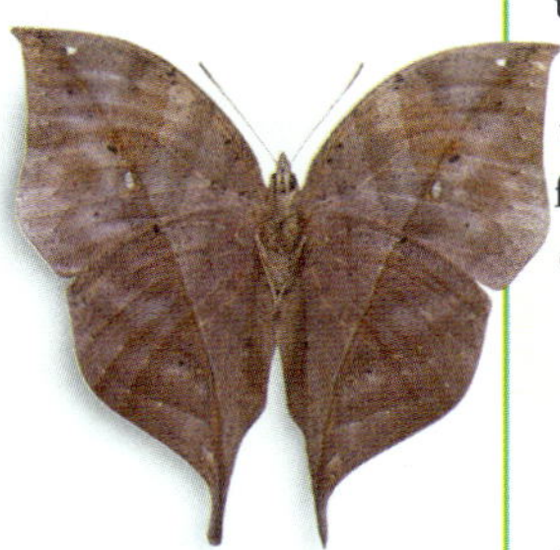

2 *Voilà le même papillon en vue ventrale, les ailes étalées. Chaque extrémité des ailes inférieures se termine par une petite queue comme le pétiole. d'une feuille.*

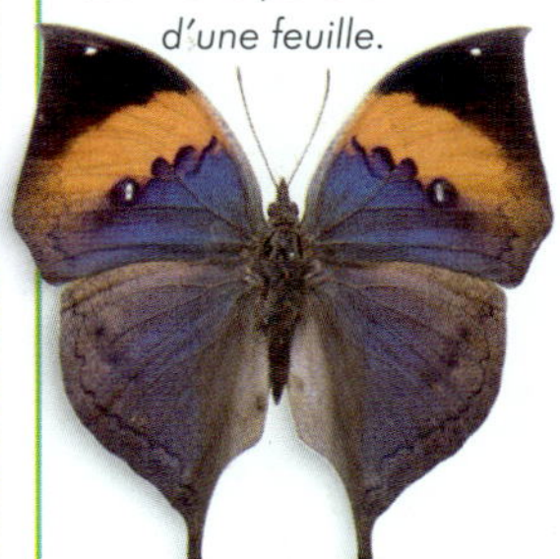

3 *Retourné en vue dorsale, le Kallima a des couleurs intenses que l'on observe en vol.*

Q Quel lézard joue à cache-cache ?

R *Uroplatus phantasticus* est une espèce de gecko nocturne très doué pour se cacher sur l'écorce des arbres. Comparé à la plupart des lézards, il a un corps plat. Il a aussi une queue qui ressemble à une feuille morte et une peau grise qui ressemble aux craquelures de l'écorce. Ces geckos chassent les insectes la nuit. Si un prédateur le guette, le lézard peut rapidement perdre sa queue, une astuce qui surprend l'ennemi et lui laisse le temps de prendre la fuite. Une nouvelle queue repoussera lentement.

Q Quel insecte se déguise en épine ?

R Posées sur une branche, les *épines* (ou *bogues*) sont difficiles à repérer car elles ressemblent aux épines d'une branche de rosier. À l'arrière de leur tête, un bouclier dur s'étire vers le haut dans une pointe en forme d'épine. Les bogues utilisent leur camouflage pour se protéger des oiseaux voraces.

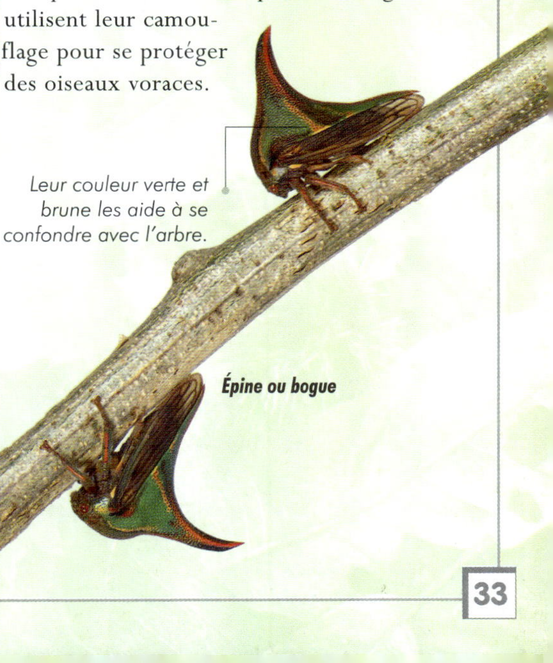

Leur couleur verte et brune les aide à se confondre avec l'arbre.

Épine ou bogue

Qui a la face la plus colorée ?

Le monde animal est plein de couleurs vives, particulièrement dans les pays chauds. Des poissons brillamment colorés nagent dans les récifs coralliens et des insectes ou des grenouilles multicolores vivent dans les forêts tropicales. La couleur aide les animaux à se reconnaître entre individus de même espèce et à distinguer les mâles des femelles. Les mammifères ont souvent des couleurs qui les camouflent, mais un singe, le mandrill, est vraiment extraordinaire. Sa face dépourvue de poils semble couverte de peinture rouge et bleue.

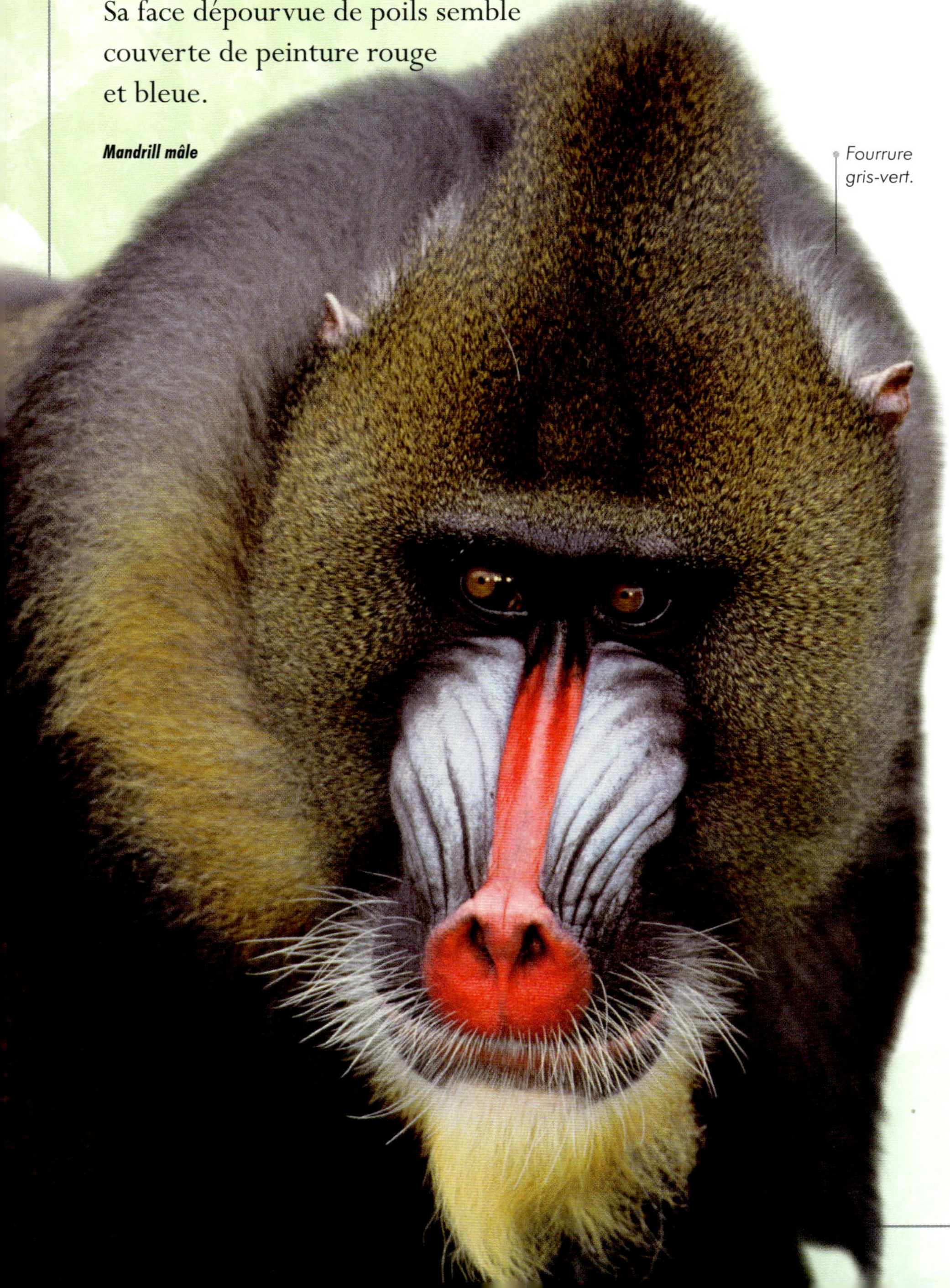

Mandrill mâle

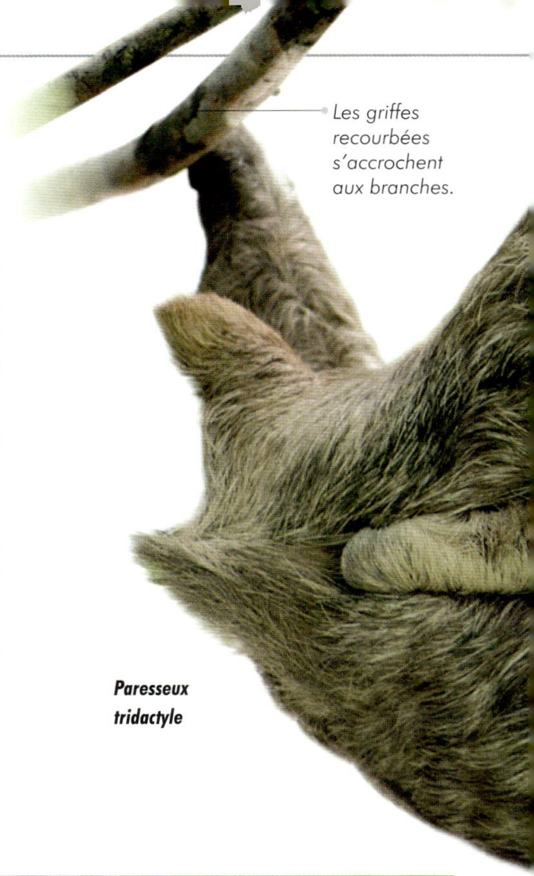

Paresseux tridactyle

Plus d' infos

- Beaucoup d'oiseaux et d'insectes voient des couleurs invisibles pour l'homme, car leurs yeux détectent les ultraviolets.
- Les poissons-anges empereurs changent de couleur et de forme au cours de leur croissance. Le jeune et l'adulte semblent appartenir à des espèces différentes.

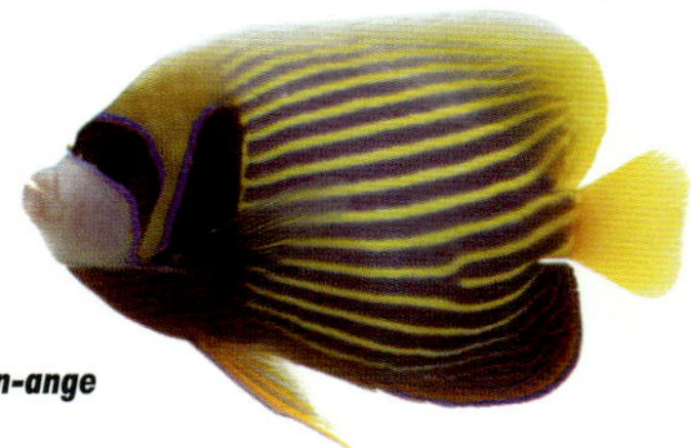

Poisson-ange adulte

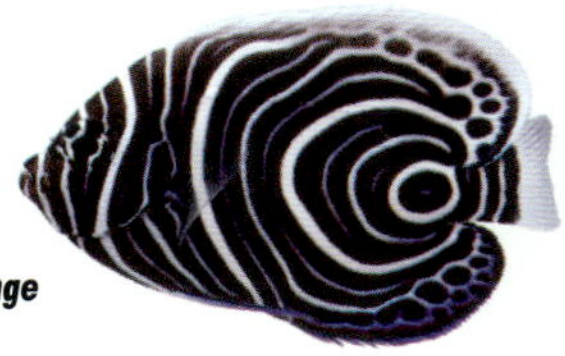

Poisson-ange jeune

- Les baleines à bosse ont un marquage noir et blanc unique, un peu comme les empreintes digitales des humains.
- Le brun est la couleur la plus répandue chez les animaux, alors que l'or est la plus rare.

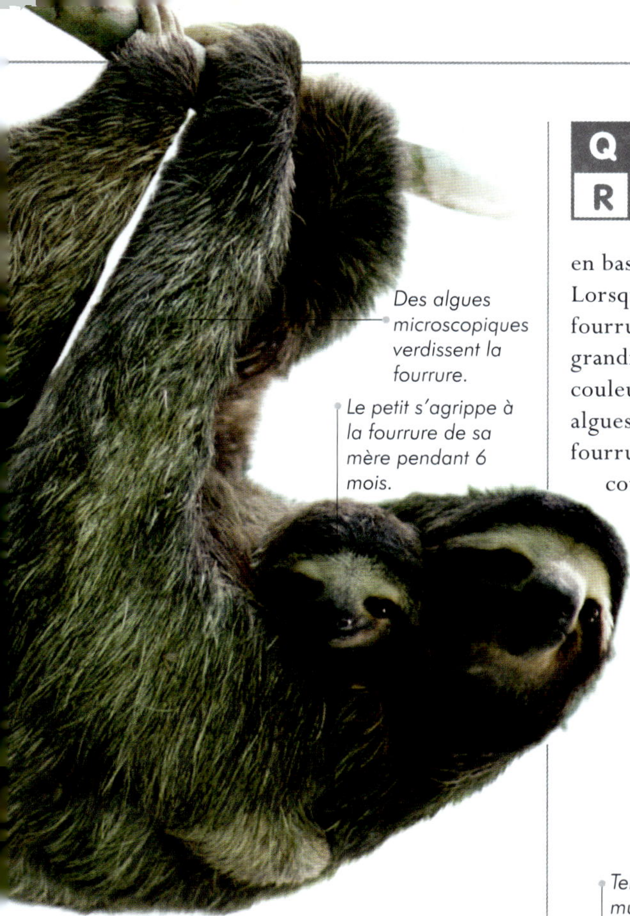

Q Pourquoi les paresseux deviennent-ils verts ?

R Les paresseux sont folivores et passent leur temps suspendus tête en bas dans les branches des arbres. Lorsqu'ils viennent de naître, ils ont une fourrure brun-jaune, mais lorsqu'ils grandissent, elle devient verte. Cette couleur vient de petits organismes appelés algues. Ces algues poussent dans la fourrure des paresseux, leur donnant cette couleur verdâtre et une légère odeur de moisi. Cette couleur verte aide les paresseux à se cacher dans les arbres, à l'abri des aigles. Étrangement, les paresseux grignotent aussi ces algues qui sont pleines de nutriments.

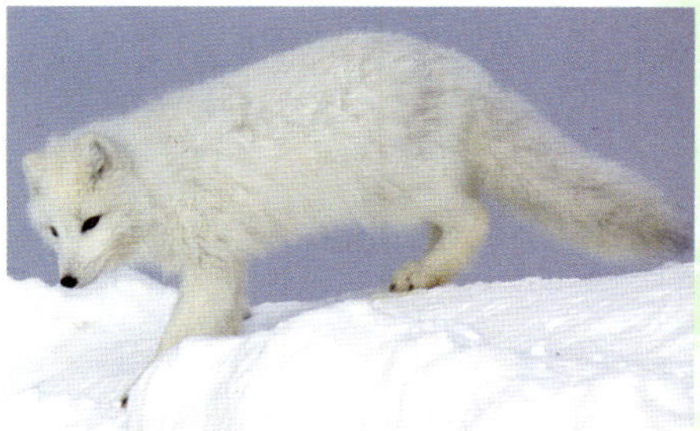

Renard polaire

Q Pourquoi les renards polaires blanchissent-ils en hiver ?

R Dans l'Arctique, un renard brun serait très facile à voir sur la blancheur de la neige. C'est pourquoi le renard polaire change de couleur selon les saisons. En été, la plupart sont gris-brun, une couleur qui se fond dans le paysage des rochers. À la fin de l'été, une fourrure d'hiver blanche pousse, beaucoup plus épaisse et chaude.

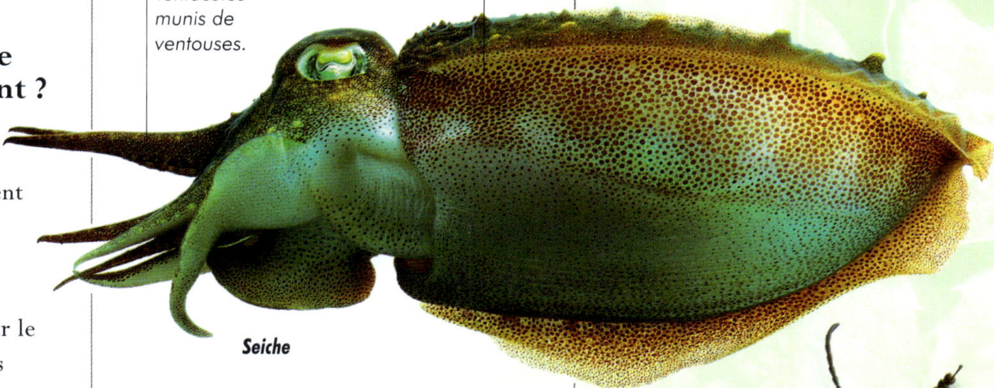

Seiche

Q Qui peut changer de couleur en un instant ?

R Certains animaux changent de couleur et de motifs pour ressembler à leur environnement ou pour montrer leur humeur. La seiche peut le faire en moins d'une seconde grâce aux petites taches de couleur sous sa peau. En nageant sur le fond de l'océan, elle se fond avec les galets, les algues ou le sable. Elle change aussi de couleur pour montrer de la colère ou surprendre un prédateur.

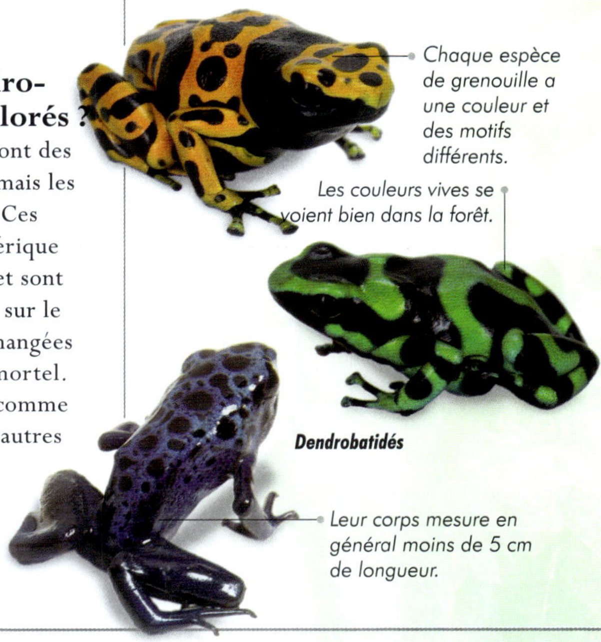

Dendrobatidés

Q Pourquoi les dendrobates sont-ils si colorés ?

R Beaucoup de grenouilles ont des couleurs de camouflage, mais les dendrobates agissent à l'inverse. Ces petites grenouilles vivent en Amérique centrale et en Amérique du Sud et sont faciles à voir lorsqu'elles sautent sur le sol. Elles n'ont pas peur d'être mangées car leur peau secrète un poison mortel. Les couleurs vives fonctionnent comme un signal d'alerte, montrant aux autres animaux qu'il est très dangereux de les toucher. Les peuples de ces forêts utilisaient ce poison pour enduire leurs flèches.

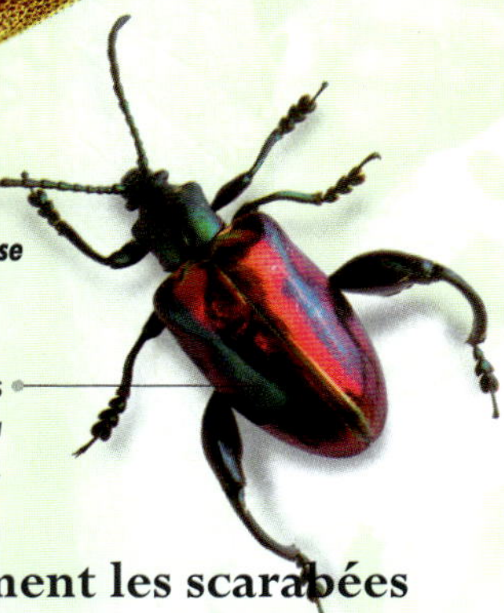

Scarabée à cuisse de grenouille

Q Comment les scarabées font-ils pour briller ?

R Ces couleurs brillantes résultent d'un procédé spécial. Au lieu d'être produites chimiquement, elles sont faites de microscopiques stries sur la carapace de l'insecte. Ces stries permettent aux rayons lumineux d'interférer entre eux, créant ainsi des couleurs aux reflets métalliques. Beaucoup d'autres animaux, y compris les oiseaux-mouches et les papillons, ont des couleurs brillantes créées de la même manière.

Qui est le meilleur acteur ?

Le milieu naturel est plein de très bons acteurs. Certains prétendent être des serpents venimeux ou des insectes piquants, alors que d'autres se font des yeux terrifiants pour faire fuir les attaquants. Tous ces animaux agissent ainsi pour la même raison : se faire passer pour beaucoup plus dangereux qu'ils ne le sont. Le meilleur comédien est le lézard à collerette du nord de l'Australie. Lorsque l'animal se sent en danger, il ouvre sa gueule en grand et déploie sa collerette comme un parapluie immense, en sifflant, frappant le sol de sa queue et fonçant sur l'adversaire. S'il se rend compte qu'il ne peut impressionner son ennemi, il va changer de tactique et s'enfuir sur ses pattes arrière.

Q R Qui sait faire une bonne imitation de serpent ?

La plupart des animaux ont peur des serpents, même s'ils n'en ont jamais vu. La chenille de papillon de nuit appelé « grand sphinx de la vigne » utilise cette peur pour se protéger. Si un oiseau repère la chenille, elle rentre la tête dans son thorax et gonfle ses premiers segments abdominaux, mettant ainsi en relief ses grands ocelles qui ressemblent alors à une paire d'yeux. Ce truc peut sauver la vie de la chenille.

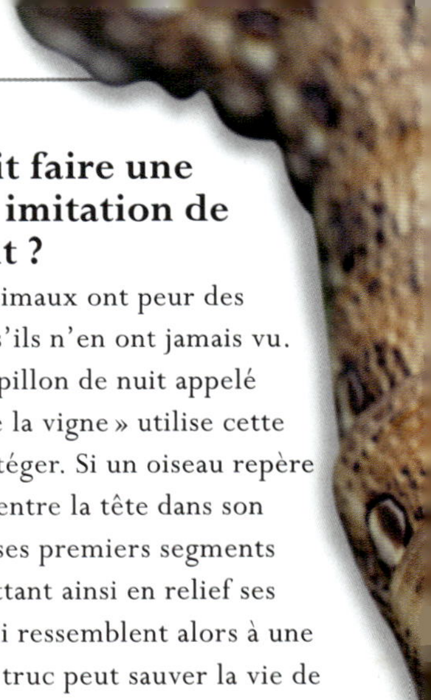

Chenille de grand sphinx de la vigne

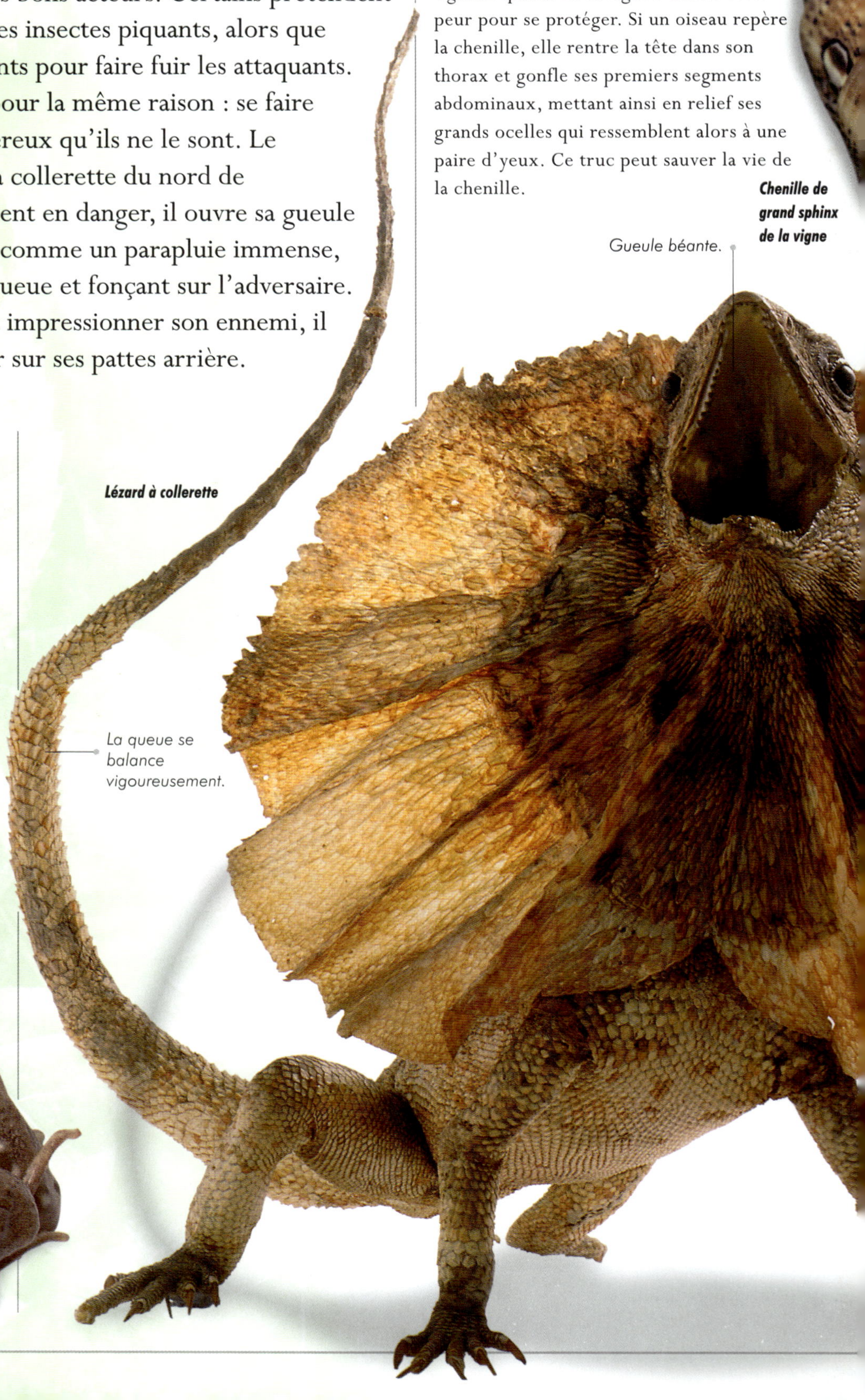

Lézard à collerette

Q R Quelle grenouille semble avoir des yeux sur le dos ?

Normalement, c'est une mauvaise idée de tourner le dos au danger. Mais c'est ce que fait la grenouille à quatre yeux de Patagonie. Elle a une paire de bosses sur les côtés qui ressemblent exactement à des yeux. Ces bosses se trouvent juste au-dessus des pattes de la grenouille et lui font une seconde face terrifiante. Ces faux yeux sont en fait des glandes bourrées de poison. Si un prédateur mord la grenouille, leur goût affreux le fera fuir très vite.

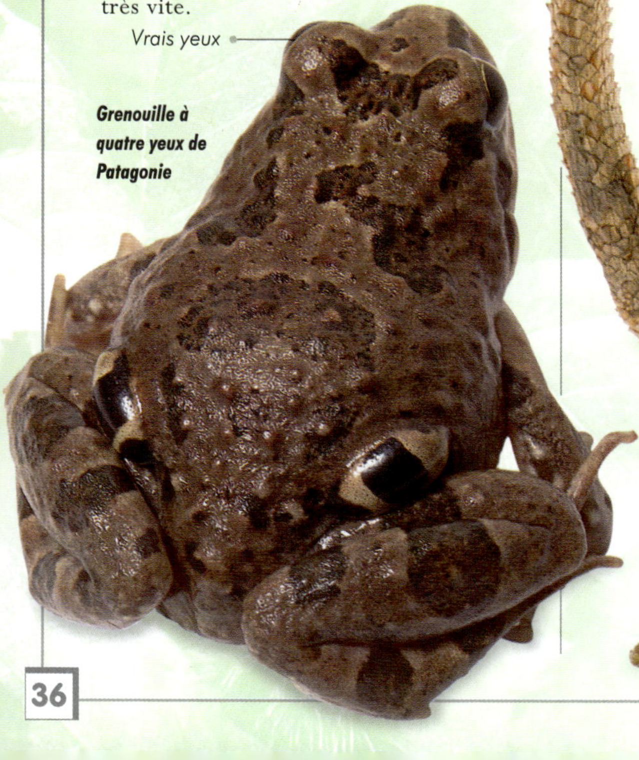

Grenouille à quatre yeux de Patagonie

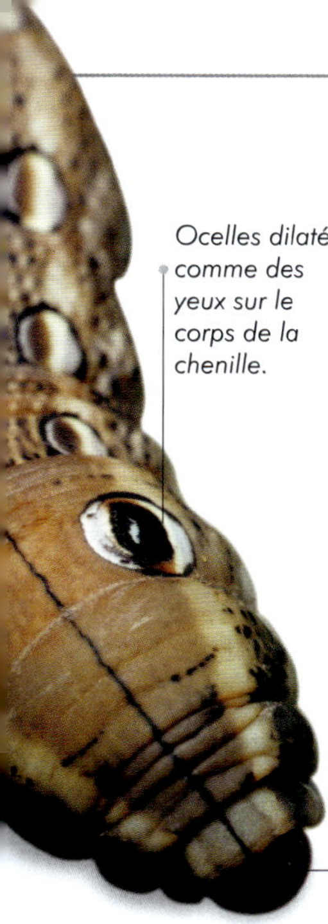

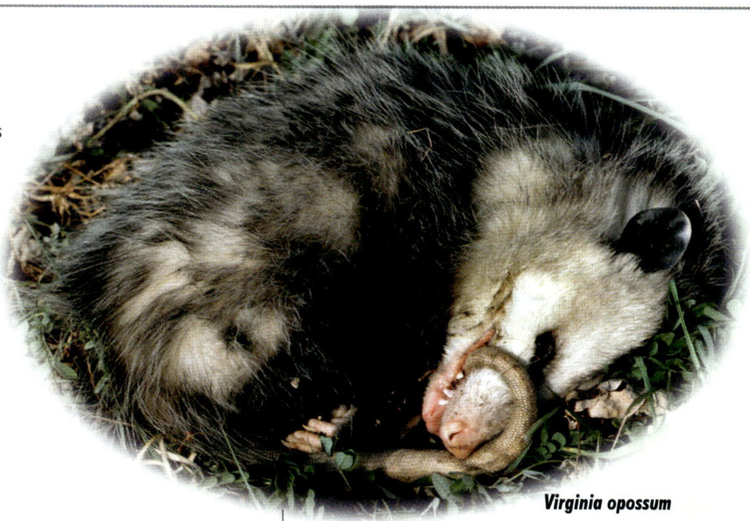

Virginia opossum

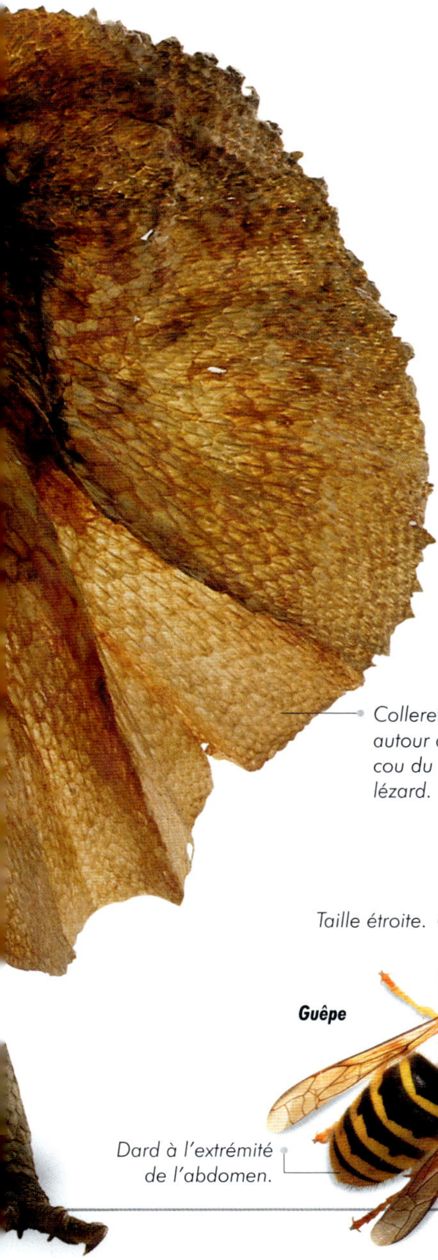

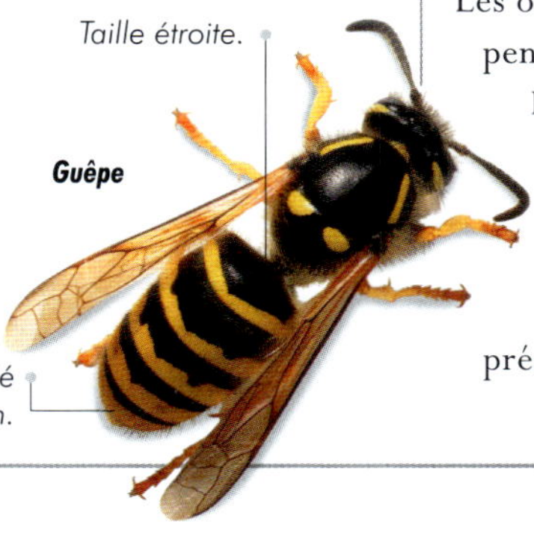

Guêpe

Un animal peut-il simuler la mort ?

Q R Oui, et c'est l'opossum de Virginie qui le fait. Cela peut lui sauver la vie. On trouve ce marsupial en Amérique du Nord. S'il est traqué par un prédateur, il s'enroule sur lui-même avec les yeux à demi ouverts, exactement comme s'il était mort. Beaucoup de prédateurs ne chassent que des proies vivantes et, si l'opossum a l'air mort, le chasseur s'en désintéressera. Lorsque le danger est passé, l'opossum revient miraculeusement à la vie.

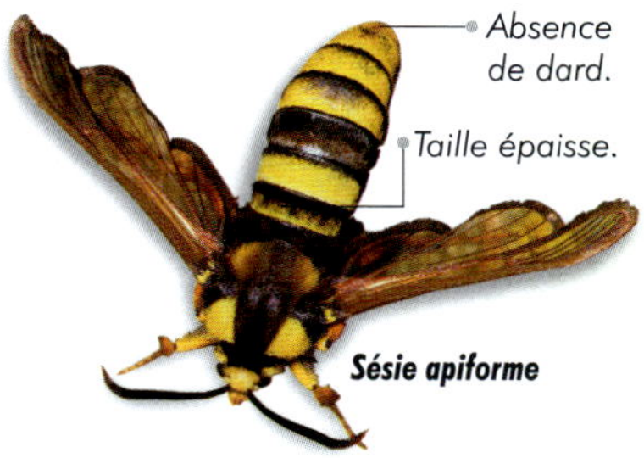

Sésie apiforme

Pourquoi certains papillons de nuit ressemblent-ils à des guêpes ?

Pour les papillons de nuit, ressembler à une guêpe est un bon moyen de se protéger. Habillés de rayures jaunes et noires et avec deux paires d'ailes transparentes, ils sont très ressemblants. Les oiseaux, et beaucoup d'être humains, pensent que ceux-ci peuvent les piquer. Imiter la guêpe est un stratagème très répandu dans le monde animal. Des milliers d'espèces de petits animaux, comme les mouches et les araignées, l'utilisent pour se préserver.

Pourquoi certains oiseaux simulent-ils une blessure ?

La femelle du pluvier niche sur le sol. Elle est donc très vulnérable. Si elle voit un animal au-dessus de ses œufs, elle va essayer de le leurrer. Elle quitte le nid et s'éloigne en boitant, comme si elle avait une patte cassée. Avec un peu de chance, l'intrus la suivra, espérant l'attraper facilement. Lorsqu'elle est suffisamment loin, elle se remet sur ses pattes et s'envole vers son nid.

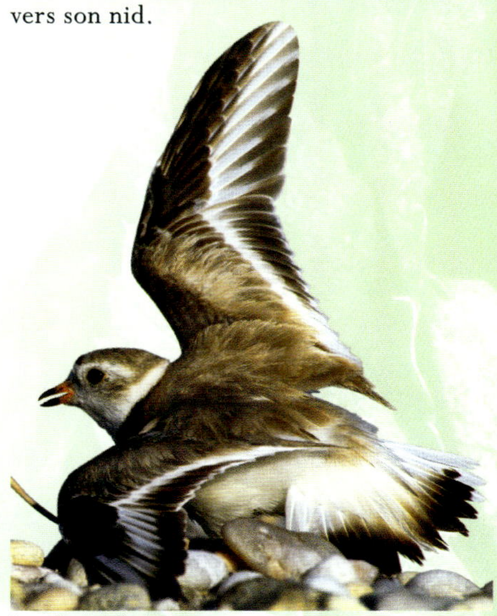

Femelle du pluvier

Plus d' infos

- Certaines araignées ressemblent à des fourmis et se meuvent de la même façon. Les fourmis peuvent mordre et piquer, donc les oiseaux et les lézards, abusés, les laissent tranquilles.
- L'Hypaurotis est un papillon qui a une fausse tête dessinée sur l'arrière de ses ailes. La fausse tête trompe les oiseaux, qui en oublient la vraie.

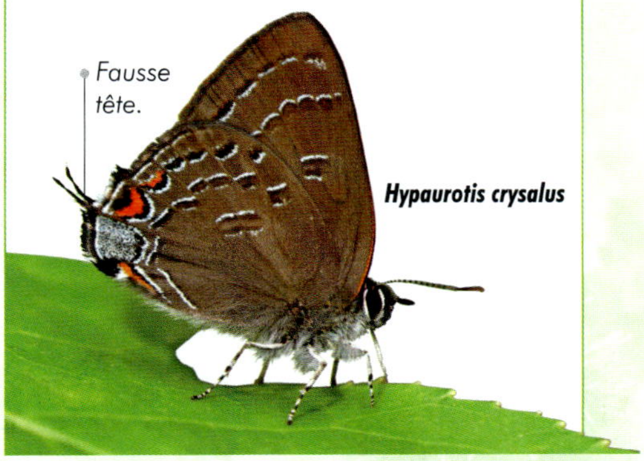

Hypaurotis crysalus

Qui utilise la couleur pour attirer son compagnon ?

Pour éviter le danger, les animaux font souvent de leur mieux pour rester invisibles. Cependant, durant la saison des amours, ils ont besoin d'attirer l'attention sur eux pour séduire un partenaire. Certains le font en appelant, en chantant ou en changeant de couleur, mais le crabe violoniste brandit une pince géante et colorée. Cette pince peut être aussi longue que le corps du crabe. Lorsqu'il agite ainsi sa pince, les femelles se précipitent vers lui à travers le sable. Les mâles utilisent aussi leur pince pour se battre entre eux.

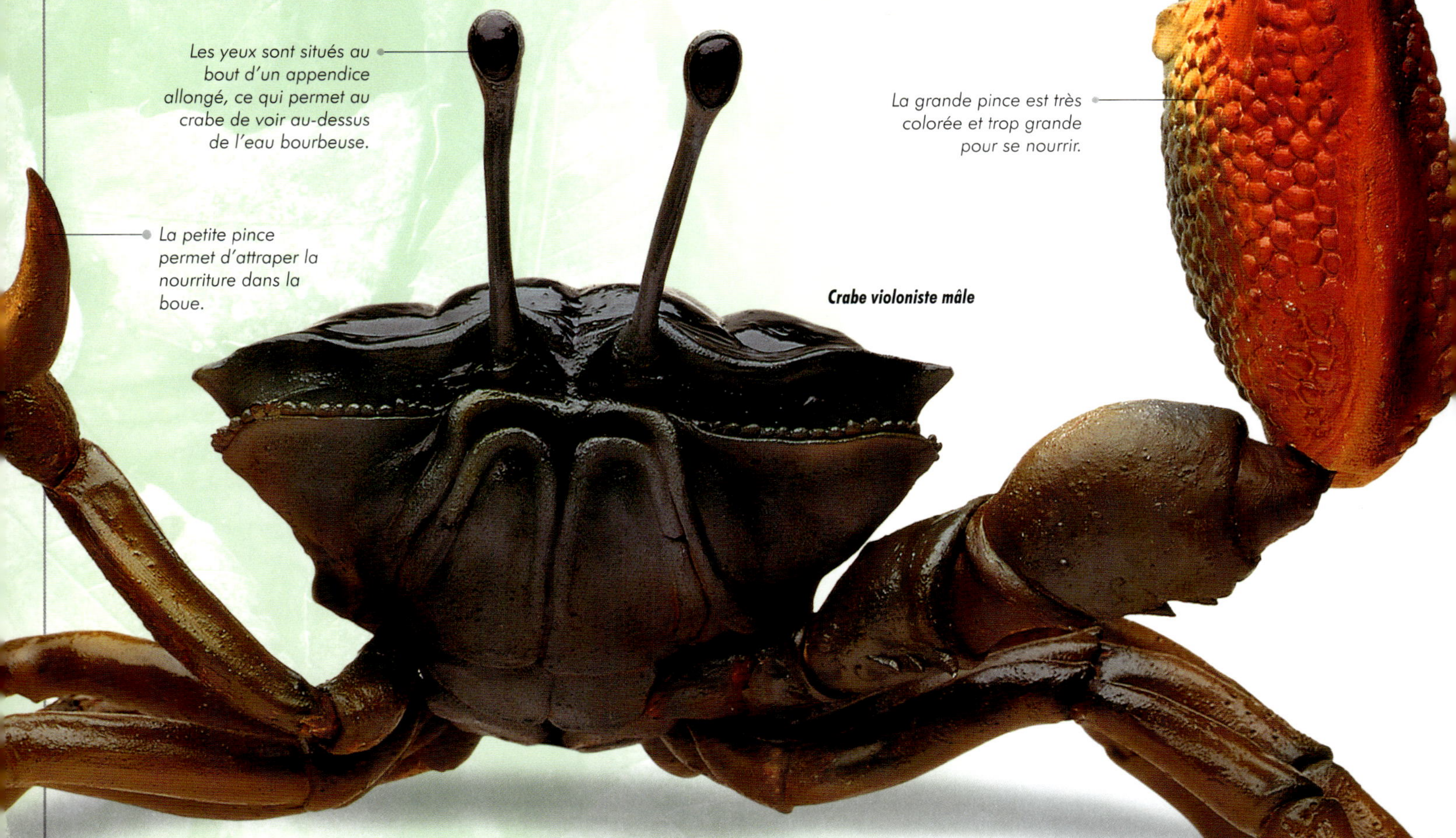

Crabe violoniste mâle

Q Qu'est-ce qui fait rougir les saumons ?

R Dans la mer, le saumon sockeye a les flancs argentés et une tête bleu acier. Juste avant la saison des amours, il devient rouge vif. Des millions d'entre eux se dirigent alors vers les côtes avant de remonter les rivières en nageant jusqu'aux lacs où ils fraient en fécondant les œufs. La couleur est le signal qui indique que l'adulte est prêt à se reproduire.

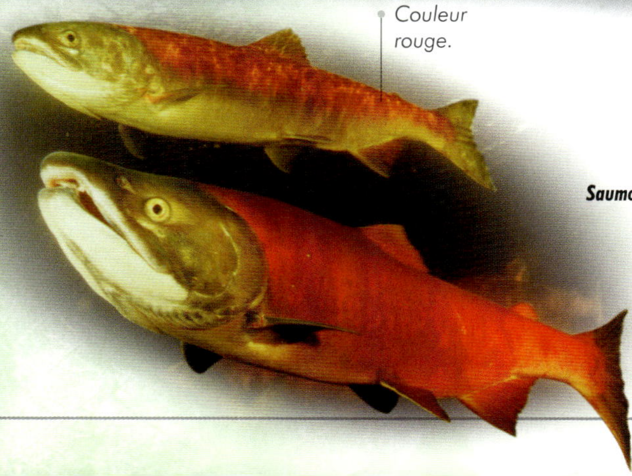

Saumon sockeye

Oiseaux satin

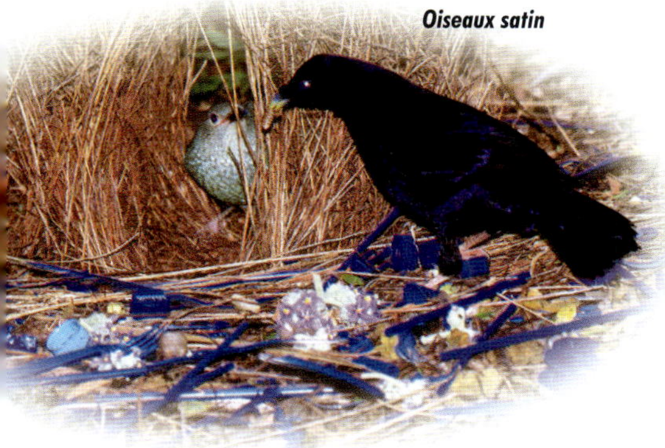

Q R Qui est attiré par la couleur bleue ?

Les oiseaux satin mâles (*Ptilonorhynchus violaceus*) ont un comportement incroyable. Pour attirer les femelles, chaque mâle ramasse des centaines de morceaux de branchages et construit une structure en forme de tonnelle ou de berceau. Puis, il décore l'entrée avec des objets brillants et colorés, et attend qu'une femelle le choisisse. Les oiseaux satin d'Australie préfèrent des objets bleus : fleurs, plumes et même bouchons de bouteilles bleus.

Q R Pourquoi les lucioles sont-elles lumineuses ?

Les lucioles sont en fait des sortes de scarabées femelles sans ailes. Pendant la saison des amours, elles doivent attirer les mâles qui volent la nuit. Pour ce faire, la femelle émet une lumière de couleur vert laser, relativement puissante. Alors, le mâle la repère et atterrit à côté d'elle pour se reproduire.

Luciole femelle

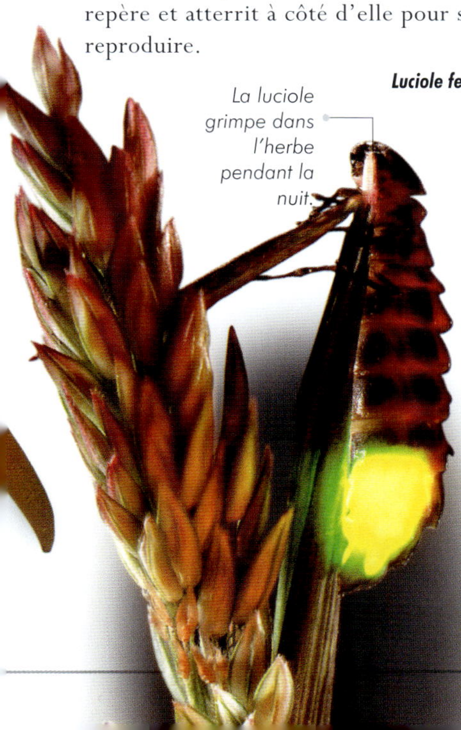

La luciole grimpe dans l'herbe pendant la nuit.

Q R Qui a une gueule repoussante ?

Chez les humains, des traits délicats font souvent un joli visage. Mais les femelles orangs-outans ont des idées bien différentes sur la séduction. Elles préfèrent que leurs partenaires aient des bourrelets très larges sur les joues, une grosse poche sous la gorge et beaucoup de poils très longs. Seuls les mâles ont ces attributs et ils deviennent de plus en plus visibles avec l'âge. Les orangs-outans passent une grande partie de leur vie seuls, les femelles n'ont donc pas beaucoup de temps pour choisir un compagnon. Les bourrelets sur les joues des mâles indiquent qu'ils sont sexuellement matures et qu'ils feront sans doute des petits forts et en bonne santé.

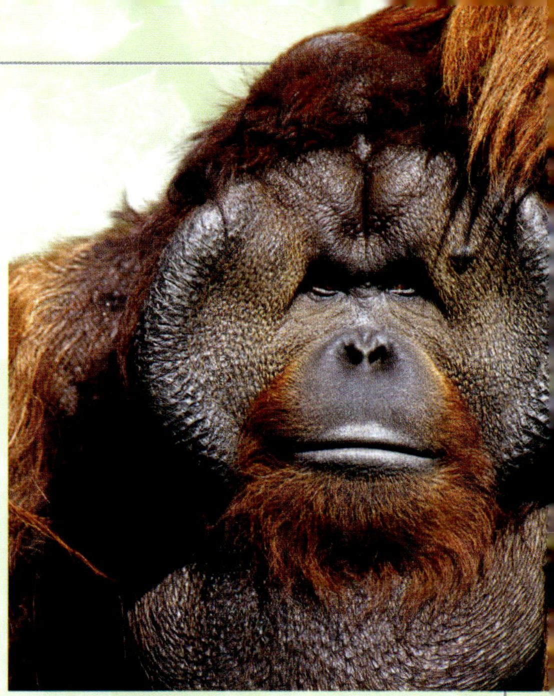

Orang-outan mâle

Plus d'infos

- Les anolis mâles sont dotés d'un fanon gulaire généralement rouge, qu'ils déploient pour séduire les femelles.

Lézard anolis

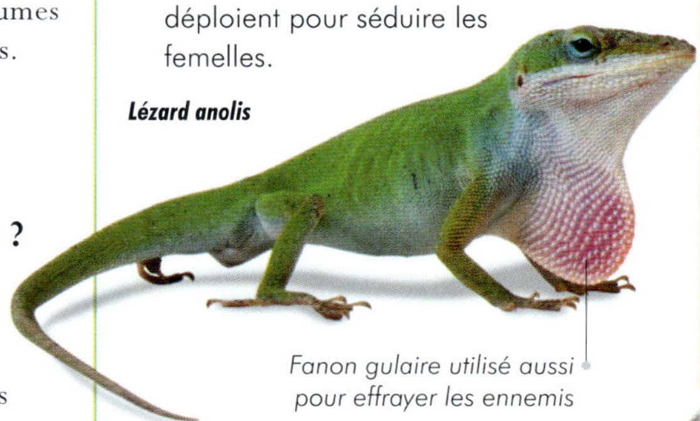

Fanon gulaire utilisé aussi pour effrayer les ennemis

- Les mâles du claqueur ou Klaké, du genre Hamadryas, sont des papillons qui font un bruit sec en volant. Ce bruit attire les femelles mais repousse les autres mâles.
- La grande outarde mâle est un oiseau qui attire les femelles en hérissant ses plumes. Au plus fort de sa performance, on pourrait croire que l'oiseau a totalement disparu à l'intérieur du plumage.

Q R Quel oiseau ressemble à un ballon ?

Les mâles et les femelles frégates du Pacifique se ressemblent beaucoup alors qu'ils volent haut dans le ciel au-dessus de la mer. Mais, pendant la saison des amours, les mâles ont une manière saisissante d'attirer les femelles. Perchés sur un buisson près du rivage, ils gonflent une poche qui ressemble alors à un gros ballon rouge. Chaque mâle conserve sa poche gonflée tant qu'il ne se sera pas accouplé.

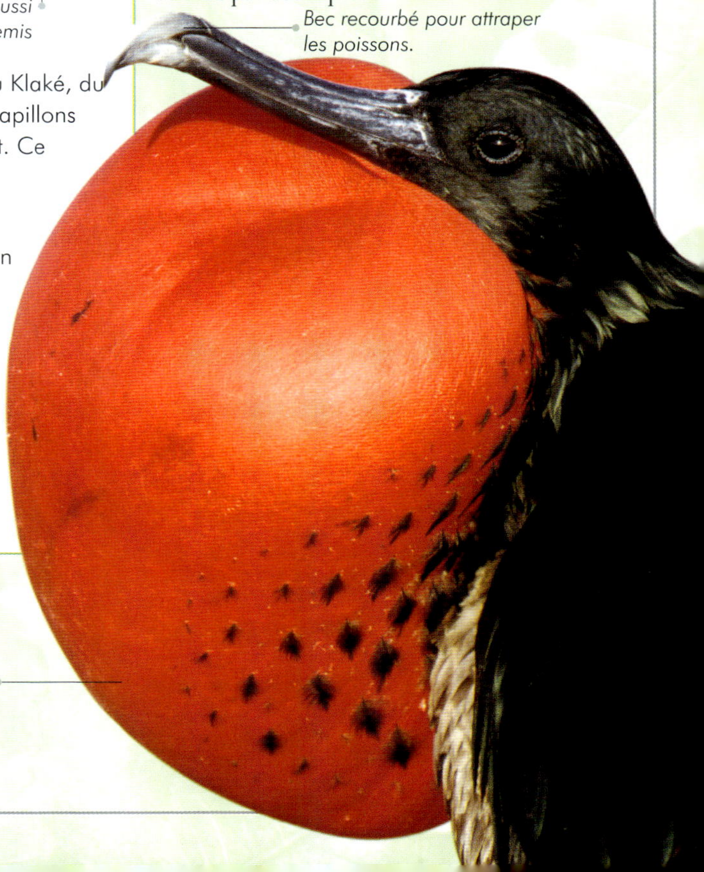

Bec recourbé pour attraper les poissons.

Frégate du Pacifique mâle

La poche passe de l'orange au rouge pendant la saison des amours.

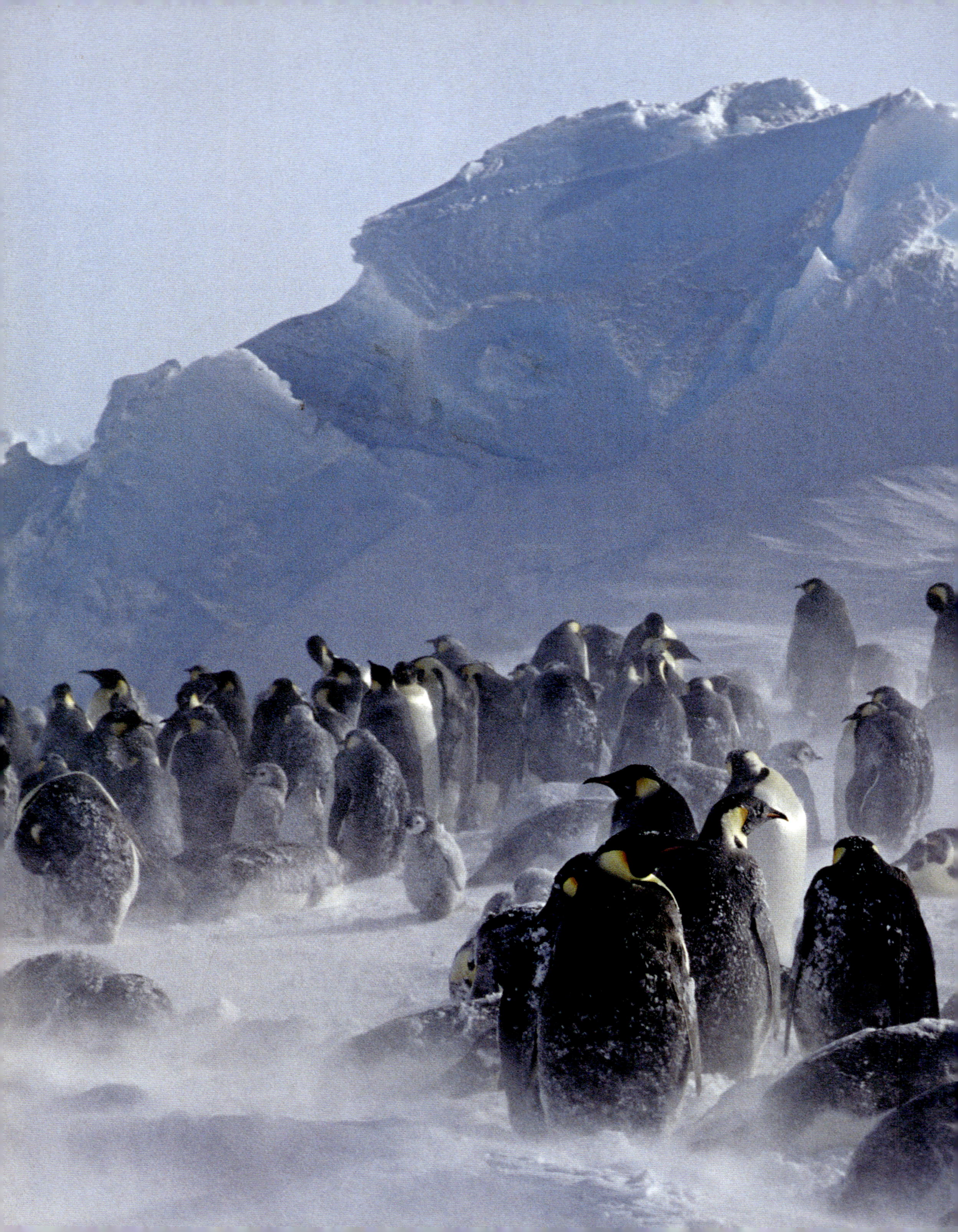

Vivre dans des conditions extrêmes

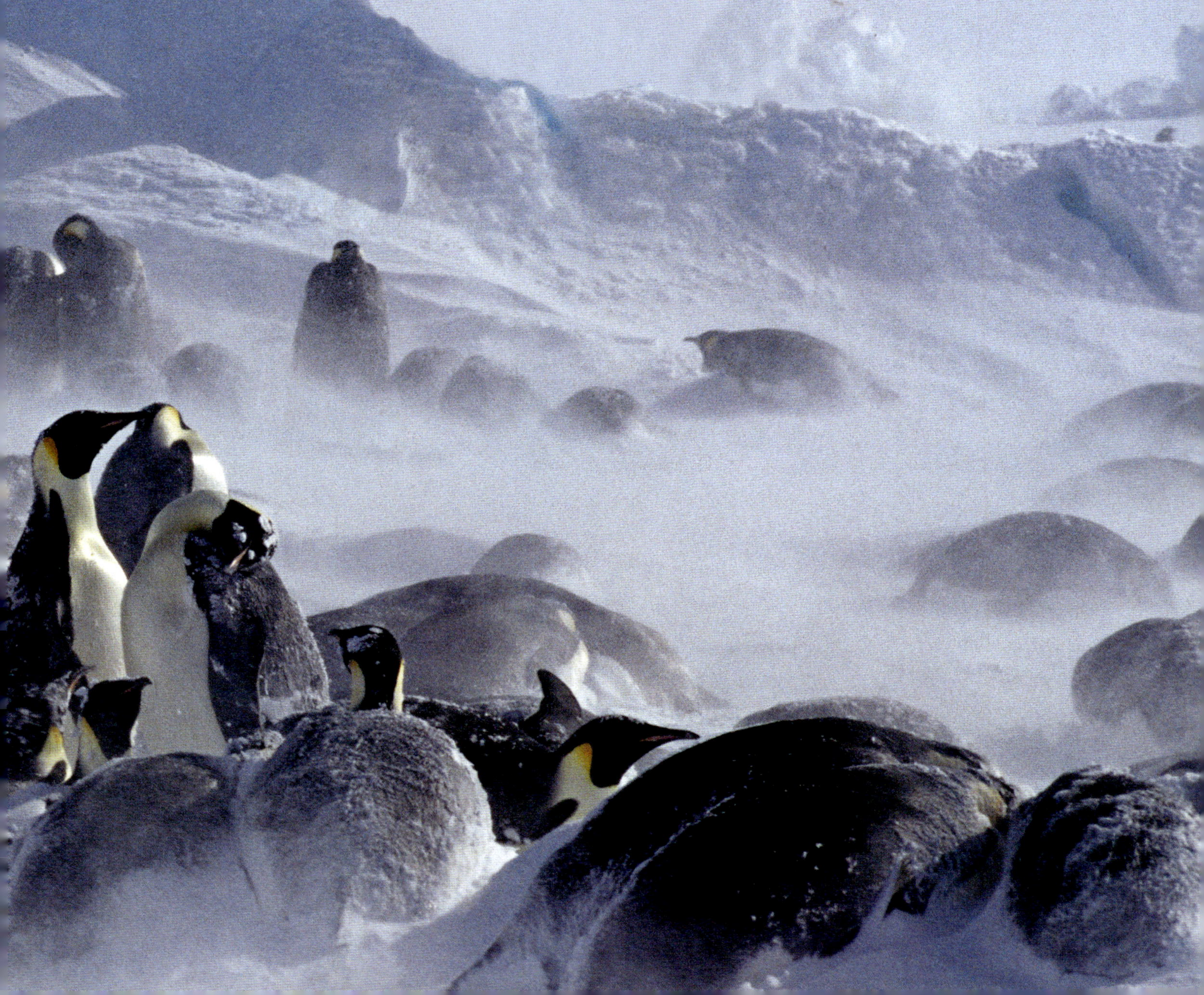

Comment les termites se protègent-ils de la chaleur ?

Pour tous les animaux, gros ou petits, avoir trop chaud peut être mortel. C'est pourquoi, dans les pays chauds, les animaux doivent pouvoir se rafraîchir. Certains se cachent du soleil de midi ou ne sortent que la nuit. Les termites se gardent de la chaleur en vivant dans des termitières climatisées. La partie où ils vivent se trouve sous le sol. Au-dessus d'eux, il y a un gigantesque tertre fait d'argile cuit par le soleil. Haut de 4 m, le tertre contient des tunnels qui rafraîchissent l'air circulant à travers le nid.

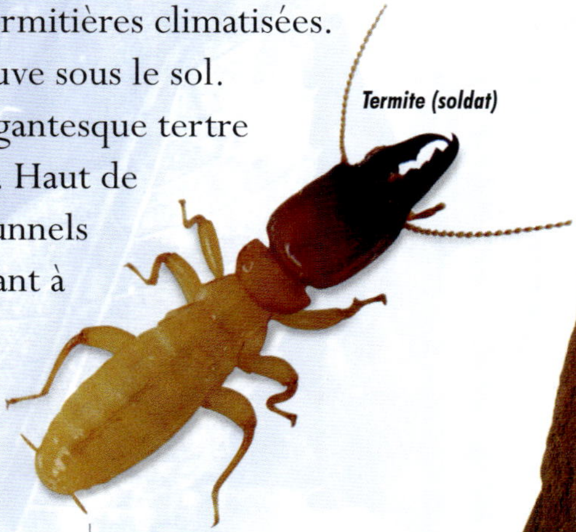
Termite (soldat)

Q R Qui se fait sa propre lotion solaire ?

Les hippopotames passent leurs journées affalés dans l'eau boueuse sous un soleil de feu. Leur fourrure est très clairsemée, mais leur peau fabrique un liquide rouge et huileux qui les protège des brûlures du soleil. Cette lotion spéciale a aussi d'autres bienfaits : elle les protège contre les piqûres des insectes.

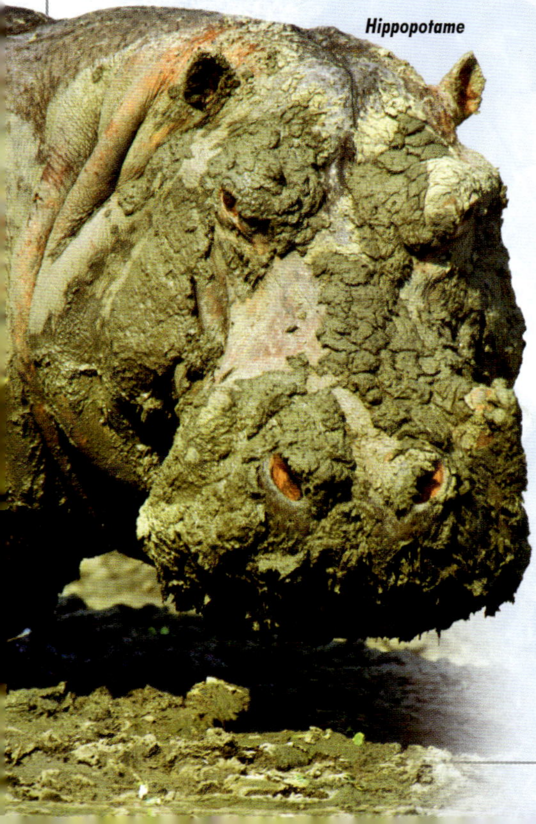
Hippopotame

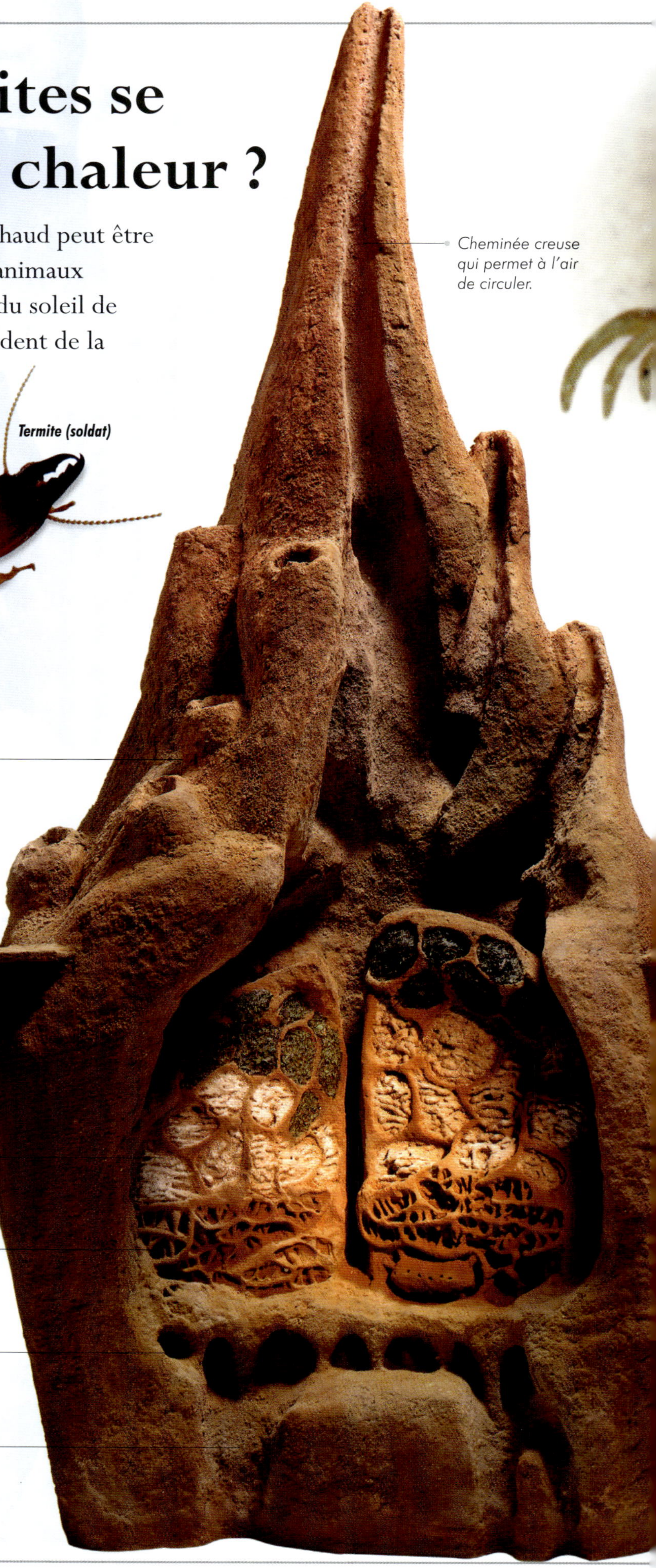

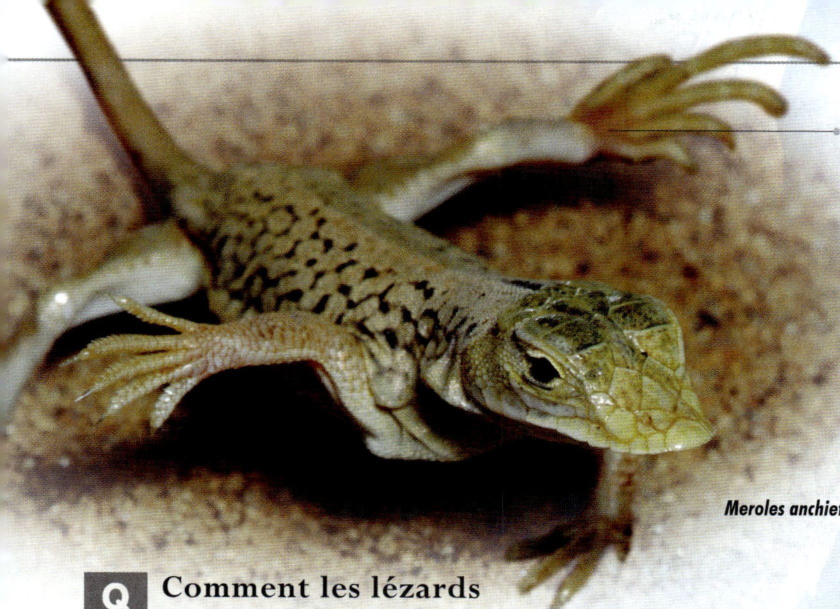

Meroles anchietae

Comment les lézards restent-ils au frais dans la chaleur ?

Dans le désert, les lézards restent au frais en se cachant sous des rochers. Le lézard *Meroles anchietae*, que l'on trouve dans le sud-ouest de l'Afrique, vit dans des dunes de sable du Namib où il est très difficile de trouver de l'ombre. Pour se protéger de la chaleur, il a de longues pattes qui maintiennent son corps loin du sable brûlant. Il agit aussi de façon amusante : il soulève deux pattes (en diagonale) en même temps, attend qu'elles se soient rafraîchies, les repose et soulève les deux autres en alternance.

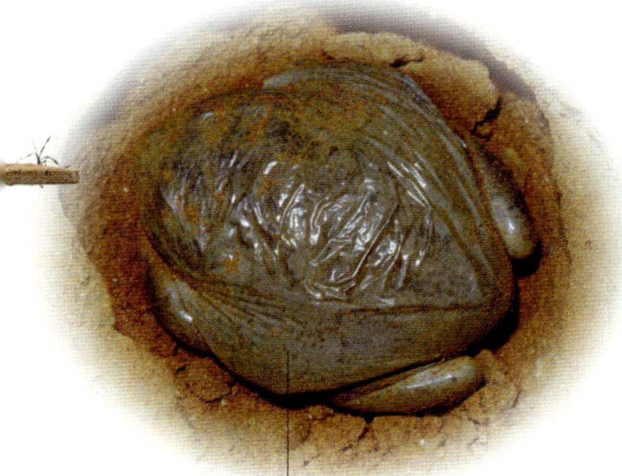

Cyclorana platycephala

Comment survivent les grenouilles dans le désert ?

Sous la surface de nombreux déserts, les grenouilles s'enterrent en attendant la pluie. Lorsqu'elle arrive enfin, la grenouille mange son cocon et remonte à l'air libre. Ces grenouilles déposent leurs œufs dans les flaques et les têtards deviennent rapidement des grenouilles. Avant que la flaque ne s'assèche, les grenouilles ont regagné le frais du sous-sol.

Plus d' infos

- La tortue du désert en Amérique du Nord passe 90% de son temps dans des terriers pour éviter la chaleur. Ces reptiles en danger sortent de préférence la nuit.

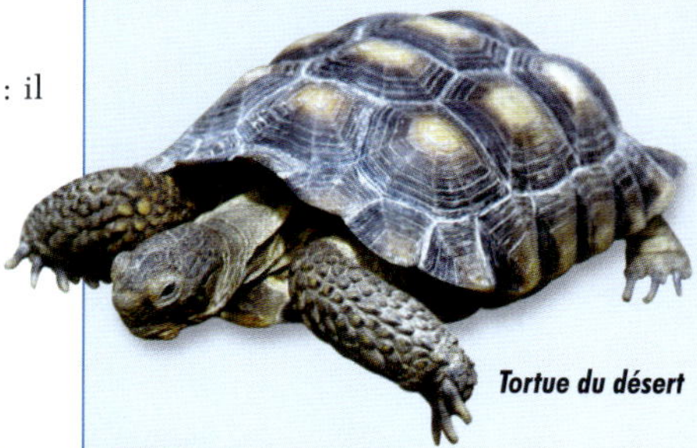

Tortue du désert

- En Australie, certaines araignées restent actives même sous des températures de 50°. Dans cette chaleur, un humain ne pourrait pas survivre.
- Les chameaux ont des naseaux qu'ils peuvent fermer pour se protéger contre les vents de sable.
- Pour réduire le contact avec le sol brûlant, les crotales avancent en se lançant dans l'air et en faisant des bonds de côté.

Pourquoi les tarentules chassent-elles la nuit ?

Contrairement à beaucoup d'araignées, les tarentules se déplacent lentement pour trouver leurs proies. Dans la lumière du jour, la tarentule serait facile à repérer pour un prédateur. C'est pourquoi elle passe la journée dans son terrier et ne sort que la nuit. Les tarentules du désert d'Amérique du Nord chassent surtout les scarabées et les criquets qui, eux aussi, sont des animaux nocturnes.

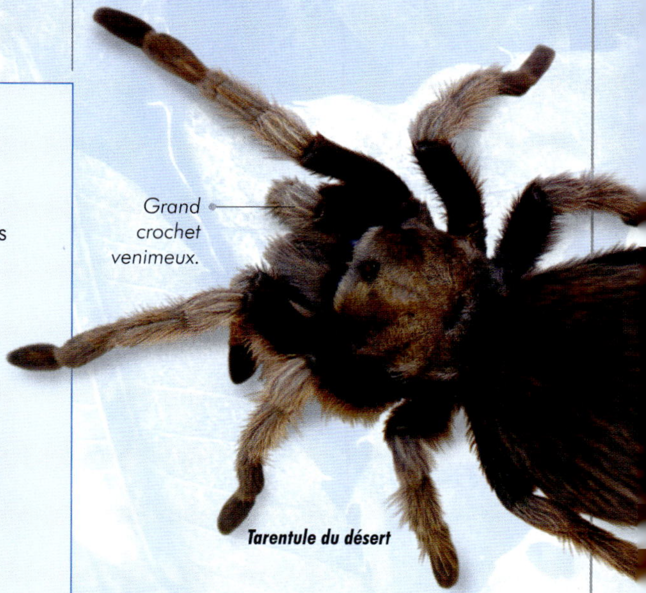

Tarentule du désert

Quel oiseau porte un « parasol » intégré ?

La plupart de ceux qui vivent dans des endroits chauds et secs, y compris les autruches d'Afrique et les émeus d'Australie. Leur « parasol » est constitué de cils en plumes, qui les protègent de la luminosité. Les calaos, oiseaux d'Afrique à face rouge, possèdent les cils les plus longs.

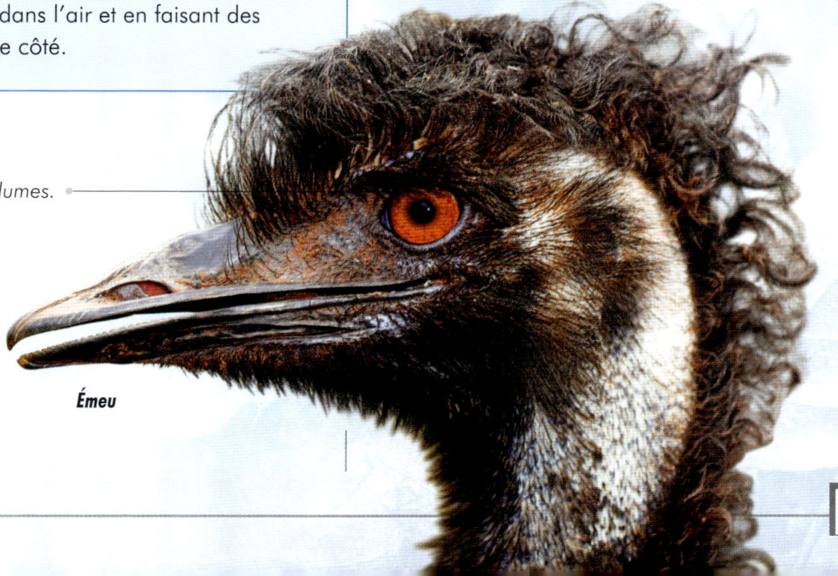

Émeu

Qui se comporte comme un réservoir d'eau ?

Les animaux ne peuvent pas vivre sans eau. Ils ont donc des astuces pour survivre aux sécheresses. Les fourmis pot-de-miel d'Australie et d'Amérique du Nord se débrouillent en sirotant le jus des plantes. Elles ont la particularité d'avoir des ouvrières qui restent dans le nid de la colonie et qui servent littéralement de réservoirs vivants. Elles accumulent le miellat récolté par les ouvrières qui reviennent au nid. Ainsi, tels des réservoirs, elles gardent dans leur abdomen cette nourriture riche en sucre, qui sera utilisée les jours de disette.

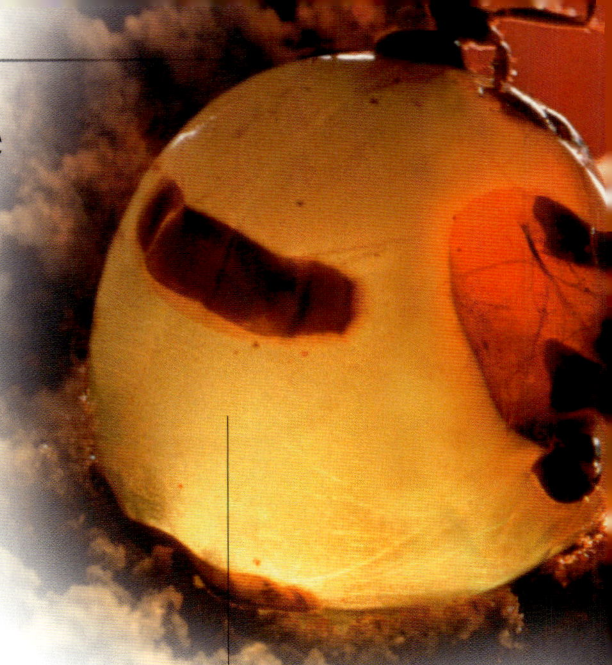

Fourmis mellifères

Q R Combien de litres un chameau assoiffé peut-il boire ?

Les chameaux et les dromadaires peuvent rester une semaine sans boire dans le désert brûlant. Mais lorsqu'ils trouvent de l'eau, ils en profitent réellement. Ils peuvent boire 50 litres en quelques minutes et en conserver la plus grande partie dans leur corps. Ils utilisent aussi leur(s) bosse(s) pour stocker des réserves alimentaires.

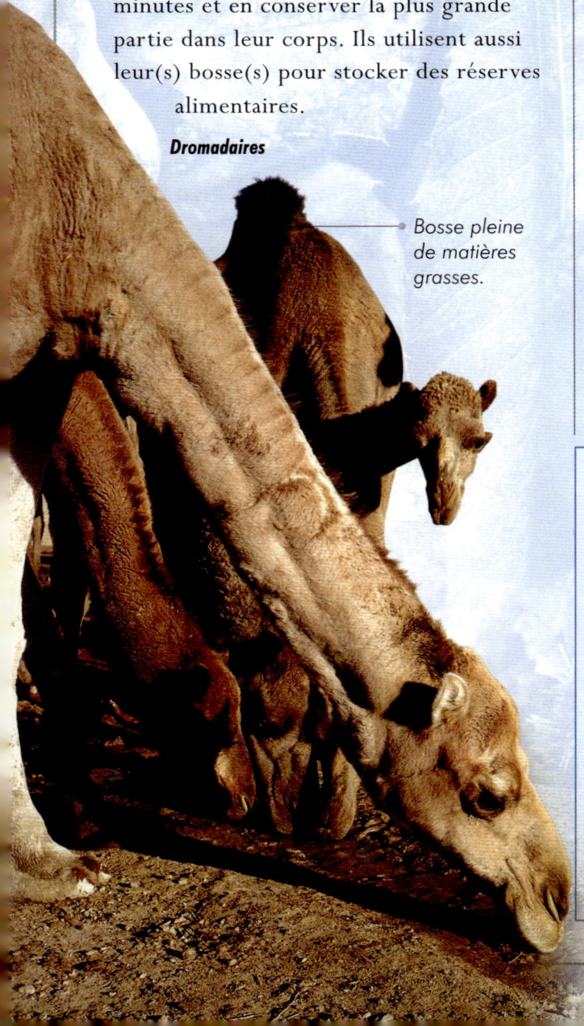

Dromadaires

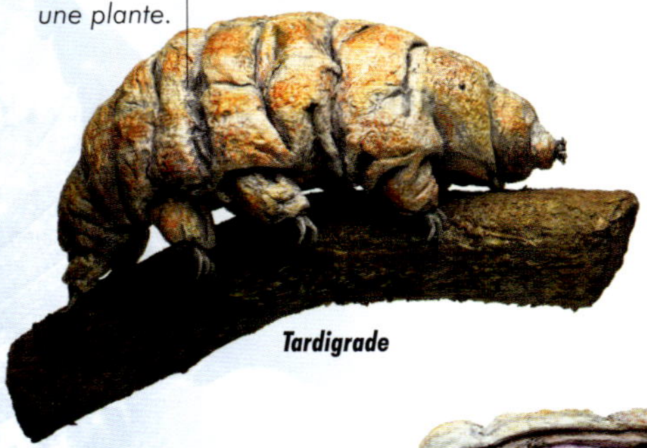

Tardigrade

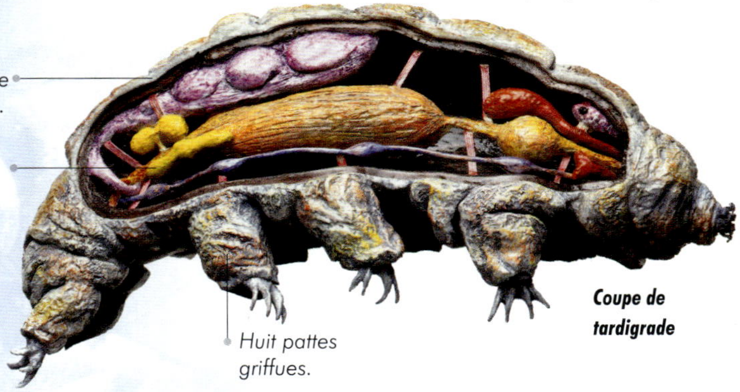

Coupe de tardigrade

Q R Un animal peut-il survivre à une totale déshydratation ?

Quelques animaux microscopiques peuvent devenir aussi secs que des chips. L'un d'eux est le tardigrade, une petite créature qui vit dans les mares. Si la mare s'assèche, le tardigrade se déshydrate aussi. Il peut rester ainsi des mois, voire des années, jusqu'à ce que l'eau revienne.

Plus d' infos

- Les pucerons peuvent boire plus de vingt fois leur propre poids de jus sucré en une journée.
- Un éléphant d'Afrique adulte doit boire 200 litres d'eau par jour.
- Les pigeons sont les seuls oiseaux qui avalent l'eau comme nous. Tous les autres commencent par remplir leur bec puis inclinent la tête vers l'arrière pour laisser couler l'eau.
- Beaucoup d'insectes passent leur vie entière sans boire une goutte d'eau. Cela inclut des coléoptères dont les larves sont les vers de farine, des mites et des vers du bois.

Tribolium brun de la farine

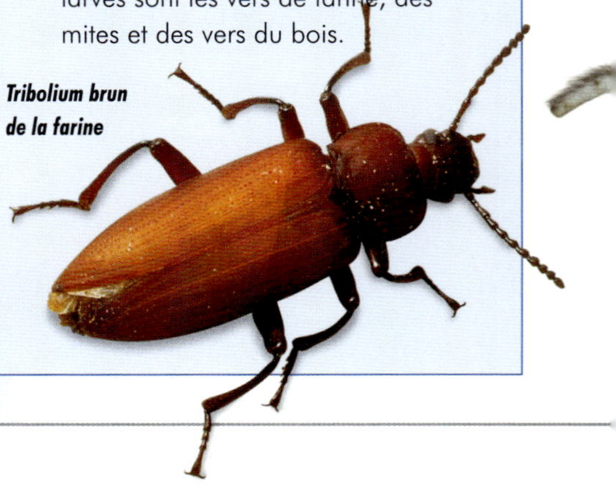

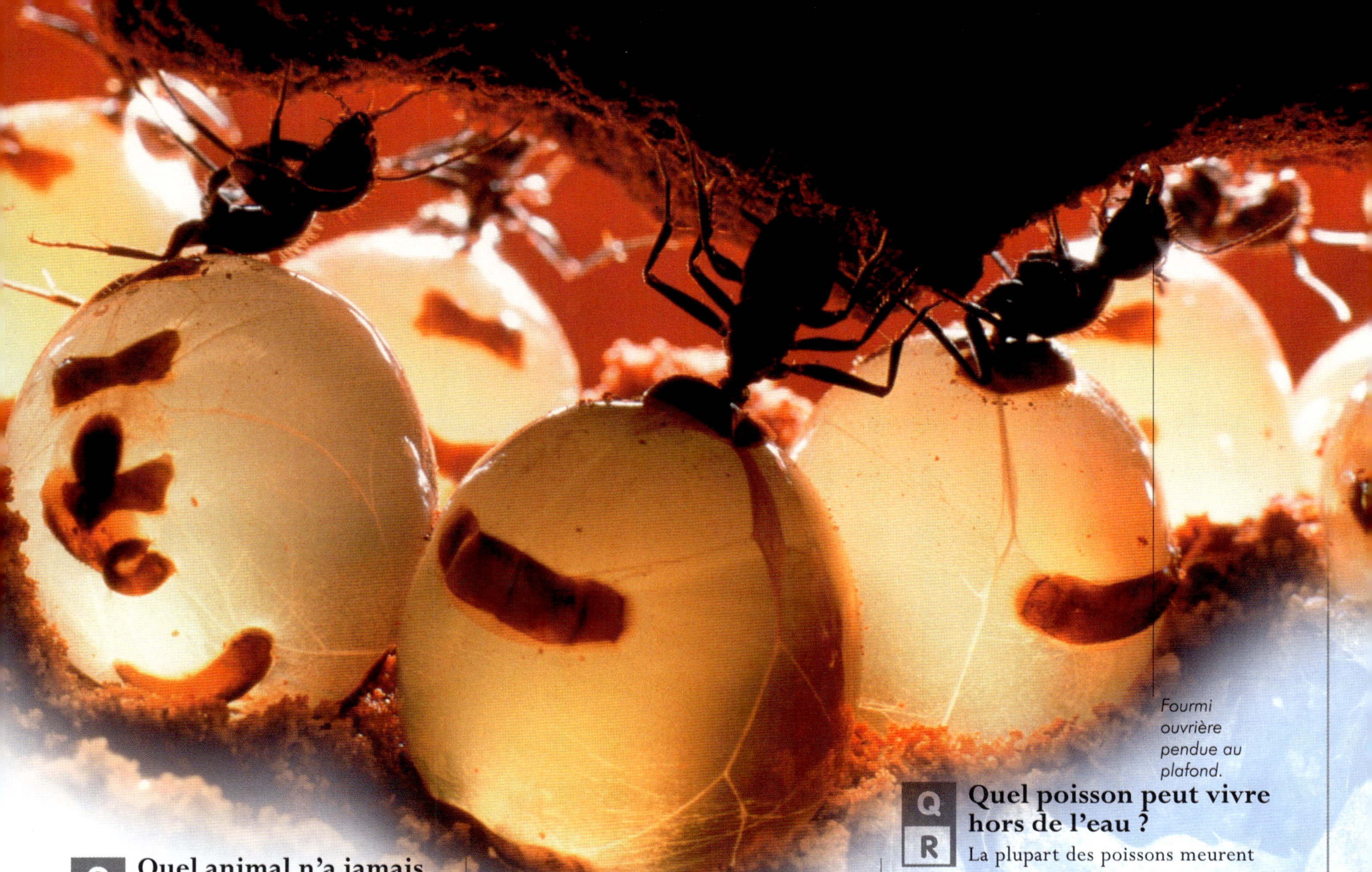

Fourmi ouvrière pendue au plafond.

Quel animal n'a jamais besoin de boire ?

Q

R Tous les animaux ont besoin d'eau, mais tous n'ont pas besoin de boire. Certains trouvent toute l'eau nécessaire dans leur nourriture. Les rats kangourous sont très forts pour cela. Ils vivent dans le désert et se nourrissent principalement de graines. Lors de la digestion, l'eau contenue dans les graines se libère et leur suffit à se maintenir en vie. Les rats kangourous vivent dans des terriers. Ils sortent principalement la nuit, à la fraîcheur, ce qui leur évite de perdre de l'eau en transpirant.

Rat kangourou

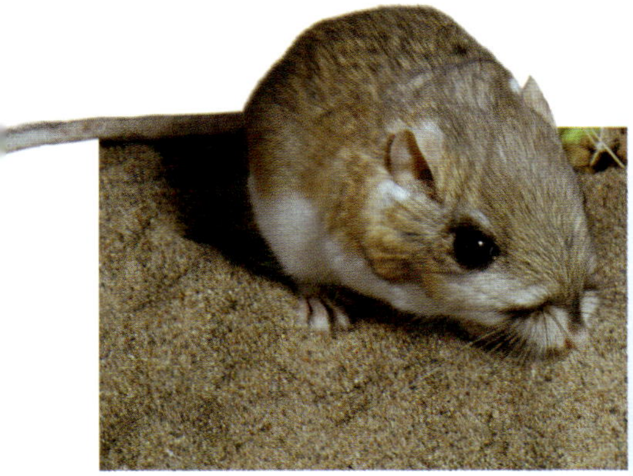

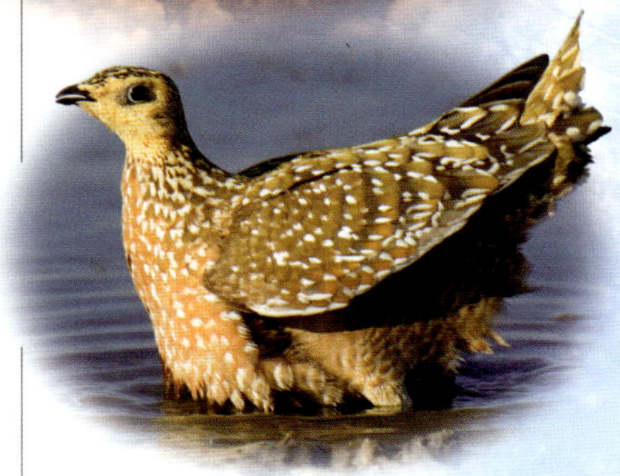

Ganga

Qui transporte de l'eau dans les airs ?

Q

R Les petits gangas ne peuvent pas aller à la recherche d'eau. Aussi, leur père effectue-t-il de vrais « ponts aériens ». Chaque matin, des volées de gangas mâles s'envolent vers des trous d'eau où ils se trempent. Une fois leurs plumes suffisamment imprégnées, ils reviennent au nid. Leurs petits, assoiffés, mordillent les plumes humides, ce qui leur apporte assez d'eau jusqu'au lendemain.

Quel poisson peut vivre hors de l'eau ?

Q

R La plupart des poissons meurent s'ils sont hors de l'eau. Mais les périophtalmes sont différents. Ces poissons aux yeux globuleux vivent dans la mangrove et peuvent rester hors de l'eau autant qu'ils le veulent à condition que leur peau soit humide. Ils utilisent leurs nageoires pectorales comme des pattes. Ils respirent principalement grâce à leur peau bien irriguée et se retirent dans leurs trous quand la marée remonte.

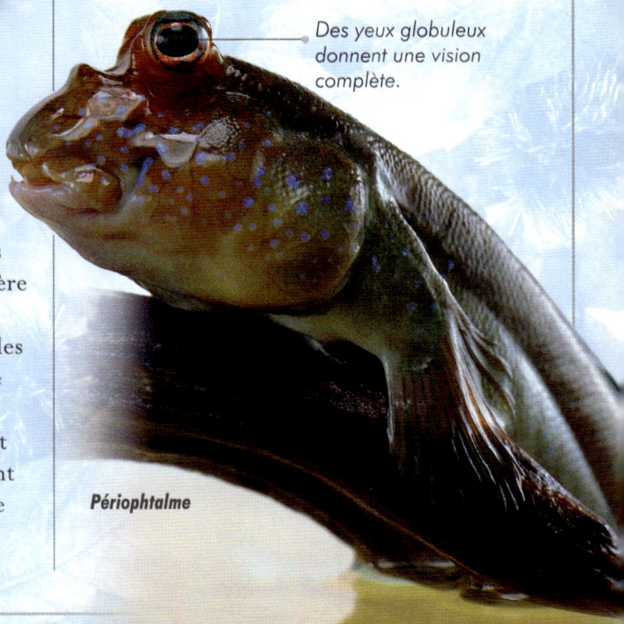

Des yeux globuleux donnent une vision complète.

Périophtalme

Les manchots ont-ils froid ?

Pour les humains, il est difficile de se sentir bien quand il gèle. Dans la nature cependant, certains animaux sont particulièrement adaptés aux températures très basses. Le manchot empereur, qui vit dans l'Antarctique, est le plus résistant de tous. Il reste sur la glace durant tout le long et sombre hiver polaire quand la température peut descendre jusqu'à - 70 °. Les manchots sont protégés du froid par leurs plumes et par une épaisse couche de graisse. Personne ne sait vraiment si les manchots ressentent le froid, mais comme d'autres animaux polaires, leur excellente isolation les garde vivants.

Phoque de Weddell

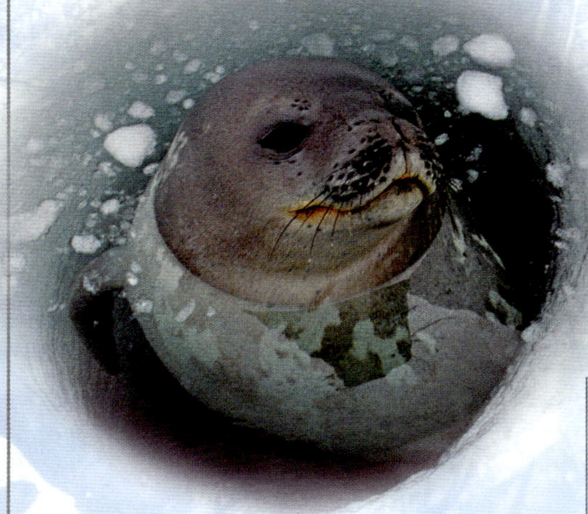

Manchot empereur

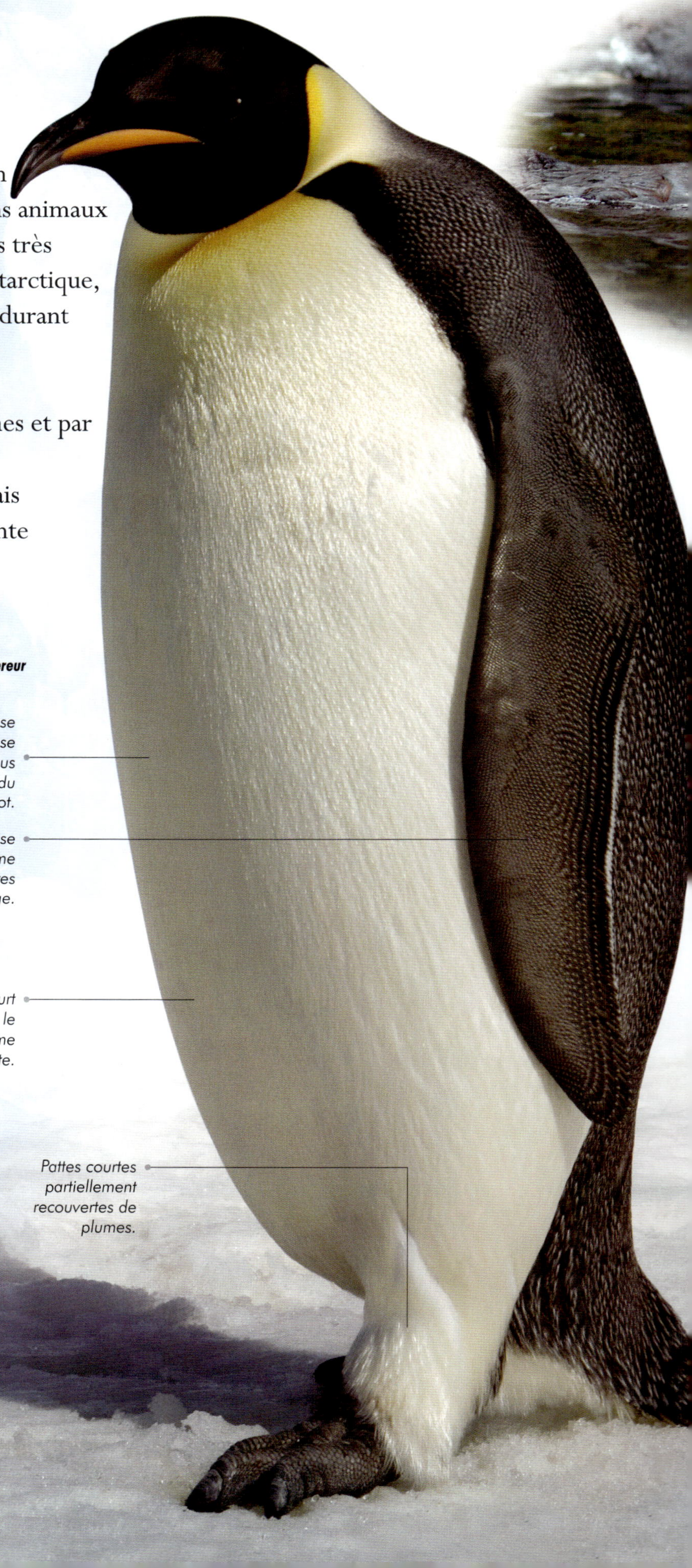

Une épaisse couche de graisse est cachée sous la peau du manchot.

Le manchot utilise ses ailes comme des nageoires lorsqu'il nage.

Un plumage court habille le manchot comme une jaquette.

Pattes courtes partiellement recouvertes de plumes.

Q R Comment respirent les phoques lorsque l'eau est gelée ?

Même au milieu de l'hiver, il y a des phoques qui vivent et se nourrissent sous les glaces polaires. Une couche de graisse les garde au chaud dans la glace, mais ils ont aussi besoin de respirer. Pour ce faire, ils utilisent leurs dents pour creuser un trou dans la glace. Les phoques commencent à faire leurs trous de respiration au début de l'hiver. Ils travaillent dur pour les conserver ouverts. Vers la fin de l'hiver, les trous peuvent mesurer jusqu'à 2 m de profondeur.

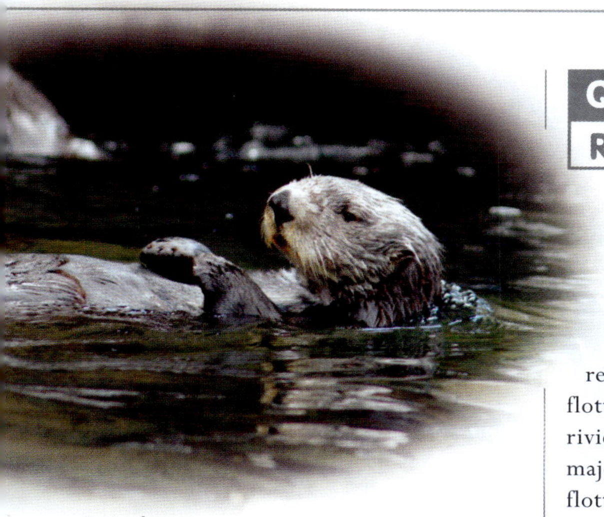

Loutre de mer

Quel animal a la fourrure la plus chaude ?

Les loutres de mer ont la plus épaisse et la plus chaude de toutes les fourrures du monde. Une seule loutre de mer a environ un million de poils. Sa fourrure est si dense que l'eau ne peut pas la pénétrer pour mouiller la peau. Cela lui permet de rester au chaud et lui assure une bonne flottaison. Contrairement aux loutres de rivière, les loutres de mer restent la majeure partie du temps dans l'eau, flottant sur leur dos en dormant.

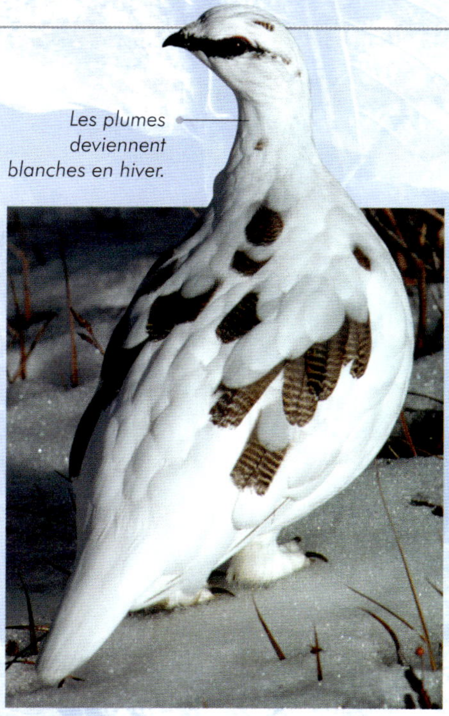

Les plumes deviennent blanches en hiver.

Lagopède

Où les ours polaires mettent-ils bas ?

La plupart des ours mettent bas dans des tanières, au fond des forêts. La femelle de l'ours polaire agit différemment. Elle creuse un trou dans un banc de glace et donne naissance à un ou deux petits, minuscules et aveugles, au début de l'hiver. Les oursons ne peuvent pas sortir sous peine de mort. Mais à l'abri de la tanière, ils ne risquent rien. La neige est un bon isolant et leur mère les garde au chaud.

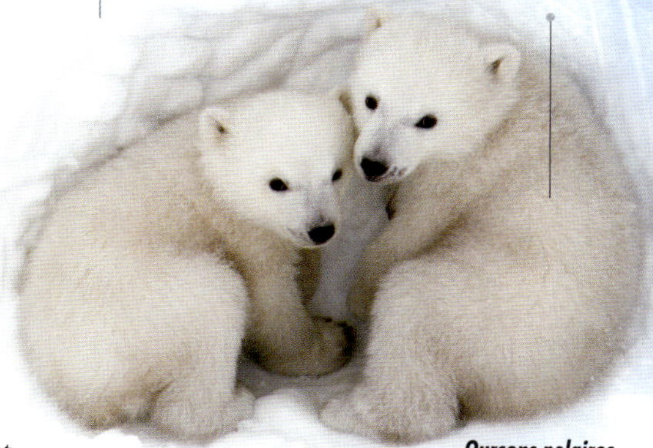

Oursons polaires âgés de trois mois.

Oursons polaires

Quel oiseau possède des « raquettes » ?

Le lagopède vit dans le Grand Nord et reste le plus souvent au sol. Ses pattes sont couvertes de plumes qui agissent comme des « raquettes ». Ces plumes, non seulement préservent le lagopède du froid, mais en élargissant la surface des pattes, l'empêchent de s'enfoncer dans la neige. Les lagopèdes sont bruns en été et deviennent blancs en automne. Ils se nourrissent de graines, de baies et de feuilles.

Qui aime se plonger dans l'eau ?

Les macaques du Japon vivent dans les forêts des montagnes du Japon où les hivers peuvent être très froids. Ils ont une fourrure très fournie mais ont aussi un moyen original de se garder au chaud. Quand les températures chutent en dessous de -5 °C, ils se réchauffent dans les eaux chaudes des sources thermales. Ils passent ainsi de nombreuses heures dans la chaleur.

Macaques du Japon

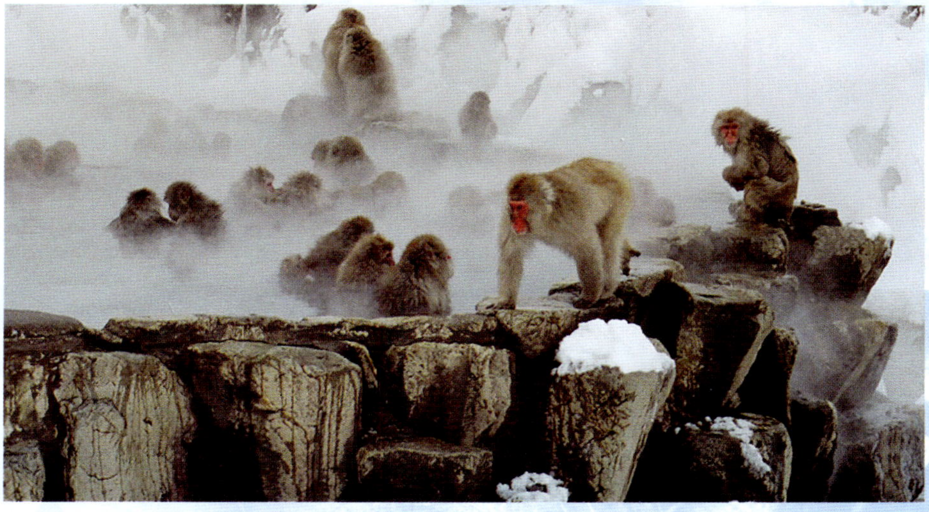

Plus d' infos

- Certains animaux, comme les grenouilles des bois, peuvent survivre même s'ils sont gelés. Des cristaux de glace se forment sous la peau des grenouilles et leur cœur arrête de battre. Elles reviennent à la vie lors du dégel.
- Le pétrel des neiges se nourrit dans les mers de l'Antarctique. C'est l'oiseau qui se reproduit le plus au sud de notre planète.

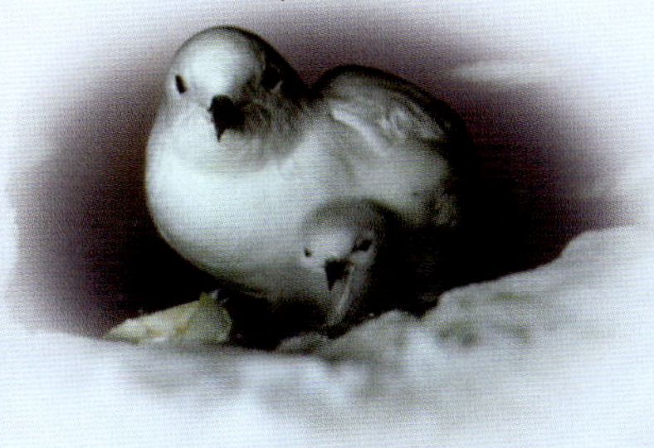

Pétrel des neiges avec un poussin

Comment les pandas survivent-ils en ne mangeant que du bambou ?

Tous les animaux ont besoin de manger, car la nourriture leur apporte l'énergie nécessaire à la vie. Certains ont une alimentation variée; d'autres, comme le panda, ont un régime alimentaire spécifique : il est constitué presque uniquement de bambous. La survie du panda est étroitement liée à son alimentation. Il passe près de 14 heures par jour à mastiquer du bambou. Son régime alimentaire se compose à 95 % de végétaux (quasi uniquement de bambous : jusqu'à 40 kg par jour) et 5 % de viande (des carcasses abandonnées).

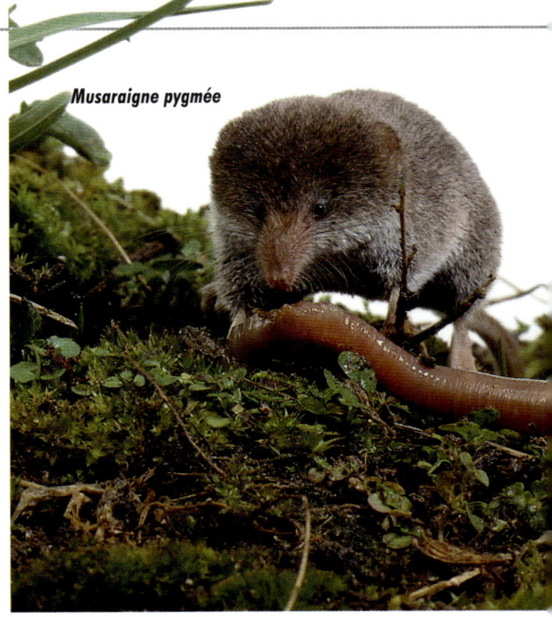

Musaraigne pygmée

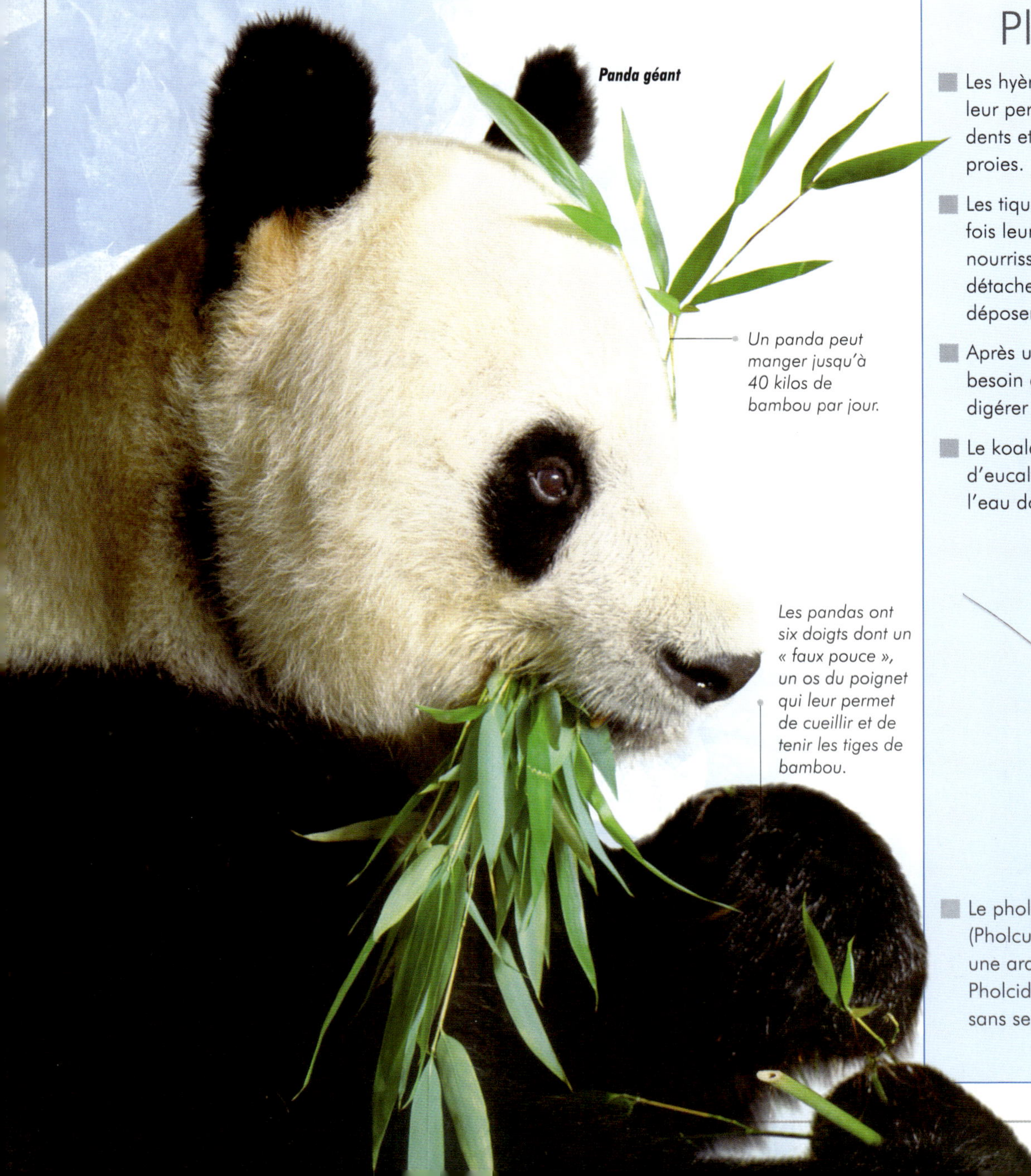

Panda géant

Un panda peut manger jusqu'à 40 kilos de bambou par jour.

Les pandas ont six doigts dont un « faux pouce », un os du poignet qui leur permet de cueillir et de tenir les tiges de bambou.

Plus d' infos

- Les hyènes ont un système digestif qui leur permet de digérer les os, les dents et même les sabots de leurs proies.
- Les tiques peuvent avaler jusqu'à 50 fois leur poids de sang lorsqu'elles se nourrissent. Après cela, les femelles se détachent de la peau de leur hôte et déposent leurs œufs au sol.
- Après un repas, un serpent peut avoir besoin de plusieurs semaines pour digérer totalement sa proie.
- Le koala mange des feuilles d'eucalyptus qui lui apportent toute l'eau dont il a besoin.

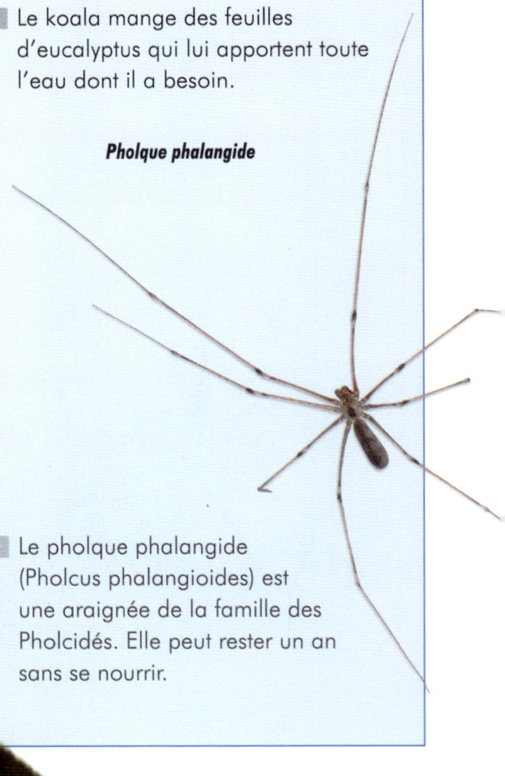

Pholque phalangide

- Le pholque phalangide (Pholcus phalangioides) est une araignée de la famille des Pholcidés. Elle peut rester un an sans se nourrir.

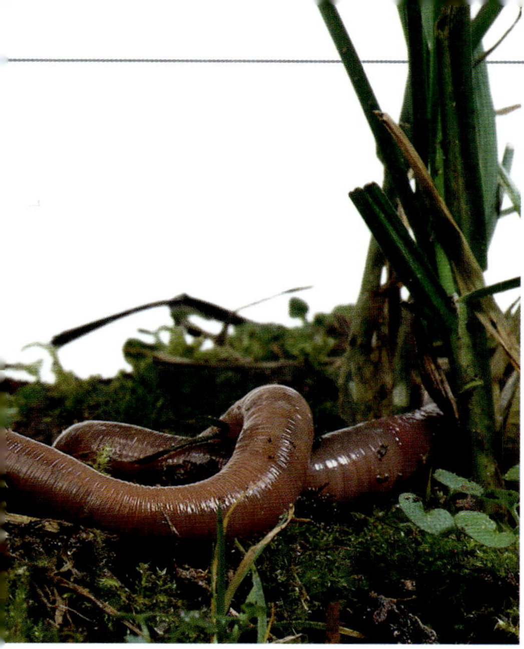

Un animal peut-il manger sans bouche ?

Cela semble impossible mais, pour les vers solitaires, c'est normal. Ce sont des parasites qui vivent dans les intestins d'autres animaux. Ils sont environnés de nourriture qu'ils absorbent à travers la surface de leur corps. La tête d'un ver solitaire a des crochets et des ventouses qui le maintiennent en place. Le ver le plus long, qui vit dans les baleines, mesure jusqu'à 30 mètres.

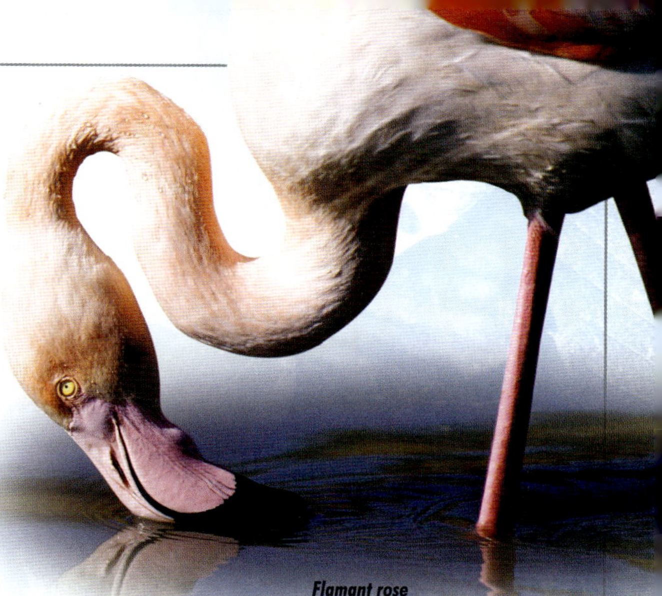

Flamant rose

Certains animaux se nourrissent-ils en permanence ?

Oui, la musaraigne pygmée doit se nourrir en permanence. C'est l'un des plus petits mammifères au monde et elle a besoin de beaucoup d'énergie pour survivre. Elle mange plus que son propre poids de nourriture chaque jour, attaquant avec férocité les vers de terre, les scarabées et les sauterelles à l'aide de ses dents pointues.

Ver solitaire

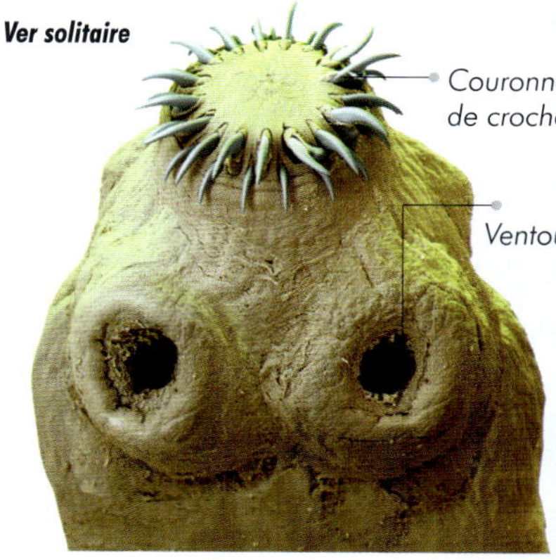

Comment un flamant rose attrape-t-il sa nourriture ?

Les flamants se nourrissent par filtrage de crustacés et d'algues. Leur bec, à la forme curieuse, est particulièrement bien adapté pour séparer la boue et la vase des aliments qu'ils consomment, et est utilisé à l'envers. Sa langue fonctionne comme une pompe. Le filtrage des éléments nutritifs est facilité par une structure en peigne des lamelles qui bordent le bec et par une langue à la surface rugueuse. Ce sont les seuls oiseaux à se nourrir de la sorte.

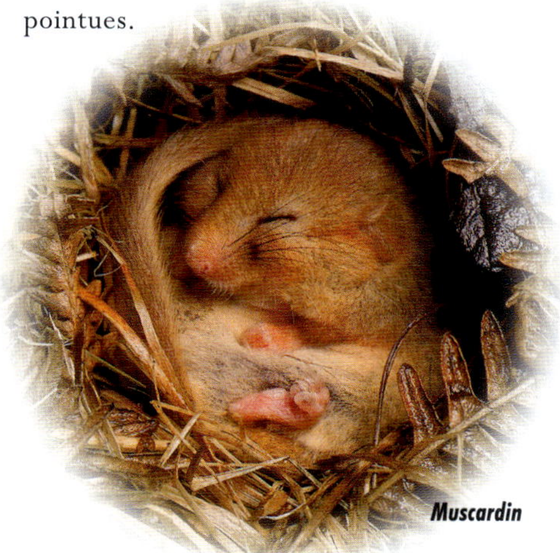

Muscardin

Qui prend du poids l'hiver ?

Beaucoup d'animaux tels que les muscardins, les marmottes, les chauves-souris et les hérissons. Tous ces animaux passent l'hiver dans un sommeil profond appelé hibernation. Ils font des réserves pendant l'automne, puis se cachent avant le début de l'hiver. Pendant l'hibernation, ils survivent grâce aux réserves accumulées. Les marmottes sont les championnes de l'hibernation : elles peuvent dormir jusqu'à 8 mois.

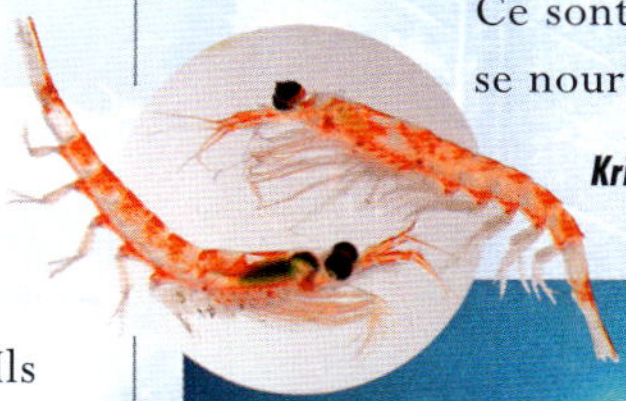

Krill

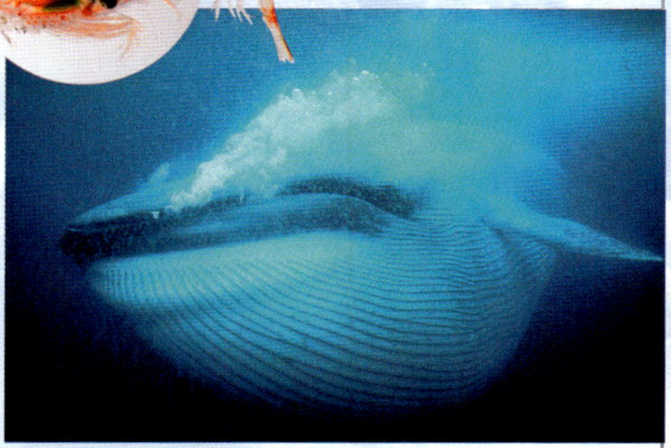

Baleine bleue

Que se passe-t-il lorsqu'un animal hiberne ?

Lorsqu'un animal comme le hérisson hiberne, la température de son corps baisse et son rythme cardiaque diminue, ce qui lui permet de survivre sans boire ni manger. Un phénomène analogue existe dans les endroits les plus chauds et les plus secs du monde : c'est l'estivation. Certains animaux, comme le hérisson du désert, entrent en léthargie pendant la saison chaude.

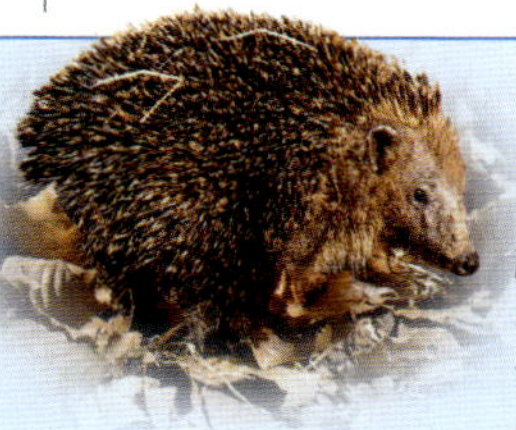

1 Les hérissons européens hibernent pendant six mois. Pendant leur long sommeil, la température de leur corps descend à 4° environ.

2 Les hérissons du désert sentent lorsque la température augmente. Ils cherchent un endroit frais où dormir durant les mois les plus chauds.

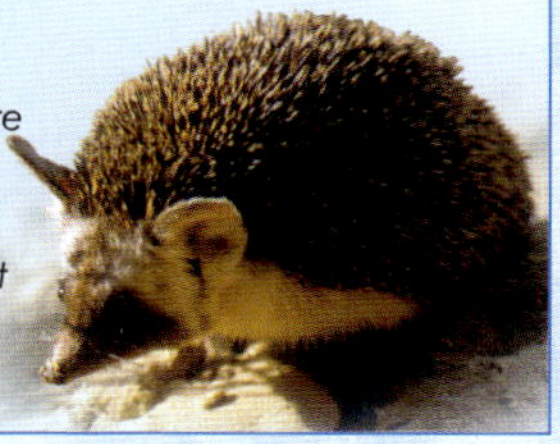

Qui mange le plus en une journée ?

La baleine bleue a le plus gros appétit. Elle se nourrit de minuscules crevettes appelées krill. Une baleine bleue peut manger jusqu'à 4 tonnes de nourriture par jour. Mais elle ne le fait pas toute l'année. Pendant la période de reproduction, elle migre vers des eaux plus chaudes et peut rester longtemps sans rien manger.

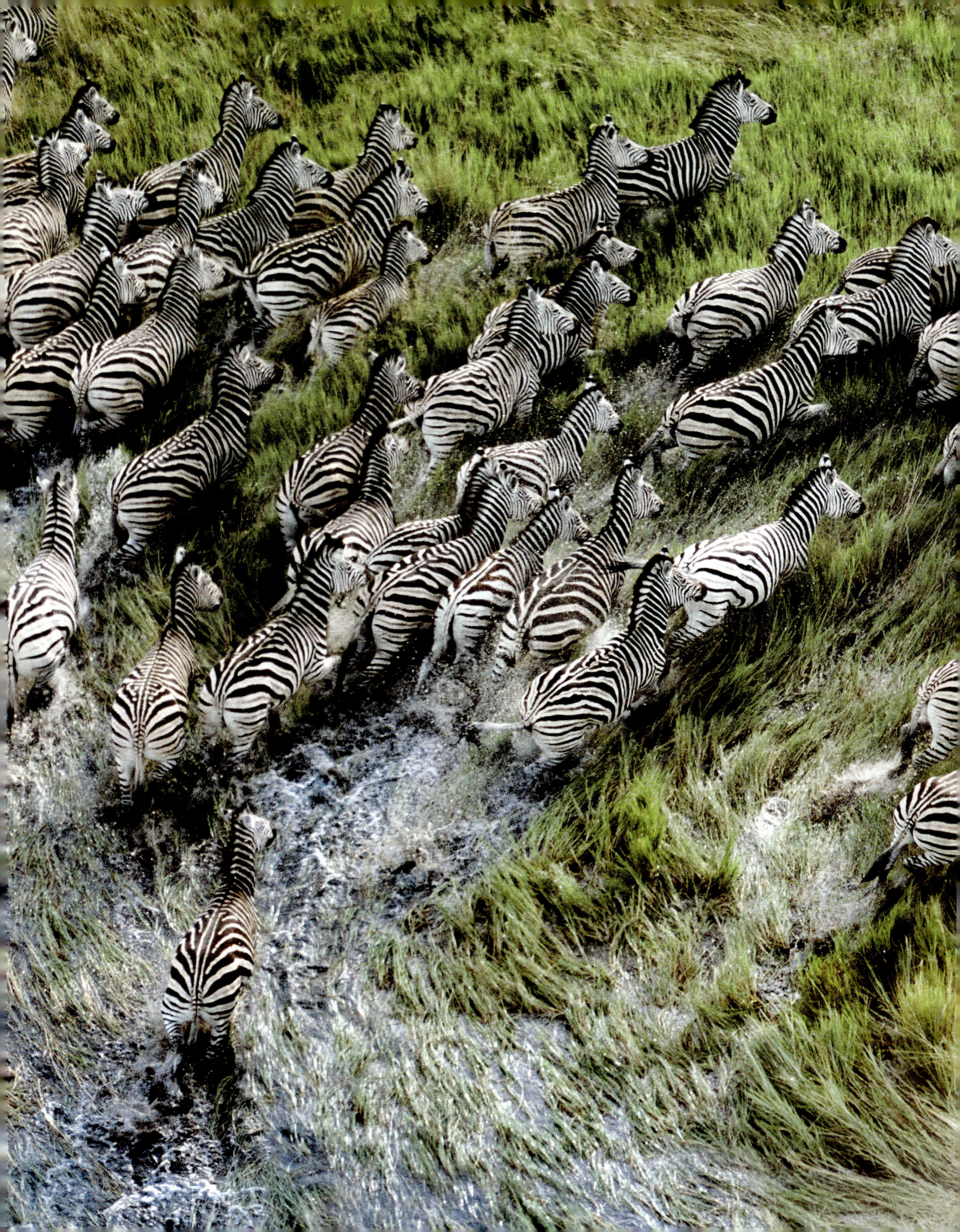

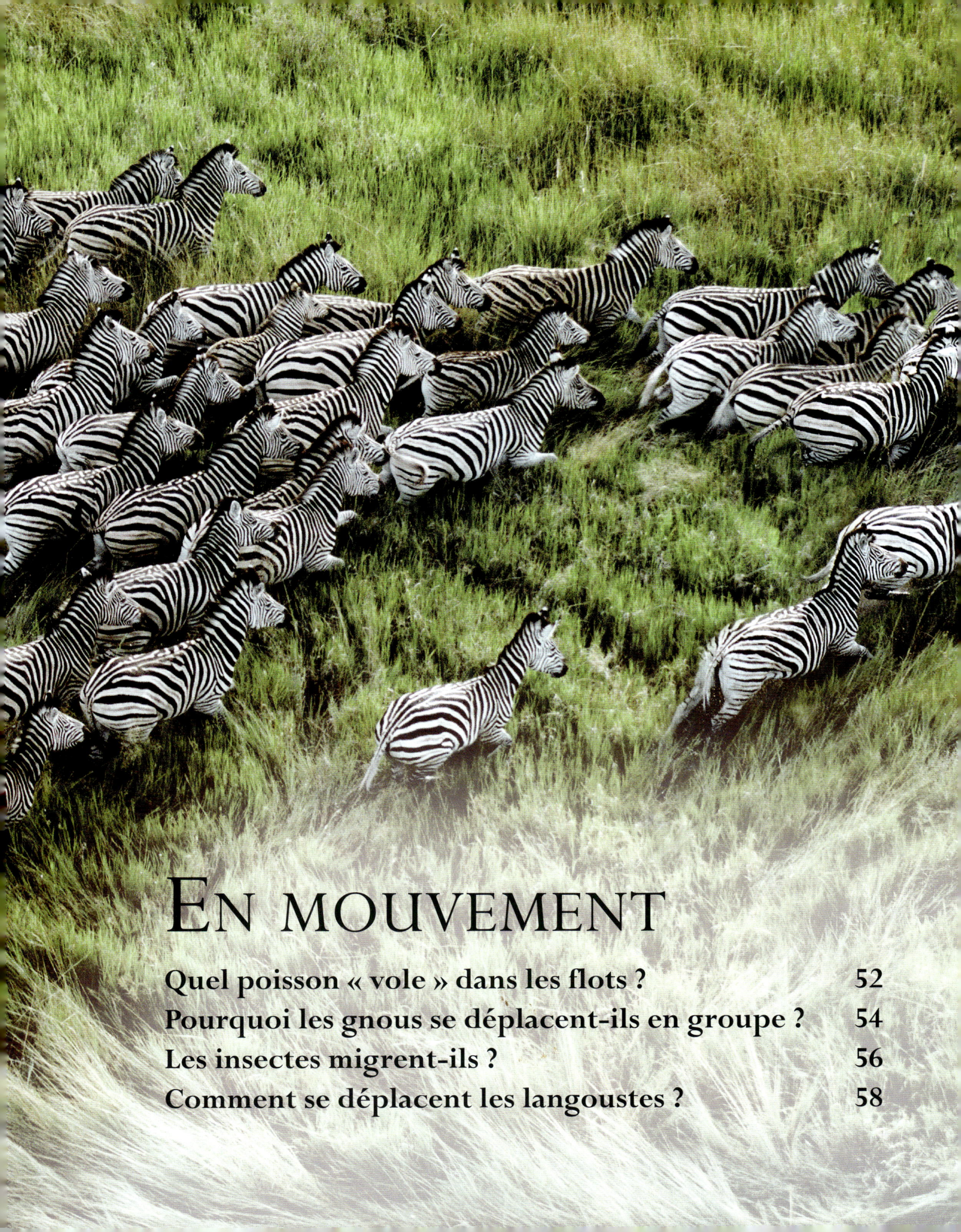

EN MOUVEMENT

Quel poisson « vole » dans les flots ?

Les animaux ont prouvé qu'ils étaient de vrais athlètes. Que ce soit sur terre, dans l'air ou dans l'eau, ils montrent de très grandes capacités à aller où ils le veulent rapidement. Mais peu d'entre eux sont aussi gracieux que la raie manta lorsqu'elle se propulse sous l'eau, utilisant ses nageoires pectorales comme les larges ailes d'un oiseau géant. Une raie adulte peut faire jusqu'à 7 m d'envergure. À la naissance, les petits n'atteignent que 1 m de large et sont roulés sur eux-mêmes comme des tubes. Ils deviennent actifs dès que leurs nageoires se sont déroulées.

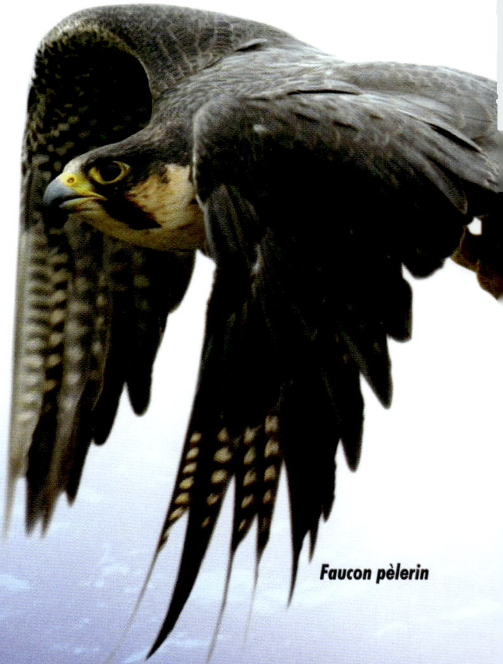

Faucon pèlerin

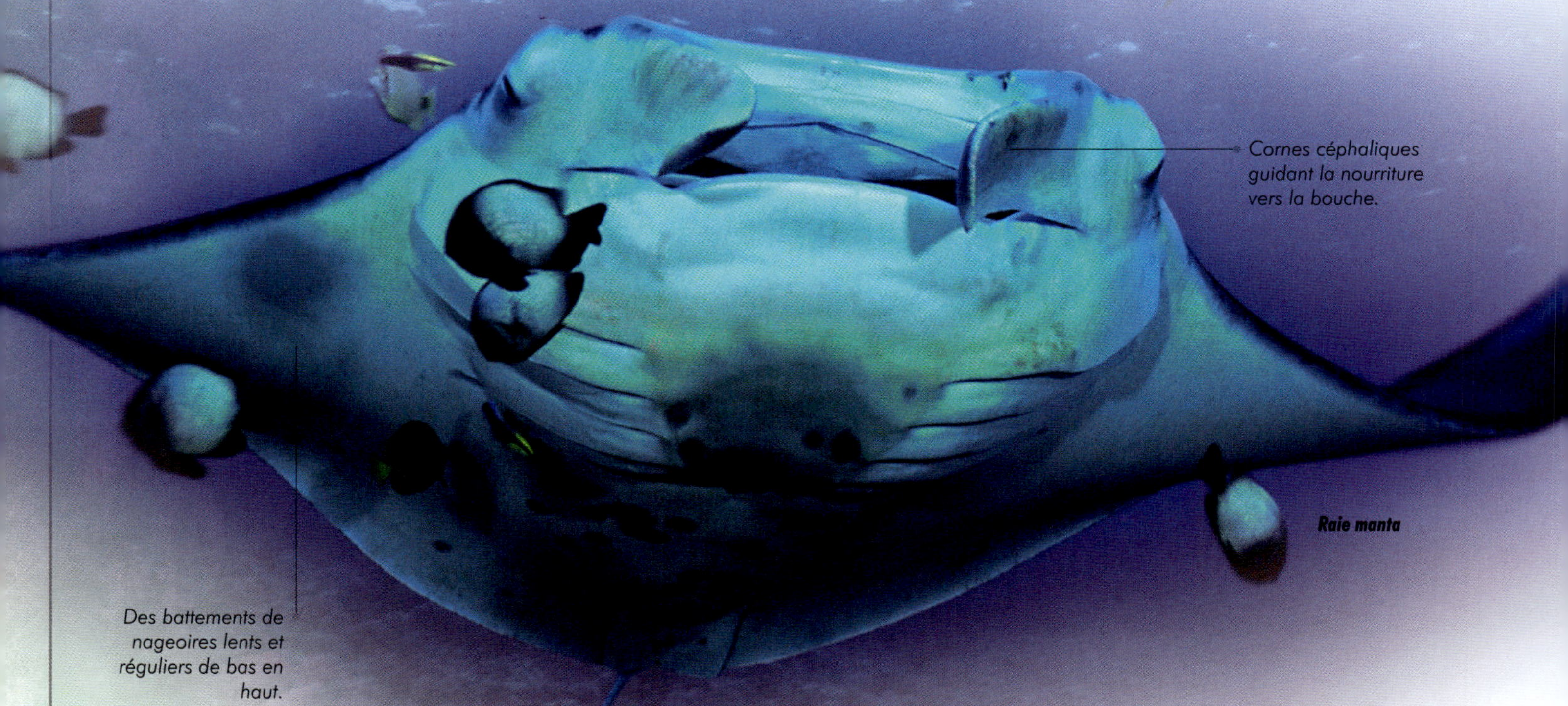

Cornes céphaliques guidant la nourriture vers la bouche.

Raie manta

Des battements de nageoires lents et réguliers de bas en haut.

Q R Quel serpent bat l'homme à la course ?

La plupart des serpents se déplacent lentement, sauf lorsqu'ils mordent. Mais le mamba noir est une exception. Sur de courtes distances, il peut atteindre la vitesse de 18 km/h, c'est plus rapide qu' un humain. Heureusement, il n'utilise ces capacités que pour s'échapper, pas pour attaquer. Il peut mesurer jusqu'à 4 m de long et est l'un des plus grands serpents venimeux d'Afrique.

Mamba noir

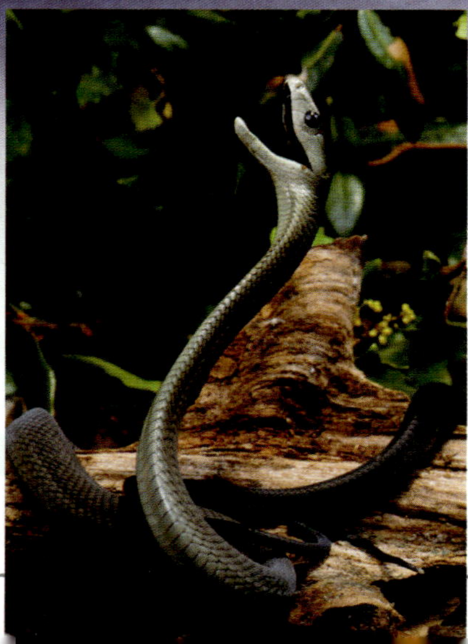

Comment les gibbons se déplacent-ils dans les arbres ?

Les gibbons sont les trapézistes de la nature, avec une agilité insensée pour se déplacer d'arbre en arbre. Ils utilisent leurs mains comme des crochets et se balancent de branche en branche. Un gibbon peut couvrir une distance de 10 m en un seul saut. Cette façon de se mouvoir est très efficace. Le gibbon utilise son corps comme le balancier d'une horloge.

Q R À quelle vitesse un oiseau peut-il voler ?

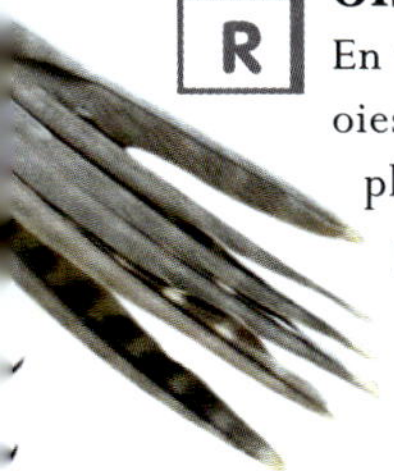

En vol d'altitude, les canards et les oies sont les plus rapides. Mais le plus rapide de tous est le faucon pèlerin. Il attaque les autres oiseaux en plongeant sur eux en plein vol. Pendant son attaque, le faucon rabat ses ailes en arrière pour rendre son corps plus aérodynamique. Cela lui permet de foncer à 200 km/h. La proie peut être directement saisie avec les serres, ou percutée avec celles-ci, et récupérée au sol.

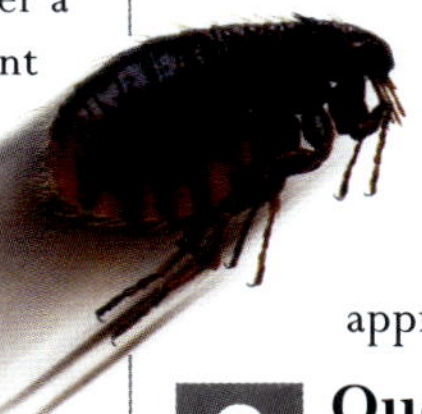

Puce

Q R Quel petit animal fait des sauts de géant ?

Par rapport à leur taille, les puces sont les meilleurs sauteurs du monde. Elles réussissent ces sauts de géant car leur corps comporte des coussinets élastiques. Pour sauter, elles compriment ces coussinets, puis subitement les relâchent, ce qui provoque une détente des pattes arrière et permet le saut. Au moment de l'extension, l'accélération est plus rapide que celle d'une fusée.

Q R Quel est l'animal le plus rapide sur six pattes ?

Les cafards ne gagneront jamais le prix de la popularité mais ils peuvent gagner un prix pour leur vitesse. Ils sont les insectes les plus rapides et peuvent couvrir une distance de 75 cm en une seconde. À pleine vitesse, ce sont les pattes arrière qui font le travail, les autres pattes ne touchant pas le sol. Ils utilisent cette capacité pour partir se cacher rapidement s'ils sentent un danger approcher.

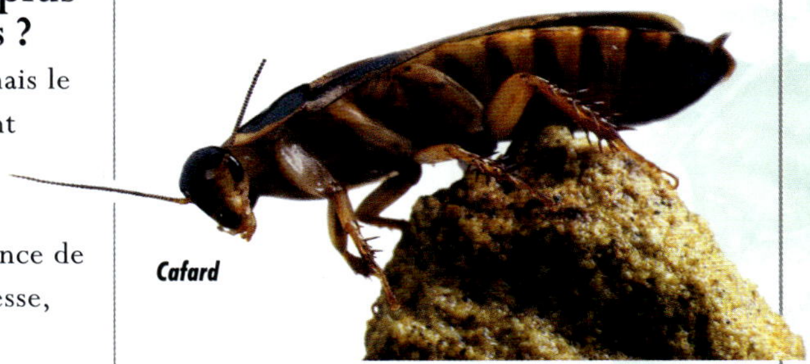

Cafard

Q R Quel est le meilleur athlète ?

Le guépard est l'animal terrestre le plus rapide mais il ne tient le sprint que quarante secondes. Le second athlète est le pronghorn. Ces antilopes ont un cœur particulièrement gros et un sang spécial qui apporte beaucoup d'oxygène à leurs muscles, ce qui leur permet un travail intensif (course) sur une longue durée.

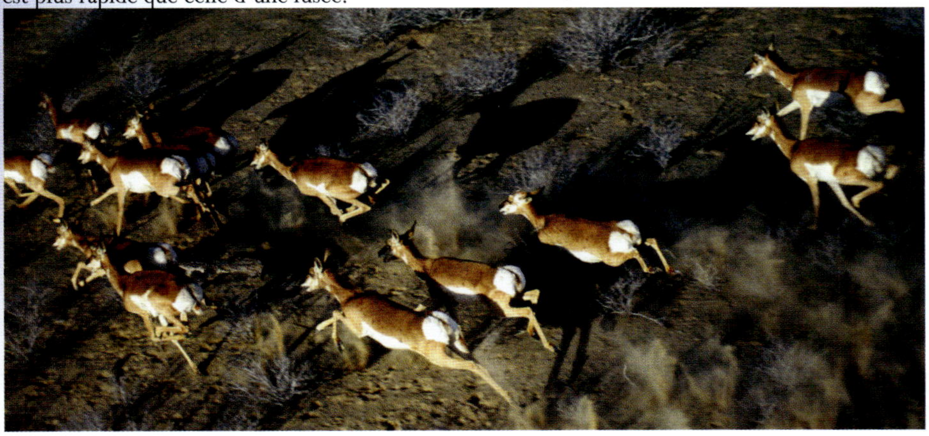

Pronghorns Antilope d'Amérique du nord

Plus d' infos

- Le crabe mal zoreille (Ocypode quadrata) vit sur les plages tropicales. Il court en zigzaguant jusqu'à son trou à 15 km/h.

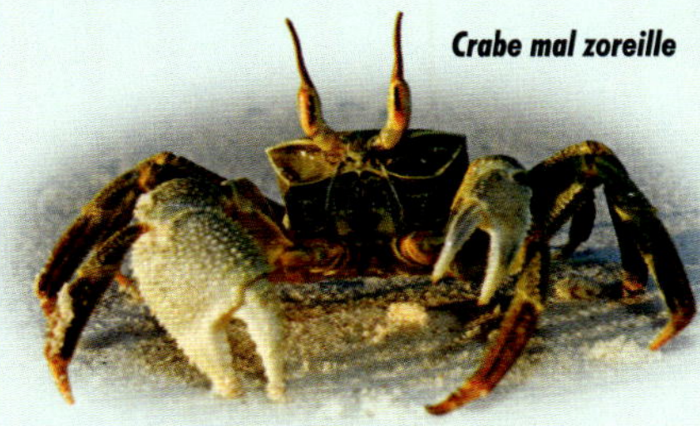

Crabe mal zoreille

- Le poisson le plus rapide du monde est le voilier. Sur une courte distance, il peut atteindre la vitesse de 100 km/h, aussi rapide qu'un guépard.
- Les calmars peuvent se propulser à 40 km/h. Ils éjectent l'eau vers l'arrière à travers un siphon qui fonctionne comme le moteur d'un jet.
- Les kangourous géants foncent à 64 km/h et font des bonds plus hauts que ceux d'un homme adulte.

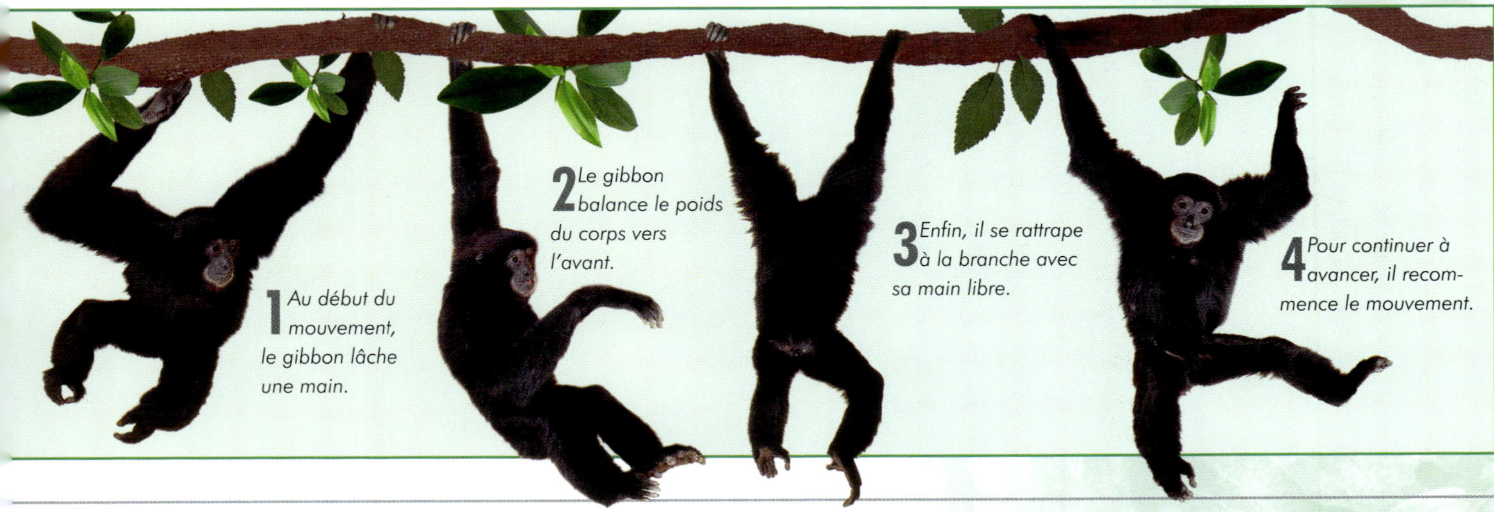

Pourquoi les gnous se déplacent-ils en groupe ?

Dans la nature, les animaux se déplacent souvent en groupe. Les poissons nagent en bancs, les oiseaux volent en colonies et les antilopes courent en troupeaux. Certains groupes ne comptent pas plus de quelques douzaines d'animaux, mais les troupeaux de gnous d'Afrique peuvent compter des centaines de milliers d'individus. Les animaux s'agglutinent, car la vie est souvent plus sûre dans la foule. Lorsque les gnous se nourrissent, ils font le guet chacun à leur tour, évitant ainsi que les prédateurs ne les attaquent par surprise. Les gnous restent en troupeaux toute l'année et un veau peut courir avec les autres une heure après sa naissance.

Q R Pourquoi les abeilles forment-elles des essaims ?

Lorsque les abeilles forment un essaim, c'est qu'elles sont à la recherche d'un nouvel abri. Chaque essaim compte une reine, quelques mâles et des dizaines de milliers d'ouvrières. La plupart des ouvrières restent près de la reine, mais certaines agissent comme des éclaireuses, cherchant un bon endroit pour établir le nid. Dans la nature, les abeilles nichent souvent dans des troncs d'arbres. Cependant, les apiculteurs essaient d'attraper les essaims. Ils les mettent dans des ruches et les abeilles y restent.

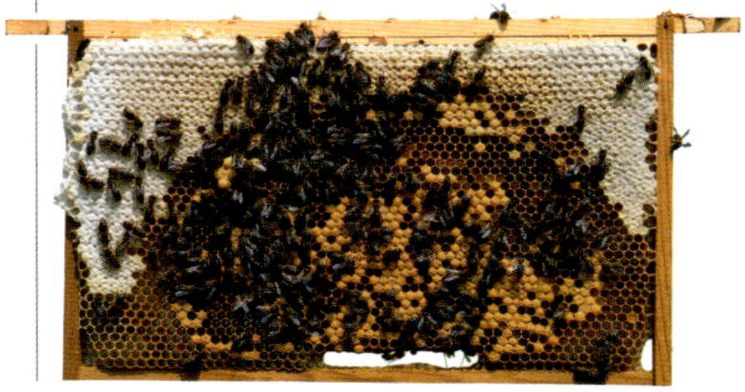

Abeilles dans une ruche

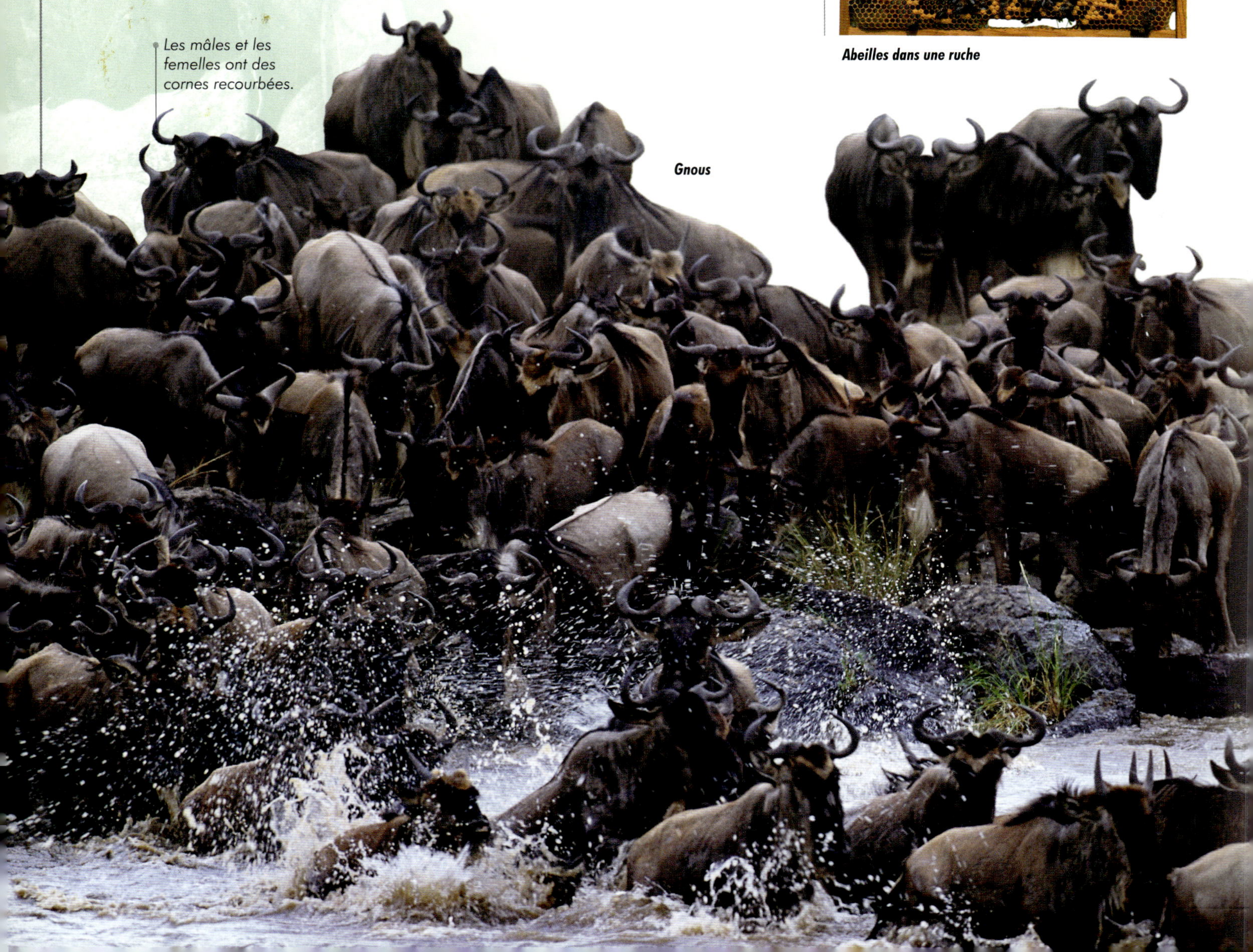

Les mâles et les femelles ont des cornes recourbées.

Gnous

Plus d'infos

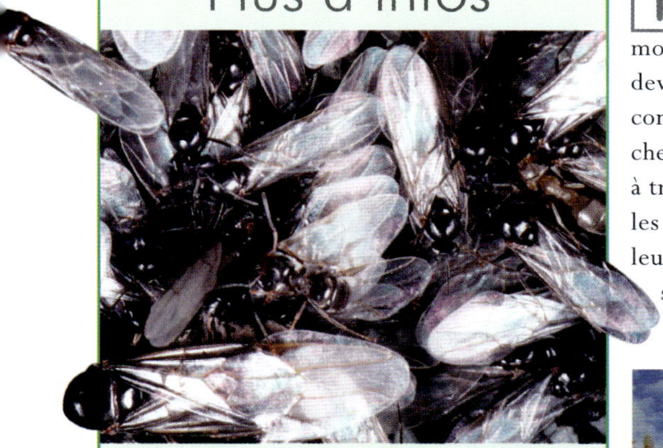

Fourmis volantes

- Les fourmis volantes ont des ailes pendant quelques jours en été lorsqu'elles doivent trouver un nouveau nid. Elles les perdent à l'atterrissage.
- Chaque soir, plus de 20 millions de chauves-souris sortent des cavernes de Bracken au Texas, États-Unis. C'est le plus important groupe de mammifères au monde.

Q Est-il vrai que les lemmings se jettent dans le vide ?

R Non, ce n'est pas vrai. À certains moments, les populations de lemmings deviennent très importantes et la nourriture commence à manquer. Alors, ils partent en chercher. Des millions de lemmings grouillent à travers la toundra arctique et nagent dans les rivières, mangeant tout ce qui tombe à leur portée. S'ils arrivent à une falaise, ils s'arrêtent, à moins d'être poussés par ceux qui sont derrière.

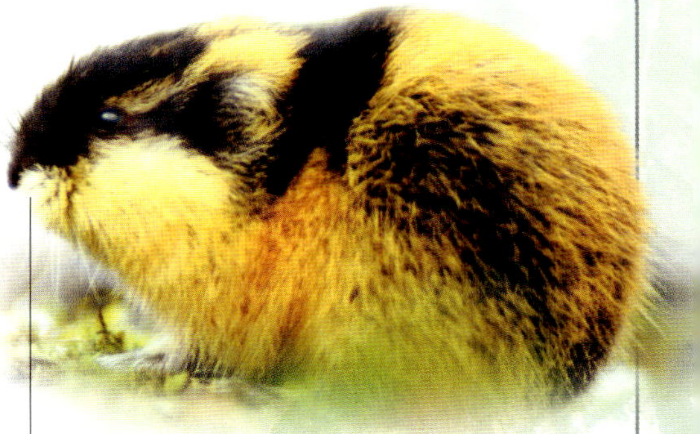

Lemming

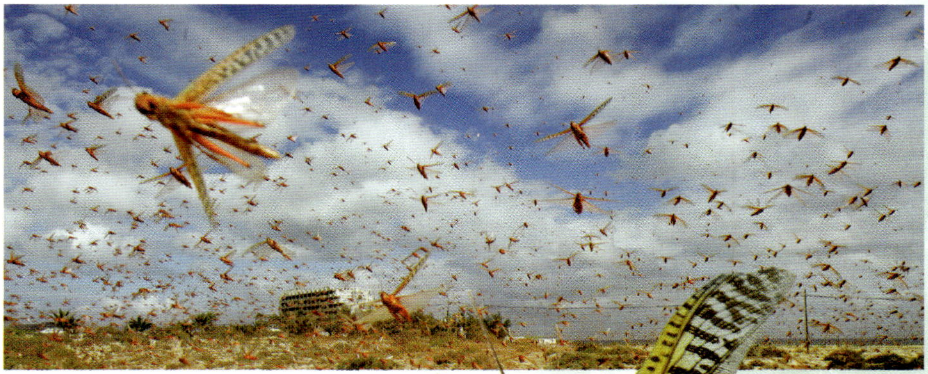

Nuage de criquets pèlerins

Q Quand les criquets forment-ils des nuages ?

R Si la nourriture vient à manquer, leur comportement et leur aspect changent et ils se rassemblent en immenses essaims. La colonie se met en route pour se nourrir ailleurs. Un seul essaim peut compter jusqu'à 10 milliards d'insectes. Lorsque les criquets s'attaquent à des cultures, il peuvent tout ravager sur leur passage.

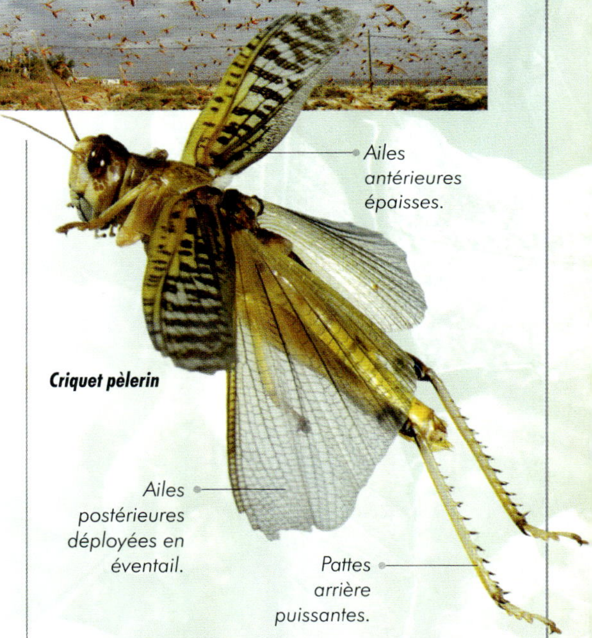

Criquet pèlerin

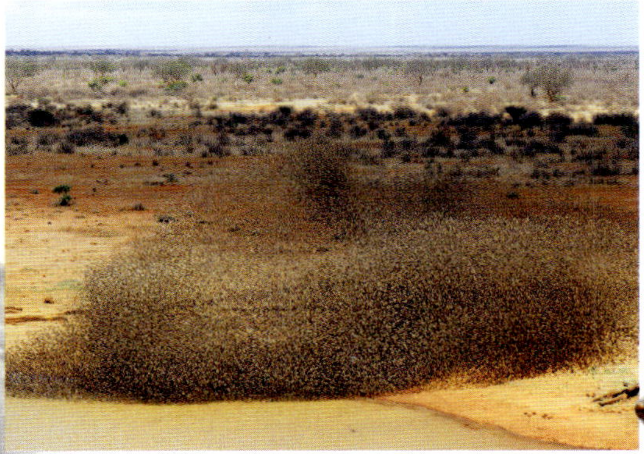

Colonie de travailleurs à bec rouge

Q Quels oiseaux se déplacent en grand groupe ?

R En Afrique, les colonies de travailleurs à bec rouge comportent plus de 5 millions d'individus. Ces oiseaux sont à peu près de la même taille que les moineaux et vivent dans les bois, les prairies et les champs. Lorsqu'une colonie se déplace, elle s'enroule sur elle-même et tourbillonne à travers le paysage comme un nuage de fumée. Ces oiseaux se nourrissent de graines et les paysans les craignent car ils ont un gros appétit. Une colonie qui traverse des terres cultivées peut dévorer des tonnes de nourriture en un jour.

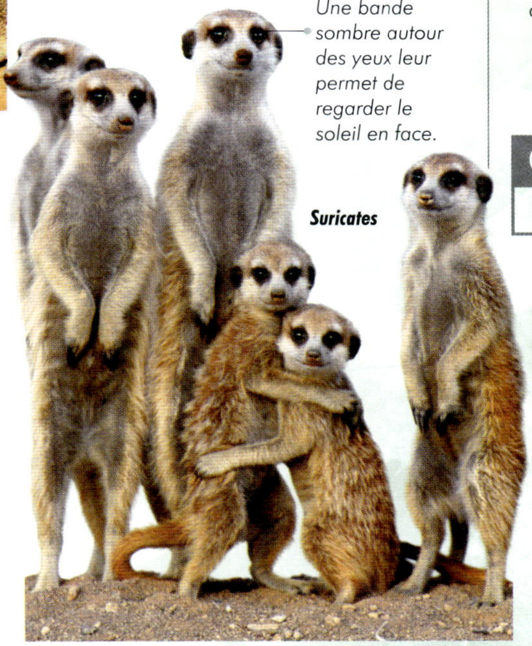

Suricates

Q Qui se déplace en bande ?

R Tous les matins, à l'aube, les suricates africains sortent de leurs terriers et commencent à chercher de la nourriture. Ils vivent en bandes et restent ensemble lors de leurs déplacements. De temps en temps, l'un d'eux s'éloigne à la recherche d'insectes ou autres petits animaux. Si un individu est resté à la traîne, la bande s'arrête pour qu'il puisse les rattraper. Les suricates ont des sens aiguisés et sont capables de se tenir debout sur leurs pattes arrières pour faire le guet.

Les insectes migrent-ils ?

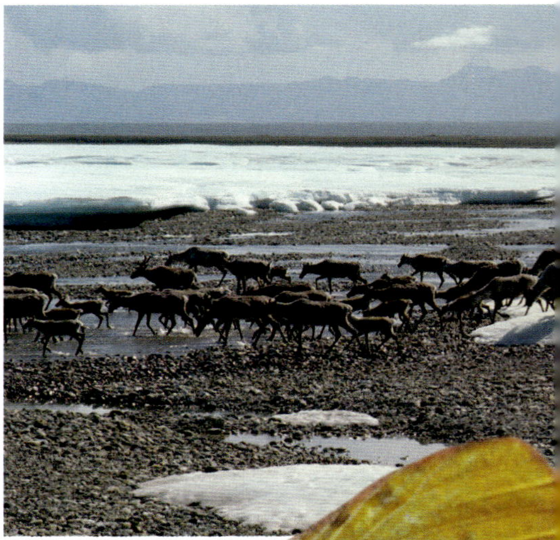

Tous les ans, des millions d'animaux se mettent en route pour un voyage appelé migration. Généralement, ils vont des lieux de leur reproduction à ceux où ils trouveront un climat plus doux en hiver et plus de nourriture. Ces voyages sont souvent longs et périlleux et tous n'arrivent pas sains et saufs. Les migrateurs comprennent toutes sortes d'animaux, des rennes aux tortues, des oiseaux aux baleines. Les insectes aussi migrent, particulièrement les papillons et les papillons de nuit. Le souci est un papillon du genre Colias, que l'on trouve l'hiver dans le nord de l'Afrique où il se reproduit. Au printemps, il peut voler aussi loin que le cercle arctique.

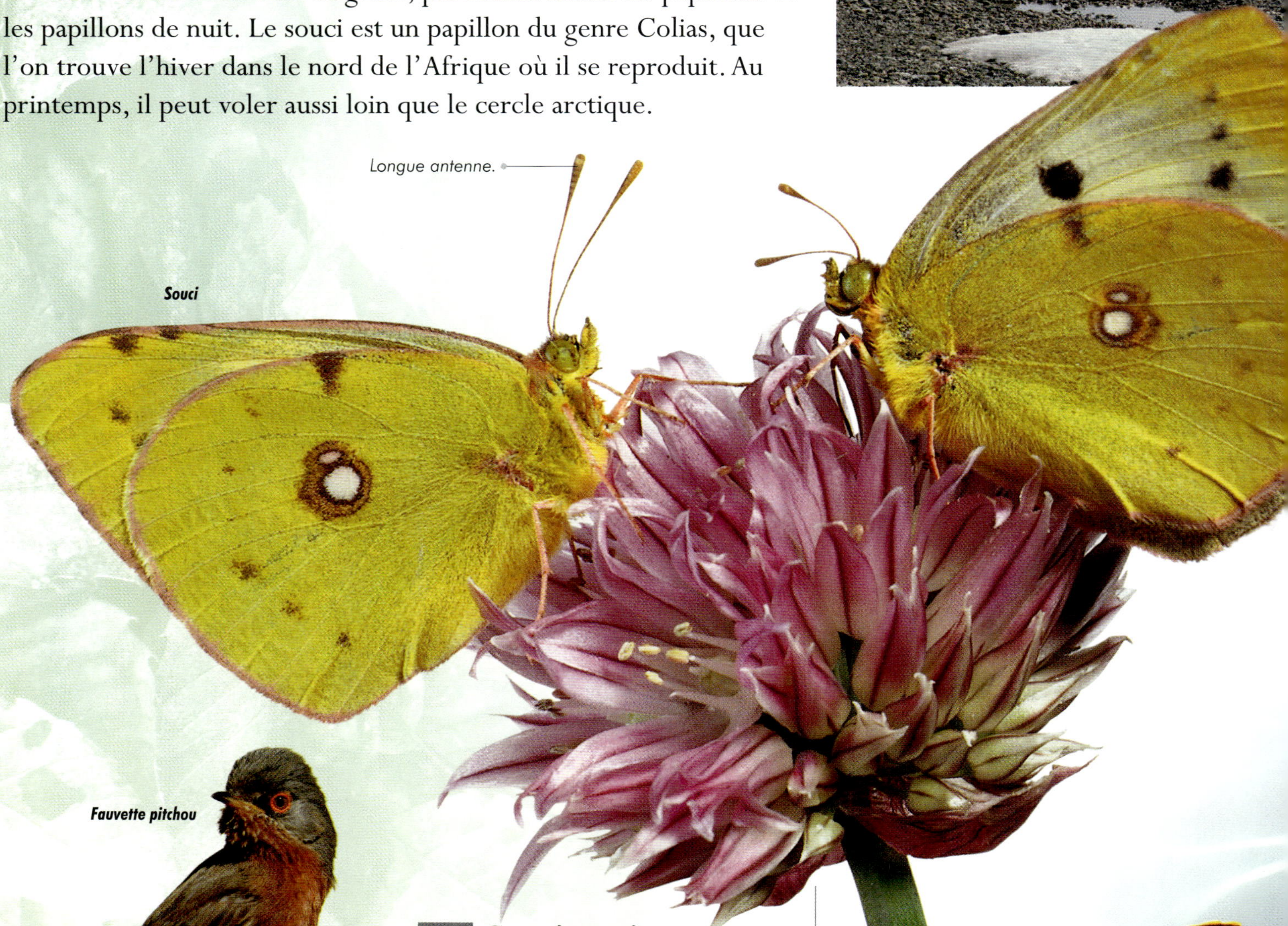

Souci

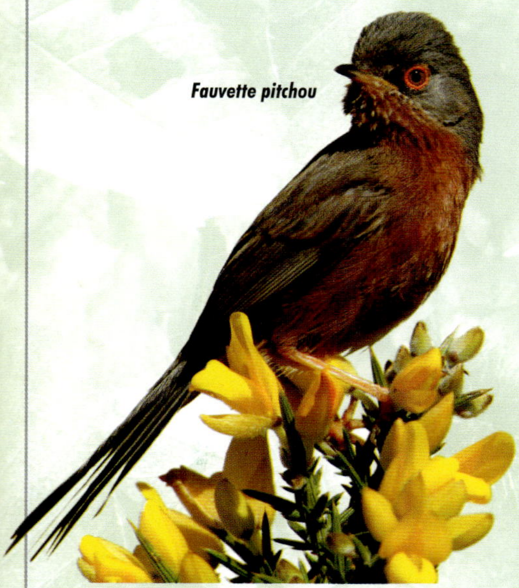

Fauvette pitchou

Q R Certains animaux restent-ils au même endroit ?

Lorsqu'il est temps de migrer, la plupart des animaux partent. Mais certaines espèces (telle la fauvette pitchou) sont divisés en voyageuses et en sédentaires. Les voyageuses quittent les endroits où les hivers sont froids. Les sédentaires occupent des territoires aux hivers suffisamment doux pour y rester.

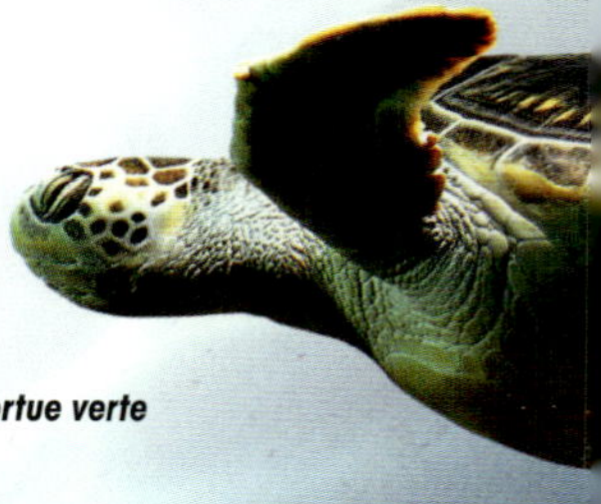

Tortue verte

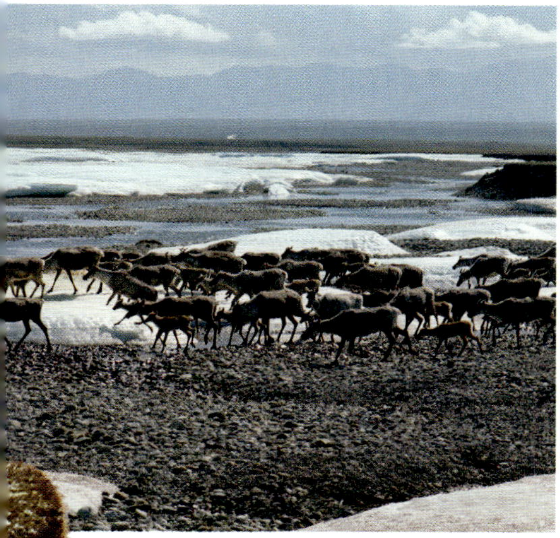

Rennes

Q Qui fait le plus long voyage terrestre ?

R Les champions sont les rennes, appelés caribous en Amérique du Nord. Au Canada et à l'ouest du Groenland, certains rennes font plus de 2 000 km chaque année. Ils passent l'été dans la toundra arctique et l'hiver ils migrent vers le sud, dans les grandes forêts.

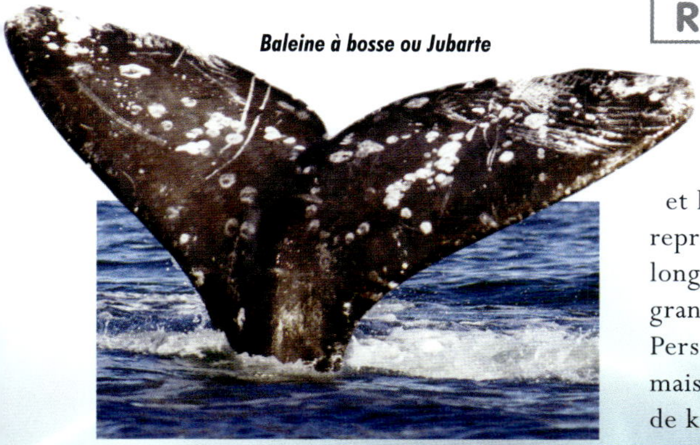

Baleine à bosse ou Jubarte

Plus d'infos

- Les hirondelles ont une mémoire incroyable. Bien qu'elles voyagent sur des distances longues de plusieurs milliers de kilomètres, elles reviennent dans le même nid d'une année à l'autre.

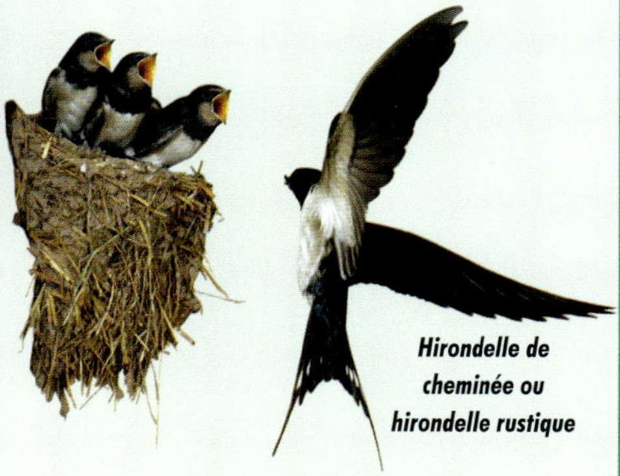

Hirondelle de cheminée ou hirondelle rustique

- Le colibri à gorge rubis pèse moins qu'un morceau de sucre, mais il peut voler depuis l'Amérique du Nord jusqu'en Amérique centrale via le Golfe du Mexique.

Q Qui voyage le plus durant sa vie ?

R La baleine à bosse appelée aussi mégaptère et la baleine grise peuvent effectuer jusqu'à 20 000 km par an, voyageant depuis les eaux froides où elles se nourrissent et les eaux tropicales où elles se reproduisent. Ces baleines vivent longtemps, elles parcourent donc de très grandes distances au cours de leur vie. Personne ne sait exactement combien, mais le record pourrait être d'un million de km. C'est plus qu'un aller-retour jusqu'à la Lune !

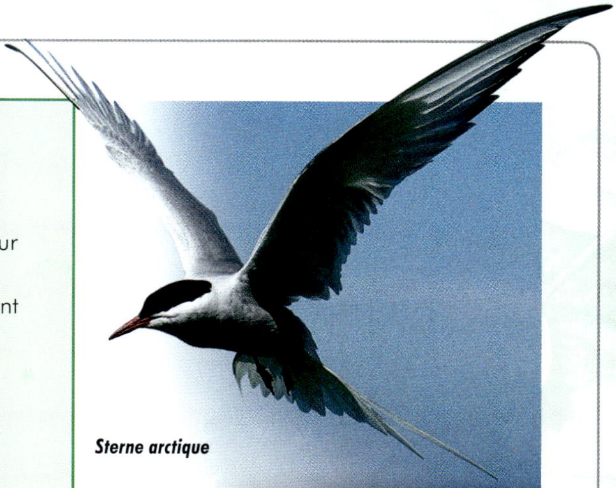

Sterne arctique

Q Qui migre le plus loin chaque année ?

R Les sternes arctiques font le plus long voyage chaque année. Elles se reproduisent dans l'Arctique, puis volent vers le sud jusqu'à l'Antarctique pour éviter l'hiver du nord. Elles couvrent ainsi plus de 50 000 km en une année, car elles suivent les côtes plutôt que de voler en ligne droite. Les albatros peuvent voler sur 10 000 km sans se poser.

Q Quelle distance parcourent les tortues ?

R Lorsque les tortues se reproduisent, elles migrent souvent des lieux où elles se nourrissent jusqu'aux plages où elles déposeront leurs œufs. Pour certaines tortues vertes, cela peut signifier un voyage de 3 000 km à travers l'océan. Mais cela n'est pas un record. La tortue caouane migre entre le Mexique et le Japon, traversant tout l'océan Pacifique. Elle utilise les courants marins, mais le voyage peut prendre plus d'un an.

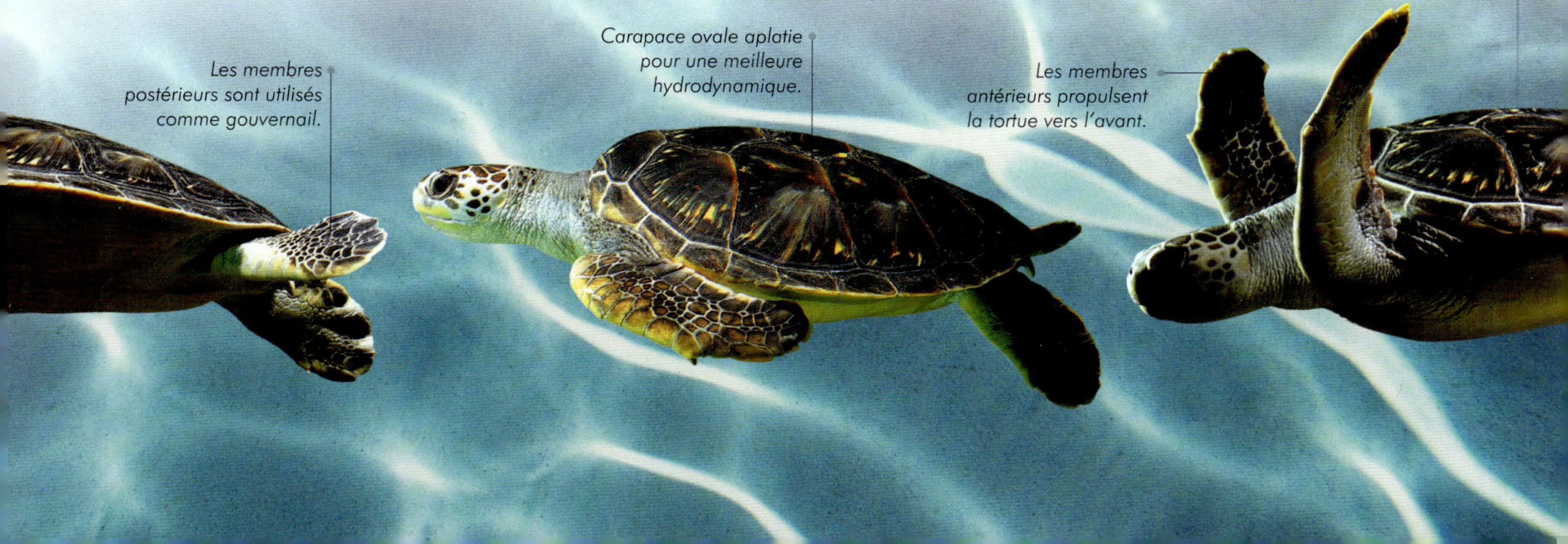

Comment se déplacent les langoustes ?

Que se soit en file indienne comme les langoustes ou en colonie comme les oiseaux, les animaux migrent souvent en groupe. Certains se guident grâce au Soleil, à la Lune et aux étoiles, ou par leur propre système de navigation, d'autres se dirigent en « goûtant » l'eau. Beaucoup retrouvent des repères familiers le long des routes que leurs ancêtres ont pratiquées pendant des centaines d'années. Les langoustes de Cuba se placent l'une derrière l'autre et voyagent ainsi en file indienne sur le fond de la mer. Les langoustes passent l'été dans les eaux peu profondes, mais, lorsque arrive l'automne, elles descendent plus profondément pour éviter les tempêtes. Les études sur cette espèce suggèrent qu'elles sont guidées par une boussole interne qui leur indique le nord.

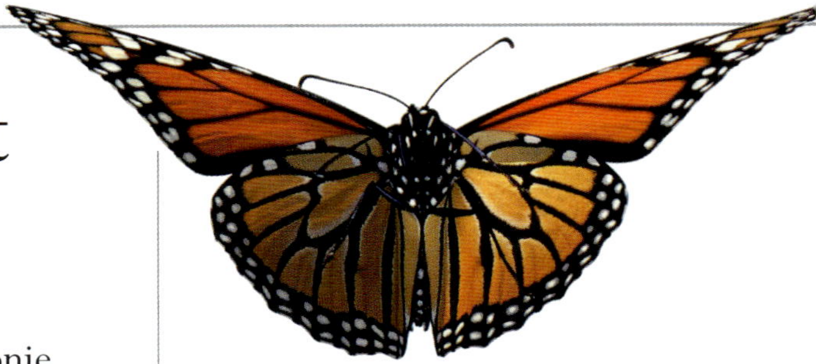

Papillon monarque

Q R Arrive-t-il que des animaux perdent leur cap ?

Même les voyageurs les plus aguerris ont parfois des soucis. S'ils perdent le cap au mauvais moment, les vents violents peuvent les éloigner fortement de leur route. Les oiseaux d'Amérique du Nord sont parfois déviés par le vent à travers l'océan, jusqu'en Europe. Cela arrive aussi aux papillons monarques. Si un insecte se perd en chemin, il est rare qu'il puisse arriver à bon port.

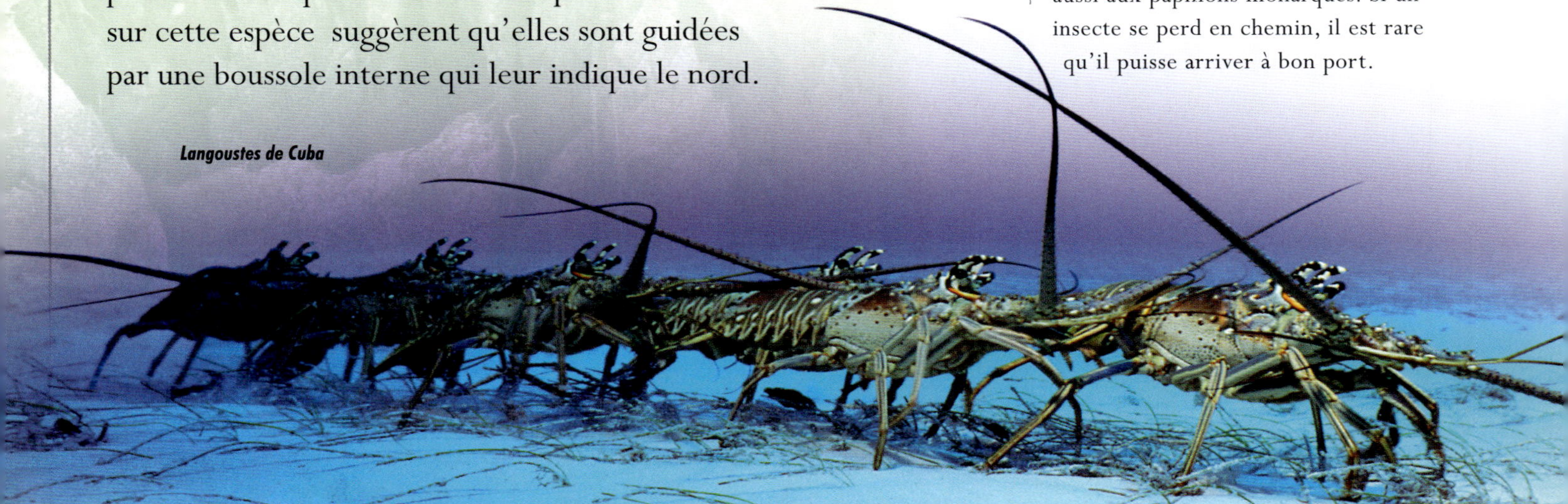

Langoustes de Cuba

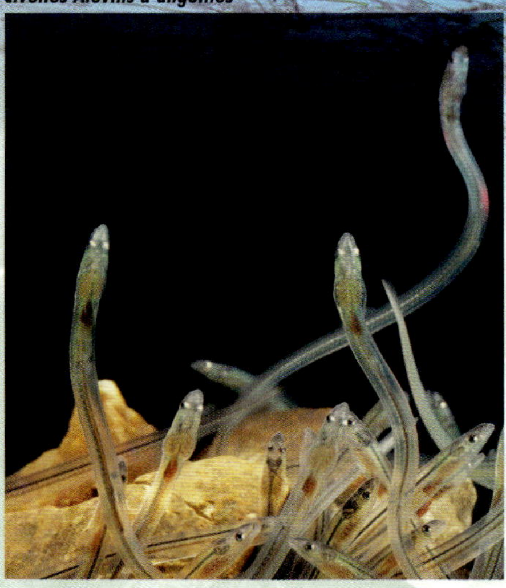

Civelles Alevins d'anguilles

Q R Comment les anguilles naviguent-elles à travers la mer ?

Les anguilles d'Europe naissent dans la mer des Sargasses située dans l'océan Atlantique. Jeunes, elles commencent leur voyage vers les côtes européennes. Ce voyage peut durer trois ans et les scientifiques ne savent pas exactement comment elles retrouvent leur chemin. Certains pensent qu'elles se dirigent en goûtant l'eau, car la saveur de l'eau change d'un bout à l'autre de l'océan.

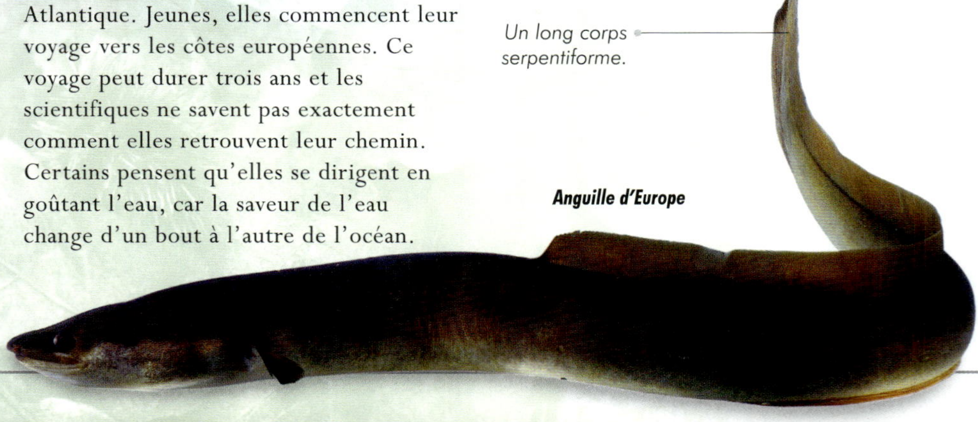

Anguille d'Europe

Q R Les oiseaux migrent-ils de nuit ?

Les oiseaux voyagent souvent de nuit, surtout si le ciel est clair. Le temps est souvent plus calme la nuit, ce qui rend le vol plus facile. La nuit, il y a aussi moins de prédateurs aux aguets, il y a donc moins de risques de se faire attaquer. Pendant leur vol nocturne, les oiseaux utilisent les étoiles comme des boussoles pour se repérer. Ces oiseaux sont difficiles à voir mais les ornithologues peuvent les observer aux jumelles, lorsqu'ils passent devant la Lune.

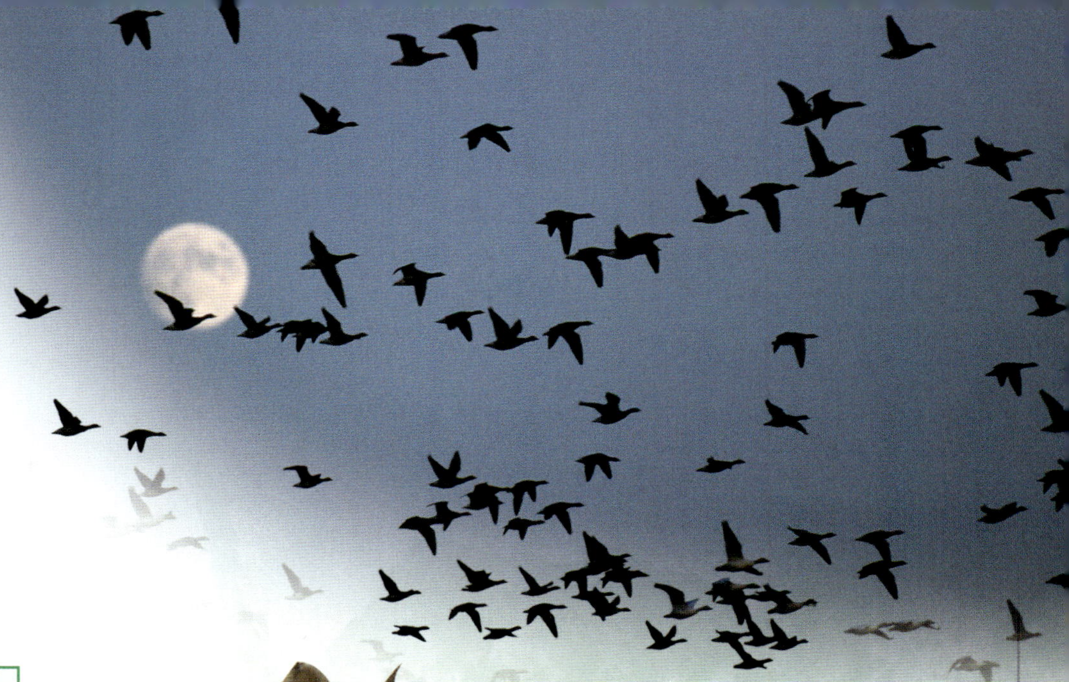

Oies sauvages

Plus d'infos

- Après leur éclosion dans le sable, les petites tortues se ruent vers la mer. Elles trouvent leur chemin en visant les points les plus lumineux de l'horizon.
- Les abeilles peuvent se dire entre elles où se trouve la nourriture et à quelle distance. Elles le font en exécutant des danses spéciales au fond de la ruche.
- Les manchots empereurs retournent chaque année se reproduire à l'endroit où ils sont nés. Ce voyage leur fait parcourir de 50 à 200 km sur la banquise. À l'arrivée, la mère pondra un seul œuf.
- Les araignées tissent un fil de soie partout où elles vont. Cela leur permet de retrouver le chemin du retour vers le nid.
- Les grenouilles rousses se reproduisent dans le même étang année après année. Elles ont une très bonne mémoire de leur environnement.

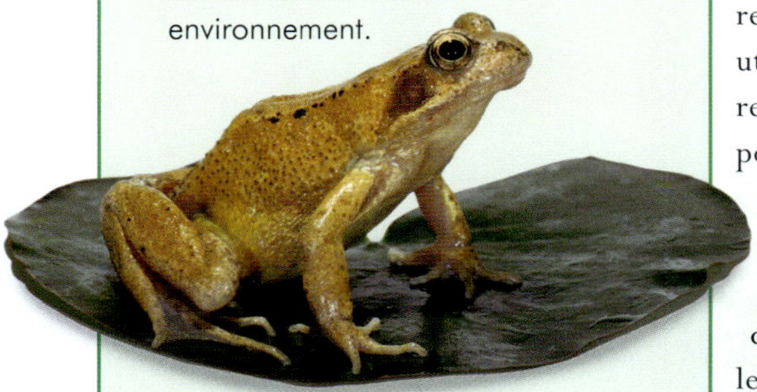

Grenouille rousse

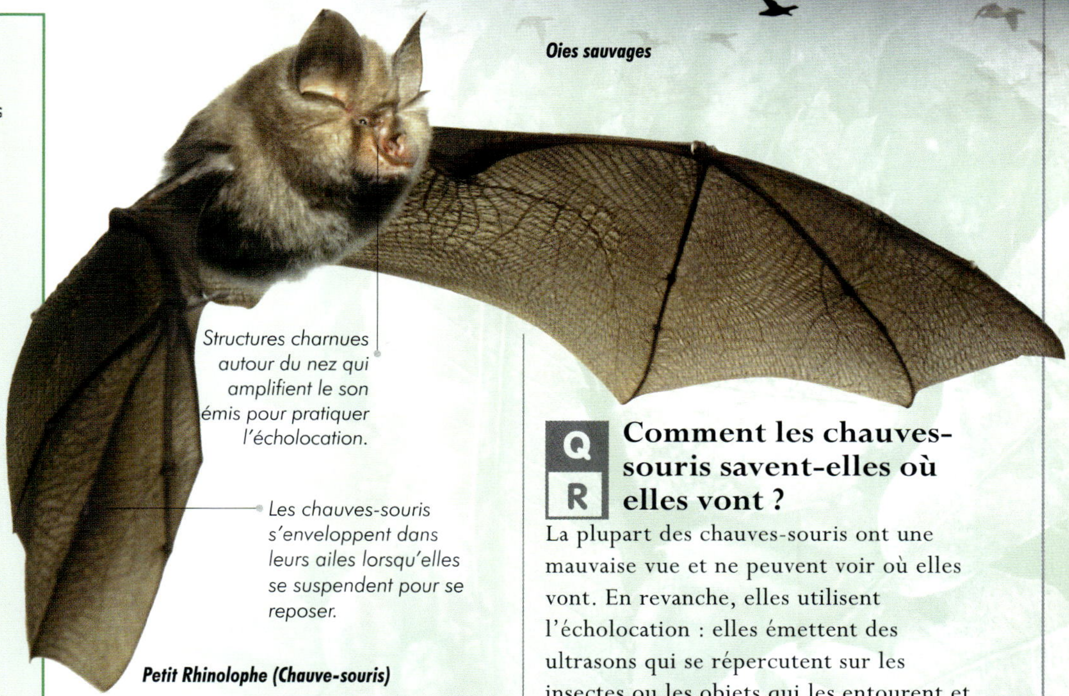

Petit Rhinolophe (Chauve-souris)

Q R Comment les pigeons retrouvent-ils le chemin de leur domicile ?

De tout temps on s'est demandé comment procédaient les pigeons pour s'orienter et retrouver leur chemin. Ils semblent utiliser plusieurs indices comme repères. Ces indices incluent la position du Soleil et aussi les variations du champ magnétique de la Terre. Ils peuvent rentrer chez eux plus vite qu'une personne en voiture sur le même trajet, car ce sont des oiseaux au vol rapide.

Q R Comment les chauves-souris savent-elles où elles vont ?

La plupart des chauves-souris ont une mauvaise vue et ne peuvent voir où elles vont. En revanche, elles utilisent l'écholocation : elles émettent des ultrasons qui se répercutent sur les insectes ou les objets qui les entourent et leur renvoient une image sonore qui leur permet de se diriger. Ainsi peuvent-elles trouver leur nourriture et situer fentes et crevasses où elles se cachent le jour.

Pigeonnier

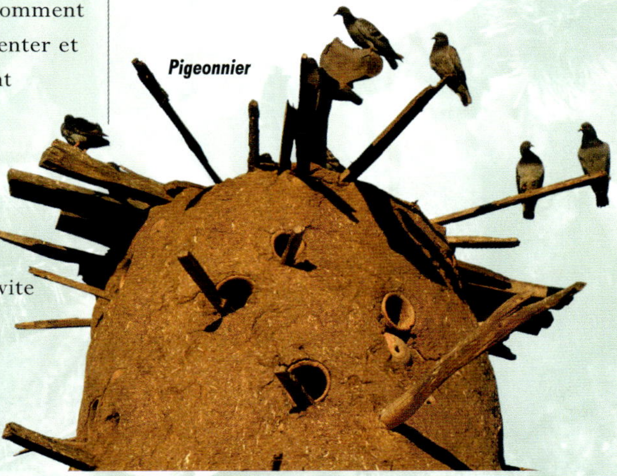

INDEX

Crédits photographiques

L'éditeur remercie ceux qui sont cités ci-après pour leur autorisation de reproduire leurs images :

h = haut ; b = bas ; c = centre ; g = gauche ; d = droite ; t = tout en haut

Alamy Images : Arco Images 52t; Troy Bartlett 37bd; blickwinkel 28bd; Bruce Coleman Inc 29ch, 53cb; Reinhard Dirscherl 11cd; Martin Harvey 53cd; Israel Images 49b; Eric Nathan 11bd; Peter Arnold Inc. 23cg; Steve Bloom Images 50-51; Barry Turner 43bd; Visual & Written SL 43d; Woodfall Wild Images 46l; Worldwide Picture Library 39bg; **Ardea :** Thomas Dressler 25td, 42l, 55bc; Steve Hopkins 55tg; Andrey Zvoznikov 12bc; **Bryan and Cherry Alexander Photography :** 46d; **Corbis :** Tom Brakefield 18bg, 25cb; Tim Davis 28t; DLILLC 34g; Peter Johnson 29bd; Steve Kaufman 47td; Martin Harvey/Gallo Images 54b; Joe McDonald 37tc; Mary Ann McDonald 25tg; Juan Medina/Reuters 55cdh; Reza; Webistan 59bd; Jenny E. Ross 47c; Jeffrey L Rotman 27cb; The Allofs 32l; Stuart Westmorland 39td; **DK Images :** Thomas Marent 8-9, 10b, 30-31, 33td, 39tl; Courtesy of The National Birds of Prey Centre, Gloucestershire 11bg; Courtesy of the Natural History Museum, London 13bg, 17bd, 53td; Courtesy of Richmond Park 25b; Jerry Young 7t, 23t, 35bd; Fred Bavendam/Minden Pictures 29tg; B. Borrell Casals 37c; Matthias Breiter 35td; Christiana Carvalho 47bg; Flip de Nooyer/Foto Natura 16g; Michael & Patricia Fogden 18t, 35tg, 43t; Mitsuaki Iwago/Minden Pictures 45t; Frans Lanting/Minden Pictures 16bd; Michio Hoshino/ Minden Pictures 56td; Tom Vezo/Minden Pictures 37cd; Norbert Wu/Minden Pictures 43c,15cb; **FLPA :** Mitsuhiko Imamori 13tg; **Natural Visions :** Heather Angel 58bg; **naturepl.com :** Barry Bland 12bd; Christophe Courteau 39bd; Bruce Davidson 55cg; Tony Heald 45c; Steven David Miller 32td; Doug Perrine 58c; Kim Taylor 27td; **OSF :** Martyn Colbeck 14d; Rudie Kuiter 33tg; **Photoshot/NHPA :** ANT Photo Library 23c, 43cg; Henry Ausloos 49td; Anthony Bannister 37tg; Bill Coster 59t; Stephen Dalton 28bg, 57tc, 58t; Robert Erwin 45bg; Bill Love 52bc; Alan Williams 56bg; Michael Reinhardt 47bd; **Science Photo Library :** Dr Jeremy Burgess 22t; Eye of Science 23bd, 49ch; Gary Meszaros 13c; Andrew Syred 12cdh; **SeaPics.com :** Jonathan Bird 23bg; Mark Conlin 38b; David B. Fleetham 52c; Saul Gonor 19cg; Steven Kazlowski 22b; Michael S. Nolan 57cg; Doc White 49cdb; **Still Pictures :** Fritz Polking 40-41; **SuperStock :** 20-21, 24b, 27b, 55td

Gardes : DK Images: Thomas Marent
Couverture avant : Corbis: DLILLC;
Couverture arrière : DK Images: Mike Linley cgb; Thomas Marent bg; **naturepl.com:** Christophe Courteau cgh; **Steve Bloom Images:** tg.

Toutes les autres photos © Dorling Kindersley
Pour plus d'informations : **www.dkimages.com**

Nos remerciements à Hazel Beynon pour sa relecture, Lynn Bresler pour l'index et Francis Enosh pour son aide à la mise en page.

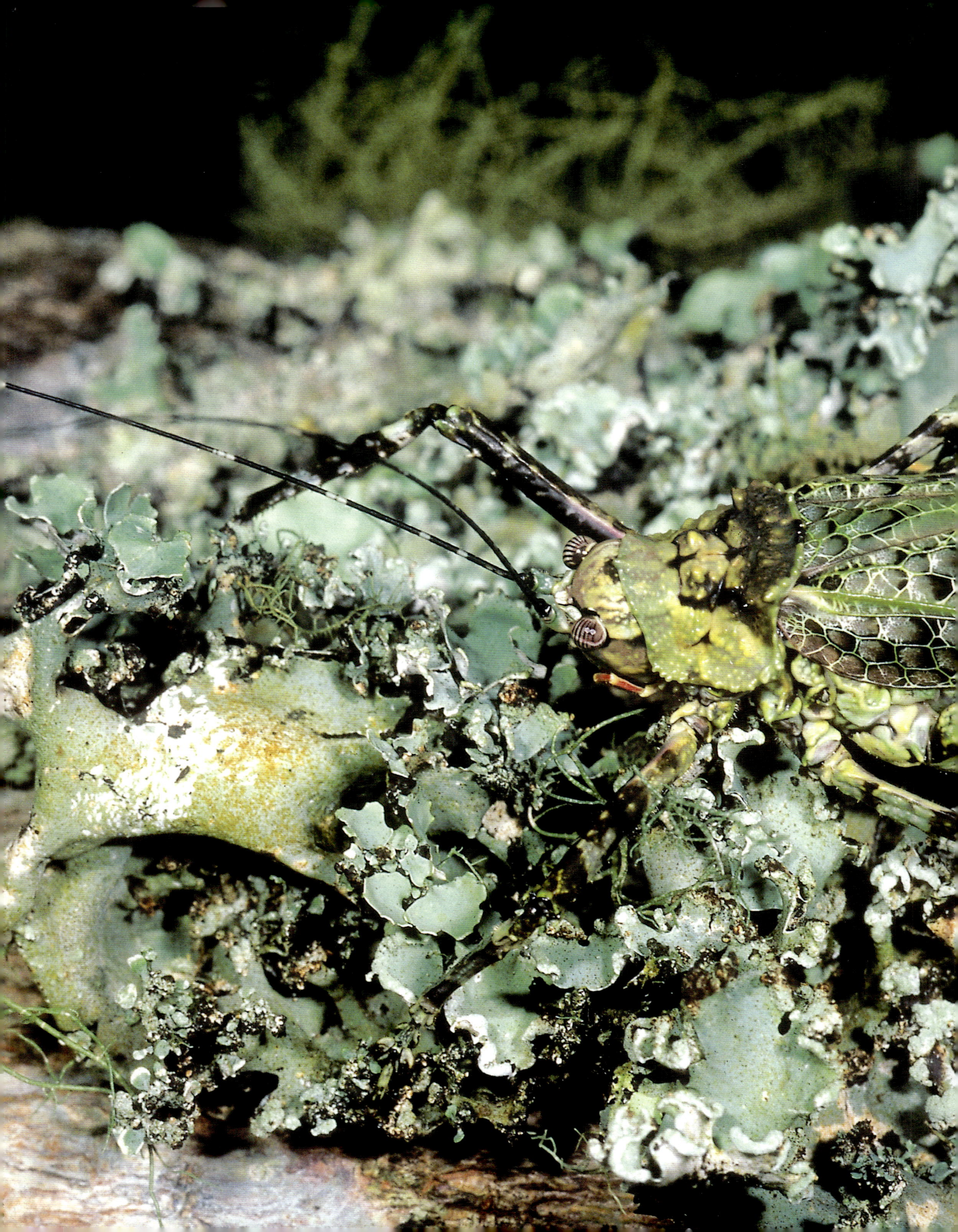